SRI LANKA

Sightseeing Highlights

Sri Lanka's beauty spots are not just to be found in its landscape. An ancient cultural heritage has survived the ages to a greater or lesser extent and is just waiting to be visited. And not least, cities such as Galle and Colombo are bustling with modern urban life. Here we've compiled a list of Sri Lanka's main highlights.

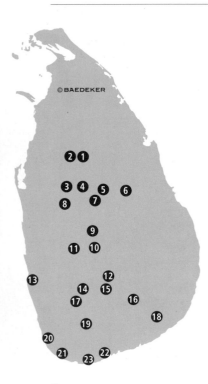

©BAEDEKER

❷ ✶✶ Anuradhapura

More than 100 Singhalese kings decorated their ancient capital Anuradhapura with magnificent palaces, large gardens, artificial lakes and many religious buildings such as monasteries and dagobas.
page 179

❸ ✶✶ Nillakgama

In this monastic complex an almost complete enclosure for a bodhi tree was found during excavations. It is the oldest found on the island of Sri Lanka so far.
page 191

❹ ✶✶ Budda statue of Aukana

The monumental figure is a magnificent example of a standing Buddha in the blessing gesture.
page 193

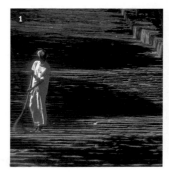

❶ ✶✶ Mihintale

Buddhism became established on Sri Lanka in Mihintale. The magnificent temples, caves and ruins of Mihintale's monastic complex are wonderfully embedded in the landscape.
page 319

⑤ ✶✶ Sigiriya
On the summit of this rock rising
up to the clouds was once a huge
palace complex with gardens and
pools. The climb is impressive and
leads past the rock with the
famous »cloud maidens«.
page 358

✶✶ Dambulla
The five cave temples in Dambulla
stand side by side like pearls on a
necklace. **page 230**

⑧ ✶✶ Yapahuwa Rock Fort
The remains of the 12th-century
rock fort are still imposing. These
days its location is remote, hidden
in the jungle.
page 382

⑨ ✶✶ Aluvihara
Here visitors can watch monks
work on the library manuscripts. In
days gone by the Buddhist canon
was written on palm leaves here.
page 309

⑩ ✶✶ Kandy
The former Singhalese royal city
is not just worth a visit during the
Perahera in July/August. It is generally regarded as the most beautiful
city in the country, its attractions
including not only its cultural heritage but also a lake and a nature
protection area within the city
boundary. **page 272**

⑥ ✶✶ Polonnaruwa
The medieval capital of the island
has plenty of archaeological attractions, including a large network of
canals and pools.
page 339

⑪ ★★ Elephant Orphanage of Pinnawalla
Elephants so close you could reach out and touch them. An attraction for adults and children alike.
page 299

⑫ ★★ Mountains around Nuwara Eliya
The pleasant climate and beautiful landscape already made this town popular in British colonial times.
page 328

⑬ ★★ Colombo
No visitor to Sri Lanka should come here without also visiting the country's capital.
page 211

⑭ ★★ Adam's Peak
Nobody should miss the opportunity to watch sunrise from the summit of Sri Lanka's most sacred mountain.
page 172

⑮ ★★ Horton Plains
This plateau at elevations of more than 2100m/6900 ft is quiet and perfect for hiking.
page 259

⑯ ★★ Rock Sculptures of Buduruvagala
In the middle of dense forest seven monumental Buddha statues rise from a rugged rock wall. They were created in the 9th and 10th centuries.
page 238

⑰ ✶✶ Ratnapura
The city of gems is situated in the middle of Sri Lanka's lowlands. It is hard work to extract the treasures from the ground.
page 354

⑱ ✶✶ Yala National Park
The park is one of the island's largest protected areas. It was founded as long ago as 1900.
page 380

⑲ ✶✶ Sinharaja Rain Forest Reserve
Real jungle adventures can still be experienced in Sri Lanka's oldest rainforest reserve.
page 358

⑳ ✶✶ Ambalangoda
The town is known for its art of mask-carving. The maskmakers there use a centuries-old tradition.
page 175

㉑ ✶✶ Galle
The heart of Galle is the fort built under the Dutch. The city is a good place to explore on foot and has relics of the colonial period.
page 238

㉒ ✶✶ Blow Hole
A natural phenomenon, of which this is one of just six in the world. On Sri Lanka it can be found close to Tangalla.
page 366

㉓ ✶✶ Matara
The island's southernmost town was already an important trading port during the colonial period. While somewhat remote, it is nicely situated on a wide bay. Cinnamon and tea are cultivated in its hinterland. **page 315**

Do You Feel Like ...

... visiting historic temple structures that attract tourists and pilgrims alike; fresh, cool air in the mountains or warm water at the most beautiful beaches; bustling, lively cities or unforgettable feasts? Then Sri Lanka is the place for you!

OLD TEMPLES

- **Anuradhapura**
  The city ruins are more than a thousand years old and also on the UNESCO world heritage list.
  page 181
- **Kandy**
  The Sacred Temple of the Tooth Relic attracts and captivates thousands of visitors daily from all over the country.
  page 281
- **Polonnaruwa** ▶
  Following the traces of history and learning to read and learn to recognize them
  page 334
- **Sigiriya**
  Incomparable wall paintings and to top it off the (strenuous!) climb to the peak plateau **page 358**

FABULOUS BEACHES

- **Hikkaduwa**
  Once a meeting place for backpackers, now it is a lively beach resort for everyone on the west coast. **page 254**
- **Arugam Bay**
  Since the end of the civil war surfing fans and surfers have begun to meet here – the slides can be up to 500m/1600ft long.
  page 348
- **Pigeon Island**
  Whether under the water or with a diving mask and snorkel, the east coast is especially interesting and colourful here.
  page 373
- ◀ **Unawatuna**
  Many claim that this is one of the most beautiful beaches in the world. **page 375**

CELEBRATING

- **Perahera in Kandy**
  The festival procession in torchlight at night with the elaborately decorated elephants is a unique experience.
  page 129
- **Climbing Adam's Peak**
  Climbing Sri Lanka's holy mountain with many hundreds of pilgrims is strenuous but an unforgettable experience.
  page 174
- **Pilgrimage to Kataragama** ▶
  Once a year this town on the southern tip of Sri Lanka overflows with thousands of pilgrims.
  page 296

LIVING TO THE HILT

- **Once a Month: Poya Day**
  Full moon is always a welcome opportunity to pay homage to Buddha, but also to hold a festival.
  page 127
- ◀ **Pettah in Colombo**
  Nowhere on the island is market life as colourful and varied as here.
  page 221

PURE NATURE

- **World's End**
  A hike across Horton Plains to the foggy World's End suits the taste of every enthusiastic nature lover.
  page 262
- **Nuwara Eliya**
  Tea plantations as far as the eye can see; colonial rulers left their architectural tracks here.
  page 334
- **Yala National Park** ▶
  This is one of the national parks on Sri Lanka with the most variety in wildlife. A park ranger is always present.
  page 380

BACKGROUND

14 »**A Radiantly Beautiful Country**«

16 Facts
17 Nature and Environment
20 ⬛ *Infographic: Tsunami – Large Wave in the Harbour*
32 Politics · Population · Economy
34 ⬛ *Facts and Figures*
44 ⬛ *Welcome to Everyday Life!*
47 Religion

54 History

72 Arts and Culture
73 Art Periods
79 Temple Architecture

85 Visual Arts
88 ⬛ *Infographic: Sitting, Standing, Walking, Lying Down ...*
94 Literature
96 Dance and Music
98 Handicraft
99 Customs and Traditions

102 Famous People

ENJOY SRI LANKA

112 Accommodation
113 Visiting Sri Lanka

116 Ayurveda
117 Life-knowledge

The largest statue in Buduruvagala depicts Buddha in the gesture of fearlessness

122 **Children in Sri Lanka**
123 An Island Full of
    Adventure

126 **Festivals · Holidays ·
    Events**
127 Many Peoples, Many
    Holidays

132 **Food and Drink**
133 Hot Stuff
134 🚹 *Typical Dishes*
136 🚹 *Special: Beyond Apples
    and Pears*

140 **Shopping**
141 Rich Seletion

144 **Sports and Outdoors**
145 Active Holidayss

TOURS

153 Tours on Sri Lanka
153 Travelling on Sri Lanka
155 Tour 1: Grand Tour of the
    Island
161 Tour 2: In Royal Footsteps
165 Tour 3: The Central
    Highlands
167 Tour 4: Combination with
    Tour 3

SIGHTS
FROM A TO Z

172 Adam's Peak
175 Ambalangoda
177 Ampara
179 Anuradhapura
192 Aukana
194 Avissawella
195 Bandarawela
198 Batticaloa

202 Bentota
206 Beruwala
208 Bundala National Park ·
    Bundula Bird Sanctuary
209 Chilaw
211 Colombo
230 Dambulla
232 🚹 *3D: Cave Temples of
    Dambulla*
235 Dedigama
236 Ella
238 Galle
247 Gal Oya National Park
249 Giritale
251 Hambantota
253 Hatton · Dikoya
254 Hikkaduwa
259 Horton Plains
262 Jaffna
266 🚹 *Infographic: A Torn
    Country*
270 Kalutara
272 Kandy
284 🚹 *3D: Dalada Maligawa*
295 Kataragama
298 Kegalle

PRICE CATEGORIES
Restaurants
(main dish)
££££ = over £12
£££ = £8–£12
££ = £5–£8
£ = up to £5
Hotels (double room)
££££ = over £90
£££ = £60–£90
££ = £40–£60
£ = up to £40

Note
Billable service telephone
numbers are marked with an
asterisk: *0800…

300	⊞ *Special: Well Protected Little Giants*
302	Kelaniya
304	Kurunegala
307	Mahiyangana
309	Matale
310	⊞ *Infographic: Dagobas*
315	Matara
317	Medirigiriya
319	Mihintale
323	Monaragala
324	Negombo
328	Nuwara Eliya
332	⊞ *Infographic: A Delicious Drink*
334	Polonnaruwa
348	Pottuvil · Arugam Bay
351	Puttalam
354	Ratnapura
356	⊞ *Special: City of Gems*
358	Sigiriya
362	⊞ *3D: Sigiriya Rock Fort*
366	Tangalla
368	Tissamaharama
370	Trincomalee
374	Uda Walawe National Park
375	Una/Unawatuna
378	Weligama
380	Yala National Park
382	Yapahuwa

PRACTICAL INFORMATION

388	Arrival · Before the Journey
392	Drugs
392	Electricity
392	Emergency
392	Etiquette and Customs
394	Health
396	Information
397	Language
400	Literature
402	Media
402	Money
404	National Parks
407	Post and Telecommunication
408	Prices
408	Prostitution
409	Safety
410	Transport
413	Time
414	Travelling with Disabilities
414	Weights and Measures
414	When to Go
416	Glossary of Religious and Cultural Terms
420	Index
424	List of Maps and Illustrations
425	Photo Credits
426	Publisher's Information
428	⊞ *Sri Lanka Curiosities*

A decorated elephant at the Perahera of Gangarama

BACKGROUND

Brief and to the point, clearly written and easy to look up:
information about the people, the economy, religion, art and
history as well as everyday life

»A Radiantly Beautiful Country«

»When Buddha came to this land he wanted to fight the evil dragons ...« the Chinese monk Fa-Haein wrote in his report in the 5th century AD after visiting Ceylon. Whether dragons ever existed on the island off the coast of the Indian subcontinent is lost in the mists of myth and religion. What is certainly a fact is that a tsunami hit Sri Lanka on 26 December 2004 and the civil war lasted for more than a decade. Now the island has recovered from the massive destruction, the civil war is over, the economy is growing and the country is seeing rising numbers of visitors every year.

There are many good reasons for visiting Sri Lanka: the turquoise water, palm trees gently swaying in the breeze, pleasant temperatures

and an enchanting, lavish landscape, and most of all the hospitality of the population, which visitors will sense as soon as they set foot on the island. The **smile** with which people are welcomed here is warm; it does not come across as fake. Tourists here do not feel as if they are only being welcomed for their deep pockets. And it seems as if the islanders want to put the ethnic conflict potential that still bubbles under the surface from time to time behind them. Those travelling through the country with open eyes will realize that most Singhalese and Tamil people co-exist quite peacefully.

Fine sandy beaches and crystal clear water

MAGNIFICENT CULTURE, DIVERSE ENVIRONMENT

Sri Lanka also has a great history, which goes back to the time before Christ. The country has unique artworks, august buildings and visible evidence of a deeply rooted religious attitude. **Buddhism**, which, coming from India, became firmly rooted here, has maintained its significant traces over the centuries. The works of the Buddhist culture are equal in beauty to those of other civilizations. Anyone who walks past the dagobas, temples and palaces without paying attention to them and just spends the days on the admittedly outstanding beaches will have experienced, but not really seen Sri Lanka because the country's true appeal is only revealed to those who venture into the interior, such as into the highlands around Nuwara Eliya, to the old royal towns of Anuradhapura and Polonnaruwa. And anyone who has ever stood at the foot of the famous rock fort of Sigiriya will fall silent in the face of this sheer unimaginable feat. Also unmissable are the traces that the Portuguese, Dutch and British colonial rulers left behind, such as imposing forts with which they tried to maintain their temporary power over Sri Lanka. The diverse **fauna** also deserves mention: this island has endemic animals, in other words ones that can be found nowhere else on earth. However, Sri Lanka's natural beauties are also unique. In addi-

Magnificent buildings: the rock fortress of Sigiriya

tion to palm-lined beaches that are amongst the most beautiful in the world, there are the mountains, the thick jungle, waterfalls and a lavish flora and fauna. Add to this the seemingly endless plantations on which the tea, popular around the world, is grown. Since the Buddhism practised in Sri Lanka is still very pure, the religious sites are the destination of many pilgrimages all year round. The colourful religious festivals, full of mysticism, are an unforgettable experience.

PEARL IN THE INDIAN OCEAN

The mere fact that on this small spot of this earth, which seems to have been casually dropped into the Indian Ocean off the coast of India, so much can be experienced that is beyond all postcard idylls makes a trip to this fascinating island state worthwhile. Sri Lanka has a lot more to offer than negative headlines. All that remains to be said by way of introduction is ayubovan, welcome, to this beautiful country!

Facts

Nature and Environment

Hundreds of miles of magnificent beaches and a diverse, evergreen mountain region with rugged peaks and gentle valleys characterize Sri Lanka's landscape.

Until about 12 million years ago the island of Sri Lanka was connected to the Indian mainland; the separation took place as a result of intense tectonic activity during the Tertiary Period, when the earth largely took on its current appearance. Previously, around 250–150 million years ago, the two supercontinents Gondwana and Laurasia had broken apart. India, which was originally part of the northern continent Laurasia, drifted south and reached Gondwana. Sri Lanka is a **tiny detached fragment of the Indian subcontinent** that was formed during this process. The strait between the Indian mainland and the island of Sri Lanka, on the Indian continental shelf, was formed as a result of a rise in sea levels. The land connection between the mainland and the island was immersed under water, but Adam's Bridge, an approx. 30km/18mi link consisting of coral reefs, sand dunes and small islands, remained.

Once part of India?

From a geological perspective the island is part of the Deccan Plateau, which makes up the entire Indian peninsula south of the 25th parallel. The factor common to both landscapes is that they are characterized by pre-Cambrian crystalline rocks with an estimated age of up to 4.3 billion years, making them some of the oldest on earth. They were formed during a time when the earth's crust was gradually cooling. Younger rocks (highly karstified tertiary limestones) can only be found in the north and northwest of Sri Lanka (on the Jaffna Peninsula) as well as on a narrow seam on the west coast, which runs south all the way to around Puttalam. They lie on top of the old crystalline base, which forms a wide depression in this area.

Ancient rocks

No less simple than the island's geological configuration is the structure of the surface, which can be divided into **just two large areas**. The island's core is dominated by a mountain range of up to 2500m/8200ft, known as the Central Highlands, which rises steeply from the plains in just a few steps. The range makes up around a fifth of the island's total area. Significantly larger are the extensive plains that surround the range. These plains are hard to classify and cover

Surface configuration

Mighty waterfalls thunder to their depths in the Central Highlands, which reach heights of up to 2500m/8200ft

the largest section of the island. In the south and west they form a narrow strip 30–50km/20–30mi wide, while the north and the east are dominated almost entirely by lowlands.

LANDSCAPES

Southwestern part of the island

The lowland strip in the southwest of the island, which is particularly affected by the rains brought by the summer monsoon, is Sri Lanka's **core area** regarding both population density and economic significance. The year-round humid climate and the fertile soils are ideal conditions for diverse agriculture. Extensive coconut-palm plantations and intensively cultivated paddy fields are supplemented by large-scale fruit and vegetable plantations. The region's high population density also creates problems, mainly impacting on small-scale agricultural businesses.

Central Highlands

The western flanks of the Central Highlands have a tropical, year-round humid climate, and are also exposed to the moist air brought inland by the summer monsoon. However, as a result of the great

Rice terraces often dominate the landscape

differences in altitude, the landscape here is completely different. With increasing height the temperatures decrease. Not least because of the **large-scale plantation agriculture**, the population density here is much lower than in the aforementioned lowland area. Although there are almost no economic problems here, in the past the region saw social tensions between Singhalese people and Tamils of Indian origin, since the latter are mainly employed on the plantations as low-paid labour. The climate of the eastern side of the Central Highlands on the other hand is shaped by the winter monsoon. However, the low temperatures as well as an extended summertime dry period do permit large tea plantations to exist here, which, naturally, are accompanied by equally large **fields of rice and vegetables**.

> **?** MARCO ⊕ POLO INSIGHT
>
> *Rubber and tea*
>
> The rubber and tea plantations are quite noticeable in this part of the island. Both plants were originally completely unknown in Sri Lanka! They were introduced by the British colonial rulers, but have since had a crucial impact on the island's landscape and economy.

Southeastern lowlands

The southeastern lowlands lie in a rain shadow and are somewhat isolated from the the the road network of the rest of the island, making them one of Sri Lanka's least densely populated regions. The five hot and dry months from October to February are a contributing factor, as they prevent profitable agriculture. This is said to have been different in the past. In the time of the ancient Singhalese kingdom this region was »**Ceylon's granary**« (the grain of course being rice).

Jaffna lowlands

Even though the conditions presented by the natural environment, particularly the poor soils, are less favourable than almost anywhere else in Sri Lanka, the inhabitants of the Jaffna lowlands in the north of the island knew how to produce fairly good agricultural yields despite all of the factors working against them. An ingenious and well-thought-out **irrigation system** that channels water collected during the rainy season to the paddy fields and vegetable plantations helped to deliver the right conditions for this development. However, the civil war left unmistakable marks on the landscape, since the military conflicts between the Tamils and Singhalese people were most severe in this region. This is also at least one of reasons why people continue to leave the rural areas for towns and cities, a phenomenon seen most strongly in the urban areas around the capital of Colombo.

Elevations

Of the many mountains in the Central Highlands, 15 are higher than 2000m/6500ft. The highest are Pidurutalagala (2524m/8281ft; military exclusion zone), Kirigalpotta (2395m/7858ft), Totapola (2359m/7740ft) and Kudahakgala (2351m/7713ft). Despite its height of »only«

»*Large Wave in the Harbour*«

Tsunamis (Japanese: large wave in the harbour) are among the most unpredictable of the marine geological events. Usually only a few minutes elapse between their starting point and the time when the gigantic waves hit the mainland with unimaginable force. This makes it practically impossible to warn the residents. Sri Lanka had this painful experience at Christmas 2004.

▶ Earthquake and the consequences

The earth's crust consists of individual plates that are constantly in motion. Great tension builds especially at the borders of the plates. If the tension becomes too great it is released with a jolt. This causes earth- or seaquakes.

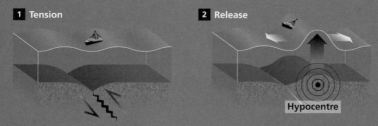

1 Tension **2** Release

Hypocentre

Tsunamis

Severe seaquakes with vertical movement near a coastline can lead to a tsunami. Characteristic are very long and low waves at sea. The waves become dangerous in shallow water where they can break on land with heights up to 30m/100ft. A tsunami can sometimes only be recognized a few minutes before it reaches land. The water then recedes a great distance and exposes the ocean floor

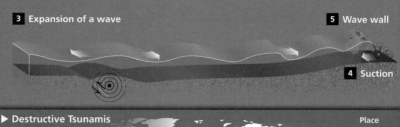

3 Expansion of a wave **5** Wave wall

4 Suction

▶ Destructive Tsunamis

Tsunamis have repeatedly caused widespread destruction and death in past history. Japan especially is effected regularly.

PORTUGAL

A

JAPAN

C D E

INDONESIA B

Place

....

Date

Cause

....

Fatalities

tastrophe on 26 December 2004

e seaquake with an intensity of 9.3 was devastating. Twelve countries were affected.
pecially Indonesia, Sri Lanka, India and Thailand are still struggling with the
nsequences.

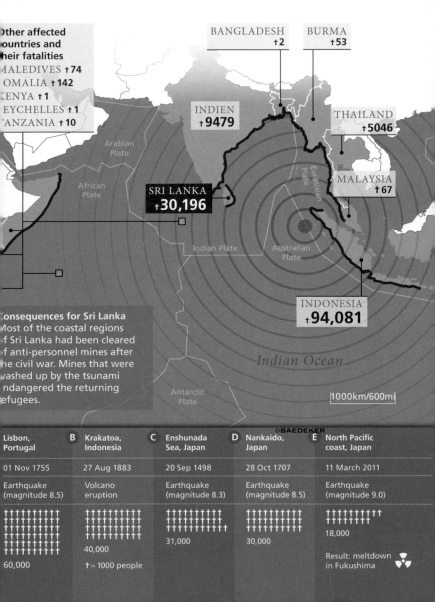

Other affected
ountries and
heir fatalities
MALEDIVES †74
SOMALIA †142
KENYA †1
EYCHELLES †1
TANZANIA †10

BANGLADESH †2

BURMA †53

INDIEN †9479

THAILAND †5046

SRI LANKA †30,196

MALAYSIA †67

INDONESIA †94,081

Indian Ocean

Consequences for Sri Lanka
Most of the coastal regions
of Sri Lanka had been cleared
of anti-personnel mines after
the civil war. Mines that were
washed up by the tsunami
endangered the returning
refugees.

1000km/600mi

©BAEDEKER

Lisbon, Portugal	B Krakatoa, Indonesia	C Enshunada Sea, Japan	D Nankaido, Japan	E North Pacific coast, Japan
01 Nov 1755	27 Aug 1883	20 Sep 1498	28 Oct 1707	11 March 2011
Earthquake (magnitude 8.5)	Volcano eruption	Earthquake (magnitude 8.3)	Earthquake (magnitude 8.5)	Earthquake (magnitude 9.0)
†††††††††† †††††††††† †††††††††† †††††††††† †††††††††† †††††††††† 60,000	†††††††††† †††††††††† †††††††††† †††††††††† 40,000 †= 1000 people	†††††††††† †††††††††† †††††††††††† 31,000	†††††††††† †††††††††† †††††††††† 30,000	†††††††††† ††††††††† 18,000 Result: meltdown in Fukushima ☢

2243m/7359ft **Sri Pada** (also known as Adam's Peak) is considered the most significant mountain; it is venerated as a holy mountain and is the destination of many thousands of pilgrims all year round.

Rivers Five rivers ensure that Sri Lanka's lowlands are well irrigated. Mahaweli Ganga, which flows into the Gulf of Bengal near Mutur (south of Trincomalee), is the longest at 332km/206mi. Further important rivers are Aruvi Aru (length: 167km/104mi, flows into the Gulf of Mannar south of Mannar), Kala Oya (length: 155km/96mi, flows into the Gulf of Mannar north of Puttalam), Kelani Ganga (154km/96mi, flows into the Gulf of Mannar north of Colombo) and Kalu Ganga (110km/68mi, flows into the Gulf of Mannar south of Colombo near Kalutara). All rivers of significance have their source on the slopes of the Central Highlands.

Irrigation system The Singhalese people achieved an almost unsurpassable feat when they constructed a carefully thought-through and practical irrigation system. As early as the 5th century AD, **wewas, artificial lakes**, were constructed in which the rain of the monsoon season was collected and channelled. This irrigation system underwent its greatest expansion in the 12th century when King Parakramabahu I put into action the insight that »no drop of water should flow into the sea without benefiting the people first«. The dense network of tanks (as the British colonial rulers called the wewa system) allows the agricultural land to receive the necessary water, generally allowing two rice harvests a year. Some of these tanks are very large in area but are very shallow, having a maximum depth of only 5m/16ft. Nevertheless these artificial lakes are also significant for fishing. They are home to **excellent edible fish** such as gourami and tilapia. Recently even carp have been farmed in them; these fish represent an enrichment to the foods available to the rural population. During the 1980s the centuries-old wewa system was **supplemented by artificial reservoirs**. Thus Mahaweli Ganga has been dammed east of Kandy by the construction of the 122m/400ft high and 520m/569yd wide Victoria Dam. It is part of the Mahaweli Project, which consists of a total of four dams. Today almost two thirds of the island's entire energy requirements are met by hydropower.

FLORA AND FAUNA

The tropical rainforest The extremely lavish vegetation on the island of Sri Lanka is primarily the result of the year-round hot and humid climate. However, what can be seen today is only a small percentage of the flora that once covered Sri Lanka. The pristine rainforest that grew over millions of years, characterized by an overwhelming diversity and home to countless plants and animals, is now only a shadow of its former self. As a result of **excessive hardwood logging** as well as **slash-and-burn farming**, only around a fifth of the rainforest, which still covered the majority of the island around two centuries ago, has remained. The government in Colombo reacted far too late to this over-exploitation of the natural environment. In the 1970s it at last began to put some of the remaining forests under **protection**. Some of the logged areas have been reforested, but usually with fast-growing woods which can only replace the tropical rainforest with regard to the wood's commercial use – that at least is one advantage. However, they are no substitute for the rainforest which is so significant for the intercontinental global climate. The tropical rainforest is structured into **five layers** that can easily be distinguished by their different heights. The average temperature, which remains relatively stable all year round at 24–30° C/75.2–86° F, and the plentiful precipitation of more than 2000mm/79in, provide the ideal conditions for the forest to flourish. Its most imposing representatives are giants that can reach a height of 50m/165ft. They are the winners in the constant battle for the light of the sun. Around sixty percent of these trees are endemic. The forest floor, which forms quite a fertile foundation for the growth of new plants, only sees a fraction of the sunlight that strikes the forest. This circumstance means the plants that want to survive must have abilities to adjust, which they have developed over millions of years. They include many types of ferns, which try to capture even the faintest ray of light by having differently shaped leaves.

The tropical rainforest is home to more **species** on a relatively small area than can be found on the entire American continent, for example. Botanists have counted more than 300 tree, shrub and flower species in just a single square kilometre. This extraordinary biodiversity means that there are often only a few specimens of each species present. Amongst the rainforest's typical trees are many Dipterocarpaceae, of which there are more than 250 different species.

MARCO POLO INSIGHT ❓

Planting trees

Every year the government of Sri Lanka hands out saplings to the population for free, to balance out the decades of excessive logging of the native forests. However, the newly planted trees are in no way enough to repair the damage done in the past.

Mountain rainforests

A subgroup of the tropical rainforests is formed by the mountain rainforests, which are found in Sri Lanka mainly in the central part of the island. The elevated location and the resulting lower temperatures prevent this type of forest from becoming so tall. Trees with a height of 22–25m/72–82ft are the giants here. However, the **diversity of flowers** such as orchids, of which there are around 125 different species in these regions alone, is remarkable.

Monsoon forest   The monsoon forests are secondary and tertiary forests, that is forests that are the result of forestation or grew again by themselves after the primary forest was logged. In Sri Lanka they can be found in the island's humid regions, i.e. the lower lying regions in the north and east. Their determining characteristics are **savannah-like vegetation** and little biodiversity. The semi-arid climate means the plants have to be undemanding.

Tropical woods   Since the early 1990s the logging of tropical hardwoods, particularly teak, has been **strictly monitored**. Distributed throughout the entire island on strategically situated roads are »Timber Check Points« where passing wood transports are inspected. With this measure the government is trying to contribute to the conservation of the tropical forest, which is an important factor in maintaining the island's climate. Violations of logging restrictions are officially punished with high fines. In order to meet the demand for tropical hardwoods, these have been cultivated in extensive plantations since the 1970s.

Development of the fauna   Considering that Sri Lanka is an island, the diversity of the fauna is remarkable. This has to do with the fact that the island was once connected to the Indian subcontinent via a **land bridge**. At this time many land animals found their way here. They looked for and found their habitats in the tropical rainforests, which covered two thirds of Sri Lanka until just a few centuries ago. The destruction of these forests by humans forced birds, insects, mammals and reptiles to retreat.

Impressive bird diversity   Of the officially registered 427 bird species, around 250 are resident on the island, while the rest are migrating birds such as the different kinds of swallow that use Sri Lanka as a stopover or winter home. Of the birds that live on the island permanently, **21 are endemic**, which means they can only be found in Sri Lanka and especially in the humid regions. Amongst this group are a few parrot species and songbirds, Brahminy kites, fish owls, one of the darter species and one of the colourful kingfisher species. The endemic species include Ceylon starlings, black-headed ibises, white-bellied sea eagles and red junglefowl. The many peacocks are considered symbols of beauty and elegance. The nature reserves marked out by the government are ideal habitats for birds. Huge numbers can be observed during a visit to **Kumana National Park** in Eastern Province or in the national parks of Bundala, Kalametiya and Wirvila in the

? MARCO POLO INSIGHT

The butterfly migration

One special event for fans of butterflies is the annual butterfly migration in March and April, when the insects fly to Adam's Peak, which as a result is also known as Samanale Kande, which means butterfly mountain.

south of the island. Bundala is known for its many flamingos, Kitulgala for its large number of endemic birds.

Butterflies

The variety of butterflies living in Sri Lanka is also striking: **no fewer than 242 species** are registered, most of them living in the lower mountain regions up to an altitude of 1000m/3300ft. Only six butterfly species live higher up than that.

Mosquitoes

Mosquitoes are amongst the less appreciated insects. They can become a particular nuisance during the evening hours.

Flying foxes

Flying foxes, or fruit bats, which hang in the trees as they sleep during the day and only become active in the evening and at night, are numerous. Then they come out to look for food, frequently surprising observers with their ghostly appearance. However, they are very shy and avoid contact with humans.

Monkeys

Sri Lanka's monkeys can be quite bold at times; some of them are endemic, including leaf monkeys, which can be recognized by their crimson faces, and purple-faced langurs, which can now only be found in the mountainous regions. The most common monkeys are macaques and langurs as well as grey monkeys, which prefer living in trees. The grey monkeys are considered holy by Hindus since, according to the Indian epic Ramayana, a grey monkey in the form of the monkey god Hanuman is said to have saved the princess Sita, who had been kidnapped by the giant Ravana and brought to Sri Lanka. Monkeys are generally vegetarians, but it is a good idea to refrain from feeding them peanuts, bananas and other fruit since the animals can **occasionally become quite aggressive** when their food stores are exhausted.

Bears and leopards

The opportunity to see bears and leopards in Sri Lanka now only exists in the nature reserves, but there the chances are good. Their numbers have been **decimated**, since they are extremely unpopular with the local population and because they seek out agricultural areas, particularly at night.

Reptiles

A total of 75 different reptile species have been counted that live nowhere else but in Sri Lanka. Amongst them is a certain species of **mugger crocodile** that can reach a length of up to 5m/16ft and a weight of several hundred kilograms, making it the **largest reptile living in Sri Lanka**. However, it is usually quite shy and lives a very withdrawn life. It is rare for crocodiles to attack humans; this has usually occurred in the past because of carelessness while bathing. Monitor lizards, which can reach a length of 3m/10ft, are also nothing to worry about; like crocodiles they have a very sensitive sense of touch, which means even the faintest vibrations on the ground make them run away. They mainly eat large insects, but also snakes, and during the hunt they develop a surprising agility. Sri Lanka is also home to **five tortoise, turtle and terrapin species**, which are all under protection. They include the vegetarian Indian star tortoise, the only land tortoise. It reaches a length of 38cm/15in and can be recognized by the star-shaped pattern on its shell.

Snakes   Only around 20 of the 83 snake species are dangerous to humans; these include cobras, Indian Ceylon krait and two species of viper (one of them is the chain viper, which can grow up to 1.6m/5.2ft and whose bite leads to certain death). Burmese pythons are impressive for their size but in their behaviour they are harmless. However, all of the snake species tend to live in remote regions of the forests. They are rarely spotted in the vicinity of humans. Mongooses are considered to be their greatest enemy. They know how to kill even the most venomous snake with a single bite.

Geckos   One of Sri Lanka's useful animals is the gecko, a lizard with adhesive toes. Geckos are attracted to artificial light sources, particularly in the

Elephant mothers spend three years looking after their offspring

evening. They make a cackling sound. They are popular because they love eating insects and will consume several dozen mosquitoes a night.

Although the lion is considered Sri Lanka's national beast, this honour should really be reserved for the elephant, not least because there have been no lions living in the wild on the island for decades. The number of Indian elephants has also been decimated; even at the start of the 20th century there were fewer than 12,000 elephants living in the wild, but today that number has dropped to **only around 3500**. Humans are largely to blame for this because of the ever more intensive agricultural use of the pristine forests, which cuts through the elephants' centuries-old routes. Like everywhere on earth where elephants exist, Sri Lanka's elephants are also hunted down by ruthless poachers for their precious ivory tusks, and countless elephants were injured or killed in the upheavals of the civil war.

Elephants

MARCO POLO INSIGHT ?

Highly respected elephant

The Maligawa elephant is highly respected on Sri Lanka. It has the task of carrying Buddha's tooth during the Esala Perahera in Kandy. Between 1950 and 1987 it was the elephant Raja who carried the relic. He enjoyed the highest reputation and was declared a national treasure in his lifetime. When he died, there was a national day of mourning. The elephant has been stuffed and is exhibited in the temple museum in Kandy.

There is an **Elephant Orphanage** in Pinnawala near Kandy for orphaned young animals who would not manage to join other herds without their mother and would wander about helplessly (▶MARCO POLO Insight p. 300).

Elephants still play an important part in forestry where they are used as work animals. They also fulfil an important role during festive ceremonies such as in Kandy, where hundreds of them participate in the annual celebrations at the Temple of the Tooth, acting as colourfully decorated relic bearers. Elephants are led by an **elephant driver (mahout)**; the animals obey only this one person and can remember around 100 words or commands. Elephants grow to a shoulder height of approx. 3m/10ft and a weight of up to four tons. They are **generally considered good-natured animals**. They can become volatile, however, during the winter months; the reason for which is a secretion produced by a small opening on the head during the mating season, which sometimes gets into their eyes. In addition their proverbial good memory (also for bad events) has surprised many a mahout and sometimes even cost his life. Elephant cows are pregnant for 23 months. Once the calf is born, they spend a **three-year »parental leave« period** during which they do nothing but look after the offspring. At birth, an elephant baby already weighs around

100kg/220lbs and has a height of around 75cm/30in. Elephants can live for a maximum of 100 years and on average reach 80; their best years are between the ages of 25 and 60. During that time they can work eight hours a day, but only during the cooler months. During the hot season the sensible animals cannot be motivated to work.

Domestic animals Amongst Sri Lanka's domesticated animals are first and foremost **water buffalo**, which have been used for hundreds of years to cultivate paddy fields and as reliable draught animals. **Cows and oxen** can be found all over the island, grazing in a leisurely manner by the side of the road. Only recently have the people of Sri Lanka, with the practical support of interested Danish companies, learned about the use and preservation of cow's milk.

Marine fauna The marine fauna all around the island of Sri Lanka is equally diverse. The sea's larger inhabitants include sharks, dolphins, rays, moray eels, tuna and barracudas, while the smaller ones include tropical fish

A water buffalo in accompaniment

such as parrotfish, heniochus and marine angelfish, who prefer to live around coral reefs. The overfishing of the world's oceans is also having an effect around Sri Lanka. Dolphins in particular are being served as delicacies. At least 5000 a year are caught and some of them are exported to Japan. However, dolphin barbecues are also quite popular in Sri Lanka amongst those who can afford them. Other underwater creatures are **corals**; corals belong to the cnidaria phylum (polyps). They surround themselves with a coat of calcium carbonate for protection. Corals prefer to settle in large colonies; warm water with a good current and strong sunshine presents the most favourable conditions for their growth. Larger coral reefs can still be found off Hikkaduwa at the southwestern end of the island, but careless divers have caused grave damage here over the past few years. The coral reefs in the northeast off Trincomalee and along the east coast are still relatively untouched; since the end of the civil war it has been possible to visit them again again.

Many streams and inland lakes are home to freshwater fish. There are said to be a total of 54 different species. Some of them were brought to the island by the British – trout, for example, which are widespread in the clear streams of the Horton Plains.

Freshwater fish

CLIMATE

Sri Lanka's climate is tropical with wet summers and temperatures that remain hot and stable throughout the year. The seasonal change in precipitation levels is significant, being tied to the Indian monsoon circulation. There are four different precipitation seasons: the pre-monsoon period (March – mid-May), the summer monsoon period (mid-May – September), the post-monsoon period (October and November) and the winter monsoon period (December – February). Sri Lanka's Central Highlands are an **effective climate barrier**. The windward and leeward effects divide the island into a southwestern »wet zone«, which covers almost half of the area, and a relatively »dry zone«.

The monsoon

Receiving around 1500mm/60in per year of rainfall, Jaffna Peninsula and parts of the northwest coast are the driest regions of Sri Lanka, closely followed by the northeast coast in the rain shadow of the mountainous interior. Yala National Park also gets relatively little rainfall. The wet southwest receives annual precipitation levels of an average of between 2400mm/95in per year in the lowlands and a maximum of 500mm/20in on the mountains' western slopes. Here it is the summer monsoon, which reaches the island with thunderstorms and torrential downpours on around 24 May, that causes the

Precipitation, storms

most precipitation. The leeward side of the Highlands is often affected by the foehn-like down-slope wind, the »kachan«, which makes the dry period and the summer heat in the northeast of the island even more intense. In the north and east the rainy season lasts from the end of November to January thanks to the winter monsoon. The foehn wind then delivers the best weather on the southwest coast. During the pre- and post-monsoon periods (March – May and October/November) the island is affected by heavy thunderstorms with veritable deluges. They are responsible for more precipitation on the southwest coast than the actual summer monsoon. The wettest months on the entire island, with up to 20 days of precipitation, tend to be October and November, the southwest is also very wet in May and June, while the northeast coast is also wet in December. **Continuous rainfall is rare even during the rainy season** – even then the sun hardly ever shines for less than six hours per day.

Temperatures   Daytime temperatures consistently reaching 29–33° C./84–91° F. and night-time temperatures of not much below 25° C./77° F., coupled with a sustained high level of humidity of 70–90 percent are **only bearable for prolonged periods of time for healthy individuals**. The Central Highlands above 1000 metres are pleasant all year round, where temperatures are 5° – 8° C./10–15° F. lower. Only the winter months are a little less muggy and somewhat cooler, whereas March and April are baking before the arrival of the summer monsoon with maximum temperatures of almost 35° C./95° F. and even 37° C./98° F. on the northeast coast.

Monsoon   The monsoon (orig. from Arabic mausim = suitable for seafaring) is a wind that changes with the seasons and occurs predominantly as a southwest (summer) monsoon and a northeast (winter) monsoon in the Indian Ocean. The cause of the large-scale air current is the warming and cooling of the Asian landmass. As a result of strong solar radiation above the Tibetan plateau in the summer, a thermal low is created, which is replaced by the major influence of the Asian cold high-pressure system. This change in air pressure, which covers large areas of the Indian Ocean and spans both sides of the equator, leads to the seasonal change in direction of the monsoonal currents flowing to equalize the pressure difference. Diverted by the Coriolis effect, the moist maritime summer monsoon blows over India and Sri Lanka from a southwesterly direction, while the dry continental winter monsoon comes from the northeast. On its journey across the Bay of Bengal, the winter monsoon, which starts off dry, takes on moisture so that places on the northeastern side of Sri Lanka, such as Trincomalee, have a wintertime precipitation maximum.

Three Typical Climates

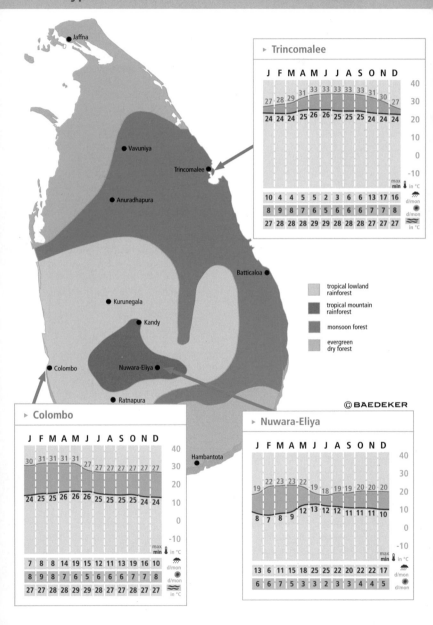

▸ Trincomalee

	J	F	M	A	M	J	J	A	S	O	N	D	
max	27	28	29	31	33	33	33	33	33	31	30	27	in °C
min	24	24	24	25	26	26	25	25	25	24	24	24	
d/mon	10	4	4	5	5	2	3	6	13	17	16		
d/mon	8	9	8	7	6	5	6	6	6	7	7	8	
in °C	27	28	28	28	29	29	28	28	28	27	27	27	

▸ Colombo

	J	F	M	A	M	J	J	A	S	O	N	D	
max	30	31	31	31	31	27	27	27	27	27	27	27	in °C
min	24	25	26	26	26	25	25	25	25	24	24		
d/mon	7	8	8	14	19	15	12	11	13	19	16	10	
d/mon	8	9	8	7	6	5	6	6	7	7	8		
in °C	27	28	28	29	29	28	27	27	28	27	27		

▸ Nuwara-Eliya

	J	F	M	A	M	J	J	A	S	O	N	D	
max	19	22	23	23	22	19	18	19	19	20	20	20	in °C
min	8	7	8	9	12	13	12	12	11	11	11	10	
d/mon	13	6	11	15	18	25	25	22	20	22	22	17	
d/mon	6	6	7	5	3	3	2	3	3	4	5		

tropical lowland rainforest

tropical mountain rainforest

monsoon forest

evergreen dry forest

© BAEDEKER

Population · Politics · Economy

Sri Lanka is primarily inhabited by Singhalese and Tamil people. Other population groups, such as the Burgher, play more of a marginal role. And then there are the indigenous Vedda.

ETHNIC GROUPS

Indigenous population

The descendants of the aboriginal island inhabitants, called Yakshas (= demons) in the Mahavamsa legend, are ethnically quite mixed, making this group difficult to capture statistically. They are known as the **Vedda** people and belong to the Australoid or proto-Australoid ethnic group. Their roots probably lie in a prehistoric hunting people that already existed during the Neolithic period. The Vedda are genetically related to Africa's indigenous population as well as to the Aborigines in Australia and Tasmania. They traditionally live in small clans ruled by a king, who holds a distinguished position in society. As a result of continuing assimilation with the Singhalese, the Vedda are threatened by the same fate as has befallen many of the Earth's primitive peoples: they will have gone extinct in the foreseeable future. Today **only an estimated 600 Vedda live in Sri Lanka**. The government granted them places of refuge in the north of the island, where they can pursue their traditions, some of which are animist in nature. Their settlements, which are hard to find in the dense jungle anyway, may only be visited with a special permit from the authorities.

MARCO POLO INSIGHT ?

Legendary Vedda chief

When Tissahami died at the age of 104 in 1998, the prime minister at the time, Kumaratunga, ordered a state funeral. Tissahami mediated between the government and the Vedda and managed to ensure that they kept part of their land for themselves.

Singhalese people

Of the approx. 20.3 million people living in Sri Lanka, the Singhalese represent **the largest group** with around 70.2 percent of the population. They are the descendants of people who came from northern India in the 5th century BC. The Singhalese expelled large numbers of Tamils, who originated from southern India and had come to Sri Lanka three centuries earlier, occupying the majority of the island. Today the Singhalese are the dominant social group, not least because of their better educational opportunities. Until 1977 the parliament in Colombo consisted almost exclusively of Singhalese, and until this date they also held all government offices. The Singhalese live mainly in the southwest and the south of the island as well as in the highlands of Kandy, a region that defied colonial conquest until 1815.

The Tamil people make up around 15.4 percent of the population, making them the **second-largest population group** in Sri Lanka; however, this figure does include the Tamils from India as well as those from Sri Lanka. They are much darker-skinned and shorter than the Singhalese and stocky rather than slim. The Tamils are mostly descendants of migrants from Malaysia, Singapore, Burma and southern and eastern Africa. However, here too there are subtle differences: only the Ceylon Tamils consider themselves native Sri Lankans. They see the Indian Tamils, the Tamil people who were mainly brought to Sri Lanka from India as cheap plantation workers during the British colonial period, to be foreigners, irrespective of the fact that these days most of them were born in Sri Lanka, i.e. have Sri Lankan citizenship. Since 1964 the Sri Lankan government has been implementing **repatriation programmes** whose goal is to send the Indian Tamils back to their original homeland. Since that time several hundred thousand have left the island. Some of them now live as refugees all around the world. The Tamils of Indian origin mainly inhabit the regions in the north of Sri Lanka and on the Jaffna Peninsula as well as along the east coast. They can also be found in other parts of the country too, however, such as in Kandy as well as around Nuwara Ekiya, where they work as pickers on the tea plantations.

Tamil people

From the 8th century AD onwards Arabs started settling in Sri Lanka. Most of them were seafarers, who initially worked as **spice exporters** and later also as **gemstone traders**. Some of their descendants, the Moors, still live as businesspeople in Colombo as well as on the southwest and south coasts. They make up the majority of the population in the district of Amparai, which stretches from the east coast far into the country's interior. They are either Sri Lankan Moors, who settled on the island before the 19th century, or Indian Moors, whose Arab ancestors only came to the island in the 19th and 20th centuries. Sri Lanka has a total of 1.9 million Moors, which is about 9.2 percent of the total population.

Moors

The Burgher people, the descendants of the Dutch and Portuguese who came to Sri Lanka during the colonial period, number only around 45,000 now. The word »Burgher« came from the Dutch term »Vry Burger«, meaning »free citizen«. Most of them left the island after 1948, when Sri Lanka was granted independence. The majority chose to emigrate to Australia. Those still living in Sri Lanka are proud of their origin: in order to stand out from the large mass of Singhalese people they often use English as their language of choice.

Burgher people

▶ Written in Singhalese:

இலங்கை ஜனநாயக சமத்துவ குடியரசு

Location: 237km/142mi east of the southern tip of the Indian subcontinent

Area:
65,610 sq km/25,330 sq mi

Length of coastline:
1340km/832mi

Population: **20.9 mil.**
Compared to
Australia: 22.5 mil.

Population density:
323 per sq km/840 per sq mi
Compared to Indonesia:
126 per sq km/48 per sq mi

Population growth:
0.86 %

INDIA

79° 54'
east longitude

6° 54'
north latitude

©BAEDEKER

Sri Lanka

432km/2

Colombo
Sri Jayawardenepura (Kotte)

Indian Ocean

225km/
135mi

▶ Government

Form of government:
Democratic socialist presidential republic
Capital (Seat of government):
Sri Jayawardenepura (Kotte)
Capital (inofficial):
Colombo
Head of State:
President Maithripala Sirisena
National holiday:
4 February

▶ Geographical data

Longest river:

Mahaweli Ganga 〰〰〰 323km/193mi

Thames, London 〰〰〰 346km/215mi
(by comparison)

Highest elevation:

2524m/8329ft   1344m/4409ft

Pidurutalagala   Ben Nevis
(by comparison)

▶ National flag and coat of arms

The Lion, which was introduced in 1978, consists of the old flag of the kingdom of Kandy (right: golden lio with sword as symbol of bravery on red background, symbol of shed blood; golden leaves of the banyan tree in the corners for »metta«/goodness, »karuna«/compassion, »mudita«/joy for others and »upekkhā«/serenity). Safran yellow on the left stands for Tamil-Hindu minority, green for the Muslim minority. The coat of arms shows the lion from the banner of the last king of Kandy, above it the blue wheel fo Buddhist teaching.

Economy

GDP 2013
(place 66 on the IWF
country list): US$134.5 bil.
Per capita income (GDP):
US$6500

Languages

Official:
Sinhala (Singhalese)
and Tamil

Tourism

About **1.5 mill visitors,**
from U.K. about 11% (2014)

Religion

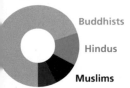

Buddhists

Hindus

Muslims

Christians
(of these 6.2%
Catholic and 1.2%
other)

▶ Climate in Colombo

Averag temperatures

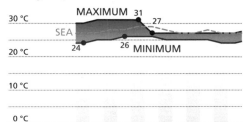

MAXIMUM 31 · · · 27
SEA
24 · · 26 MINIMUM

30 °C
20 °C
10 °C
0 °C
J F M A M J J A S O N D

Precipitation

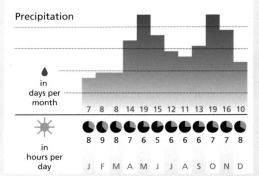

in days per month: 7 8 8 14 19 15 12 11 13 19 16 10

in hours per day: 8 9 8 7 6 5 6 6 6 7 7 8

J F M A M J J A S O N D

Composition of population

The largest ethnic group on
Sri Lanka is the Singhalese.

■ Singhalese   ■ Indian Tamil
■ Moors   ■ Ceylon Tamil
               ■ other

70.2
% 11.2
9.2
4.2
5.2 (Malays, Burghers, Veddas,
the Sri Lankan aboriginals,
only a few hundred)

Colombo
Sri Jayawardenepura (Kotte)

Conflicts
(►MARCO
POLO Insight
p. 266)

Conflicts between the different population groups erupted even in early centuries. They usually emanated from members of the ruling families. Thus, Tamil mercenaries from southern India were at the centre of the conflicts between the rich Hindus in India and the Lambakanna and Moriya rulers in Sri Lanka. Today it is mainly the Tamils living in the north and on the east coast who feel themselves to be second-class citizens. Their political representation, the **Tamil United Liberation Front** (TULF), had been demanding not just political equality since the 1980s, but also an independent Tamil state under the name of Eelam. While the TULF rejects violence to implement its political goals, another group that came into existence in the 1980s was the **Liberation Tigers of Tamil Eelam** (LTTE), which led to an escalation of the conflicts. The civil war in Sri Lanka that broke out in 1983 and lasted for more than a decade claimed more than 50,000 lives. **Contacts** between the Singhalese and Tamil populations are closer than one might think. Even today, just like many centuries ago, marriages between Singhalese and Tamil people are no rarity.

Welfare
system

The welfare system is quite well established considering Sri Lanka is still a developing country. There are several state-organized Social Assistance Services that can be taken advantage of during emergencies and illnesses. Pregnant women also have the right to financial support; however, there is no unemployment pay. While civil servants have their own pensions system, widows' and orphans' pensions are not mandatory. Medical care is also good compared with other developing countries. It is free of charge. Hospitals and clinics are available in sufficient numbers. The traditional natural medicine of ayurveda plays a special role in Sri Lanka.

Education

Compared with other countries with a similar structure Sri Lanka has an outstanding position regarding education. Intense government efforts have contributed to a literacy rate of more than 90 percent. In Sri Lanka education is compulsory for children for five years, between the ages of six and eleven; attendance at state schools and preparatory kindergartens is free.
The education system is based on the British model; primary school is followed by junior secondary school and senior secondary school. In order to get into university students have to sit an entry exam. They are then selected by a quota system; as well as their attainment, the population and the level of development of the relevant district is taken into account. The University of Peradeniya near Kandy is considered to be the island's best.

Caste system

Since a modern constitution was passed in 1972, there are **officially no more castes in Sri Lanka**; however, this separation of the social classes which has a religious basis and follows the Indian model, is still ubiquitous and leads to separation and hierarchical structures. Even though the boundaries have become somewhat blurred, particularly amongst the smaller castes, members of a low caste have a hard time improving their professional position regardless of how much hard work they put. It is virtually impossible for the rural population to marry into a higher caste. This can be seen in the marriage advertisements in Sri Lanka's newspapers. Membership of a certain caste is an absolute must for the desired partner and if the star signs are a fit too, there is nothing in the way of future happiness anymore. While the term »varna« (= colours) for castes is customary in India, the word »caste« is of Portuguese origin (casta); **it means »pure« or »chaste«**. The term was coined by Portuguese seafarers who arrived on the Indian subcontinent, and was probably a reference to the fact that the members of the different classes of Hindu society had highly specific purity rules.

The caste system is based on religion. Its basis is the understanding that every Hindu is born into a very specific, closed religious and social group; upholding the rights and duties of this group is a lifelong requirement. Moving from one caste to another is generally only possible as a result of the process of **rebirth**, i.e. only in the next life and after an existence full of good thoughts and deeds.

Originally there were only four castes in India: Brahmins (priests), Kshatriyas (warriors), Vaishyas (farmers and craftsmen) and Shudras (labourers). Over time, around 3000 smaller castes were added, whose members were recruited from the different professions. The Brahmin caste naturally enjoys the highest standing, since princes, officials and intellectuals consider themselves as belonging to it. Singhalese and Tamil people generally use different castes or give their castes different names. There are **four Tamil castes** in Sri Lanka, of which the Pujavis, the Hindu priests, have the highest standing. Below this caste are the people born into the Velalla caste (its main group of members are large landowners), the members of the Kovias caste (farmers in the service of the Velallas) and finally the Pallas and Nevalas (landless farm labourers). Anyone not belonging to a caste is largely ostracized by society, and in India the person is considered to be »dalit«, »**untouchable**«. In Sri Lanka the term for this social class is »paravas«; members of this group are forbidden, for example, to enter certain Hindu temples. **The Singhalese in Sri Lanka have 43 castes**, but more than half belong to the Goyigama caste, the caste of large landowners and free farmers. Below this is the Karava caste, which once included fishermen and seafarers, but is now made up of merchants and entrepreneurs. Amongst the lower castes, the Navamdama caste is worth mentioning. It is reserved to blacksmiths. The members of the Velli-duraya caste are the »guardians of the Bodhi tree«, the tree under which Buddha achieved enlightenment.

STATE AND ADMINISTRATION

Official name Since 1972 the island's official name has been Sri Lanka Prajathan-thrika Samajavadi Janaraiaya (Democratic Socialist Republic of Sri Lanka). Until this time Ceylon was the standard name, but of course only since the period of the British colonial rule. The current short name, Sri Lanka, means »**resplendent land**«.

Forms of government Since 1972, when the constitution was passed, Sri Lanka has been **a democratic and at the same time socialist republic**. With this constitution, largely written by the United National Party (UNP), Ceylon became a republic and the governor general in place since 1948 was replaced by a prime minister appointed by the president.

Government Since as far back as 2005 Sri Lanka was led by the **state president** Mahinda Rajapaksa, who surprisingly lost January 2015 elections against opposition candidate **Maithripala Sirisena** (»Maithri« or »MY3«). He appointed UNP leader **Ranil Wickremasinghe** as Prime Minister.

Parliament The parliament consists of 225 deputies, who are elected by the population every six years.

Administrative structure The island of Sri Lanka is divided into **nine provinces** (Southern Province, Sabaragamuwa Province, Western Province, Uva Province, Eastern Province, Central Province, North Western Province, North Central Province und Northern Province), which are in turn divided into 24 districts.

Political parties Sri Lanka's party system is very diverse. There are dozens of parties that represent the very different interests of the population. The social democratic, **United People's Freedom Alliance** (UPFA) was victorious at the last parliamentary elections in 2010, which were held on a party-list system of proportional representation. Since then 144 members of parliament and the prime minister, Dissanayake Mudiyanselage Jayaratne, have come from the UPFA.
The **United National Party** (UNP), which dominated the political scene for years, won only 60 seats, while the rather insignificant **Democratic National Alliance** (DNA) obtained a mere seven.
14 MPs from the nationalist **Tamil National Alliance** (TNA) represent the interests of the Tamil population.

Foreign policy With regard to foreign policy, the government has pursued the goals of the Non-Aligned Movement, but did maintain close relations with some eastern bloc states until the latter were reordered or dissolved.

As early as 1948, when the country's independence constitution came into force, Sri Lanka entered the **Commonwealth of Nations**, whose member states consider the British crown as the symbol of their voluntary association. In 1955 the island state joined the United Nations and has since sent representatives to the UN's many special and sub-organizations. The **Colombo Plan** (in full Colombo Plan for Cooperative Economic and Social Development in Asia and the Pacific) was named after the place where it was ratified in 1950, initially by seven member states of the Commonwealth. The purpose of the alliance, which now has 54 member states, is the co-ordination and promotion of the economic development of its Asian and Pacific members.

International affiliations

The many trade unions play an important role over and above their function of representing employees, since they also pursue political goals and are associated with a party. This fact was particularly significant during the time when the United National Party (UNP) was in power and the unions formed an extension to the opposition parties. Traditionally unions are also represented in parliament. Wildcat strikes were made illegal in 1979 when a law to that effect was passed.

Trade Unions

Sri Lanka does not have compulsory military service. Many social classes consider employment in the army as desirable, for women too, since it provides sufficient social security, including pensions.

No compulsory military service

ECONOMY

The location of the island of Sri Lanka as an »outpost« in the Indian Ocean allowed it to benefit from a **favourable economic development** soon after the first settlers arrived. The first inhabitants were farmers who cultivated paddy fields. They developed the method of artificial field irrigation using dams and reservoirs that is still in use today. This 12th-century system has allowed two rice harvests a year ever since. The **period of colonization** of large parts of the Asian continent by Europeans brought the **Portuguese** first to Sri Lanka in the 16th century. They wanted to created a trading post in Colombo and were helped by the fact that the largest part of the island, which they called Ceilao, had fallen apart into three kingdoms at this time, and the kings were fighting for power. In around 1610 the Portuguese controlled almost the entire southwestern part of the island as well as some regions on the eastern end. Their area of influence ended below Kandy, however, whose king, Senerath, initially resisted the foreigners, but then came to contractual agreements with the Portuguese on trade in 1617. When the **Dutch** arrived in the mid-16th century, Senarat's son Rajasimha II signed a pact whose goal was to put an end

Development

to Portuguese power in Sri Lanka. At this time trading in spices had reached a first climax. The Dutch did not, however, stick to the agreements; although they helped the kings of Kandy oust the Portuguese from the strategically important ports of Galle and Negombo, they subsequently declared Galle to be their territory. The income from exporting spices subsequently formed the most important source of revenue for the state.

A good century later the **British** arrived, and their traces are still clearly visible today. After bringing the majority of the island under their control, they set about restructuring the economy to their liking. During the first half of the 19th century they introduced coffee cultivation, which soon became so successful that it exceeded the profits from the spice trade, which had dominated until then. This development ended again however in around 1865 when the plants were affected by coffee rust. This disease spread from Sri Lanka all around the world. For the British, the abrupt end of coffee cultivation was the reason why other profitable crops were brought to Ceylon. The plantation economy they had created was suitable for tea, rubber and coconut palms. These three plants still make up Sri Lanka's agricultural backbone. Around a fifth of GNP comes from the agricultural sector.

The annual per capita income of just under US$ 5700 (UK: US$ 36,600) **means Sri Lanka is still a developing country**, but in comparison with other south Asian states it has an outstanding position. According to the Human Development Index of the United Nations, Sri Lanka held 73th place amongst the world's 186 states in 2013.

Tea cultivation (▶MARCO POLO Insight p.332)   The fact that Sri Lanka, after Kenya, is now the world's second-biggest tea exporter with approx. 300,000 tons a year is mainly due to British colonial rule. Around 14 percent of the agricultural area, which corresponds to around 260,000 ha/640,000 acres, is used for tea crops. In Sri Lanka tea grows at altitudes of around 1500–2000m/4900–6500ft. The young shoots are harvested and brought to factories where they are dried.

The cultivation of this land illustrates the division in the Sri Lankan population. Almost all plantation workers are Tamil people, who are some of the worst-paid labourers here.

Rice cultivation   A further important role in Sri Lankan agriculture is played by rice, the vast majority of which is grown in watery fields or paddies. The foundation for this is the centuries-old irrigation system that brings sufficient water even to the most remote parts of the island. Visitors should not be fooled by the apparent large-scale nature of rice cultivation in Sri Lanka. It has no significance as an agricultural export. The quantities produced are not even enough for the country to cover its own demands! During difficult climatic years Sri Lanka has to import rice from, for example, the United States, which has a significant impact on the state budget. The government has been implementing targeted measures such as the **Mahaweli irrigation project** to make sure rice imports will soon be a thing of the past.

Coconut palms are also cultivated on large, mostly privately owned plantations. Every year around 2.5 million coconuts are harvested. Copra, the flesh obtained from them, is an important export, most commonly used in the cosmetics industry.

Coconut palms

Picking tea is a laborious and yet badly paid job

Rubber Even though Sri Lanka's rubber plantations take up six percent of the country's agricultural land, the profits from exporting rubber are playing an ever decreasing role. Competition from other east Asian countries in particular, and also the devaluation of the currencies of Thailand and Malaysia, have led to a big drop in prices. Small farmers, whose rubber plantations often only consist of a few hundred square metres, are suffering the most. There has even been talk of planting tea between the rubber trees to compensate for the small profits. The annual production in 2012 was approx. 150,000 tons.

Forest areas Two thirds of the island of Sri Lanka was once covered by jungle, but human interference has left its mark. Unchecked logging for many decades means the island now only has around 1.7 million ha/4.2 million acres of forest left. The government has only recently begun making efforts to increase this percentage again by reforestation measures. Around 90 percent of the wood from logging is used to supply the population with fuel.

Fishing Fishing is surprisingly underdeveloped. Coastal fishing is not even capable of covering the country's own demands. One negative aspect here is that after the 2004 tsunami, aid organizations donated new fishing boats, which are now lying on the beaches »unemployed« because of overfishing. It is only high-seas fishing that is worthwhile, but even here ruthless exploitation of tuna stocks for example means that they are threatened by extinction. Most high-seas fishing is done by Japanese trawlers, with whom the Sri Lankan government has an agreement. This in turn means that the catches by the local population have been falling for years. Inland, the reservoirs from centuries ago are now being used to farm freshwater fish.

Industry, mining, energy Sri Lanka does not have a noteworthy energy and mining industry. One reason for this is the **lack of natural resources and raw materials**. All around Colombo an extensive free trade zone was set up, causing dozens of **textile factories** to be opened, but the raw fabrics are imported from India and Europe rather than produced in Sri Lanka. As a result of the exceptionally low wages for seamstresses (less than £75 a month), this is nonetheless lucrative. As a result of the abolition of the internationally agreed textile quotas, more than 25,000 people lost their jobs in 2005 alone.

More than two thirds of the country's energy requirements are now met from **hydropower**. The damming of Mahaweli Ganga east of Kandy and the construction of further dams in the country's interior were ambitious government projects to reduce dependence on expensive oil imports. Although Sri Lanka does not have any coal

Toddy tappers acrobatically climb coconut palm trees to a height of 30m/100ft to tap their sap from which arak is made

deposits, **gemstones** are very significant for the island's economy. Rubies, sapphires and other gemstones are found, mainly in the south of the island around Ratnapura. The export of gemstones is officially worth £60 million annually (►MARCO POLO Insight p. 356).

Sri Lanka is **one of the most popular Asian destinations**, maybe because tourists remained almost unaffected by the civil war. Sri Lanka is also an inexpensive destination, and the islanders' hospitality is almost proverbial. The year 2013 saw record numbers; a total of around 1.27 million visitors came to the island. Tourism, after the export of tea and textiles, is the **largest source of foreign exchange**, bringing in around US$ 1 billion. It contributes more than a fifth of the national income. An estimated 67,000 people are employed in the tourism sector.

Tourism

Welcome to Everyday Life

Experience Sri Lanka away from the standard tourist trails and meet »completely normal« people. The islanders are incredibly friendly and it is easy to find a guide to show visitors around. Here are some tips:

MARKET LIFE

Markets in Asia have the reputation of being an olfactory trial for unaccustomed Western noses. Hold your nose and go for it is the best motto, especially when exploring one of the more rural markets. Sensitive noses will note the differences; the various smells are the most intense around the stalls that trade in spices and spice mixes (the famous curries that are particularly typical of Sri Lanka).

CRICKET IS THE NATIONAL SPORT

Cricket is a very English game but it also attracts large crowds on Sri Lanka. The Sri Lankan national team has won international titles after all. Every larger town has a cricket stadium. The matches are announced in the daily newspapers. There are differences in ticket prices. A premium is charged for fixtures against the arch rival India.

LIVING WITH SRI LANKANS

It is hardly possible to get a more direct contact to the native population. And since this is a real alternative to comfortable hotel rooms fitted with all the bells and whistles, there are some websites that find accommodation for visitors with Sri Lankan families. Eat breakfast together before taking up the suggestion of the man of the house for a good place to visit. Reunite over the evening meal with many new impressions. Many small guesthouses also offer such an individual atmosphere. They are known as ›homestays‹. They often have only a few rooms, are very inexpensive and the contacts come on their own.
en.homeforhome.com

CELEBRATING

Sri Lankans generally live their everyday lives in accordance with the recommendations of the Enlightened Buddha. And he is omnipresent, but especially so on the Poya Days that take place once a month. They are somewhat like points of reference in the course of the year, on which devout Buddhists take the opportunity to engage in self-contemplation. The pilgrims, dressed in white, flood en masse to the country's sacred sites; but keep in mind that Buddhism is not a religion that prohibits enjoyment. The Poya Days are also used to visit friends and family again. To make it all worthwhile, it is common for a day or two to be added to allow Sri Lankans to eat, drink and celebrate together. However, these celebrations are not purely family affairs and anyone visiting Sri Lanka during these days will experience the locals' full cordiality, especially in smaller towns and villages.

VOLUNTEERING

Near Polonnaruwa there is an organizer of elephant safaris who also has a programme that supports the local schools. Anyone wishing to stay for a longer period of time who can speak English can work as a teacher in the local school. Interested parties need to be at least 18 years old and have to pay for their own accommodation.
Samagi Villa Safari
Polonnaruwa
Tel. 077 758 73 27
www.samagivillasafari.com

Religion

More than two thirds of the people in Sri Lanka are Buddhists. They belong to the Singhalese people. The Tamil population is Hindu.

BUDDHISM

Strictly speaking Buddhism is more a philosophy than a religion. However even today it is still considered a counter-movement to Hinduism; Buddha wanted to reform the Brahmin culture of India, particularly the old caste system, and break the dominance of the Brahmins in society. Buddha, meaning »the enlightened one«, was born as the son of a king in Nepal at the foot of the Himalayas and was called **Siddharta Gautama** (▶Famous People). During his esti-mated 80-year life, which he largely spent as an itinerant monk and hermit, he developed teachings that have spread around the world. After Buddha's death, which took place in 480 BC according to his-torical sources, but is said by Buddhists to have occurred in 543 BC, his teachings quickly spread. During the time of the Indian king Ashoka (approx. 272–236 BC), who was converted by a monk called Ugagupta, Buddhism experienced its **first great heyday**. It spread from India to Sri Lanka and far beyond to southeast Asia and China. An estimated 150 to 500 million people now live by the principles of Buddhism, but it should be noted that they may at the same time be followers of other religions too.

Most Buddhists in Sri Lanka invoke the rules of the **Theravada school**, which was founded only shortly after Buddha entered nir-vana. This school claims to follow the unadulterated teachings of the Enlightened One and cites as evidence three councils, of which one took place a few years after Buddha's death, the second 100 years later and the third in around 245 BC. While different schools formed at this time spread different teachings, the followers of the Theravada school held on to what they believe were Buddha's original teachings. Theravada monks can be recognized by their dark robes.

Buddhist schools of thought

From Hinduism, Buddhism took over the term **karma**, the insur-mountable cosmic law. According to tradition Buddha was only able to break free from this cycle after more than 500 lives in different incarnations. However, this does not mean the soul leaves one body for another. Instead, after the third step of the cycle, death, a new be-

The depiction of Buddha with the Gesture of Argument

ing comes into existence from the karma of the being that has just passed away. According to dominant opinion, those closest to breaking free from this cycle are the monks living in monasteries, which explains the high standing monks enjoy in Sri Lanka.

The most important difference between **Mahayana Buddhism**, which has now become dominant in China, Korea, Japan and Vietnam, and **Hinayana Buddhism**, which has followers in Sri Lanka, Thailand, Cambodia and Laos, consists in the possibilities of breaking out of the cycle of birth, death and rebirth. While Hinayana Buddhism, the teaching of the »low vehicle«, starts with the idea that this has to be achieved by every single believer without any support, Mahayana Buddhism, »high vehicle«, which developed in the 1st and 2nd centuries AD, has bodhisattvas. These venerable people, who have already achieved the state of enlightenment, have chosen to remain on earth in order to help others find the way to enlightenment via the »Eightfold Path«. Mahayana Buddhism has far more followers, presumably because it prescribes far less strict rules than Hinayana Buddhism, and shows the path to breaking free from the eternal cycle to a much greater number of Buddhists.

Buddhism in Sri Lanka

Sri Lanka was the first country outside India in which the teachings of the Enlightened One became established. In around 250 BC King Ashoka sent his son (according to other sources his brother or his nephew) Mahinda to King Devanampiya Tissa of Sri Lanka, who was soon converted to Buddhism and had the new teachings spread through the entire country. He founded **the island's Buddhist monastery** in Anuradhapura and had the first dagoba, the Thuparama Dagoba, built to house a Buddha relic. After Ashoka's death his powerful empire fell apart into several individual states and a few centuries later Buddhism had almost disappeared entirely from India. It was only under the Gupta dynasty (around AD 310–500) that it flourished once more. The teachings suffered temporarily from the **split** that produced Hinayana and Mahayana Buddhism as well as the different schools. An important role was also played by Vishnu worship, which the Gupta rulers also participated in. Thus by the 8th century Buddhism disappeared once more from the Indian subcontinent and was replaced by Hinduism. Buddhism had nevertheless spread to other parts of Asia: to China from the second half of the 1st century, Korea from 372, to Japan, Burma, Java and Sumatra from the 5th century, to Siam from 720 (but possibly already during the reign of Ashoka) and to the Khmer Empire, whose core area roughly corresponds to modern Cambodia, from the year 800.

In Sri Lanka, in Burma and in Siam both types co-existed for a long time until the **Theravada school**, the most important school of Hinayana Buddhism, became dominant. It has remained dominant in these countries to this day. The monks living in Sri Lanka have claimed to be the ones maintaining Buddha's original teachings, but they too have been exposed to attacks on a number of occasions. Already in the 1st century BC the monks split, and later Mahayana and Tantra Buddhism also became established in Sri Lanka. It was only under King Parakramabahu I (1153–86) that the Buddhist teachings were reunified. More recently Buddhism in Sri Lanka has experienced a **multifaceted renewal**. Under the governments of Salomon and Sirimavo Bandaranaike it was employed to convey socialist values. They were able use monks for political ends and they were lucky in that Buddhism was still one of the country's most important social forces.

Strictly speaking only monks (Bikkhu), novices (Samahera), nuns (Bikkhuni) and hermits are considered Buddhists, because only they live in a world that is free from the pursuit of possessions and wealth. This is one of the most important conditions for a life according to the teachings of Buddha, who said the **Eightfold Path** was the only way by which to break free from the eternal cycle of rebirth. Hinayana Buddhism, the more dominant type in Sri Lanka, only permitted this possibility to monks, not to lay people. This is maybe the most important difference between this type of Buddhism and Mahayana Buddhism.

Buddhist
monks

Monks, nuns, novices and hermits make up the monastic community (Sangha) or **monastic order**. At the head of every large monastery is an abbot, who also usually has jurisdiction over several small monasteries in the surrounding area. There are currently around 16,000 monks in Sri Lanka. Every man can enter a monastery regardless of his caste and is also free to leave again if and when he chooses. In Sri Lanka the tradition that every man spends at least a few months in a monastery during his lifetime is less widespread than in Thailand, however. Most monks remain loyal to their decision to become a Bikkhu and spend their life in the monastery. There is no prescribed minimum age and there are even 12 to 14-year-old boy monks who wear a white novice robe until their ceremonial ordination amongst family, friends and acquaintances. When they enter the order proper, they are given the saffron-coloured monk's robe and a new name – often one of a meritorious old monk. During the ceremony the young monk recites the »**Three Jewels« of the Buddhist teachings**: »I take refuge in Buddha«, »I take refuge in the Dharma«, »I take refuge in the Sangha«. Then the monk vows to adhere strictly to the **five principles of the monks' rules**: no killing, no deception, no adultery, no stealing and no alcohol. Only over time does the monk learn the 227 detailed rules (Vinaya), of which the vows of poverty, celibacy and peaceableness are the most important. A monk is not allowed to possess more than his robes, an alms bowl, a needle, a belt, a razor and a filter to remove bugs from drinking water. **He may not have any other property** and he may not han-

dle money: for that there are nuns, who generally take care of the monastic budget. When it comes to contact with women, the monks in Sri Lanka are far more uncomplicated than the monks of Thailand, for example: in Thailand monks are not permitted to have direct contact with women, whereas those in Sri Lanka are generally quite willing to have a conversation and are also allowed to receive objects. Monks are not allowed to ingest any solid food after noon, but are restricted to drinks; they use their time to study the scriptures or to meditate. Monks begging for their food are a rare sight in Sri Lanka, by the way, because here the people living around the monastery are responsible for providing sufficient food for them. If you do see a monk going from door to door with an alms bowl, this should not really be called begging: quite the opposite in fact, as it is a good opportunity for the population to gain more merit by aiding the monks. In order to achieve enlightenment and enter nirvana it is important to follow the »**Three Noble Disciplines**« which Buddha taught. The first prescribes sacrifices for gods and demons in their many different guises, the second consists of the pursuit of knowledge and insight, and veneration for others, particularly priests and old people. The third holds that self-contemplation, meditation, will bring about release from the clutches of the five elements, which is necessary in order to achieve unification with the divine principle.

HINDUISM

Around 900 million people on Earth call themselves Hindus. The term Hinduism arose from the translation of the Sanskrit word »Indu« into Iranian (»Hindu«), where it was originally reserved for those people who lived along the Indian river Indus; the term Hinduism for their religious beliefs is an invention of the Western world. In contrast to monotheistic faith in a single personified divinity, Indian Hinduism is a **monistic religion** oriented to a de-personified principle (cf. Buddhism, Confucianism and Taoism).

Principles

The foundations of Hinduism have grown over the millennia; Hinduism is not a rigid religious principle. One of the basic elements of Hinduism today is **Brahmanism**, which only developed in the first millennium AD; it took its basic ideas from Vedism, a religion of ancient India. According to Hindu beliefs all living beings – plants, animals and people – have a place on a **symbolic ladder**, at the top of which is the pantheon. This highest rung is reserved to the gods and deities living on Mount Meru, a mountain inconceivably high to human beings.

There is no minimum age for monks

On the rung below are saints, kings, spirits and demons, while human beings are located around half way up the ladder. Hinduism has a large number of gods, the most important of which are the trinity (Trimurti) of Brahma, Vishnu and Shiva. They can, however, take on any guise they wish. They could, for example, enter the body of an object or a living being during a visit to earth and take possession of it for a certain amount of time. The four-headed god Brahma is the personification of the supreme cosmic spirit Brahman. He is considered the creator of the world and was once the highest god of Hinduism. Today he is on the same rank as Vishnu, the preserver of the world, who is popularly depicted as the shepherd god Krishna, and Shiva, the destroyer of the world. In Sri Lanka the god of war Skanda, who appears in various incarnations, including Kataragama, is particularly highly venerated. The most important principle of Hinduism (as also of Buddhism) is the notion that every living being is subjected to the **eternal cycle of rebirth**.

This cycle of birth, death and rebirth of the soul (Samsara) is inescapable for all living things, unless they manage to enter nirvana after many lives filled with good thoughts and deeds. In what shell the soul is reborn is just as unpredictable as the number of lives. The cycle can be influenced, however, by good and bad deeds (karma) that are rewarded or punished in the next life as a better or worse existence. The goal of every Hindu is to escape from having to be reborn, thus breaking free from the cycle forever. Hindus also have a relatively fixed notion of the cosmos, which is based both on mythological and philosophical ideas and on the simple observation of natural processes. The world, put together from the essential constituent of the universe (prakriti), is thus in a constant **cycle of development and destruction**; between these two phases is a phase of rest separating the two. Human beings consider themselves as a small world (Buwana Alit) in a large world (Buwana Agung).

ISLAM AND CHRISTIANITY

Islam   Somewhat more than 7 percent of Sri Lanka's population follow the Islamic faith. They are largely found amongst the descendants of the Moors, who came to the island from the 8th century AD onwards as Arab seafarers and merchants. Islam (translated »surrender« or »submission«) is a monotheistic religion. Its teachings go back to **Mohammed**, Allah's last prophet, who was probably born in Mecca (in what is now Saudi Arabia) in around AD 570. Islam's most important sacred site is the Kaaba (cube) in Mecca, a cubical building on which the »Black Stone« can be found. By touching or kissing it the pilgrims show it the highest veneration during the hajj, the **pilgrimage to Mecca**. The Kaaba dates back to before Mohammed's time, when it was already a popular place of pilgrimage. According to a revelation made by Allah to Mohammed in the Koran, it was built by Abraham and one of his sons at God's behest. Mohammed had the Kaaba freed from all images of gods. The foundation of the Islamic faith, written down by the followers of Mohammed, is the **Koran** (»that which is to be recited«). It consists of 114 suras (sections) in free verse and contains all the commandments and laws a devout Muslim has to obey. The most important part consists of the »**Five Pillars of Islam**« (arkan): the affirmation that there is no other deity besides Allah and that Mohammed is His prophet; the ritual prayers (salat) that have to be performed; the giving of alms (zakat), the pilgrimage to Mecca (hajj), and the requirement to fast during the month of Ramadan, the 9th month of the Islamic lunar calendar. Even though almost all towns and villages in Sri Lanka have not just Buddhist and Hindu temples but also mosques, there is little evidence of missionary work on the island. Few women wear veils.

Again somewhat more than 7 percent of the Singhalese population are of Christian faith, most of them Roman Catholics. In contrast to other Asian countries, where missionaries from Europe arrived very early on, Christianity only became established in Sri Lanka from the 16th century, when the Portuguese, then the Dutch and finally the British came to the island. Missionary activity in Sri Lanka was never particularly strong.

Christianity

History

The Royally Luminous Land

The island's history has been influenced throughout the centuries by Buddhism. Even when the various colonial rulers came and took control of the country's riches, the people did not stray from their faith. In the 20th century a civil war broke out which claimed thousands of victims. And then the island was hit by the tsunami, which destroyed large parts of the country.

SRI LANKA HAS HAD MANY NAMES

Over the course of its history, Sri Lanka has had different names. The current one has only been the island's official name since 1972, when a new democratic constitution came into effect. The Singhalese term Lanka goes back to a Sanskrit word and means »luminous«. This name already appears in some ancient Indian sources, such as the Ramayana epic. The addition of the word Sri is a Singhalese honorary title and means something like divine, royal or holy. If the current official name is translated it means the **royally luminous land**.

During the time of the Romans and Greeks, Sri Lanka was also known by the name Taprobane (**copper island**), or at least the Egyptian Ptolemy called it thus in his geographical work of the 2nd century. The island chronicle Mahavamsa penned by the Buddhist monk Mahanama in Pali at the start of the 6th century knew modern-day Sri Lanka by the name of Tambapanni (**copper-coloured land**). In the 8th century the Arabs called the island Serendib (**the enchanting one**).

In later times the Singhalese who had migrated to the island gave it a name that befitted their high self-confidence: Singhala Dvipa (**lion island**); it was named thus after the sons of the lion who came from southern India. Finally, the Tamil people had and have their own names for Sri Lanka: Singhalam, Singhala-divu and Ilankai (the latter stands for **jewel island**).

Last but not least the colonial rulers left their marks; the name of Ceilao introduced by the Portuguese later became **Ceylon** during the Dutch occupation and remained in place until 1972. The British also used the name Ceylon.

Dagobas, such as the Ruwanweli Dagoba in Anuradhapura, commemorate Buddha and act as a reminder of the right path to Enlightenment

PREHISTORY

1st millennium BC	Farmers come to Sri Lanka from southern India.
250 BC	The first irrigation system is built.
80 BC	The First Buddhist Council is held.

Around 500,000 years ago
Until the 1960s historians had assumed that it could not be proved whether settlers had come to the island in prehistory. However, **stone tools** were then found and dated to around 500,000 years ago. Further discoveries in the form of clay tableware presumably date to the Iron Age; their appearances resemble those found in southern India. The discoveries indicate that there may have been trade relations between India and Sri Lanka. There is no certain knowledge about the ancestry of the people who lived in Sri Lanka during this time.

Balangaloda culture
During the period of the Balangaloda culture tools were made of stone. They were probably made by people who came to the island from southern India.

Settlement
The first parts of the Indian chronicle Mahavamsa contain clues to a settlement of Sri Lanka. In verse this reputed mix of legend and reality describes the arrival of the Singhalese, probably people of Indo-Aryan ancestry. They were followed three centuries later by the first Tamils, who were most likely merchants.

Vedda
The Vedda, members of a Caucasian race who are related to different Vedic tribes of the Indian subcontinent, some of which live in the jungle, are still considered to be the island's aboriginal inhabitants. However, the Mahavamsa does not provide information about whether the beings identified with them were really human. In it they are described as yakshas and nagas, ghost-like beings.

The first settlers
During the first half of the 1st millennium BC farmers came to the island of Lanka, that being the old name of Sri Lanka in Sanskrit, from southern India. They are now known as Ancient Singhalese. While many aboriginals, robbed of their lands, were pushed back ever further into the jungle regions where they led a hunter-gatherer existence, many others assimilated with other, more recent arrivals. Many sites dating from the prehistory of the first settlement in Sri Lanka have been discovered, such as the caves around Bandarawela.

Irrigation system
Long before channels were built to irrigate the paddy fields on the island of Bali, for example, Sri Lanka already had such a system. Archaeologists have found man-made structures that were in place as

early as 250 BC; they captured the water running off from the mountains, stored it artificially and distributed it on to the fields using an ingenious system.

During this time the city of Anuradhapura became the island's first flourishing capital and a centre of Buddhist teaching, which had spread here from the Indian subcontinent. The king in power there, Ashoka, sent Mahinda, his son or a different close relative – it is not known exactly – to Sri Lanka, where he spread the Buddhist teachings at his behest. King Devanampiya Tissa readily accepted them and soon declared Buddhism the universal religion. The town of Anuradhapura itself was extended. The basis of the wealth of its population primarily came from the irrigation system, which had been built long before but had since undergone comprehensive extensions. Many sacred buildings were constructed within the town. Travellers reported »golden stupas that could be seen from far away«. By far the most imposing was the stupa of Jetavaranama with a height of 120m/394ft. It was followed by the stupa of Abhayagiri, which had a height of 70m/230ft.

Anuradha-pura

In around 200 BC Tamil people from southern India occupied the majority of the island. This episode did not last long, however. The invaders were soon ousted by King Dutthagamani (161–137 BC). To this day Dutthagamani is considered a national hero amongst the Singhalese population for this reason.

Indian Tamils

Rock relief in Anuradhapura

First Buddhist Council   Around 500 Buddhist monks gathered in the monastery of Alu Vihara near Matala, north of Kandy, in 80 BC in order to write down those sermons of Buddha that were considered authentic. They were given the name »Tripitaka« (three baskets) and became a fundamental and still valid component of Buddhist teaching.

THE YEARS OF THE FIRST VISITORS

1st century	Greek seafarers come to Sri Lanka; Ptolemy describes more than 50 places on the island.
around 450	The rock fortress of Sigiriya is built; Fa Xian, a monk from China, travels around Ceylon.
993	The Chola dynasty conquers the entire island; Polonnaruwa becomes the capital.

Visit and return visit   Greek seafarers came to the island of Sri Lanka on their way to India at the start of the 1st century AD. They called it »Taprobane« (copper island). In the year 45 Sri Lankan merchants responded to a visit by Roman emissaries by visiting Rome themselves. The astronomer, mathematician and geographer **Claudius Ptolemy** (around AD 100–160) described more than 50 places in Sri Lanka. However, he presumably got his knowledge from the reports made by the Greek seafarers. An early map of the island is also attributed to Ptolemy.

A father-son conflict   The **rock fortress of Sigiriya** was built under King Kashyapa, one of the two sons of King Dhatusena of Anuradhapura. He feared revenge by his half-brother Moggallana, since, according to tradition, he is said to have chained their father naked to a wall and immured him alive. When Moggallana approached with his troops in 495, Kashyapa left the fortress (located at an elevation of 200m/660ft and considered impregnable) in order to ride out towards his half-brother, but committed suicide before falling into his hands.

Fa Xian and Buddhaghosa   In the 5th century BC the wandering Chinese monk Fa Xian visited the island of Sri Lanka. He walked all the way from China and stayed for two years. During this time wrote incredibly accurate **descriptions of the situation** there, although he often referred to legends from the Mahavamsa. Fa Xian does seem to have travelled through large parts of the island himself. Thus he reported a temple in which a shrine contained one of Buddha's teeth. The town of Mihintale, which is still considered the birthplace of Buddhism in Sri Lanka, was also mentioned in his records. Around the same time as Fa Xian and during the reign of King Manama (406–428 AD) the Buddhist dogmatist Buddhaghosa was working in the monastery of

Anuradhapura. He wrote many commentaries on Buddhist teaching written in Pali, a central-Indian language related to Vedic Sanskrit.

Although King Mahinda V acceded to the throne in 982, he had to accept the fact just a few years later that King Raja Raja the Great was not just conquering large parts of southern India but Sri Lanka as well. This ruler of the southern Indian Chola dynasty invaded Sri Lanka with his troops in 993, thereby beating other powerful Pandya rulers from southern India to it. He conquered the entire island and made it a province of his empire. He declared Polonnaruwa to be his administrative capital and Hinduism to be the valid religion. Anuradhapura had been the most flourishing town in Sri Lanka until this point, but then it was drawn into conflicts. In 1017 Mahinda V was deposed, taken prisoner and carried off to southern India. His capital, Anuradhapura, largely fell victim to destruction and the population was deported.

A Chola province

The occupation by the Chola rulers was to last many centuries. It was only in 1070 that the Singhalese king Vijaya Bahu I was able to push them back to the Indian mainland. This was naturally too late for Anuradhapura. Polonnaruwa not only had a strategically more favourable location than the old capital, but also better agricultural conditions as a result of its proximity to the Mahaweli River. Instead of Hinduism, Vijaya Bahu I reintroduced Buddhism and made a name for himself as a reformer of the administration and public life. This was, however, a relatively short-lived golden age. After his death the country was divided up.

Polonnaruwa

When King Parakrama Bahu I ascended the throne in 1153 he found a country whose people were deeply at odds with each other. By ruling with an iron fist he nevertheless managed to unify the country into one Singhalese kingdom again within just a few years. The new state structure with its capital in Polonnaruwa subsequently flourished, a development that also expressed itself in increased political influence towards the Indian mainland. The irrigation system, which was already centuries old at this time, was also expanded. The biggest part of this project was the construction of the 24 sq km/9 sq mi **Parakrama Samudra Reservoir**, which allowed more than three times as much land to be cultivated as had been possible before.
Artistically speaking Parakrama Bahu's successor Nissanka Malla (1187–96) made a name for himself despite his short reign by commissioning several sacred works of art such as the monumental Buddha statues of Gal Vihara and the Vatadage of Polonnaruwa. Politically, however, he did not succeed in stabilizing the situation in the long term. Shortly after his death a new conflict erupted between the Sin-

Fighting and reunification

ghalese dynasties. Mercenaries from southern India (amongst them also countless Cholas), who were called in to help by various members, marched across the island, plundering as they went. An Indian pirate by the name of Magha finally brought matters to a sad head: he took his band to Polonnaruwa, overran the city and sacked it. The inhabitants were forced to leave and flee to the surrounding areas.

THE COLONIAL ERA

16th century	The Portuguese discover Ceylon.
Around 1640	The Dutch expel the Portuguese.
1815	The British conquer Kandy.

Years of uncertainty
The 14th and 15th centuries were marked by uncertainty. It was only during the reign of King Parakrama Bahu V (1411–67), a ruler who knew how to bring fractured kingdoms back together again, that this period ended. His residence was located in Kotte, a fact unpopular with the rulers of Kandy. Confrontations occurred time and time again, and after Bahu's death Kotte fell into the hands of Kandy entirely, which thus succeeded in subjecting a large part of the island to its rule.

The Portuguese
Even though Sri Lanka had been known since ancient times, and not just by seafarers, foreign powers, apart from the ruling dynasties of southern India of course, did not show much interest in the island. This was to change at the start of the 16th century, when the Portuguese began extending their colonial efforts to Asia. Initially they only tried to establish a trading post en route between Europe and Asia where ships could call in. As early as 1510 Goa in the west of India had been conquered by the seafarer and viceroy **Alfonso de Albuquerque** and declared a Portuguese colony. Macao near Hong Kong followed in 1557. Ceilao, as the Portuguese called Sri Lanka, was ideal for the Portuguese because it helped them **secure their shipping routes**, and soon the trading post they had been granted became an area of influence that covered the entire southwest of the island. However, they had no luck with the rulers of Kandy. The Portuguese even left the island temporarily, only to return in 1610 at the express wish of King Senerath (1604–35). Senerath, too, soon had enough of the Portuguese attempts to gain control of the island, particularly the strategically important ports of Trincomalee and Batticaloa. When Raja Sinha II came to power after Senerath's death, the Dutch appeared on the scene.

The Dutch
The Netherlands also had overseas territories such as modern-day Indonesia. The **Vereenigde Oost-Indische Compagnie** (VOC) was

Foreign Rulers on Sri Lanka

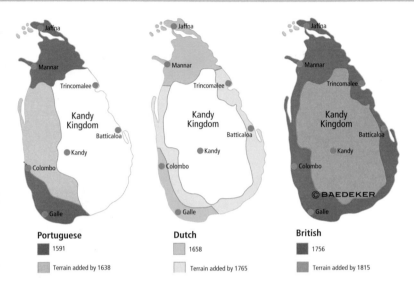

Portuguese
- 1591
- Terrain added by 1638

Dutch
- 1658
- Terrain added by 1765

British
- 1756
- Terrain added by 1815

©BAEDEKER

responsible for trading with them. They were primarily interested in spices and gemstones, two commodities the Singhalese had in plenty. Raja Sinha II offered them a treaty giving the Dutch the sole right to trade in both. This treaty was conditional on the Dutch assisting the Singhalese in their fight against the Portuguese. However, Raja Sinha II had misjudged the Dutch. After winning the ports of Galle and Negombo back from the Portuguese they quickly declared them to be their own territory. They had recognized how valuable these two ports were and a few years later they added Jaffna on the island's north coast. Though the Portuguese had been expelled from Sri Lanka, the Dutch had now taken their place. In 1656 they had the fortifications of Colombo demolished.

They showed almost no interest in **Kandy**, however, which at this point still had the Singhalese name Srivardhanapura. This allowed King Raja Sinha II to secure the continued existence of his kingdom. He was unable to prevent the colonial rulers from trying to impose their Christian faith on the island population. At least they proved tolerant enough towards the Buddhist and Muslim faiths too. The **trade in spices** started to flourish, and of course it was firmly in the hands of the Dutch. Some of the export profits went into the state coffers and thus contributed to the growing affluence of the Singhalese islanders.

The British After some unsuccessful attempts the British managed to become established on Ceilao. Bit by bit they took the most important ports, an endeavour they did not find difficult in view of their military superiority. They managed to achieve what the Dutch could not: in 1803 the rulers of Kandy were able to fend off a British attack but twelve years later their days were numbered. The British benefited from the fact that the rulers of Kandy were at odds with each other, which made them an easy target for attack.

Singhalese rebellion Nevertheless the British took several years to secure their power in Kandy and had to use force. A Singhalese rebellion that arose in 1817 and lasted almost two years, claiming hundreds of victims, was brutally put down. Kandy henceforth became the capital of the entire island of **Ceylon**, a name that was to remain until 1972. In 1815 King Shirivikramarashasimha's days were also over; he was deposed by his own noblemen. In the Kandyan Convention that was passed by mutual agreement, the king acquiesced to his entire kingdom being made subject to the British crown. In return the British guaranteed to maintain the administrative system and protect the Buddhist religion.

Indian Tamils are recruited The British soon began creating large coffee plantations, for which they needed more, and cheaper, labour than they could find on the island. Their solution was to recruit Tamil workers from southern India, who initially willingly followed the call of their new masters, but by 1848 realized their labour was being exploited. A rebellion broke out, which the British put down in a bloody confrontation. Then came the problem of **coffee rust**; the disease began affecting the delicate coffee plants of Ceylon in 1865 and quickly spread to all the world's coffee-growing regions. The British soon had a solution, however: they replaced the coffee plants with tea bushes.

CEYLON BECOMES INDEPENDENT

1931	Universal suffrage for all the island population.
4 February 1948	Ceylon gains its independence.

Elite and patriotism The wealth that came to the island as a result of its coffee and tea plantations created an intellectual and moneyed elite amongst the Singhalese population. They succeeded in obtaining certain **rights of self-administration** from the British. However, even in the less well educated strata of society a certain patriotism, which had been a Singhalese characteristic since time immemorial, emerged in a more pronounced manner. They started fighting their foreign rulers. Buddhist monks played an important role in this endeavour. However, the British had managed to obtain enough influence amongst the

Singhalese early on. For this reason the efforts of individuals to escape from the rule of the British crown came to nothing. In 1915, on the anniversary of Kandy's capitulation to the British, renewed **unrest** broke out. It had clear nationalistic tendencies and the refusal of the British to give at least the Singhalese elite a certain voice in government now came back to bite them. The violence was not aimed primarily at the British but rather at the Moors, the enterprising descendants of Arab seafarers who were living on the coast. However, when the British started to worry that the unrest would spread further and possibly bring about the end of their rule, they intervened and arrested the ringleaders without further ado.

Although the Singhalese and Tamils were largely agreed in their desire to expel the British colonial power from the island in the not too distant future, some Tamils were worried as early as 1920 that the Singhalese were being given greater political power than themselves. Even a commission put in place by Sir Hugh Clifford, the governor at the time, could not change this. Its purpose was to advise on a new constitution and take the special ethnic needs of Ceylon into account.

Tamils against Singhalese

Clifford had been in office for less than four years when the commission finally came to an agreement in 1931. It not only proposed a government that included Singhalese and Tamil politicians, but also permitted the introduction of universal suffrage for all island inhabitants from the age of 21. This made Ceylon the first British overseas territory that had such a suffrage.

Universal suffrage

The right to vote ignited more and more **nationalistic tendencies** amongst the population. The people became more self-confident in dealing with their British rulers; a labour movement developed and social conditions were improved. Don Stephen Senanayake earned himself particular merit in his efforts to improve the country's agriculture. It was also he with whom the British chose to negotiate about Ceylon's independence. Senanayake suggested handing over possession step by step. The British agreed to this proposal when Senanayake, whose parents had given him an English first name as a sign of their loyalty, said he would make sure this transition would be a peaceful one.

Efforts to gain autonomy

The Second World War put the efforts of the independence movement on hold. The ports of Colombo, Trincomalee and Batticaloa were important British bases between Europe and Asia. When the Japanese bombed these ports in 1942 more than 1200 Allied (mainly British) and Singhalese soldiers were killed, but the attacks ultimately remained unsuccessful. Maybe, historians suggest, Japanese control of Ceylon would have given the war a different direction.

Second World War

Independence

The first years after the end of the Second World War were dominated by renewed efforts for independence. Britain once again set up a commission to draw up proposals. Although the draft would have allowed the Singhalese to govern themselves in the future, the British still wanted to determine foreign policy, but gave in surprisingly quickly when the Singhalese people were against this. On **4 February 1948** Britain granted the island of Ceylon independence and Don Stephen Senanayake became the country's first prime minister.

BUILDING A NEW STATE

from 1948	Economic boom
1950	The Colombo Plan is born.
1972	Ceylon is renamed »Sri Lanka« and becomes a socialist republic.
1978	The presidential system is introduced.

Determined development

Senanayake immediately set about developing the young state of Ceylon. He aimed for a **strict separation of religion and state** and worked on building up the economy. His great skill in handling public opinion was a reason why the socialist-oriented opposition had little chance. The weakened economy recovered and the money from the tea and natural rubber exports filled the treasury; the government invested a large percentage of this money into improving welfare, but also into the first big irrigation project. This is how the **Gal Oya project** along with Senanayake Samudra came into existence. This reservoir is almost four times bigger than Parakrama Samudra.

Tamils lose their right to vote

Senanayake must admittedly take some of the blame for the civil war that broke out in 1983. In 1948 he not only revoked the Indian Tamils' right to vote, he even took away their citizenship and thus clearly made them second-class inhabitants. Their **exploitation as cheap workers** was thus legitimized by law. In addition he made Singhala the only official language.

Colombo Plan

The Commonwealth heads of government met in Colombo in 1950 in order to develop a mutual framework for their economic development. The resulting plan was named after the city in which this conference took place: the »Colombo Plan for Cooperative Economic and Social Development in Asia and the Pacific«, or »Colombo Plan« for short. It is an important instrument for co-ordinating development aid in Asia, which is paid for to this day by Great Britain, Australia, Canada, the United States and New Zealand. Nineteen further states joined the seven founding states over the years.

The Gal Oya Project was implemented to irrigate the country

The Bandara-naike dynasty

When Don Senanayake suffered a fatal riding accident in 1952, his son Dudley (►Famous People) took over as prime minister, but could not build on his father's successes and had to step down just a year later. In the meantime the opposition had re-formed: with the participation of the minister Solomon West Ridgeway Dias Bandaranaike (►Famous People), who had left the United National Party, the **Sri Lanka Freedom Party** (SLFP) was formed. They won the elections of 1956 with Solomon Bandaranaike as the prime minister. When he was assassinated in September 1959 by a fanatical Buddhist monk, the UNP, under Dudley Senanayake, managed to win the elections of March 1960. After the new elections just four months later the UNP had to accept a heavy defeat. Sirimavo Bandaranaike (►Famous People), the widow of the murdered prime minister, took over with the stated goal of continuing her late husband's policies, making her **the modern world's first female head of government**. However, she was only partially successful in that goal and met with particular resistance over nationalizing the tea and rubber plantations. The UNP triumphed at the 1965 elections, and Dudley Senanayake became the head of government once again. Since he again did not manage to solve the country's problems (increasing unemployment, rising costs of living), he held office for only five years and in 1970 was in turn replaced by Mrs Bandaranaike once more. She had a **new constitution** drawn up that came into effect in 1972. Ceylon was henceforth the Democratic Socialist Republic of Sri Lanka.

Nationalizing the economy

Sirimavo Bandaranaike set about continuing her firm programme of nationalizing the economy, particularly the plantations. Possession of land was limited to 20ha/50 acres per family, monthly income to a maximum of 2000 rupees. In return she promised the people that »everyone would receive their rice for free«, which soon caused huge deficits in the state budget. Just in time for the elections of 1977, **accusations of corruption** materialized, which helped the opposition win. Junius Richard Jayawardene of the UNP became president by introducing a presidential system based on the French model in 1978. Ranasinghe Premadasa (►Famous People) was elected prime minister. Both changed the policies of their predecessor in that they tried to reverse some of the nationalization programmes and win foreign investors for Sri Lanka. For this reason large **free trade zones** were set up north of Colombo, which were primarily used by the textile industry.

THE CIVIL WAR BREAKS OUT

1976	The Tamil people demand their own state.
from 1983	Attacks on Singhalese institutions
1995	First ceasefire

Even though there were economic successes, Premadasa did not manage to keep the growing social tensions between the Singhalese and the Tamil people under control. More and more Tamils were demanding an independent state called »Eelam«. When these demands were rejected the military wing of the Tamil United Liberation Front (TULF), the »Liberation Tigers of Tamil Eelam« (LTTE) was formed. This **guerrilla organization** started attacking the Singhalese and their institutions all over the country.

Growing tensions (►MARCO POLO Insight p.266)

When Premadasa's government lost control of the confrontations it called for help from **Indian soldiers** in 1987. They too were unable to solve the conflict and only stayed until March 1990. On 29 July 1987 Premadasa's government decided to implement an autonomy statute for the north and east of the island where the Tamil people

After the attack on the Temple of the Tooth, security gates were added at the entrance to the temple complex

live. The rights they were given were not enough for the LTTE, who continued to cause unrest under the leadership of their founder Velupillai Prabhakaran (1954–2009). Prabhakaran, who lived in the underground, succeeded in winning over young Tamils, some of whom were even willing to commit suicide attacks. The LTTE did not even stop at recruiting women and children.

LTTE terrorism LTTE terrorism primarily targeted the Singhalese population, but victims also included Tamils considered moderates. At the heart of the confrontations was the Jaffna Peninsula in the north; however, acts of terrorism were also committed in Colombo and elsewhere. The LTTE was also accused of having murdered Indian prime minister Rajiv Gandhi on 21 May 1991. The targets of these attacks were initially people and buildings, but from the mid-1990s LTTE increasingly targeted the country's infrastructure, such as electricity substations.

Peace talks When President Chandrika Kumaratunga took office in 1994 she promised she would soon start peace talks with the LTTE. Later she even declared the »liberation tigers« to be negotiation partners, an offer which Prabhakaran firmly ignored, however. However, the ceasefire declared on 8 January 1995 was broken again just three months later.

Pope John Paul II On 20 and 21 January 1995 Pope John Paul II visited Sri Lanka. Buddhist dignitaries boycotted the visit since derogatory statements about Buddhism from the Vatican were made public prior to the visit.

Wave of terrorism The country was affected by a wave of terrorism in 1995. A bomb exploded in a commuter train in Colombo, killing 78 people. Further attacks followed, causing Kumaratunga to extend the **state of emergency** to the entire country on 8 April 1996; up until this point it had been restricted to Colombo and the northern and eastern parts of the island. The army and police were thus given far-reaching powers; moreover the freedom of assembly and the freedom of the press could be limited by the president.

Attack on Kandy In the opinion of the general population the LTTE committed a big mistake when it carried out a bomb attack on **the country's largest Buddhist shrine**, the Temple of the Tooth in Kandy, on 25 January 1998. This suicide attack killed eight people and seriously damaged part of the complex. Although President Kumaratunga continued her policy of holding peace talks, a significant number of Singhalese people believed only military means could solve a conflict that had killed and injured more than 69,000 people since 1984.

IN THE NEW MILLENNIUM

| **Since 2002** | Official peace negotiations |
| **December 2004** | The tsunami disaster kills around 30,000 and makes more than 500,000 homeless. |

With Norway, which took over the UN mandate, as an intermediary, the Sri Lankan government and the LTTE agreed to a ceasefire and to hold peace talks. For the first time the LTTE foreswore its demand for a Tamil state and the government promised not just to work for a federal structure for the Tamil regions but also to lift the prohibition on the Tamil Tigers. Some progress was made during several peace conferences. One problem was that the government was led by different parties with different goals. President Kumaratunga had a sceptical attitude towards the peace talks, while the prime minister was committed to a policy of negotiation. Since they could not agree on a common strategy, Kumaratunga dissolved parliament ahead of time in 2004 and called for **new elections**, which she also won. After that the ceasefire entered on fragile ground, a state of affairs that continued when Kumaratunga's successor Mahinda Rajapaksa took office in 2005. Although it was not destroyed by spectacular violence, its sustainability was compromised as a result of several LTTE attacks. There were also disagreements among the LTTE leaders themselves, further compromising the peace talks.

Peace negotiations

The tsunami that struck the island on 26 December 2004 caused no change in the situation. While in Sumatra for example the civil war parties put down their weapons and got to work helping the affected population, the government of Sri Lanka was faced with the accusation that it first helped the Singhalese population, leaving the Tamil people to make do with whatever was left. In addition, Sri Lanka's east coast, the main Tamil settlement area, was the most affected. Help, including foreign aid, only reached these areas days and even weeks after the disaster.
In June 2005 the two parties signed an agreement about the **equal distribution of aid money**, which was immediately declared invalid by the Supreme Court in Colombo. According to official figures the tsunami claimed more than 36,000 lives and more than half a million people lost their homes. Large parts of Sri Lanka's south and east coasts were flooded.

Accusation of partisan tsunami aid

More than 25,000 textile workers have lost their jobs since the beginning of 2005; the reason, it is believed, being the **abolition of the textile quotas** in international trade. This is a serious economic strain for Sri Lanka since production has increasingly been moved to even less expensive factories in other countries.

Economic strain

Assassination of the foreign minister

In August 2005 the 73-year-old Sri Lankan foreign minister Lakshman Kadirgamar was murdered in his villa in Colombo; he was considered a hardliner on the Tamil issue. The **LTTE vehemently denied responsibility** for the assassination, which was a minor sensation in itself because the LTTE had not commented on any other assassination before this event. Many houses belonging to Tamils were searched, but the person or persons responsible were not found.

No chance of autonomy

Mahinda Rajapakse won the presidential elections in November, but the people in the northeast of the country still largely continued to boycott the polling booths. Rajapakse was considered a strict opponent of autonomy for the largely Tamil regions. The former foreign minister Ratnasiri Wickremanayake became the new prime minister.

Latest developments

The LTTE leader Prabhakaran then invited the government in Colombo to participate in talks about autonomy for the north of the island. The government refused but did declare itself willing to negotiate on a »united Sri Lanka« with a special status for the Tamil regions. In June 2006, the opposing parties met in Norway for peace talks, which however came to nothing. Just one month later the government started a first major offensive against the Tamils and thus definitively abandoned the ceasefire agreed in 2002, which was supposed to hold until January 2008. On 8 January 2009 government forces took the Jaffna Peninsula and hence were able to exercise a large degree of control over the area. Once India started patrolling the Palk Strait between Sri Lanka and the mainland more closely, fewer and fewer weapons could get through to the insurgents, who were pushed back to a small area around their final stronghold of Mullaittivu. The flow of money from Tamils living abroad was also visibly drying up. When government forces took Mullaittivu on 23 January 2009, the end was already in sight, and after one last major offensive, on 16 May 2009 President Rajapaksa **officially declared the LTTE defeated** and the civil war to be at an end after 26 years. The leader and chief strategist of the LTTE, Velupillai Prabharakan, was shot dead two days later »while trying to escape«, and his body was put on public display. The people who suffer, as usual, are the civilian population. Hundreds of thousands of Tamils were caught between the fronts and fled. Reception camps were set up for them. The government in Colombo categorically rejects foreign help, and refuses to allow aid organizations or journalists to the refugee camps. In a speech to parliament President Rajapaksa promised the Tamil population a certain degree of autonomy in their ancestral territories. For the time being, however, all the Tamils in the camps will be interned until it is certain that there are no longer any LTTE members among them.

Mahinda Rajapaksa was re-elected in the elections in January 2010 that had been brought forward. His former friend, the retired general Sarath Fonseka, was a formidable opposition candidate, who accused Rajapaksa of nepotism and electoral fraud. Indeed, almost the entire government apparatus was in the hands of the Rajapaksa family and their friends. Rajapaksa had Fonseka arrested and the parliament dissolved.

Presidential elections in **January 2015** brought a major and unexpected change when oppostion candidate **Maithripala Sirisena**, the former Minister of Health in Rajapaksa's government, replaced Rajapaksa.

Latest elections

Arts and Culture

Art Periods

The island's most impressive cultural treasures are in an area known as the cultural triangle with its three corners of Anuradhapura, Polonnaruwa and Kandy. The remains of old royal cities, some of which have been reclaimed from the jungle that covered them for centuries, can still be seen in this area. For many the highly visible rock fortress of Sigiriya is the absolute highlight.

THE AGE OF CLASSICAL ART

First Anuradhapura period

The influence of the Indian Amaravathi style is clearly recognizable during the first Anuradhapura period (250 BC–AD 432) in Sri Lanka. It is named after a place in southern India which was the cultural centre of south Indian Buddhism from the 2nd century BC to the 2nd century AD. The characteristic features of the Buddha statues of this this time are majestic poses, a raised right arm that symbolized protection (abhaya mudra), a round face and an ushnisha or topknot. This way of depicting Buddha continued until the end of the Polonnaruwa period, so that it is often difficult to say which standing Buddha statue came from which period.

Buddha poses

Towards the end of the 4th century Buddha was no longer just represented in a standing pose but also seated. This period also saw the **first likenesses of bodhisattvas**, a development that went hand in hand with the spread of Mahayana Buddhism. They were mostly made of bronze. The preferred way of depicting the sitting Buddha was to show him meditating (Samadhi mudra), but contrary to the practice in northern India and many other Buddhist countries the legs in the hero pose (virasana) were placed on top of each other and not crossed.

The round face was retained while the bodies were given softer shapes than the earlier examples. There is a fine difference in **how the facial features were modelled**; they are more hinted at than fully portrayed, giving them an air of inapproachability. This tendency for simplification and abstraction reveals the desire to depict the eternally valid rather than something with contemporary individuality.

Unique forms

While the artists of that time made use of Indian models for their Buddha statues, they deviated from these and created unique forms

The Lion Gate marks the entrance to Sigiriya rock fortress. Only the paws remain of what was once a huge lion.

typical of Sri Lankan Buddha likenesses: the sitting Buddhas in particular were crowned by the splayed shield of the seven-headed naga. While the period of monumental buildings and imposing dagobas was over in architecture, production began of **colossal stone sculptures**, either as free-standing statues or as high reliefs. Examples from this time can still be seen in Buduruvagala, Sasseruwa and Aukana, which has a beautiful, approx. 14m/46ft depiction of Buddha. It is the largest sculpture in Sri Lanka to survive from this period and was carved from a single boulder!

THE PERIOD OF THE CHOLA KINGS

New perfection in sculpture

The period of the Chola kings (996–1070) also brought a new kind of perfection to art. A large number of **bronze statues** were made, most of which depict Brahman deities; the artists' extraordinary feeling for depicting individual facial expressions and modelling very elegant postures is remarkable. Statues from Indian Pallava art, which was characterized by exactly this style of representation, may have been used as models.

The **stone reliefs** from this period (such as the rock reliefs of Isurumuniya near Anuradhapura) and the depictions of figures on friezes and cornices were also rendered with a stronger design, giving them an impressive refinement. Moonstones, the sculpted thresholds at the base of staircases, guard stones and steles, as well as the makaras (fabled creatures) of the balustrades, were given their classical appearance. New motifs increasingly appeared on the steles serving as architectural ornamentation, such as the seven-headed naga under a parasol, the vase of abundance as well as mythical dwarfs with lotus blossoms on their heads.

Architecture

In architecture a new sense for proportions developed during this period. The dagobas were smaller and were crowned by a rounded cone structured by rings. One striking feature was that the boundary wall of the base was now also decorated (sparingly) with three-dimensional ornamentation. Fine examples of this can be seen on Ruvanveliseya Dagoba in Anuradhapura.

Amongst the rulers of this period the **desire for display** also grew. Palace complexes, such as those in Anuradhapura and Sigiriya, were given pleasure gardens and baths; the latter were often carved from the rock, such as the Lion Pond and Naga Pond in Mihintale. While few remains have survived from the palaces of this time, these artistically designed ponds can still be seen today. The only evidence of Tamil architecture from the time of the Chola kings is the fairly plain Hindu temple in Dondra (in the district of Matara) dating from the 7th–8th centuries. It is probably the first purely stone building in Sri

Lanka, replacing the wooden structures that had been customary up until then.

The paintings of this period reached extremely high artistic standards. Well-preserved examples are the world-famous **Cloud Maidens** on the walls of the gallery in the palace of Sigiriya. Their design is **World-famous paintings**

very graphic but their bodies, with their tumescent forms, elegant and graceful from head to toe, seem almost three-dimensional. The exceptionally individual drawing style used in the design of the facial features is quite remarkable. It is not yet known who was depicted, but the maidens came from different cultural circles – one is clearly Mongolian, another Indian and yet another African. Originally there were more than 500 paintings of this nature, but now only 22 survive. Cave paintings of impressive quality were created in Hindalga, not far from Kandy in the 6th century. They tell the story of the god Indra visiting Buddha; they captivate beholders with their attention to detail.

Graceful down to the fingertips

POLONNARUWA PERIOD

The first king to choose Polonnaruwa as his permanent capital was Vijaya Bahu I. After putting an end to the rule of the Chola kings in 1070, he began a programme of construction. Of these buildings, which must have been very impressive, few remains are still extant. There is one building in Sri Lanka, the **Temple of the Tooth** in Kandy, that contains elements of this new stylistic direction. Thus the cella, the temple's central room, was no longer round but rectangular in form. The ornamentation also became richer, as is demonstrated by the decorative bas-reliefs on the temple's 54 stone columns. They are characteristics of the Polonnaruwa style, which was much more showy than its predecessors. Under King Nissanka Malla the style reached its highest perfection, as can be seen on the Vatadage of Polonnaruwa, where an older sacred structure was fundamentally remodelled and to gain a far richer ornamentation than before. An-

Only fragments of architecture survive

other good example of the display-conscious Polonnaruwa style is the Missamkalata Mandapa, a hall where the sacred tooth relic was worshipped.

With the Polonnaruwa style, Singhalese art departed almost completely from its Indian model and became **very independent**. No one worried about pulling down a large number of Brahman buildings from the time of the Chola kings or altering them in such a way that they were only distantly reminiscent of former days. However, not only sacred but also secular structures underwent changes to their exterior. **The palaces of Kings** Nissanka Malla and Parakrama Bahu I were extensive complexes with large halls and many chambers, which according to ancient chronicles reached heights of up to seven storeys. King Parakrama Bahu's audience hall for example demonstrates a remarkable self-sufficiency of design. Substantial parts of this hall still exist today.

Monumental rock sculptures Buddhist sculpture was enriched during the Polonnaruwa period through the introduction of the recumbent depiction of Buddha, symbolic of the moment in which the Enlightened One entered nirvana; the most famous example is the monumental rock sculpture of **Gal Vihara** near Polonnaruwa. The highest degree of solemnity, dignity, harmony and internalization was achieved with very sparing means. Amongst the masterpieces of this period is also the 3.5m/11ft rock sculpture of Potgul Vihara; it is not known, however, whom it depicts. While stone was the main material used for making sculptures of Buddha, **bronze** was often used to depict Brahman deities. The works are characterized by sophisticated lines, elegant postures and a fine working of the details.

Lost painting The painterly production of this period, which was so important for the development of Sri Lankan art, must also have been significant. According to old chronicles elaborately painted fabrics as well as high-quality wall paintings existed, but unfortunately none of this has survived.

THE PERIOD OF THE SHORT-LIVED CAPITALS

Kingdoms The two centuries between 1235 and 1415 were characterized by the fragmentation of the Singhalese kingdom into several principalities. The capital also changed several times: Yapahuwa, Dambadeniya, Kurunegala and Gampola. Naturally not much remains, which is why information about any changes that may have taken place in art can only be obtained from written sources. One exception is the **rock fortress of Yapahuwa**; its surviving ruins allow an insight into the powerful desire of the rulers to create buildings for display.

Of Gampola it is known that several significant temple complexes were constructed during this period in a mixed Brahman-Buddhist architectural style. The reason was probably that deities from both religions were worshipped within them. The depiction of figures and the floral ornamentation on the sculpted wooden pillars of Gadaladeniya Vihara and Embekke Devale are evidence of a high level of craftsmanship and also of great vitality. A certain Burmese influence cannot be denied, particularly in Lankatilaka Vihara near Kandy.

THE KOTTE PERIOD

Nor has much survived of the period from 1415 to 1597, when Kotte in the west of Sri Lanka was the capital of a small kingdom. The few artefacts from this time do not reveal whether any significant developments occurred on the artistic front. Several friezes, now in the National Museum in Colombo, are, however, evidence of a great creative power.

Few artefacts extant

THE KANDY PERIOD

The few fragments of building still remaining from the early Kandy period (1597 – approx. 1650) show how the architecture of that period tied in with that of the Gampola period. **Simple, occasionally wide halls** with artistically sculpted and carved wooden pillars were built. During the heyday of the Kandy period, on the other hand, there were a few new developments, which are particularly obvious on the Temple of the Tooth in Kandy. More and more elements from the sacred art of other Buddhist countries, such as the Kingdom of Siam, modern-day Thailand, were incorporated.

Architecture

The renaissance experienced by wall painting during this period, **in a much more vernacular form** however, was remarkable. The reason for this may have been that it was not so much artists as craftsmen who worked in this area. At the centre of the paintings was the Jataka, tales from the lives of the Buddha, supplemented by scenes from Singhalese history. Generally speaking only the colours red and yellow were used, but because of the many different tints the paintings still seem very colourful.

Remarkable painting

FROM THE COLONIAL PERIOD TO THE PRESENT

The British also left unmistakable traces in Sri Lanka. As becomes obvious when visiting places such as Colombo, they introduced **Eu-**

British and Dutch influences

ropean architectural features that still shape large parts of the cityscape, even though much, such as parts of the old forts, has since been demolished. Colombo, still the island's economic centre, is aiming to treat the remains left by colonial rulers with more care than it has done to date. The Dutch, whose centre was in the south of the island, also left their mark, for example in Galle. Fortresses, churches and public buildings have typical features of **colonial architecture**, while homes and commercial buildings have arcades, for example, and ornamentation on the windowsills.

Contemp-
orary
architecture

There are certain trends that aim to revive old building styles; one case in point being the Independence Memorial Hall built in Colombo during the 1980s. Nevertheless the city council is very much at pains to give Colombo a modern appearance on the Western model. Sri Lanka's most famous architect of the modern era is Geoffrey Bawa (▶Famous People), who was influential in the whole of Asia.

Dutch Baroque church in Galle

Temple Architecture

Despite the dependence of Singhalese art on India's Hindu art, a striking independence developed in Sri Lanka over the centuries. This is expressed in the incorporation of Buddhist artistic forms of expression and the conviction with which Buddhism was represented, believed in and lived amongst the Singhalese. For more than one and a half millennia the majority of all Singhalese art was Buddhist art.

BUDDHIST TEMPLES

Every town in Sri Lanka has a sacred complex that includes a temple, a bodhi tree and a monastery. Further buildings are the vihara (image gallery), the bana maduwa (preaching hall) and the pansala (house of the priest).

Temple complex

A dagoba is not a temple the way we know it; rather it is an **inaccessible cult building** containing the relics of Buddha, his disciples or other sacred individuals. The dagoba's form and symbolism in Sri Lanka go back to the Indian stupa, which developed from burial mounds constructed over the relics of holy monks.

Dagoba (MARCO POLO Insight p.310)

The oldest stupas are said to have been built under King Ashoka (273–231 BC), who made Buddhism the official religion. Examples include the five stupas in Pattan/Nepal. The Thuparama dagoba in Anuradhapura from the 3rd century is also one of the oldest. It is said to have contained a shrine with **one of Buddha's collarbones** that King Ashoka sent from India after the king of Anuradhapura converted to Buddhism.

Dagobas, also known as thupas in Sri Lanka, form the conspicuous centre of the monastery and usually consist of round, or, occasionally square or polygonal, stepped foundations, known as maluva or medhi, on which there is a terrace, which is in turn surrounded by a stone balustrade. Above this is the anda (egg), the usually hemispherical superstructure, which is symbolic of the firmament or also of the all-embracing principle of enlightenment. The anda is usually a brick structure coated in plaster or stucco. Above the anda is the harmika, which symbolizes the holy place above the world beyond all rebirths, nirvana. In the past it contained the actual relic, but later the preferred method was to immure the relic in the lower third of the anda. Above the harmika is the conical, ringed chattra, whose lower section is often surrounded by standing Buddha statues. The (in most cases) eight rings of the chattra stand for the Eightfold Path

? Inventor of the stupas

Buddha is alleged to have said to his first disciples »Build heaps out of sand, like rice, which everybody needs« in response to their request for visible symbols to commemorate him, which inspired the idea for stupas.

that Buddha taught. The structure is completed by the tip, which is often coated in gold and sometimes decorated with precious stones. The **access to the base** of a stupa, which people always walk around in a clockwise direction during holy ceremonies, is designed using the arrangement for stairs that is typical in Sri Lanka. It consists of a moonstone in front of the steps, guard steles on both sides of the first step, the steps themselves as well as the stringers, which were often in the shape of a naga (a mythical snake).

Moonstone   The moonstone has a special role: by walking across this symbolic stone slab a person leaves the world of material possessions and human weaknesses and enters a world of the senses, the world of the enlightened Buddha. **The best moonstone** in Sri Lanka is at the staircase to Mahasena Palace in Anuradhapura. It is composed of four semicircular rings. The first, outer ring represents the flaming wreath as a symbol of human desire; the second ring depicts the sacred animals (elephant, lion, stag and horse). The third ring is decorated with plant ornaments, and the innermost ring with a half-open lotus blossom that symbolizes nirvana. Four or five steps lead up from the moonstone to the sacred temple complex. They symbolize the stages of meditation.

Vatadage (stupa house)   A further creation of sacred Singhalese architecture is the vatadage, the stupa house (also known as chetiya-ghara). It is a small stupa surrounded by concentric rings of stone columns that support a wooden beam ceiling. This stupa house was **used by monks and pilgrims as accommodation** and provided protection against the weather. The stupa itself, although it often did not contain an actual reliquary, was the object of a cult of veneration that took the form of a walking around it several times. Similar buildings can also be found in India but there they are known as chaitya halls and have a central nave and aisles and are built into the rock. In Sri Lanka the vatadage stood above ground and had a far simpler artistic design.

Asana-ghara   The asana-ghara, **the temple of the (empty) throne**, a place commemorating Buddha's first sermon at Varanasi (Benares), was characteristic of Sri Lankan sacred architecture until well into the European Middle Ages. The temple's focal point is a sculpted stone slab symbolizing Buddha's throne. Around it is a series of stone columns that support a wooden beam ceiling. This building method also dates

Moonstones symbolize a transitional area

back to the early Buddhist period, during which there were no likenesses of Buddha; instead there were these asana-ghara as well as
bodhi trees, stupas and symbolic footprints that referred to the teacher and his teachings. The emergence of Buddha likenesses caused the
asana-ghara to be replaced more and more by the statue house (patima-ghara). This was often a high, narrow building with thick, often
richly painted walls that housed the monumental statue of a sitting
or standing Buddha. The Thuparama statue house in Polonnaruwa is
considered to be the best example.

In addition to the stupa house, the patima-ghara and the bodhi-ghara, the uposatha-ghara (house of ordination), an often generously
proportioned building with a trapezoidal floor plan, is also part of the
monastic sacred complex. This is where ordinations take place, for
which the members of the religious community assemble under their
leader, the abbot. A Buddha image is obligatory here, while the holy
scriptures are kept in a small room separate from the actual hall.

**Uposatha-
ghara**

The temple complex also contains the monks' living cells (known as
arama or pansala), the refectory and the baths as well as the bell-

Living areas

Bathing pools in the monastery of Anuradhapura

frame (ghantara). In monasteries of the Dhammarucika order, which claims to follow the teachings of Buddha particularly closely, the individual areas are clearly separated from each other by stone walls or ditches. Other monasteries do not have such divisions.

Cave temples Since the earliest times Buddhist monks have lived in caves, either alone or in groups; at first they were scantily equipped, for example with a pipe to catch and channel rainwater; later their interiors were decorated more lavishly with statues and frescoes. Cave temples are very plentiful in Sri Lanka, one excellent example being the **Dambulla complex**. Even before the birth of Christ it was inhabited by monks who founded a significant Buddhist monastery here in around 80 BC. The model for this cave temple came from the complexes in India (Bhaja, Karli and Ajanta), but it cannot be compared directly to them.

Bodhi tree The bodhi tree (Ficus religiosa), also a standard component of every temple complex, is highly venerated by Buddhists because Buddha is said to have attained enlightenment while sitting under such a tree in India. Bodhi trees, which can be several hundred years old, usually stand on their own terrace (bodhi-ghara) surrounded by a wall decorated with reliefs or at least by a balustrade. They are decorated with colourful ribbons to reveal their sacred nature. The oldest known still extant bodhi-ghara was uncovered by archaeologists in the Kurunegala complex. It dates from the 8th–10th centuries and is surrounded by nicely sculpted entrance gates.

BRAHMAN SHRINES

Deities

The main Brahman deities worshipped in Sri Lanka are Shiva, Isvara and Skanda, Vishnu, Ganesha and the goddesses Kali, Tara and Pattani. The largest numbers of Brahman temples are consecrated to them. However, it is not unusual for the abovementioned gods from the Hindu pantheon to be joined by beings from Mahayana Buddhism (such as bodhisattvas) and Vedic (ancient Indian) deities, since the devout Tamil population hoped to get special protection from them. This syncretist tendency has varied in strength over the centuries. It reached a peak at the start of the 13th century. This also explains the mixture of architectural styles from the Gampola and Kandy periods.

Models from India

Pure Brahman architecture does not have any great past in Sri Lanka; no real creative impulses came from it. Hinduism had long become the popular religion in India, while in Sri Lanka Buddhism first had to establish itself and its architecture had to develop its own creative force. Elements were incorporated for this purpose, albeit only to a modest extent, from some of the art forms developed in India, particularly from the southern Indian Chola and Pandy styles. It is thought the northern ports of Jaffna and Trincomalee must have once had many sacred buildings modelled on Indian examples, but not much of them has survived.

Temple architecture

Good examples of Brahman temple architecture can nevertheless be found in Polonnaruwa: a Shiva Devale, reminiscent of the Chola style, and another that has the characteristics of the Pandy style. They are difficult to distinguish, differing in just a few details such as the vertical and the horizontal structuring of the external façade. The biggest difference is on the crest, which is a modification of the basic shape of early Indian tower temple: at the base there is a stepped terrace, upon which is a cubic block with the main room, the cella, above which is a pyramidal, usually stepped tower. The highest point is often given a dome-shaped design. The cella's exterior wall was adorned with blind arcades, niches, small chapels and balconies, while the roof is divided into several storeys and small towers whose niches were decorated with statues of gods, people, animals and demons. These statues, sculpted in the round, emerge from the wall and at times even appear separated from it. Many Hindu temples in Sri Lanka are also based on **Chola architecture**, which reached its peak between the 8th and 10th centuries. Characteristic of this Dravidian style are the steep, multi-storeyed pyramid tower, whose angular tip is crowned by several lights, and also the secondary temples around the main temple, the processional corridors and the gates. Successful syntheses of Buddhist patima-ghara (picture house) and Hindu temple are Galadeniya Vihara and Vijayotpaya, both of which are in Galadeniya not far from Gampola. They were built in the mid-14th century. The **Satmahal Prasada** in Polonnaruwa is quite unusual. The very high, simple stepped tower consists of six elements roughly cubic in shape placed on top of each other, with the largest at the bottom and the smallest at the top. At the centre of each side of the cubes is a niche that may have contained a statue of a standing deity (possibly also Buddha statues). This 12th-century building, in its atypical design, resembles the stupas built in the Mon architectural style that was widespread in Burma and Thailand. The only evidence of artists from these countries influencing Sri Lanka's architecture is that it is thought that wandering Burmese or Siamese monks must have come to Sri Lanka for Buddhist congresses and donated funds for the construction of the Satmahal Prasada.

SECULAR ARCHITECTURE

Victims of time The use of wood as a construction material must have been known about in Sri Lanka from very early on. One case in point is the eight wooden storeys of the Lohapasada (copper palace) in Anuradhapura. Most of these buildings, which must have once been very artistic, have fallen victim to the centuries, so that much is very difficult to make out with certainty. The buildings that used other materials as well, such as those made of both stone and wood, have survived. They were primarily built during the Gampola and the Kandy periods, while hardly anything remains of those buildings that were constructed centuries earlier, such as in Anuradhapura.

The employees of the Archaeological Survey of Sri Lanka, a government body that has the task of saving and preserving significant antiquities, have spent the past 25 years working very hard on uncovering the unique but overgrown **palace buildings of King Parakrama Bahu I in Anuradhapura**, so that they at least give an impression of their former magnificence. It is the island's second-largest excavation site.

Visual Arts

During the early Buddhist period there were no depictions of Buddha himself, and it seems they may even have been taboo. In any case there is no proof of figural representations of Buddha having existed at this time. The reason was probably that it was neither possible nor desirable to capture the Enlightened One in an image.

DEPICTIONS OF BUDDHA
(►MARCO POLO INSIGHT p.88)

Initially, symbols were used instead of depictions of Buddha and they were intended to give Buddha a physical presence: **lotus blossoms** were symbols of the beautiful and the consummate harmony that appears to emerge from the nothing, or the **Bodhi tree** (Ficus religiosa), the tree under which Siddharta Gautama reached the state of enlightenment. The symbolic and thus oversized **footprint** that is found in every country with a Buddhist following was also very popular at this time. All of these symbols were enough at first to bring to life Buddha's life-path and teachings to the hearts of Buddha's followers. Since the first likenesses of Buddha appeared there have been hardly any changes to them. Buddhist artists strive not for artistic freedom and individuality but to follow the old canon. Of course the artist's individual expression of his personal religious experience is not ruled out. The artist, incidentally, always remains anonymous. The works are not marked with names.

Buddha symbols

The Bodhi tree is one of Buddha's symbols that pilgrims seek out on holidays

Early depictions of Buddha

Early depictions of Buddha are known from around the 1st century AD. They were presumably made in the northern Indian kingdom of Kubhana in the reign of King Kanishka, who was devoted to art. Around the same time the Indian towns of Mathura and Ghandara, centres of art at the time, also already had depictions of Buddha. During this time an artistic style developed in Ghandara that was most likely influenced by **artists from Persia**, which was then part of Alexander the Great's empire. For this reason it is known as the Greco-Buddhist style. These early depictions show Buddha Shakyami either standing or sitting; the fixed and still valid **canon of proportions, attributes and gestures** seems to have started to develop here. This iconographic canon emerged from the desire to create the »right« likeness and give it eternal validity. It is meant to point to the right path to enlightenment beyond worldliness and finiteness. Thus there are speculations about the existence of cosmic number relationships in the physical proportions.

To this day the old canon is taken into account when creating likenesses of Buddha, such as here, in the 20th-century Weherahena Temple

Buddha's transfigured body exhibits 32 main characteristics, which were later supplemented by a further 80. One is the topknot on Buddha's head (ushnisha), which has the shape of a serpent with a flickering tongue (in other Buddhist countries such as Thailand it has the shape of a lotus bud). Other characteristics are the curl (uma) between the eyebrows, which is often shown as a mark or gem; Buddha's main head of hair, styled into small curls or waves; and the symbolized halo around Buddha's head or around the entire body as a symbol of energy. Depictions of Buddha are **always gender-neutral**. The hands and soles of the feet always show religious symbols or Sanskrit words. The overly long earlobes are also remarkable; different interpretations have been given as to their significance. Some say they are symbols of Siddharta Gautama's noble origin, because only the rich were able to afford weighty jewellery to elongate the earlobes. Other scholars believe this form of representation is a further symbol of the Enlightened Buddha's omniscience.

Symbolism

The insights about the structure and movement of the human body, used in Greek sculptures for example, only play a subordinate role in the design of Buddhist sculptures. According to Hindu beliefs movement is the expression of the sensual and fertile energy that inhabits the body. On this interpretation it seems completely natural that Vishnu, for example, is depicted as a god with many arms, and other gods (such as the elephant god Ganesha) are shown to have many heads.

Movement is energy

Buddhism has four ways in which the first Enlightened One can be depicted: in standing, sitting, walking and recumbent positions. There are five different standing postures and five sitting ones, all with exactly prescribed hand positions, each of which has its own symbolic significance. The **standing postures** include Buddha standing upright or sometimes bent at the hip, with the head and body in alignment. In another common posture one leg is stretched out, while the other is at a slight angle. Less common is the posture where one leg is bent and the other slightly pulled towards the body (dance posture).

Buddha's postures

The **recumbent posture** stands for the time when Siddharta Gautama reached the state of enlightenment. Other scholars think this is the moment when Buddha enters nirvana, i.e. dies. This latter opinion is strengthened by the particularly large number of depictions in Sri Lanka where Buddha is lying on a bed with his first disciples sitting in front of him in a semi-circle. This contradicts the first interpretation, because Siddharta Gautama is said to have been alone at the moment when he found enlightenment.

The classical **sitting postures** require a much larger number of interpretations. One well-known posture shows Buddha sitting with

Sitting, Standing, Walking, Lying Down ...

... are the most common classical poses of Buddha. Every pose has a meaning attributed to it, which is supplemented by a mudra. A mudra (Sanskrit: seal) is a sign of the hand or a gesture with a concrete symbolic meaning that refers to a specific statement made by Buddha. Monks and believers use mudras in daily prayers; even the ordinary gesture of folding hands is considered to be a mudra.

▶ **A Buddha for every day of the week**
Seven different statues of Buddha stand for the seven days of the week.
Every day has its own colour too.

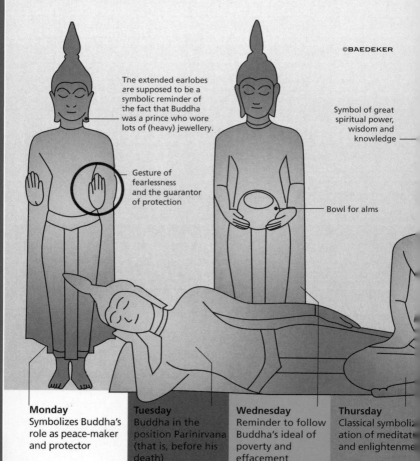

©BAEDEKER

The extended earlobes are supposed to be a symbolic reminder of the fact that Buddha was a prince who wore lots of (heavy) jewellery.

Symbol of great spiritual power, wisdom and knowledge

Gesture of fearlessness and the guarantor of protection

Bowl for alms

Monday
Symbolizes Buddha's role as peace-maker and protector

Tuesday
Buddha in the position Parinirvana (that is, before his death)

Wednesday
Reminder to follow Buddha's ideal of poverty and effacement

Thursday
Classical symboliz ation of meditat and enlightenme

The Mudras

Codified and symbolic positions of the hands are iconic characteristics to differentiate Buddha statues.

Varada Mudra
Fulfillment, gift, hospitality, generosity

▶ **Fat or thin Buddha?**

The slender Buddha is the historic founder of Buddhism. The fat, laughing Buddha goes back to the Chinese Zen monk Pu-Tai and is considered to be an incarnation of the Buddha of the future (Maitreya).

Anjali Mudra
Gesture of reverence

Vitarka Mudra
Gesture of guidance

Yoga Mudra
Meditation, contemplation

Gesture of self-confidencs

»Naga«
naga (snake with 7 heads) protects the head against wind and rain.

Friday
Reminiscent of hesitation in the difficult task of communicating the teaching after attaining enlightenment

Saturday
Represents deep meditation while being protected by the naga snake.

Sunday
stands for the time after Buddha attained enlightenment.

crossed legs with the feet over the knees, making the soles visible – lotus position, meditation position; others show Buddha with one bent leg, while the other is dangling down, or sitting in the European fashion with both legs hanging down vertically – naturally a very rare depiction, which is typical of »the Buddha of the future« known as Maitreya. A very common depiction shows Buddha sitting under a serpent with five, or sometimes seven, heads. It goes back to an event in Buddha's life: Muchalinda, one of the naga or serpent kings protected the meditating Buddha from a torrential downpour by spreading out his heads like a fan.

Hand postures Amongst the hand postures, the »seals« (mudra), which are possibly given the most attention by the sculptors, are the **gesture of confidence and security** (abhaya-mudra) – the right hand is raised and the palm is facing forwards – and the gesture of **adoration or worship** (anjali-mudra) – the palms of the hands are pressed together, the fingers are slightly angled and are pointing upwards. The second gesture is less common when depicting Buddha Shakyami himself; it tends to occur more in depictions of his followers and future Buddhas. A further gesture, known as asiva-mudra, is the **gesture of granting blessings**. A particularly good example of this is the monumental Buddha statue in Aukana.

The gesture of **calling the earth to witness** (bhumisparsa-mudra) goes back to a legend; in this mudra the right hand is resting on Buddha's crossed legs with the back of the hand facing upwards and the fingertips pointing downwards. Once, when Buddha was deep in meditation, Mara, evil, appeared in order to prevent enlightenment. Siddharta Gautama called the earth goddess Thorani to be a witness of his virtue by touching the earth with his fingertips. Thorani's hair was full of water because after every good deed Gautama made a sacrifice of water to her, as was the custom. Thorani appeared and wrung her hair, whereupon Mara and his helpers were washed away and Gautama became the »vanquisher of Mara« (maravijaya). This depiction is one of the most common representations of Buddha in Sri Lanka. The dhyana-mudra or samadhi-mudra, the gesture of meditation, involves Buddha's hands lying over each other on his lap with the palms facing upwards. Finally there is the gesture of fulfilment (karana-mudra), where the little finger and the index finger are pointing upwards, while the middle finger and the ring finger are bent downwards and are covered by the thumb. There are a few depictions of Buddha in a posture known as vajradhara or primordial Buddha. This is the mystical Buddha of the Vajarayana school (Adi Buddha), who stands for unification with the world principle (sakti): the arms are crossed in front of the chest, while the hands are enclosing a bell and thunderbolt.

BRAHMANIC DEPICTIONS

Since the Shiva cult has a special significance in Sri Lanka, the sculptural representation of the dancing Shiva (Nataraja) is important. The statue is made exclusively of bronze and is almost one metre tall. **Every detail is filled with symbolism**: the lambent flames of the wreath surrounding Shiva symbolize the power of the Hindu religion. Shiva's face has three eyes; the central eye is a symbol for omniscience. In his right earlobe the deity has a »male« earring and in his left a »female«, proof that he embodies both sexes. The hair on his head is plaited until it forms a crown. There is a human skull at his feet, which symbolizes the principle of destruction Shiva that stands for. The lower plaits are following the whirling movements of the dance, the girl on the right is emblematic of the Indian river Ganges, the symbol of fertility, while the crescent in Shiva's left hand represents magnanimity and fame. **The finest depiction of a dancing Shiva** is to be found in the national museum in Colombo. There are, however, countless replicas of varying quality, including artificially aged ones that can be bought in every antique shop or even department store.

Shiva

The dancing Shiva in one of his countless manifestations

PAINTING

Early
examples

The oldest paintings and drawings, dating back to the Neolithic age, were found in caves in Central Province (in Tantrimalai, Madagala, Kadurupoluna and Mahalenama). The motifs include plant patterns and animals that were painted on the rock wall in red paint. During the Buddhist period many monks and hermits lived in caves, and there too the walls were painted. However, the painters could not have been the inhabitants themselves, because the rules of Buddhism forbid monks to paint. It is much more likely that **donors** – maybe kings – commissioned the paintings. Amongst the various depictions, common ones are of Buddhas, bodhisattvas and worshippers. Characteristic of these paintings in Sri Lanka is the preliminary drawing in red. This tradition continued until the end of the Polonnaruwa period, thus differing from the Indian practice, where the outlines of figures and floral elements were drawn in black. Famous examples of early Buddhist painting in Sri Lanka can be seen in the **caves of Kurandaka Lena** (2nd century BC) near Ambalantota and in **Karambagalla** (also 2nd century BC) as well as near **Ridigama** in Yala National Park. The figures are simple in their shapes, highly abstract and almost schematic. However, the clear and confident lines and the lovingly worked details are striking. Sri Lanka's paintings always emphasize the graphic aspect, but they lack perspective so that the people and scenes depicted are right in the foreground and come across directly to the beholder. The fresco technique seems to have been almost entirely unknown in Sri Lanka. The area to be painted was often covered in a layer of lime or clay but the paints, usually bound with a mixture of tempera and oil, were only applied after this layer had dried. The range of colours was limited because the pigments were obtained from natural raw materials: white from lime or magnesia, black from coal, yellow and red from ochre, green from plants and blue from lapis lazuli.

Rock dra-
wings of
Sigiriya

Amongst the rock-painting masterpieces are undoubtedly the images on the gallery wall below the rock palace of Sigiriya, **the famous Cloud Maidens**. They date from the late 5th century, but experts are still debating who they represent. In 1897 the first archaeological commissioner of the government of Sri Lanka, the Englishman H.C.P. Bell, opined that it was a procession of queens, daughters or concubines living at the court of King Kassyapa, specifically a scene depicting an offering. This seems most likely, while other suggestions, such as that the women are mythical beings from the world of legend or that the painter was an Indian artist, are speculative. Even more significant than the quality of the colours are the confidence of the lines, the desire to capture a great degree of individuality, and the depiction of the corporeal.

The ceiling paintings in the second cave of Dambulla reveal a great wealth of detail and a lavish use of colour

No less significant are the wall paintings in the cave temples of Dambulla, whose beginnings probably go back to the 1st century AD. They were only given their current appearance in the 12th century when King Nissanka Malla commissioned artists to renew the existing murals and to add some new ones. The paintings in the third cave temple date back to the 18th century, when King Kirti Sri Raja Sinha commissioned its decoration.

Wall paintings of Dambulla

The wall paintings of the Polonnaruwa period are predominantly to be found inside patima-ghara (picture houses). The number of motifs expanded to include **scenic depictions** that reveal the artists' evident joy in story-telling (such as the wall paintings in the cella of the Tivanka Pilimage in Polonnaruwa). They depict events from the Jataka, Buddha's previous lives, of which there were more than 500.

Polonnaruwa period

Gampola period
Some high-quality wall paintings from the Gampola period have survived, as in Gadaladeniya and in Lankatilaka Vihara in Polonnaruwa; their style however, ties in with tradition.

18th century to modern times
From around the 16th century the art of painting seems to have disappeared for some time, and when it reappeared two centuries later (including in Telwatta near Hikkaduwa and in Kathaluwa near Galle as well as around Kandy, in the Degaldoruwa cave temple) it had a fundamentally different character. From then on **the paintings were folksy, almost naïve,** filling up large sections of wall space. An unselfconscious enjoyment of narrative becomes clear, making the hand of the anonymous artist paint the worlds of people, animals and plants as well as scenes from the Jataka.

The 19th century saw the painting of further high-quality murals, such as in the temple of Kelaniya (not far from Colombo). They reveal a Burmese and sometimes even a European influence, which can be seen both in the hint of perspective and in the postures of the figures, as well as in the fall of the lavish robes.

Literature

The beginnings of Sri Lankan literature lie in chronicles that go back to the 5th century BC and have been passed down through the ages under the names Dipavamsa and Mahavamsa.

Beginnings during the 5th century BC
In the 4th century AD the Indian monk Buddhagosa, who had spent some years living in Sri Lanka, was credited with having translated Sanskrit Buddhist texts and commentaries and written them down in Pali. He is also a potential candidate for the authorship of a **Buddhist textbook**, the Visuddhimagga. A little later, in around the 5th and 6th centuries, a number of **biographical poems and novels** were written in Sanskrit. In the 12th century Singhalese-language literature finally emerged and immediately flourished during the reign of King Parakrama Bahu I (1153–86). He is also credited with having set up the first **public libraries** in order to allow the literate monks to read the texts that had been written down on palm leaves. The subjects of this time included religious, scientific and medical insights as well as countless stories (usually in verse) as well as poems. Parakrama Bahu's successor Nissanka Malla (1187–96) is believed to be the author of a **chronicle carved in stone** that reports on his (alleged) military campaigns, but also on his relations with other countries. This granite block, 8m/27ft long, 4.5m/15ft wide and richly orna-

The Gal Pota is about the military campaigns of King Nissanka Malla

mented all round, known as Gal Pota (»stone book«), is in Polonnaruwa. In the 14th century literature also enjoyed a high standing
under King Parakrama Bahu IV (1302–26). It was during this time
that a **Singhalese grammar** was developed as well as a detailed description of the Jataka.

Two long literary works, the *Mahabharata* and the *Ramayana*, are of
great significance to Buddhism, whose teachings spread from India
to the rest of the Asian continent during the reign of King Ashoka
(approx. 272–236 BC). While the former, consisting of 18 books with
more than 90,000 verses, probably has a historical core that many
»reporters« helped write, the *Ramayana*, consisting of seven books
and around 24,000 verses, is more likely to be a collection of legends.
The *Mahabharata* largely consists of **descriptions of battles and
festivals**. The connective elements between these episodes are elegies
written in lyrical form, such as love poems, as well as mythological,
fabulous and at times also instructive interspersions. Indian women,
whose much-quoted qualities of purity and chastity play an important role in Indian literature, are often at the centre of these stories,

Mahabharata
and
Ramayana

which are not, however, historically verifiable. It is, on the other hand, considered certain that the Mahabharata was written between the 4th century BC and the 6th century AD. Rama, who is described as the divine incarnation of the Hindu god Vishnu in books I and VII, which may have been written at a later date, is at the centre of the *Ramayana* (»in honour of Rama«); its poetry is more chivalric than priestly in nature. It is believed the Ramayana was written between the 3rd century BC and the 3rd century AD.

The chronicle of the island of Sri Lanka
In around AD 320 Buddhist monks began writing the *Dipavamsa*, the great chronicle of events in Sri Lanka. This work still provides detailed information about this lively period, during which Buddhism became established on the island. It encompasses a period from pre-history to the year 303, the year King Mahasena died, describing life in prehistoric Sri Lanka and the arrival of the Aryans, following the development of Buddhism and also reporting on the three visits the Enlightened One is said to have made to the island. Furthermore it names the early Singhalese kings, describes their reigns and thus **permits conclusions about the social, economic and cultural conditions** of this period.

Dance and Music

Singhalese dance and the dance theatre based on it are a true popular art form, and although it is becoming more refined, it has never become separated from the popular soul. In some Sri Lankan dances Indian influences are unmistakable, but they now only play a very subordinate role.

Different forms
Dances have always been the main component of exorcist rituals, where dialogues are not so much spoken as danced. Thus demons, a dramatic component of the mostly traditional stories, are integrated into the play by embodying their role in a highly fearsome appearance that is increased through commanding behaviour in the form of a dance. There are two types of Singhalese dances in Sri Lanka. While the **Up-Country Dances** (also known as Kandy Dances) are performed in the highlands, the **Low-Country Dances** are performed in the southwest of the island. They differ in the nature of the performance, in the dance rhythms and in the different accompanying instruments. The clearest difference lies in the dancers' appearance: the Kandy dancers wear headdresses and facial ornamentation but no masks; their transformation is mainly demonstrated by the dancers' expressive power. The dancers of the lowlands, on the other

hand, do wear masks and thus complete their transformation into other beings, into gods and demons.

The classical Singhalese orchestra is made up of **three types of drums** in addition to cymbals, a small metal percussion instrument and a clarinet-like instrument. Drums are indispensable for accompanying dances; they are usually beaten directly with the hands. They are covered with one or two skins and there are also various types of flat drum. Drums set the rhythm for dances, but they can also emphasize the nature of a certain being through their pitch. Thus the Yak Bera (devil's drum), for example, is used exclusively for devils and demons. It accentuates their character because its sound resembles that of a deep human voice. The most-used drum is the rahana, which is available in many different sizes, from the large drums that stand on the floor to the small types that the musician can hold in his hands. The getaberaya is often used for religious ceremonies. This drum has one skin of cow leather and one of monkey hide, so that different sounds can be made on it. The getaberaya is carried around the neck so it can be played with both hands.

Music

Religious ceremonies are opened with the hakgediya, a shell. When it is blown a deep, drawn-out sound is produced. A slightly modified version of this is the saksinnam, where a shell has a mouthpiece attached. The wind instrument known as bata nawala is also popular. It consists of a bamboo pipe with seven holes. The brass horn known as kombu on the other hand has almost fallen into oblivion. It was once used as a signal horn.

The drums set the rhythm for the dance

Handicrafts

Handicrafts in Sri Lanka have a tradition going back many centuries, particularly in the manufacture of dance masks.

Mask-carving   The small town of Ambalangoda on the southwest coast, where the island's most famous carvers live, is the centre of mask carving. There is a good reason for this: the inhabitants of this fishing village on the southwest coast of Sri Lanka have held on to a variety of customs. The masked plays (kolam maduwa) play a significant role.

Kolam maduwa   There are few certainties about the origins of the **masked plays** in Sri Lanka. It seems, however, that the participants incorporated political, historical and social elements over the years as well as myths that have been passed down across the centuries.

Like so much in Sri Lanka the development of the masked plays is also connected to legend: a queen is said to have felt the insatiable desire for masked dances. However, nobody knew how to perform them, so in her need she appealed to the god Sakra, who in turn appealed to the god Visvakarma, the god of the craftsmen, to ask him to make the required masks. The next day, not just the masks were found in the royal garden but also the right verses for a masked play. After the plot had been studied, the kolam maduwa was performed and the queen was happy. By the way, this legend still plays a role in every kolam maduwa and is incorporated into the action. A traditional kolam maduwa also uses current events from the lives of the village community; and since the characters actually exist in real life the plays often produce great amusement amongst the spectators.

> **! MARCO ⊕ POLO TIP**
>
> *Mask museum*   **Insider Tip**
>
> There is a museum full of valuable old masks in Ambalangoda. The museum also issues a booklet in which describes some kolam plays (426 Patabendimulla, daily 8am – 7pm, free entry).

Making the masks   Larger masks are carved from very light materials such as sandalwood and balsa wood, while the wood of the kaduru tree (Nux vomica) is used for smaller ones. In the old masks all facial features are carved, whereas more recent masks tend to have some of these features merely drawn on. The **purpose of the masks** is to be found in the dances in which they are used. Their colourful appearance is designed to produce as much tension and excitement as possible. When the dancer holding the mask in front of his face moves, the light of the oil lamps is reflected from the painted surface in the half-dark, giving the impression that supernatural forces are at work. Amongst the particularly imaginative performances are the naga masks, which embody the snake god and often consist of several faces and upright cobras.

The batik technique is not originally Singhalese, but a craft imported from Indonesia. Nevertheless, the batik items produced in Sri Lanka, mainly for tourists, are of exceptionally high quality, almost as good as the original, in fact. In this method of dyeing, certain areas of the fabric are sealed with wax, preventing them from taking up the dye when the fabric is dunked into the dye bath.

Batik

Among the few resources found in Sri Lanka that can be exploited are metals such as copper, which is used as the raw material for statues, containers of various sizes, and also vases. Silver is often used to make pretty pieces of jewellery.

Metalwork

Customs and Traditions

Even though ordinary visitors are most likely to find out only by chance about the penchant of the people of Sri Lanka to believe in spirits, animism continues to play an important role in everyday life.

Many temples throughout the country still have **cans for donations** at which some drivers stop and throw in a few rupees, while reciting a spell. They thereby hope to drive accident-free. The Sri Lankan belief in spirits also plays an important role when it comes to funerals. **Small white flags** hung on string over a street reveal that a person has died. They are hung all along the route between the home of the deceased and the burial site. Sometimes banners honouring the deceased's achievements are also hung up. The flags are meant to keep evil spirits away from the last journey of the body. If the small flags hanging across the street are yellow, it is a monk who has died.

Animism

The dead are only buried after four to five days in Sri Lanka (members of certain castes as well as monks are cremated), but until then they are kept in their homes, where relatives, friends and acquaintances have sufficient time to say goodbye and wish them a better existence in their next life. The magical rituals to ward off evil spirits were developed as early as the 1st millennium BC. Details about them can be found in the earliest recorded written accounts. Together with the Singhalese invasion of the island, northern Indian influ-

Coconuts can also be sacrificial goods

ences were added. By the 17th century the ceremonies had already reached the level of development which characterizes them today.

Demons Of the countless demons which, according to popular belief, have lost their way in the mountains and forests, in rivers and lakes or linger on remote streets or three-way intersections, there are about 20 that have to be driven out and banished. The predominant group amongst these are the spirits that bring diseases (cholera, dysentery, fever etc.) and those that put curses on people. The Singhalese believe the ceremony of the **thovil** to cast out spirits is the one most likely to be successful. It takes place in the relevant person's home and lasts from dusk till dawn. The ritual dances are performed by a kattadiya, **an exorcist**, in front of an altar-like set-up. The exorcist wears various colourful masks to prevent the spirit or demon from recognizing that a person is behind all of it. Various gifts such as betel leaves, blossoms, fruits or linseed cake are placed on the altar. Since it is believed that the demon will slip into the betel leaves when it believes its harmful machinations to be over, they are wrapped in seven threads that are pulled tight as soon as the demon is in the leaves. Then the bunch is hung up on nails that were previously banged into a tree. At the end of the ceremony, which is particularly popular with the people of the southern part of the island, all the other gifts are taken to a remote location.

Planets Since the people of Sri Lanka imagine the planets to be deities influencing the lives of the people on earth, they too need to be placated through certain rituals, particularly when a person has been affected by disease or misfortune. The most important of these rituals, called

bali, is also held at night, and is conducted outside the home. Instead, a spot in the garden is chosen and then cleaned with a mixture of fresh cow-dung, milk and pulverized sandalwood. Next an image of the planet deity, formed out of mud and covered in a white cloth, is set up in this spot. The priest begins the ceremony by scattering rice kernels on the ground and putting down various sacrificial gifts. Then he takes a thread spun by a virgin, attaches one end to the statue, then draws it around the entire ceremonial area and ties the other end to a branch, which he hands to the affected person. The dances, which now begin amidst intense drumming, can bring the participants to ecstasy. They are interrupted by songs and calls from the spectators. Once the ritual's climax has been reached, the afflicted person approaches the image (or is carried there), attaches the thread to it and throws the branch on to it. For safety's sake the statue stays in place for three days after the ceremony. Then it is placed under a tree and sprinkled with magic water.

Spells

The belief in the efficacy of spells (**mantras**) is also widespread in Sri Lanka. They are very old; some were written down in Singhalese infused with Sanskrit words, others in the Dravidian languages. Before the magician (kattadiya) can put them into effect he has to fill them with life or supernatural power through incantations and certain rituals. For this purpose the kattadiya could use a cobra or scorpion, whom he would order to kill the enemies, by stinging them, strangling them or biting them.

Amulets

Amulets also have magic powers against all things evil. They are worn around the neck, waist or wrist. The complicated patterns that bring about the desired effect are drawn on copper or aluminium foil or onto a palm leaf that is rolled up and carried in a small gold or silver container.

le liure marc pau

Cy dist de lisle de seilan.

auint len se part de lisle de augamanain. et on va entour mil
le milles par ponent. aucune choseu a mais alar vers garb
adont truue len lisle de seilan. qui est tout verement la
meillur isle qui soit ou monde de la grandese. Et sachies
que elle dure bien .iiii. mil. milles. mais ancianement e
stoit grigneur. car elle duoit bien enuiron trois mille selone ce que les bons
mariners dient de celle mer. Mais le vent de tramontaine y vente si fort qi
a fait une grant quantite de celle souls aigue. Et ceste est la choison pour
quoy elle nest si grant comme elle iadis. Mais sachies que de la ou
vent a tramontaine vient. est lisle moult basse et toute plaine. Et quant
len vient de haultemer a tout autant nef. len ne puet veoir la terre tant laut
que on est dessus. Or vous compterons des fais de ceste isle. Ils ont roy q
ils appellent seudinain. et nen sont tréage a nul. ils sont ydolatres t von
tous nuds fors que il cueuurent leur nature. ils nont nulz bles. mais tres
sulement de quoy ils sont humiles. il viuent de char et de lait et ont vin de ca
arbres que ie vous ay dit autres fois. Et ils ont de buesil moult le meillur
du monde. Or vous lairray a compter de ces choses. et vous dirray de la plu
precieuse chose qui soit ou monde. Car sachies que en ceste isle truue len
les rubis. et cumille autre contree du monde ne nouissent fors que en ceste
isle. Et ce y truue len aussy les saphins. et les topazes. et les amasites et de
maintes pieres precieuses. Et cy a un roy de ceste isle un rubis le plus bel et
le plus gros qui soit ou monde. Et vous dirray comment il est fait il est

SIRIMAVO BANDARANAIKE (1916–2000)

Sirimavo Ratwatte Bandaranaike was born in Balangoda near Rat-   Politician
napura as the daughter of a large landowner. Her political career began after her marriage to the lawyer and politician Solomon Bandaranaike (1940). After his assassination in 1959 she took over the
leadership of the **Sri Lanka Freedom Party (SLFP)**, which was the
opposition party at this time. A year later she managed to be elected
prime minister, not least because of her promise to hand out free rice
for all the people of Sri Lanka. She was therefore the first woman in
the modern world to achieve the position of head of government. In
order to achieve this goal she pursued a strict course of nationalization
of many tea and rubber plantations as well as of banks and oil companies. Nevertheless the programme tore huge holes in the state budget
with the consequence that she lost the general elections in 1965.
After five years in opposition Mrs Bandaranaike managed a political
comeback in 1970, when she once again ran as the SLFP candidate
and won. However, great resistance soon developed to her leadership:
when a commission appointed by the government accused her of
abusing her powers and of favouritism, she was deprived of the right
either to vote or to stand for office, which meant her only option was
to withdraw from political life. Her banishment from the political
stage only lasted until 1986, and after her daughter Chandrika Kumaratunga became president when early elections were held (1994),
she managed to become prime minister the following year.

SOLOMON BANDARANAIKE (1899–1959)

Solomon West Ridgeway Dias Bandaranaike was born in Colombo.   Politician
After studying law he first worked as a lawyer and then as a politician
in the United National Party (UNP). After he left this party he founded the **Sri Lanka Freedom Party (SLFP)**, whose leader he became in
1952. Four years later he managed to secure the election with the help
of the People's United Front led by the SLFP, and at the head of a four-
party coalition he was elected prime minister. During his time in office, which lasted only three years, he implemented a first phase of
introducing socialism to Sri Lanka, which his wife Sirimavo rigor-
ously continued. In addition he made Singhala the official language
in 1957. Politically he pursued a strictly nationalist course, while taking a neutral stance in foreign affairs. Solomon Bandaranaike was
assassinated by a Buddhist monk on 25 September 1959. It is not
clear whether the monk was acting on orders from anyone else.

**Marco Polo described the inhabitants of Sri Lanka as dog-headed. An
illustrator (around 1412) depicted them like this, while trading spices**

IBN BATTUTA (1304 TO APPROX. 1368)

Arab globetrotter

If there is one man of the 14th century who can rightly be called a globetrotter, it must be the Islamic scholar Ibn Battuta. Thanks to his wanderlust there are relatively reliable accounts about the Islamic world and neighbouring regions at this time. Ibn Battuta was born in **Tangier (Morocco)** as the son of a noble family. After training in law he left his home city when he was just 21 in order to go on his first pilgrimage to Mecca. It was not long, however, before he was off the beaten pilgrimage paths and without the protection of the pilgrims' caravans on much more dangerous routes. This journey was followed by others from 1328 onwards, which took him through Arabia to the coasts of east Africa, Anatolia and the Crimea. After working as a judge for the sultan of Delhi, Ibn Battuta once again went on several trips that brought him to the Maldives and to Sri Lanka, where he stayed for two years. It is not proved whether he reached Beijing, but it can be deduced from Battuta's detailed travel accounts that he was in China. He wrote down this travel account together with the scholar Ibn Juzayy in the form of a rihla. In his time this form of literature was a highly popular kind of travelogue; it superficially dealt with religious subjects but also described the experiences of travellers in faraway countries as well as the idiosyncrasies of the landscapes, cultures and people.

Ibn Battuta's travel routes

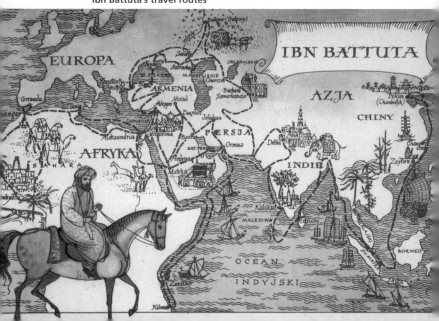

GEOFFREY BAWA (1919 – 2003)

Those who climb the steps in the exclusive Jetwing Lighthouse Hotel in Galle will be accompanied by mystical metal creatures along the banister. They are proof of the creativity of Sri Lanka's most famous architect, Geoffrey Bawa, who demonstrated his artistic liberties in other places too. Born on 23 July 1919 as the son of a well-off Burgher family, the individualist shaped several other buildings on the island with his unique style. His list of works include buildings commissioned by public and religious clients as well as private ones. Shorty before the Second World War Bawa went to Great Britain, where he initially studied law and graduated in 1946. However, the life of a lawyer, determined by strict regulations, was not for him, which is why, after a brief intermezzo in Colombo, he set off on an extensive trip around the world. He obtained his first architectural experience in Italy, but just a few years later he was drawn back to Sri Lanka. In 1949 he acquired a disused rubber plantation near Bentota, which he shaped using Italian gardens as the model. From 1951 onwards Bawa started working for the renowned architectural office of Edwards, Reid & Begg in Colombo. In 1954 he returned to Great Britain to study architecture. After graduating in 1957, he once again went back to Sri Lanka, where he and some designers opened an office whose architecture combined traditional elements and modern construction methods. His signature was obvious even for his first buildings, such as the modern-day Gallery Café in Colombo: it combined local and colonial elements that produced a unique symbiosis in their openness. Light and water played an important role in Bawa's architecture. He used local construction materials such as coconut trees and the semi-circular fired clay tiles typical of his style. Form, material and space always created a fascinating unit in his designs. Bawa's many architectural creations include the Bentota Beach Hotel (1967), the Heritance in Ahungalla (1981), the new parliament in Kotte (1982) and the Kandalama Hotel near Dambulla (1994). The latter is considered an exceptionally successful example of green architecture. Bawa's buildings can be found in India, Pakistan, Japan, Egypt and Singapore as well.

Geoffrey Bawa died highly respected, the recipient of many national and international awards, in Colombo on 27 May 2003.

Architect

SIDDHARTA GAUTAMA, KNOWN AS BUDDHA (APPROX. 560 – 480 BC)

Siddharta Gautama was probably born in Nepal at the foot of the Himalayas in around 560 BC. He was the son of a tribal leader who called himself a king. His children grew up as members of the noble

Buddha

Sakya dynasty. At first he was shaped by the luxury of his parents' court, but on three trips he was confronted with human suffering, when he encountered an old man, a sick person and a corpse. His meeting with a hermit during his fourth trip was crucial for how he spent the rest of his life. It gave the 29-year-old the impetus to give up the life he had led so far and as a **wandering ascetic** to search for answers to questions about the purpose of life.

After intense meditation and strict asceticism as well as many years spent wandering, Siddharta Gautama achieved the state of enlightenment under a fig tree (bodhi tree) by the Indian river Neraya, when he went through the »four stages of Jhana«. During this time he discovered the Four Noble Truths: »the nature of suffering«, »the cause of suffering«, »salvation from suffering« and »the way leading to the end of all human suffering«. Soon afterwards he gave his first sermon near the Indian town of Varanasi, which addressed these Four Noble Truths.

Just a few months later Buddha, which means »**the enlightened one**« or »the awakened one«, had a few dozen followers, whom he asked to teach his principles to the people. He himself spent 45 years as an itinerant preacher to proclaim his teaching of the »Wheel of Law«. While Buddhist tradition believes Buddha entered nirvana, a stage that releases every living thing on earth from the eternal cycle of birth, life and death, when he died in 543 BC at the age of 82, the historical account puts Buddha's death in the year 480 BC. Nevertheless, in the countries that have adopted Buddhism as their state religion, the assumed year of death, 543 BC, is important for the calendar. The year 2014 thus becomes the year 2557 in these countries.

MICHAEL ONDAATJE (BORN 12 SEPTEMBER 1974)

Writer The writer Michael Ondaatje, born in Colombo as the son of a Burgher family, is the best-known author in Sri Lanka. He moved to Canada when he was eleven and later he acquired Canadian citizenship. After studying at the Universities of Toronto and Kingston (Ontario), he started teaching at York University Toronto in the mid-1960s. Here he quickly developed a reputation as a poet and novelist. His detailed, vivid language earned him an interested international audience. For his early work *The Collected Works of Billy the Kid: Left-Handed Poems* (1970) he received the Governor General's Award for Poetry the following year. The abrupt jumps between narrator perspectives as well as the different story lines are typical of his early works. In his novel *Running in the Family*, Ondaatje took a nuanced, visual approach to dealing with the political and social problems of the country of his birth. This memoir, rich in metaphors, was written

The Temple of the Tooth in Kandy possesses a number of pictures
with depictions from Buddha's life and work, here his death

in the form of a fictionalized childhood memory. However, his best-
known work is the love story *The English Patient*, which was made
into a film in 1996, directed by Anthony Minghella and starring
Ralph Fiennes, Juliette Binoche and Kristin Scott Thomas. The film
won nine Academy Awards at the Oscars in 1997, including Best Picture and Best Director. In 1988 Ondaatje was awarded the Order of
Canada, the country's highest honour. He received special recogni-
tion when the near-Earth Amor asteroid (6569) was named after
him. Michael Ondaatje now lives in Toronto.

His brother, **Philip Christopher Ondaatje**, born in Kandy on 22
February 1933, is almost as famous. He made a name for himself as
a writer, philanthropist and adventurer, as well as a participant in the
Olympic Games.

MARCO POLO (1254–1324)

Marco Polo, whose name has become the epitome of travel, was born   **Merchant**
in Venice in 1254. His birth came at a time when Venice's trade rela-   **and traveller**
tions were not just limited to well-known ports around the Mediter-

ranean, but extended far beyond. There was particular interest in Asia. Together with his father Nicolao and his uncle Matteo, Marco Polo, having just turned 17, travelled to what is now Pakistan via Iran and from there via the Hindu Kush to China, where the small group was warmly welcomed at **the court of Kublai Khan**. The khan liked the young, well-travelled Venetian so much he employed him as a diplomat and a special representative for trade with the Western world. Marco Polo spent 17 years in China. During this time he went on many trips throughout Asia and wrote the first »travel guide«. His most famous book is called »Il Milione« (»The Travels of Marco Polo«), in which he wrote less about his routes than about his personal experiences when coming into contact with foreign cultures. At times his reports are rather fantastical, especially when he relies on the accounts of others.

When Marco Polo set off for home in 1292 he chose the sea route, which took him via Malaya and Sumatra as well as the Andaman Islands and Sri Lanka. He spent a few months here, possibly in search of a precious ruby, which had allegedly been in the possession of the king of Lanka and had the diameter of a man's arm.

Marco Polo died in his home city of Venice in 1324, having married just a few years earlier and become the father of three children.

RANASINGHE PREMADASA (1924–93)

Politician   Ranasinghe Premadasa was born the son of a labourer in Kehelwatte, a slum in Colombo. After working as a journalist he joined the Ceylon Labour Party (CLP) and in 1955 was elected vice-mayor of Colombo. Just a year later he left the CLP in order to become a member of the **United National Party (UNP)** and enter the House of Representatives. After the Sri Lanka Freedom Party (SLFP) lost the elections of 1965, Premadasa first became the parliamentary secretary of the minister of local government, whose office he took over in 1968. Premadasa's political career was interrupted by a new election victory of Sirimavo Bandaranaike. It was only in 1977 that the UNP came into office again. Premadasa returned to the post he had held in 1965 and in 1978 became prime minister under President Junius Jayawardene. During the course of the severe confrontations between the Singhalese and Tamil people, Premadasa played an important role. In 1987 he was given special powers when the rebels of the Liberation Tigers of Tamil Eelam (LTTE) threatened to violently take the control of government in their stronghold of the town of Jaffna. However, Premadasa managed to prevent this with a large-scale military operation. In 1988 he won elections by a narrow margin, defeating the former prime minister Mrs Bandaranaike, and in the following year succeeded President Junius Jayawardene, who was already 82 at the time. He gave the Indian troops stationed in Sri Lanka since 1987, an ultimatum for their withdrawal; at the same time he also opened talks with the rebels. This led to a temporary truce. Even though Premadasa was given a lot of credit, particularly for the many social measures he implemented for people of low income, his authoritarian leadership style was often criticized and caused one of the country's biggest governmental crises in August 1991. Even though the vote of no confidence directed at him was no more successful than the official impeachment proceedings, Premadasa's power declined. During a UNP election rally in Colombo on 1 May 1993 a young man armed with grenades blew himself up, killing the president and 23 others.

DUDLEY SHELTON SENANAYAKE (1911–73)

Dudley Shelton Senanayake was born in Colombo as the eldest son   Politician
of the first prime minister of Ceylon, Don Stephen Senanayake. He studied natural sciences and law in Cambridge, England. In 1934 he was called to the bar in London but shortly afterwards he returned to his home, where he spent some time working as a lawyer. In 1936 Senanayake was elected to the Legislative Assembly for the UNP, from 1974 onwards he was also a member of parliament and the minister of agriculture.

When his father died on 22 March 1952, Senanayake was invited by the governor-general, Lord Soulbury, to form a government. The many problems with which the Sri Lankan economy had to deal with during this time caused Senanayake to step down. He subsequently dedicated himself to the study of Buddhist scripture, but in 1957 returned to the political stage and took over the leadership of the UNP. After Solomon Bandaranaike fell victim to an assassin, he took his place, but only for four months. Then he was replaced by Sirimavo Bandaranaike, whose socialist course he now attacked. During the parliamentary elections of 22 March 1965 the governing SLFP suffered heavy losses, while the UNP more than doubled its number of seats in parliament. Senanayake became prime minister for the third time. He reversed the socialist direction of his predecessor and worked at achieving a more balanced foreign policy.

He was no match for the growing agitation of the opposition under the leadership of Mrs Bandaranaike, however. In 1970 in another political landslide his party lost 55 seats. In May 1970 he stepped down to make way for Mrs Bandaranaike; a short while later he also resigned as party leader.

ENJOY
SRI LANKA

Why do Sri Lankans celebrate on full-moon days? What rice varieties are good enough for a feast? Who would take an Ayurveda break? What must visitors pay attention to when eating? What fruit is available on the island?

Accommodation

Visiting Sri Lanka

Even though the country is not stingy with its natural beauties and cultural highlights, for many years the Sri Lanka hotel industry lagged behind that of other Asian countries. The civil war prevented any steady development. When the tsunami devastated the eastern coastal regions in 2004, the tourist industry struggled once more. All this is now history, and it seems that Sri Lanka is trying to put the problems of the past behind it at lightning speed.

More and more international hotel operators as well as local consortia have discovered Sri Lanka. Even if they already offered accommodation in the large towns on the west coast, they have been looking for suitable plots in the east for some years now as this coast is wild and romantic in some places, and great for swimming, snorkelling, surfing and lazing around in others. Now that the transport infrastructure is being improved all the time through the construction of new roads, there is virtually nothing in the way of a positive development of the hotel industry anymore.

Development

There is now the full spectrum of accommodation to choose from, from simple guesthouses to five star hotels. Visitors will be able to tailor their holidays to their needs and budgets. The boutique hotels are quite new. Their special feature is their charm, which is often based on their historical appeal. Of course the accommodation options are still focused on the towns and regions frequented by tourists. Since there are virtually no limits to the personal initiative of local entrepreneurs, accommodation can now also be found in somewhat more remote locations.

Guesthouses can be found all over the island. The level of comfort tends to be at least adequate and if something is missing, this is almost always made up for by the willingness or ability of the owner to improvise. Some guesthouses are run by ex-pat Europeans who are at pains to make a stay in Sri Lanka an experience. In many guesthouses it is almost the norm to live under the same roof as the owner's family, literally and metaphorically. There is virtually no better way of getting to know the locals.

Guesthouses

The Sri Lankan government maintains a number of rest houses, for example in Dambulla, Habarana, Sigiriya, Mihintale, Polonnaruwa

Rest Houses

The famous Galle Face Hotel in Colombo was opened in 1864 and is still a highlight and Ella. They are modest when it comes to creature comforts, but very cheap. Early reservations are therefore vital.

Living with the locals
In **homestays**, an inexpensive form of accommodation, visitors usually live with the family and will also often participate in the daily meals. (www.srilankanhomestay.com).

Home swap
The idea of swapping your home with someone in another country has not yet really established itself on Sri Lanka. Some options for this relatively new way of going on holiday can be found at www.knok.com.

Youth hostels
There are **no youth hostels** on Sri Lanka. Travellers with a tight budget will find inexpensive accommodation in the abovementioned guesthouses and homestays.

Camping
There are no campsites on Sri Lanka either. In theory, it is permitted to camp with your own equipment if the landowner gives his permission – this is not the case in the national parks unless it is expressly permitted. However, staying in one of the island's many rest houses is so cheap that it is hardly worth exploring Sri Lanka with a rucksack and tent.

Accommodation in national parks
Some national parks have chalets, which tend to be basic and inexpensive. During holiday times and in the peak season a reservation here is a must. The relevant contact details are available in the main section of this travel guide under ▶Sights from A to Z.

Reservation
Making timely reservations is particularly recommended during the main travel period between November and March. It is absolutely essential for Christmas and New Year. Accommodation near significant Buddhist shrines is often fully booked around the monthly Poya Days. There is no need for reservation during the low season.

HOTEL PRICES
Price categories
The hotels recommended in this guide in the chapter »Destinations from A to Z« are in the following price categories (double room incl. breakfast):
£ £ £ £ = over £90
£ £ £ = £60–£90
£ £ = £40–£60
£ = up to £40

HOTEL GUIDE
Tourism Authority of Sri Lanka
www.srilanka.travel
There is a register of all kinds of accommodation here, some of which can be booked online.
Ceylon Hotels Corporation
www.ceylonhotelscorporation.com
The Ceylon Hotels Corporation also finds hotels for visitors.

THE BEST AYURVEDA HOTELS IN SRI LANKA

Hotels offering Ayurveda are naturally a lot more expensive because the treatments and medications and also the ayurvedic meals are included in the price. For this reason they are not in line with the standard accommodation categories in this guide.

Ayurveda Centre Lawrence Hill Paradise £ £   **Insider Tip**
en.ayurvedakurlaub.de
(website in English)
Peace and quiet is guaranteed here because this hotel, which is reserved solely for ayurveda guests and is under German management, is set in a lovely garden a few hundred metres from the lively beach of Hikkaduwa. Only 14 rooms – hence a place of individuality and contemplation.

Ayurveda Hotel Paragon £ £ £
www.paragonsrilanka.com
This resort is situated between Galle and Matara. It was designed by a pupil of the well-known architect Geoffrey Bawa, a reason why it is one of the most exclusive Ayurveda resorts on the island. It is just a few metres to the beach. Visitors fancying a change of scene can also use the freshwater pool.

Vattersgarden £ £ – £ £ £
www.vattersgarden.com
This resort, which has been around for 20 years now, is located around 40km/25mi to the south of Colombo. The extensive park that surrounds the small living units is a great place for relaxation. There is a co-operative agreement with a state-run ayurveda clinic and the Buddhist community in Kottegoda.

Greystones Villa £ £ – £ £ £
www.greystones-villa.de
This ayurveda resort is located near Bandarawela in among some glorious mountain landscape. It was the first to receive official permission in 1992 to offer panchakarma treatments to foreigners.

Barberyn Reef Ayurveda Resort £ £ – £ £ £
www.barberynresorts.com
Right by the sea. This ayurveda resort has been well-known for more than two decades now. Since the surrounding natural environment plays an important role, the landscape architect Lucky Senanayake, who is famous on Sri Lanka, was commissioned to design of the garden.

Ayurveda

Life-knowledge

The word Ayurveda comes from the ancient Indian language, Sanskrit, and refers to a collection of insights developed over a period of more than 3000 years: »veda« means »knowledge« and »ayus« means »life«, so both together mean »life-knowledge«. Ayurveda focuses not just on medical insights, but also on those that deal with everyday habits. Therefore it aims to be holistic and preventive. Anyone looking for a wellness holiday should look elsewhere.

Since every person has different life energies and temperaments, ayurvedic teaching has doshas that can be attributed to an individual. They consist of three types – **vata, kapha and pitta** – to which the five elements – air, space, fire, water and earth – are assigned: the vata dosha is given air and space, the kapha dosha water and earth and the pitta dosha the element of fire. However, there are mixed types as well: vata-pitta, vata-kapha, pitta-kapha and the rarer tridosha type (vata-pitta-kapha). One central goal of ayurvedic treatments is to maintain the doshas in balance or to get them into such a state. To do this, disturbances need to be recognized as they could lead the patient to feel unwell and later to become sick. If someone's body temperature is too high or that person has visual problems, it indicates a disturbed pitta; migraines and sleep disturbances as well as poor appetite are signs of a problematic vata.

The Doshas

In ayurvedic medicine, no technical aids or synthetic ingredients are used in the manufacture of essences and oils. In ayurvedic medicine, pharmacology (dravyaguna) is considered the most important science. Recipes have always been guarded as secrets and often only handed down to family members following in the tradition. Many complaints can be alleviated or even cured using this knowledge of the healing **power of herbs and spices**. Ayurveda's medicinal use of plants is thus both successfully applied in the home as well as in the clinical sphere. The healing power of the substances is said to come from the extent to which the five eternal elements are present in them. Five factors determine how a recipe is put together: flavour (rasa), properties (guna), thermal qualities (virya), the effect after digestion (vipaka) and the specific healing effect (prabhava). Every recipe is individually tailored to the mental and physical state of the patient.

Ayurvedic medicines

A shirodhara massage with warm oil poured over the forehead is the best-known ayurvedic treatment

Nutrition The doshas also play a special role when it comes to nutrition: food and health are inextricably linked in ayurvedic medicine. **»We are what we eat and digest«** is one of Ayurveda's central tenets. To every type are attributed certain foods that are particularly beneficial or deleterious. Hot, wet foods balance out vata disturbances. They include hot, mildly salted soups and broths, soaked dried fruit and nuts. Easily digestible hot foods such as fennel are also recommended. The daily menu should contain dairy products as well as spices such as ginger, cloves, saffron and cinnamon. Too much raw food should be avoided, as should bitter vegetables (e.g. cabbage) and dried food. The pitta type, which should consume their main meals at midday, will find that cold, sweet and bitter foods have a harmonizing effect; spices such as turmeric, cardamom and coriander as well as bitter herbs also play an important role. Green vegetables are also recommended, such as broccoli, lettuce, root vegetables and leafy vegetables. Raw food and salads are a valuable addition. Pitta types

For Vata types: an ayurvedic Lassi drink

should stay away from tomatoes, citrus fruits and dairy products. Meat and alcohol should on principle only be enjoyed in small quantities. The kapha type should limit their meals to a nutritious one at midday and a lighter one in the evening: spicy and bitter foods are no less positive for this type than light and dry dishes. Aromatically spiced vegetables should be on the menu as should light, cooked dishes and bitter herbs: chilli, mung beans and barley. The kapha type should avoid fatty or fried foods as well as salty and sweet foods.

During **mealtimes** the silence is almost devout. The fork is consciously guided to the mouth. Every bite is carefully chewed. Instead of beer and wine, water and tea are served. Alcoholic drinks are frowned upon. The only place it is acceptable for guests to drink them is within their own rooms. Still, ayurveda is not a philosophy that is anti-pleasure. It does not deny the pleasures of life; instead it promotes conscious enjoyment.

Ayurveda focuses first and foremost on detoxing and purging the body and then on recreating the balance between body, mind and soul that has been disturbed by unhealthy influences. This is to be achieved with heat treatments, massages and oil treatments but also with yoga. Breathing exercises, steam and herb baths as well as a special diet are also firm components of any treatment following ayurvedic principles. Precise and detailed conversions of the specifications in Indian texts are available. They are so old that their origin is lost in the realm of Indian mythology. Even the treatment table is carved from a single massive block of wood, as is required by the ancient writings. *Cleansing techniques*

The Panchakarma cleansing methods have been in use for many centuries now. Using a complex system of five (panch) actions (karma), toxic substances and metabolic waste is removed. The number of methods matches that of the individual ailments according to which they are chosen. They are tailored to the diagnosed state of health. *Panchakarma*

The panchakarma is not equally good for all ailments. The intensive cleansing procedures achieve the best results with chronic illnesses and psychosomatic complaints. They can help with many skin conditions, with digestive problems and diseases of the auto-immune system. Diabetes, cardiovascular diseases and mobility issues can all be successfully treated this way. The purifying treatments – laxatives (virecana), enemas (basti), emetics (vamana), nose and sinus treatments (nasya) and blood letting (rakta moska) – do not just cleanse the digestive tract. The combination of preparation, purification and post-treatment lastingly restores body and mind. The waste products and tissue toxins are released and are removed from the body through subsequent sweat treatments. It takes a certain amount of time to complete a panchakarma treatment. Three weeks is considered the minimum. Many complaints can be improved or even healed and the original balance of the doshas returns. This is not a holiday with a mere health component; rather it is a challenge.

Ayurvedic massage

Ayurvedic massages are used both as preparations for a panchakarma treatment as well as an accompaniment to any medical treatment. When practised regularly, the ayurveda treatments have a **rejuvenating and invigorating effect, renewing the body's cells**. In addition they strengthen the immune system and produce a general sense of wellbeing. A distinction is made between tissue-reducing and tissue-building treatments. Tissue-building massages include the various massages with carefully and individually chosen oils. These oil massages are called snehana. The whole body (abhyanga) or only certain areas (face, abdomen, back, feet) are massaged with oils that are tailored to the skin type, constitution and ailments of the patient. This reduces stress and is helpful for anyone suffering from problems sleeping. It strengthens the skin, bones and muscles, it helps with mobility issues and it generally improves the immune system.

The best-known ayurvedic treatment is the **shirodhara** massage: warm, fragrant oil is continuously poured in a fine trickle over the forehead. This shirodhara does not just produce a state of deep relaxation. It also helps with sleeplessness and headaches, and with depression. It is easy to relax fully during such a treatment. The quiet hissing of the flame heating the oil seems very far away.

A foot massage reduces stress

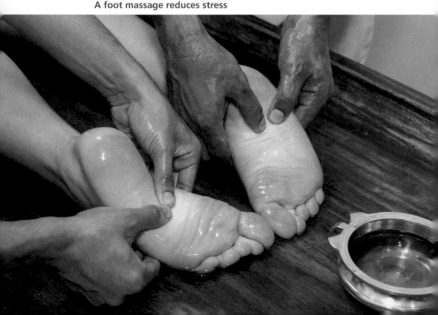

It takes five years before anyone on Sri Lanka is allowed to call him or herself an ayurvedic doctor – that is comparable to the time it takes in Europe to train as a medical specialist. This makes it very clear that the many courses lasting just a few days or at best a few weeks that claim to train participants as ayurveda therapists can only impart superficial knowledge. In Europe, the title **»ayurvedic practitioner«** is not adequately protected, but it still looks good on the sign of a doctor or alternative therapist. However, what is currently on offer in Europe as ayurveda often has little to do with the ancient Indian art of healing. That is not to say that these practitioners are charlatans. Since wellness has become an umbrella term for anything that feels good in some way, many therapists have discovered ayurveda. However, there is a danger that unprofessional practitioners could make misdiagnoses and choose the wrong treatments, thereby worsening the health problems. A good dose of scepticism is essential when ayurvedic practitioners make excessive promises of healing, even when it comes to serious diseases, such as cancer. Ayurveda is no cure-all, even though a trusting following swear by the powers of this millennia-old natural medicine. What has been proved, however, is that Ayurveda can relieve chronic illnesses and guard against future ailments.

Ayurvedic training

▶p. 115

Ayurveda hotels

Children in Sri Lanka

An Island Full of Adventure

Even though children do not generally have a strong interest in ruins and temples, riding on elephants and visiting national parks with their impressive fauna compensate for the long flight or visits to cultural sites. There are also lovely beaches that are great for swimming, while the many colourful festivals bring life into any vacation.

When travelling with children it is advisable to see their family doctor in good time. They will definitely need adequate **vaccinations**. There are sometimes special drugs for children, such as for malaria. Generally speaking, any **travel first-aid kit** should include drugs that are suitable for children (e.g. to treat diarrhoea and feverish colds), since they are often not available even in larger towns and if they are, then often under an unfamiliar name. The stray cats and dogs are a hygienic problem; as they carry parasites, it is best to keep children away from them. **Wash fruit thoroughly** before eating it.

Health care

Baby food and nappies can be found in supermarkets in large towns. Bottles are quite rare, however, so it is best to bring them. Children's **cots** are also rare. However, many hotels offer an additional bed. Hotel receptions stock mosquito nets. Anyone hiring a car should make sure it comes with a **child's car seat**. This cannot be taken for granted on Sri Lanka.

Some more advice

The temperatures on land and in the water are pleasant all year round, making fun in the water an inviting prospect.
The **nicest beaches, which are also child-friendly**, can be found on the west coast near Negombo, Hikkaduwa and Bentota, while Unawatuna Beach and the beach at Matara in the south are legendary. There are some glorious beaches above Trincomalee on the east coast (e.g. on Pigeon Island) or further south near Pottuvil. Hotels are now being built here that cater to the needs of children.

Fun in the water

What would a round trip of Sri Lanka be without a visit to a **national park**? This is a very special experience for children of all ages. Here they can observe in the wild animals they otherwise only see in zoos. Driving through such a park in a car and spotting wild animals is definitely a highlight they won't forget in a hurry (►Practical information, p.404).

Discovering animals

A ride on an elephant's back is a must for children

Attractions for children

COLOMBO
National Museum
Sir Marcus Fernando Mawatha
Colombo 7
Daily 9am–5pm, except holidays
Admission charge: 500 Rs, children half-price
(photography permit: 1000 Rs)
tel. 011 269 43 46
www.museum.gov.lk
For older children who are already a little bit interested in the history of a country – they would enjoy visiting the National Museum in Colombo, the largest museum in Sri Lanka. It is housed in a two-storey building in the Victorian colonial style and displays numerous artefacts from the island's history.

National Museum of Natural History
Ananda Coomaraswamy Mawatha
Colombo 7
Mon – Sun 9am – 6pm, except on holidays
Admission charge: 500 Rs, children half-price
(photography permit: 1000 Rs)
tel. 011 269 13 99
www.museum.gov.lk
Lots of photographs and stuffed animals exhibited in their artificially created habitats should be of interest to all children. The tiger, although stuffed, is nevertheless fearsome. It was killed near Batticaloa on 16 August 1924 by no fewer than 13 people.

National Zoological Gardens
Dehiwala
Mon – Sun 8.30am – 6pm
Admission charge: 2000 Rs, children half-price
tel. 011 269 13 99
www.colombozoo.gov.lk
Colombo's zoo is considered to be one of the best in Asia. Its origins go back to the German zoo expert Jon Hagenbeck, the half-brother of the man who founded Hamburg zoo, Carl Hagenbeck. He spent some time in Sri Lanka. However, some animals are not kept in the way they should be, which is criticized by animal welfare activists.

KEGALLA
Pinawela Elephant Orphanage
Near Kegalla on the Maha Oya River
Mon – Sun 8.30am – 6pm
Admission charge: 1000 Rs, with a ride on an elephant 2000/3000 Rs; Children aged 3 and up half-price
Twice a day, in the morning and in the afternoon the app. 75 elephants of all ages are herded through the village to the Maha Oya river, where they are allowed to bathe. Sometimes it is possible to participate in this refreshing dip or let the elephants splash water over you.

Insider Tip

KOSGODA
Turtles and their offspring
Not far from Kosgoda and Bentota there are some facilities for looking after freshly hatched turtles that could scarcely survive without human help. One such facility is the Victor Hasselblad

Feeding turtles in the hatchery

Turtle Hatchery to the south of Bentota. It can be visited between 8am and 6pm (admission charge: 300 Rs, children half-price). With a bit of luck visitors will be able to experience how the young turtles that have been given a helping hand are released back into the wild, preferably in the evenings at around 6.30pm. There are also some permanent guests, such as older turtles injured by fishing nets which are being nursed back to health by the hatchery. There are two further facilities nearby. Watch out of the signs on the road to Galle.

WELIGAMA
Watch dolphins and whales

The Indian Ocean is full of interesting animals. The far south of the island, near Dondra Head, is an outstanding place to watch dolphins and whales. Entire schools of these marine mammals can be seen just a few kilometres offshore. Several operators run trips from Mirissa near Weligama all year round. They last up to four hours. They are not cheap but they will definitely be an absolute highlight for children (www.mirissawatersports.com)!

Festivals · Holidays · Events

Many Peoples, Many Holidays

The people of Sri Lanka enjoy celebrating and they do so often. There are plenty of occasions in the calendar because Sri Lanka is home to many peoples, which expresses itself in a large number of religious holidays. On the island, which is where Buddhism became widespread for the first time, events from the life of the Enlightened Buddha Siddharta Gautama are naturally at the heart of the festivities.

The full moon day (**Poya Day**) that takes place once a month is a public holiday during which public life rests. Depending on the occasion, hundreds or thousands of pilgrims make their way to the historic Buddhist sites. On these days monks and laypeople will focus on inner contemplation. The most pious fast on these days and abstain from all pleasures. Full moon days do not have to coincide with those in Europe. Because of the astronomical calculations they can take place up to two days earlier or later. By the way, it is against the law to serve alcoholic drinks on Poya Days. This is not the case for hotels where alcohol is generally only served via room service.

Full moon day

It is possible in a hotel or restaurant on Sri Lanka that the familiar service will cease to be the same high standard it had recently been. If almost all the employees gather in front of a television, it is definitely because a cricket match has entered a crucial phase. Cricket is the country's top national sport and **every match is an event**. Even the youngest boys learn to play cricket and every self-respecting school in the country has its own team. There are two large cricket grounds in Sri Lanka. One of them is in Colombo, while a second was built in Galle in 1998. International matches are held here too.

Cricket has a mass following

An English-language calendar with the dates of all the important moveable festivals and holidays in Sri Lanka is available as a download at www.srilanka.travel.

Calendar

Festival calendar

HOLIDAYS

1 January (New Year)	22 May (Day of the Republic)
4 February (Independence Day to commemorate 4 February 1948)	30 June (Bankers Holiday)
	25 December (Christmas)
1 May (Labour Day)	31 December (New Year's Eve)

Magnificently decorated elephants during the Perahera of Gangarama

Traditional Singhalese orchestra in Kandy during Perahera

cred tooth. Hundreds of decorated elephants take part in this ceremony.

Perahera of Kataragama
The Perahera in honour of the god of war, Skanda, lasts nine days. All ceremonies begin with a bath in the Menik Ganga. The actual procession begins with festively decorated elephants; one of them carries the relics. On the final day believers flagellate themselves or walk on hot coals.

Vel (in Colombo and Jaffna)
A holiday in honour of the god of war, Skanda, which is celebrated both in the capital Colombo and in Jaffna. A procession is held in Colombo that centres on the

golden chariot of the god of war. It starts in the Pettah district and ends in Bambalapitiya.

Nallur Festival
The Nallur Kandaswamy Temple in Nallur on the lagoon is at the heart of this festival. It is the largest Hindu temple in Sri Lanka. It is predominantly frequented by Sri Lanka's Tamils, the majority of whom are of the Hindu faith.

AUGUST
Nikini Poya (nationwide)
The Full Moon Day of August is a much more modest and quiet celebration. For the monks who live in the monasteries this day centres on prayer and meditation.

SEPTEMBER
Binara Poya
(nationwide)
All over the country this Full Moon Day is celebrated in memory of the day Buddha entered the heaven of the gods in order to spread his teachings there.

OCTOBER
Wap Poya
(nationwide)
Two events from the life of the Enlightened One are at the heart of this event: the day he gave up his existence as a lay person and the day he returned from the heaven of the gods.

NOVEMBER
Dipavalee Festival
(nationwide)
This Hindu festival revolves around Vishnu and Krishna and the victory of light over darkness. Thousands of small oil lamps are symbolically lit in temples on this day.

Il Poya
(nationwide)
Buddhists commemorate the sending out of the first 60 monks who were to spread the teachings of the enlightened Buddha.

NOVEMBER/DECEMBER
Hajj Festival
(nationwide)
Moslems celebrate this festival in the country's mosques; some also go on the pilgrimage to Mecca.

? MARCO❀POLO *Pilgrims under way*

Around the middle of December the pilgrimage season to Adam's Peak, Sri Lanka's sacred mountain, begins; it lasts until mid-May

DECEMBER
Unduwap Poya
(nationwide)
The sacred bodhi tree in Anuradhapura is at the centre of the December full moon festival. Major celebrations take place all around the temple that houses the more than 2200-year-old tree, which was created from a cutting of the tree under which Buddha found enlightenment.

Food and Drink

Hot Stuff

The influence of the Indian subcontinent on Sri Lanka's cuisine is obvious. Just as in India, rice and curry are the staple foods and ingredients of the national dish. However, the term curry means something different from what it does in Europe. That is also true with regard to spiciness, which is almost a trade-mark of Sri Lankan cuisine.

In Sri Lanka, curry is not a single spice, it is a spicy mix of up to 20 ingredients. The most important is turmeric. Others include ginger, nutmeg, pepper, allspice, paprika and chilli. Every cook and every chef who prides himself in what he does uses an individual curry mix. It is added as soon as the fish, meat, poultry or veg is seared. Coconut milk is added to refine the dish, which lessens the bite somewhat and produces a rounded flavour. The meals tend to be **very spicy**. Be especially careful when it comes to curries. A typical speciality is a simple curry that includes chopped onions, green chilli and aromatic spices such as coriander, vanilla, cloves, nutmeg, cinnamon and saffron as well as coconut milk. All this is used to flavour chicken, beef or pork. A curry as a main meal often consists of a number of different meat and vegetable variations.

Curry

> **MARCO ⬤ POLO TIP**
>
> **Beware! Spicy!**   **Insider Tip**
>
> Those who do not like their food too spicy (hot) should say »without chilli please« when ordering. The food will still be spicy enough and European palates tend to be more sensitive than Sri Lankan ones.

Sri Lankan cuisine is also known for its excellent fish dishes. Almost everything caught in the sea is also put on the plate: tuna – here the particularly tasty bonito – herring and goatfish. The local chefs know how to prepare lobster, shrimps and shellfish to make them just right. Fish curries are a very tasty option. Whether boiled, fried or grilled, seafood only costs a fraction of what it does in Europe. Grilled king prawns in a garlic sauce are just one of the many delicacies on offer.

Seafood

There are no fewer than 15 different rice varieties in Sri Lanka. The reddish rice (kakuluhaal) is the best. The way in which the rice is prepared plays an important role, as it does everywhere in Asia. It is not boiled in water, but slowly and carefully steamed in special pots. That

Rice

Spices are at the heart of Sri Lankan cuisine, hence they are sold in large quantities at the country's markets

Only Fresh Ingredients

There is far more to Sri Lankan cuisine than just the rice and curry specialities mentioned above. It is more diverse than one might think and fresh ingredients are always indispensable, as are the spices that flourish in such variety on Sri Lanka – the island has always been considered the spice island after all. They do not just make the dishes tasty, they also make them digestible. Ayurvedic cuisine is noteworthy because its dishes consist of very specific ingredients.

Rice with curry: the classic dish of Sri Lankan cuisine. It largely consists of rice, to which fish, shrimps and other seafood are added. The local population are more likely to put chunks of pork or beef into their curries instead. Vegetarians will not be short-changed either because there are not just meat curries but vegetable ones too (elawalu).

Jaggery: a kind of caramel made from the crystalized juice of the jaggery palm. The most popular desserts also include wattalapam, a pudding that is cooked and is made of the sugar of palm nectar, coconut milk, eggs and spices such as cinnamon. Kiribath is another popular dessert. It is a tasty rice pudding made with many different spices.

Dhal: served as a side or as a main, it is a very nutritious dish. Dhal consists of red lentils that are cooked with various spices. Sometimes coconut milk and dried fish are also added.

Roti: flat bread made of flour and grated coconut, served with various fillings. There are also papadums, which are made of lentil flour and deep-fried in oil, which makes them nice and crispy. They are used as the basis for breakfast or as a snack.

Hoppers: a cross between a muffin and a tea cake with a crunchy exterior. If they are served with a freshly cooked egg on top, they are called egg hoppers (biththara appa). They are often made of rice flour, palm sugar and coconut milk and are stuffed with finely chopped vegetables. Hoppers are also a popular dessert, for example when they are filled with honey or coconut honey. One variation is the string hopper. String hoppers are steamed rings of rice flour and coconut milk that are popular at breakfast and as side dishes for a curry.

Pickles: pickled fruit or vegetables that are served as a spicy side to meat, rice or bread. The most common fruits and vegetables to be pickled in oil, spices and salt in this way are (unripe) mangos, lemons, limes, green chillis, cloves of garlic, ginger, carrots and radishes.

Lychee   Durian

Beyond Apples and Pears

Visitors from northern Europe will see Sri Lanka as a lavish orchard with many, maybe hitherto unknown tropical fruits. Fresh fruit is sold cheaply all over the island, depending on the season, and is available in every restaurant. Fruit bought on the market should be washed thoroughly to neutralize potential residues of pesticide, which is much used on the island.

Pineapple (annasi) is available fresh from April to July in various varieties. Pineapples are rich in vitamin C and low in calories. Some varieties are eaten slightly fermented, which can have a laxative effect.

Bananas (kessel) are also available in various varieties all year round. A tip: the smaller the banana, the sweeter it tastes. One delicious treat for anyone with a sweet tooth would be bananas dunked in sweet coconut milk and then grilled, baked or fried in hot coconut fat.

The somewhat floury flesh of **durians** – known to Europeans because of its strong odour – is considered a delicacy by Asians (April to June). However, many hotels ask their guests not to bring durians back to their room.

Guavas (pera) are usually eaten with sugar and a pinch of salt and are harvested between September and January.

The sweet, aromatic **jackfruit** (waraka), a round fruit weighing several kilograms, is cut into slices and served on ice (August to September).

The milk from **coconuts** (pol) is a refreshing, healthy drink. After drinking, the flesh is scraped out with a pointy spoon.

Langsats (con) are a tasty, light-brown berry with a thin but hard shell that has to be removed with a knife. Careful: the sweet flesh of this berry covers a very bitter pip (June to September).

Limes, green and round, are the local version of lemons. They are available all year round.

Longans

Mangosteens

Longans come from higher parts of the island. Since the fruit only keeps for a few days and has to be transported over long distances, it is expensive (July to September)

Lychees used to only be available as a luxury import in tins. Now they are grown in the country as well. There are various price categories, but they taste almost the same. Get them fresh and ripe with a red skin between May and August.

After pineapples, **mangos** (ambe) are the most popular fruit among tourists. They are only sweet, juicy and flavoursome when ripe (yellow skin, limited shelf life). The stone is cut out and the flesh is eaten with a spoon or even sucked (March to June).

Mangosteens (manjustin) are purple on the outside and are available from June to November. The flesh is white and has a sweet flavour that is similar to that of lychees.

Oranges (dodam) have a thin, green peel in Asia. They are particularly sweet when yellow. They are available all year round.

Grapefruits (bambelosi), usually with delicious pink flesh and available fresh all year round, are popularly served with a pinch of salt.

Papayas or pawpaws (pepol) are served in halves with a lime at hotel breakfasts. It is the cheapest of all the fruits and available all year round from every market stall. Careful: if eaten in larger quantities, papayas are a definite laxative!

Rambutan (rambutan) were called »hairy« by the Americans because of their green and, when ripe, greenish-red hairs. Cut open the shell with a knife and enjoy the juicy flesh but not the stone (May to October).

The **rose apple** (jambu) has the shape of a pear with a rust-coloured waxy skin and a porous, white flesh. Since this fruit is somewhat sour, it is commonly eaten with sugar and a pinch of salt.

The yellow-green to dark-blue oval **passion fruit** (passion) is also widespread. Its juicy flesh is particularly popular as a dessert.

is the only way the valuable ingredients can be preserved. White rice is used for daily cooking, while the more expensive basmati rice or the brown, unprocessed rice is used for special occasions.

Eating habits

It is not customary to eat with cutlery on Sri Lanka – people eat with their hands. Or rather, with their right hand, since the left one is considered impure as that hand is used to clean oneself on the toilet. To eat without cutlery, shape your fingers in such a way that everything on the plate can be mixed. Pick up a portion of it and form it into a ball and eat it. Wet cloths are used to clean the fingers. Tourists are naturally provided with the cutlery they are accustomed to.

Cookshops and restaurants (▶price categories p.9)

The markets in particular are likely to feature the cookshops that are so typical of Asia. Simple meals are produced while the customer waits. It is up to the individual to assess the hygienic conditions and decide whether to consume the food or not. It goes without saying that it's worth leaving the hotel complex and visiting one of the restaurants, which are particularly plentiful in the seaside resorts. The quality is generally good and the selection is also tailored to visitors from Europe. The more expensive restaurants require timely reservations. It is also customary to wait to be seated. The menus are generally available in English.

Tea

Tea is Sri Lanka's national drink and a lot of care and effort is put into its preparation. The four elements that make up a Ceylon tea are altitude, climate, leaf quality and processing. Green tea is not commonly produced in Sri Lanka, but the different types of black tea are popularly drunk with a lot of milk and sugar. The practice, widespread in continental Europe, of flavouring teas with alien aromas is as abhorrent to Sri Lankans as it is in the British Isles. The best tea, called High Grow, is largely planted in the Uva district, where the excellent climate and the altitude of at least 1300m/4300ft give it a special flavour. However, the best tea varieties tend to be exported. Recently there have been attempts to produce tea following organic principles. This method makes do without fertilizers and pesticides, while the drying facilities are powered by wood fires (▶MARCO POLO Insight p.332).

Alcohol-free drinks

Drinking water is sold everywhere and when bottled there is no problem drinking it. Soft drinks such as Coca Cola, Pepsi Cola, Sprite and tonic water are also available everywhere.
Fresh coconut milk is very tasty. Connoisseurs also spoon out the white flesh of the king coconut (thambili), which is plentiful on Sri Lanka. Another popular drink, known as curd, is made from buffalo milk. Curd is consumed in a small, clay bowl: to find out if it is fresh, turn the latter upside down. If the milk stays in, it is.

Popular options brewed in Sri Lanka include Lions Lager, which in recent years has received strong competition from Lion Strong Beer. Alcoholic drinks

Another brand is called Three Lions; one thing all these varieties have in common is their relatively high price, since hops and malt have to be imported as they do not grow on Sri Lanka. Many restaurants and hotel bars now stock European beers, such as the Danish Carlsberg, which is brewed in Sri Lanka near Colombo. Pricier restaurants serve wine, which also does not grow on the island and has to be imported, mostly from Europe or Australia, making it among the most expensive drinks. Arrak definitely takes first place when it comes to intoxicating drinks. It is made by taking the sap of palm trees and processing it into toddy, a kind of palm wine. Once distilled, it becomes arrak.

Curd is sold in clay bowls

Rich Selection

The long-standing tradition of Sri Lankan handicrafts makes it easier for visitors to find suitable souvenirs. Be it carved masks, batik fabrics or gemstones: the choice is broad and inexpensive.

When shopping, it is nonetheless worthwhile not to go for the first price that is given; haggling is part of the shopping experience almost everywhere, except in department stores and up-market shops. The Arts and Crafts Centers that can be found in every larger town offer a wide variety of goods and the state-owned Laksala shops are also a good place to look for souvenirs. They sell high-quality handicrafts made of wood, metal, silver, reed, natural fibres, buffalo horns, coconuts and bamboo as well as textiles, batik goods and silk. Laksala has a total of ten branches, the main one being at 60 York Street, Fort, Colombo 1, www.laksala.lk.ge. Local artisans sell their products in small stalls in the hotel grounds.

Art market

The art market, Kala Pola, which is held on the third Sunday in January, has become a fixture in Colombo. It is primarily local artists presenting their works to a wide and sometimes expert audience.

Batiks

Along the road between Colombo and Kandy a large number of small businesses laboriously make elaborate batik goods by hand. It is often possible to watch how the colourful fabrics are made. Strictly speaking the art of batik is not originally Sri Lankan, but was imported from Indonesia. However, its quality is coming closer and closer to the original.

Designer knock-offs

The market for designer knock-offs is flourishing in Sri Lanka, because many designers also have their clothes made here and so even the originals are cheaper in Sri Lanka than they are in Europe. But beware: many items are under trademark protection and if it is too obvious, they can be confiscated by customs when you return home, and you may even face prosecution.

Lacemaking

In the south of the island all around the port of Galle the art of lacemaking, brought here by the Portuguese, has survived to this day. The main goods are tablecloths, handkerchiefs and similar items.

Traditional masks, woodwork

The mask carvers of Ambalangoda, a small town on the southwest coast, are well-known for their traditional masks. As a result a large

Get an artistic henna tattoo on the market

Masks made in the workshops of Ambalangoda

number of shops selling a wide variety of masks have opened up here. However, there is no place frequented by tourists in Sri Lanka that does not also sell masks as souvenirs. Visitors will also find everything else that can be made of wood, such as elephants or Buddha figurines. It is wise, however, for ecological reasons, to avoid all teak products in favour of goods made from other types of wood.

Furniture   Amongst the larger souvenir items are complete furniture suites, made for example of rosewood or bamboo. The stores that sell these also organize shipping to Europe and deal with the customs formalities.

Gemstones   The region around Ratnapura is a Mecca for gemstone prospectors. It has rubies, sapphires, topazes and many other precious stones. They can be found carefully cut and polished in jewellers' shops all over the island, where of course they are also sold as part of finished pieces of jewellery. However, the latter items can be disappointing in terms of quality. It might be better to buy the stones in Sri Lanka and have them made into jewellery at home.

Like everywhere else in Asia, Sri Lanka also has itinerant hawkers who try to sell tourists, on the beach, for example, »high-quality stones at exceptionally good prices«. It should be obvious that these stones are either very poor quality or even imitations. It is also not advisable to buy gemstones directly from the mines around Ratnapura, because the dealers there can be very pushy at times. In general it is a good idea to have some knowledge of gemstones in order to judge their quality. Many a purchase made without this knowledge has turned out to be an expensive and disappointing mistake. If in doubt, turn to the National Gem & Jewellery Authority, which will test the authenticity of gemstones for free. In addition they issue a list of inspected jeweller's stores (25 Galle Face Terrace, Colombo 03, tel. 011 239 06 45, www.srilankagemautho.com).

MARCO POLO TIP

! *Ayurveda cosmetics* **Insider Tip**

Western toiletries are quite expensive on Sri Lanka. But if you run out of something, fear not, the local ayurveda products are excellent and inexpensive.

Brass goods

All over the island there are small companies that sell artistic brass goods. They are usually hand-made and the motifs are often of a religious nature, but can also be secular.

Tea

Those who leave Sri Lanka without a few packets of tea will probably be missing out on the best-tasting souvenir of all. Particularly in the highlands around Nuwara Eliya there are many tea factories that also have tea-tasting facilities and a shop. The prices even for the best varieties are low – no wonder, given the low wages the pickers get paid.

Spices

The highlands are also home to a number of spice farms that sell fresh spices such as nutmeg, vanilla, cardamom, cinnamon and many others straight from the producer, meaning they will be fresh and inexpensive. A further place to buy spices is at one of the markets that are held in every town.

Opening times

Since shop opening times are not regulated by law in Sri Lanka, there is no single time when shops close. Shops are generally open Mon–Fri 8.30am–7pm and often close for lunch between 1pm and 2pm. Many shops also open on Saturdays; most stay closed on Sundays.

Sport and Outdoors

Active Holidays

Of course it is possible to experience Sri Lanka as a package tourist, but there are virtually no limits to what visitors can do under their own steam. The choice of sports is growing all the time, since the Sri Lankans want to do more than just spoil their guests and give them a comfortable stay. They also want to make sure their visitors have plenty of experiences.

A holiday on Sri Lanka is not limited to spending lazy days on one of the glorious beaches. Anyone active enough will have a choice of a variety of active alternatives. Be it golfing, surfing, diving, mountain biking or hiking: the options of enjoying an active and varied holiday on Sri Lanka are growing all the time.

Stressed individuals will find some happiness here: leave the hustle and bustle of everyday life behind in the seclusion of a Buddhist monastery. Search for the self or the »Four Noble Truths«. This is quite possible on Sri Lanka and information about it is available in Colombo in the **International Vipassama Meditation Center** (tel. 011 269 41 00, www.vipassana.com). The website also lists addresses of meditation centres that teach in English. One of the oldest institutions of this nature is the **Kanduboda Meditation Centre** in Delgoda (tel. 011 257 03 06), founded in 1957. In Kandy the **Nilambe Meditation Center** (tel. 081 222 54 71) also offers stays for foreign visitors. Things are somewhat Spartan at the **Polgasduwa Island Hermitage** 5km/3mi outside of Hikkaduwa, which follows the principles of Theravada Buddhism. Only men are allowed on the island here – and only if they registered at least six weeks in advance and they have a confirmation letter. This can be obtained from the Monk in Charge, Polgasduwa Island Hermitage, Dodanduwa 80250. *Meditation*

There are currently several golf courses of international standard on Sri Lanka. They can be found in places such as Colombo, Rajawella and Nuwara Eliya. One of the most beautiful golf courses is app. 115km/71mi to the west of Kandy near Mahinyangana. There are also comfortable chalets available to rent here. There are plans to set up more golf courses in the coming years. *Golf*

The landscape of the Central Highlands is a paradise for mountain bikers. Bikes can be hired but it is best if passionate bikers bring their own. *Mountain biking*

The east coast of Sri Lanka is very popular with surfers. International surfing competitions are regularly held in Arugam Bay.

Hiking
Sri Lanka is not a traditional destination for hikers but there are nonetheless some attractive regions that can be explored on foot. The Horton Plains, a unique natural landscape with an interesting flora, is just one example. There is a very well signposted hiking trail here. Hiking is also possible in the Sinharaja Rain Forest Sanctuary near Ratnapura, but only in the company of a licensed guide. Climbing Adam's Peak could also be considered a hike.

Tennis
Tennis courts, some of which are floodlit, can be found all over the island, especially in the better hotels. They will often hire out equipment and have coaches available.

Ballooning
For some years now it has been possible to enjoy the scenic beauty of Sri Lanka from above, in a hot air balloon. Tours above the Cultural Triangle are particularly enchanting (Dambulla, Anuradhapura or Polonnaruwa and Sigiriya). The baskets hold up to 16 passengers (www.srilankaballooning.com).

The highlands around Kandy are particularly good for hiking because the temperatures here are pleasant

Information and organizers

WILDLIFE SPOTTING
Eco Adventure Travels
58, Dudley Senanayaka Mawatha
Colombo 8
tel. 011 268 56 01
www.slwcs.org
Website of the Sri Lanka Wildlife
Conservation Society with lots of
addresses.

GOLF
Royal Colombo Golf Club
Model Farm Road, Colombo 8
tel. 011 69 14 01
18 holes, total course length
5776m/6317yd, par 71
This golf course was opened in
1879 and is the oldest in Sri Lanka. Lots of water obstacles.

**Victoria International Golf
and Country Resort Kandy**
18 holes, total course length of
6288m/6877yd, par 73
tel. 081 237 63 76
www.golfsrilanka.com
The newest golf course is also one
of the best.

Nuwara Eliya Golf Club
tel. 052 52 28 35
18 holes, total course length of
5550/6070yd, par 70
Sri Lanka's best golf course is situated in a valley near Nuwara Eliya.
It has long, narrow fairways.

Waters Edge Golf Club
18 holes, total course length of
6288m/6877yd, par 73
tel. 081 237 63 76
www.golfsrilanka.com
The newest golf course is also one
of the best.

Nuwara Eliya Golf Club
tel. 011 286 38 63
Battaramulla (app. 10 km/6mi
north of Colombo)
www.watersedge.lk
18 holes, 3 courses of different
lengths, Par 72 or 73
Very nicely situated golf course
with an international layout.

ACTIVE HOLIDAY
OPERATORS
Lanka Sportreizen
29-B, S.DES. Yayasinghe Mawatha
Kalubowila, Dehiwela
tel. 011 282 45 00, 282 49 55
www.lsr-srilanka.com

CANOEING
Jetwing Eco Holidays
Jetwing House 46/26
Navam Mawatha Colombo 2
tel. 011 234 57 00
www.jetwingeco.com

RAFTING
Rafters Retreat
Hilland Estate, Kitugala
tel. 036 228 75 98
chnnap@jtmin.com

DIVING
Poseidon Diving Station
Galle Road
Hikkaduwa
tel. 091 227 72 94
www.divingsrilanka.com

Unawatuna Diving Centre
Matara Road
Peellagoda/Unawatunabei Galle
tel. 091 224 46 93
www.srilankadiving.com

WATER SPORTS

Sailing, surfing   Countless hotels on the west coast hire out sail boats. Most of them are small boats in the dinghy class. Surfboard hires are even more common.

Canoeing   Canoeing is possible on the upper reaches of Kelani Ganga and Kalu Ganga, which flow through a superb mountain landscape. White-water rafters also get their thrills on some sections.

Rafting   The little village of Kitulgala is situated on the banks of Kelani Ganga. Together with the Rafter's Retreat, this is a great place to stay. It was built as a tree house from the wood of the surrounding forests. It is a good base for many rafting tours. The 6km/3.5mi trip through gorges and rapids takes two hours.

Snorkelling, diving   The once magnificent underwater world around Sri Lanka has also been damaged by coral bleaching. Diving is nonetheless very worthwhile, not least because of the incredible number of fish. Some tourist towns have diving schools and operators who will put on trips to dive sites. Between November and April there is a good chance of seeing large fish as well as blue whales and sperm whales.

It is possible to spot nurse sharks when diving in Sri Lanka's rich underwater world

BATHING BEACHES

The best beaches can be found along Sri Lanka's east coast. However, this area was not just badly affected by the civil war but also by the tsunami, which is why every precaution should be taken when visiting these beaches. It will also be difficult to find accommodation in places because not many hotels and guesthouses have re-opened yet. It would be impudent, though, to play down the quality of the beaches in the western and southwestern parts of the island. There is the wonderful beach of Unawatuna near Galle for example, or the beaches of Hikkaduwa, Bentota and Negombo. Apart from Negombo the other beaches were also affected by the tsunami, but almost all the hotels have now been rebuilt.

Beautiful but not without their dangers

During the **summer monsoon** period, between the end of March and mid-November, bathing on the southwest coast and the west coast can become a life-threatening »pleasure«. Warnings about dangerous undercurrents, which, unlike high waves, are not apparent at first glance, should be heeded in the interest of self-preservation! A **red flag** on a beach means no swimming. During the other months it can be dangerous to bathe on the east coast.

MARCO ⊕ POLO INSIGHT ?

The best beaches

- Unawatuna Beach: one of the ten most beautiful beaches in the world – almost all the hotels there are new.
- Mirissa Beach: the town is a bit quieter than Hikkaduwa and the flat beaches and bays are stunning.
- Beaches near Hikkaduwa: not so much the main beach, but the long palm-lined beaches somewhat further south are gorgeous.
- Arugam Bay: this is where the world's surfing elite meet, but it is also a great spot for bathing.
- Rekawa Beach: straight out of a picture book: golden sand and turquoise water.

Nude bathing is officially forbidden on Sri Lanka, since it goes against the moral principles of the population. However, bathing topless is tacitly tolerated on individual hotel beaches.

Naturism

TOURS

These routes visit the island's most beautiful and historic locations as well as the scenic highlights. In addition, check here for the best places to stay on these tours.

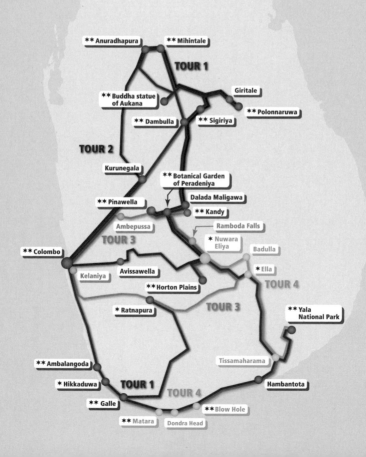

100 km

©BAEDEKER

INDIAN OCEAN

** Anuradhapura   ** Mihintale

TOUR 1

Giritale

** Buddha statue
of Aukana

** Polonnaruwa

** Dambulla   ** Sigiriya

TOUR 2

Kurunegala

** Botanical Garden
of Peradeniya

** Pinawella   Dalada Maligawa

Ambepussa   ** Kandy

Ramboda Falls

TOUR 3

* Nuwara
Eliya

** Colombo   Badulla

Kelaniya   Avissawella   * Ella

TOUR 4

** Horton Plains

* Ratnapura   TOUR 3

** Yala
National Park

** Ambalangoda   Tissamaharama

* Hikkaduwa   TOUR 1   TOUR 4   Hambantota

** Galle   ** Blow Hole

** Matara   Dondra Head

Tours on Sri Lanka

There is no need to complete all four tours to get an insight into life in Sri Lanka. That said, one tour will leave everyone wanting more and it is also possible to combine tours. Before setting off it is best to read through the following tips.

Tour 1   Grand Tour of the Island
Even the Arabs called Sri Lanka »the serendipitous island«. This trip includes everything that makes it so attractive: old temples, lush green tea plantations, wonderful beaches and last but not least, friendly people.
►page 155

Tour 2   In Royal Footsteps
This tour goes to Sri Lanka's royal cities, where many historic buildings reveal what a rich past this island has. In addition it grazes attractive landscapes such as the Central Highlands.
►page 161

Tour 3   The Central Highlands
Tea plantations as far as the eye can see. Tumbling waterfalls, one of Buddha's sacred teeth and the town that was visited by British colonial rulers in need of relaxation: this tour, which goes to the island's Central Highlands, delivers on all of this.
►page 165

Tour 4   Combination with Tour 3
This round trip is based on the abovementioned Tour 3, but also makes room for experiencing Sri Lanka's fauna and the still extant tropical rainforest.
►page 167

Travelling on Sri Lanka

The island of Sri Lanka has so many sights that one week is just about enough to get a brief insight. Visits to the religious and historical sites of **Anuradhapura** and **Polonnaruwa** are a must. A drive through the Central Highlands, covered in lush green vegetation, should also not be missed. In the middle of the magnificent landscape is **Kandy**,

Enough time

with its Temple of the Tooth; the town has comfortable accommodation, making it a good place to spend the night.

Since the end of the civil war between the Singhalese and Tamil populations, both the island's **northern** and **eastern coasts** have been undergoing a remarkable, positive development in the tourism sector. Even though the effects of the military confrontations are still very much visible in many locations, all of Sri Lanka can now be visited without restrictions. Naturally, these areas have fewer accommodation options. Animal lovers will get their money's worth in Sri Lanka's **national parks**. In addition to wild elephants there are many other animals, some of which have long since gone extinct elsewhere. Yala National Park is probably the best-known amongst Sri Lanka's protected regions, albeit not necessarily the most biodiverse.

The perfect Sri Lanka holiday could consist of part round trip, part beach holiday. A week to ten days should be allowed for the first part before enjoying some well deserved rest and relaxation while thinking about all the different experiences of the past few days.

Sri Lanka's **best sandy beaches** are to be found on the east coast, which can currently be visited without restrictions. Since they were hard to access during the civil war and since there is an increasing amount of decent accommodation in this region, visiting this part of the island is definitely worthwhile. Nevertheless it is easy to find a quiet place to go swimming and laze around. Attractive, well-tended beaches with fine sand can also be found on the southwest coast, near the seaside resort of Hikkaduwa, which became legendary as long ago as the 1970s. Although the tsunami destroyed most of the hotels along the coast, they have been rebuilt in a more attractive and comfortable manner. Alternatively there are a good number of seaside towns near Negombo north of the capital of Colombo.

Travelling   At first glance travelling through Sri Lanka by vehicle could look like an unproblematic undertaking, given the dense road network. The actual conditions make the express warning to visitors not to drive themselves but to hire a local driver a sensible suggestion. Having **a driver with knowledge of the country** also has the advantage that visitors do not have to concentrate on the occasionally anarchic traffic conditions and can instead pay attention to the beautiful scenery outside. The round trips described in the following section have been put together on this understanding. Further information is available under »transport« in the section »Practical Information«. Travelling by bus in Sri Lanka can be quite an experience, but not necessarily a positive one. The fares are cheap but the buses are usually hopelessly overcrowded. At times some drivers appear to have suicidal intentions when they race along the narrow and winding roads in the interior in a manner that appears rather gung-ho to Western sentiments. **Official timetables are rare**; so the buses often only leave when they are full.

Regardless of the time of year, the sea around Sri Lanka is always warm enough for swimming

Grand Tour of the Island   Tour 1

Start and End: Colombo
Duration: 12 – 14 days

Distance: approx. 1100 km/690 mi
(without day trip to Ratnapura)

The grand tour of Sri Lanka touches on almost all of the island's significant sites. Anyone visiting Sri Lanka for the first time will gain a comprehensive insight from this tour. The route has been designed in such a way that places off the main route can also be visited.

Leave ❶****Colombo** early in the morning northbound. Reach the city of Raja Maha Vihara in **Kelaniya**, one of the most sacred Buddhist sites in Sri Lanka, after heading northeast for around 11 km/6

Day 1:
Colombo

mi. The oldest sections of the temple date from the 13th century; some of the stunning wall paintings are exceptionally well preserved. For the next 100 km/60 mi the landscape towards the island's interior now becomes very changeable.

❷**Kurunegala** will be reached by about noon. It is notable for strangely shaped rocks above the town that are named after animals. They can also be seen from the nicely situated **Lake Batalagoda**. Allow for plenty of time for the famous cave temples of ❸****Dambulla**, approx. 60 km/40 mi away. The temple complex is the largest in the country and covers an area of 2100 sq m/21,000 sq ft. The approx. 80 temples were already inhabited in prehistoric times, but the majority of their magnificent interiors date back to the 1st century BC (accommodation in Dambulla).

An early start is a good idea for this day too so as to have enough time to view the monastery of Mihintale and go on to Anuradhapura in the afternoon. The first stop is ❹****Mihintale**, 62 km/40 mi from Dambulla, the birthplace of Buddhism in Sri Lanka. It is said King Ashoka sent the monk Mahinda here in around 250 BC to spread the teachings of the enlightened one. Every year on the day of the June full moon tens of thousands of pilgrims celebrate this event. ❺****Anuradhapura** is just 17 km/11 mi from Mihintale; exploring the extensive ruins, protected by UNESCO, gives an insight into the architecture of earlier Singhalese kings. If sufficient time remains, the ❻****Buddha statue of Aukana** 48 km/30 mi away deserves a visit; it is a masterpiece by an unknown artist. If there is not enough time, this really worthwhile detour could be moved to the following morning (accommodation in Dambulla).

Day 2:
Mihintale

Two further highlights in the area known as Sri Lanka's **cultural triangle** are on the agenda on day 3. The route first goes to ❼****Polonnaruwa** 70 km/45 mi away, which replaced Anuradhapura as the capital in around 1073. Here too a large number of (in some cases) quite well preserved ruins await. The highlight of this morning is viewing the famous **Buddha statues in the Gal Vihara**. Around 55 km/35 mi from Polunnaruwa is the unique rock fort of ❽****Sigiriya**, the destination of the afternoon. After seeing the world-famous »**cloud maidens of Sigiriya**«, the somewhat laborious climb up to the actual rock fort is an absolute must. It is not just the thought of how the workers under King Kassyapa brought the building materials up here that takes your breath away (quite literally). A distant, magnificent view makes up for the tiring climb (accommodation in Dambulla, approx. 18 km/12 mi away).

Day 3:
Polonnaruwa

What was already hinted at during the drive from Sigirya back to Dambulla is the focus of the days to come. The landscape becomes

Day 4:
Dambulla

more lavish and the **Central Highlands** come into view during the approx. 70 km/45 mi drive. Around 20 km/13 mi outside of Kandy a detour to the Alu Vihara near **Matale** is a good idea. It draws visitors in for its impressive location in a fantastic rocky landscape. The temple played an important role for Buddhism: a council of around 500 monks is said to have met here and during this council, Buddha's teachings were written down for the first time.

On the way to **Kandy**, which should be reached by around noon, it is a good idea to stop at one of the many **spice gardens** along the A9 road. Visitors will learn a lot about the traditional naturopathic medicine known as **ayurveda**, which has been experiencing a revival for quite a while now. Spices can also be purchased here. On the way, such as between Dambulla and Matale, make a quick stop at the ***Nalanda Gedige**. This 7th-century Buddhist temple has a similar architecture to the Hindu temples near Mahabalipuram in India. The complex consists of a statue house (gedige) and had become derelict, but in around 1980 it was reconstructed to look like the 8th-century original. The combination of Buddhist and Hindu elements is quite interesting and it is them that give this gedige its particular appeal.

MARCO POLO TIP

Kandyan Dance Show   **Insider Tip**

When in Kandy, plan to visit the Kandyan Dance Show in the evening. The performance includes dances from all parts of the country (Cultural Centre of the Kandyan Art Association, 72 Sangaraja Mawatha.

Before visiting Kandy's Temple of the Tooth why not enjoy a short visit to the ❾****Botanical Gardens of Peradeniya** created in the 14th century as a royal pleasure garden. They are among the most beautiful gardens of their kind in the world. Viewing Sri Lanka's most important temple is the culmination of this eventful day. The Sacred Tooth, which is said to have been one of the Buddha's own, and which over the centuries went on an odyssey through different parts of the country, attracts thousands of devout Buddhists every day to the ❿****Dalada Maligawa**, the »Temple of the Tooth« (accommodation in Kandy).

Day 5   Once again an early morning start is rewarded by a very special experience. The ⓫****Elephant Orphanage of Pinawela** is located around 42km/25mi west of Kandy near Kegalla. Start no later than 8.30am so as not to miss the feeding of the young animals. The elephant bath in the river afterwards is also very enjoyable. It is even possible to participate in it (accommodation in Kandy).

Day 6: Kandy   Day six of the round trip sees an increase in altitude, namely to the »city above the clouds« as ⓬***Nuwara Eliya** is also called. It is around 75km/45 mi away. The difference in temperature is quite noticeable and the air becomes fresh and clear. The landscape, which is densely vegetated with tea bushes, is one of the most beautiful in Sri Lanka, but it is also one that is most intensively farmed. Of course visiting a **tea factory** en route is an obvious choice and there are several here to choose from. The town of Nureliya, as the name is pronounced by the locals, has some sites of its own and also places to go shopping (accommodation in Nuwara Eliya).

A hike through the ⓭****Horton Plains** is one of the best experiences nature-lovers can have. Needless to labour the point, but once again an early start is advisable, even though the distance is a mere 32km/20mi. The place known as **World's End** is covered by shreds of mist in the late morning, making the otherwise magnificent view from the steep rock almost invisible.

Day 7:
Nuwara Eliya
– Bandara-
wela

The route then goes back to Nuwara Eliya, and then southeastwards to Bandarawela (just under 50km/30mi). En route, after about 12km/7mi, are the well-known **Botanical Gardens of Hakgala**, which developed from a coffee plantation. There are some fabulous views of an impressive landscape to be had during the onward drive to **Bandarawela**. In good weather they extend all the way down to Sri Lanka's south coast. Near Bandarawela, a further centre of tea growing, there is the opportunity to visit the caves in Istripura, time permitting (accommodation in Bandarawela).

At 117km/75mi, this leg is one of the longest of this round trip and heads back again to the lowlands, which is noticeable from the higher temperatures alone. ⓮**Hambantota** was a very lively fishing town on the southeast coast of Sri Lanka until the tsunami on 26 December 2004. The destruction is still visible in some places; however, most of the buildings destroyed have since been rebuilt. Hambantota was considered the government's showcase example of the reconstruction efforts. The harbour was extended with Chinese help to accommodate big ships as well. This work was completed in 2012. New residential neighbourhoods were no longer built close to the sea but in a more protected location. The reconstruction of the former royal capital of **Tissamaharama**, in which the kings created an impressive irrigation system, has now been achieved (accommodation in Hambantota).

Day 8:
Bandarawela
– Hambantota

A trip through ⓯****Yala National Park** can be done in two ways: either with an early morning start or an afternoon start. There is not much of a difference because at both times there are many animals to be seen, including wild elephants, water buffalo, crocodiles and plenty of birds. Renting an off-road vehicle with a knowledgeable guide at the entrance to the park is a good idea (accommodation in Ham-

Day 9: Yala
National Park

People with carts can often be seen on Sri Lanka's beaches looking for shells – like here in Galle

bantota). However, the national park is closed during the dry season between August and October!

Day 10:
Hambantota
– Galle

The route now runs along the coastal road to Galle (131km/85mi) through several **fishing villages** that were badly damaged by the tsunami but have almost been completely rebuilt and equipped with new roads. It is worth taking a detour to the **Blow Hole**, a gap in the rock where seawater is compressed, making it shoot up as if from a fountain. This phenomenon is at its most impressive during the monsoon season, when the waves are higher than at other times of the year.

The town of ⑯**∗∗Galle** already had a significant harbour many centuries ago, but it long ago had to hand over its status to Colombo. One pleasant option is a stroll through the **Fort**, which was completely spared by the tsunami because of its exposed location, while most of the city itself was flooded. The Fort provides a good impression of the typical architecture of the Dutch colonial period. The still extant, massive **fortifications** are particularly impressive, although they were unable to prevent the British from taking the city in 1796 (accommodation in Galle).

It is only around a 20km/12mi, 30-minute drive from Galle to ⑰*
Hikkaduwa. This seaside resort, which became world famous in the
1970s, is appealing not so much because of its sights as because of its
excellent beaches and diving opportunities. Hikkaduwa is also a good
base for excursions. This is a further reason for the recommendation
to plan several nights here and spend the eleventh even-ing in one of
the excellent fish restaurants, for example.

Day 11: Galle
– Hikkaduwa

A further day on the beach would be a relaxing option but another
possibility would be to take a trip to ⑱*Ratnapura. The distance is
approx. 135km/90mi, which can be completed in around two hours.
The **City of Gems** is worthy of its name, because this is where most
of Sri Lanka's sapphires, rubies and other mineral treasures are found.
The entire town lives off searching for or trading in these precious
stones and there are naturally many inexpensive **places to buy** them.
The **mines** can also be viewed, but they are not a good place to buy
because the dealers there can be very pushy (accommodation in Hikkaduwa)!

Day 12 or 13:
Ratnapura

The final day of this round trip is spent travelling along the southwest
coast back to the starting point of Colombo 110km/70mi away. After
around 13km/7mi, take the opportunity to take a break in ⑲**Ambalangoda**, the centre of mask carving. **Kalutara**, with its imposing
dagoba right on the road is also worth a quick stop. Taking both of
these stops into account, visitors should get to **Colombo** in the early
afternoon.

Day 14:
Hikkaduwa
– Colombo

In Royal Footsteps

Tour 2

Start and Destination: Colombo   **Distance:** approx. 690km/450mi
Duration: 8 days

This round trip takes in all the former royal cities in Sri Lanka,
and many ancient sites of significance await the visitor. The
attractions of scenic interest such as the Central Highlands
should not be neglected either.

The round trip begins in ❶**Colombo**. On the first day there is
plenty of time to visit the city's attractions. One recommendation for
the morning is a walk through the colourful and lively quarter of **Pettah**. The afternoon could, for example, be spent in the **National Museum** of Colombo. An alternative could be to walk through the quarter known as **Cinnamon Garden**, which could also be done after
visiting the museum (accommodation in Colombo).

Day 1:
Colombo

Day 2:
Colombo
– Anuradha-
pura

The drive for day 2 covers 200 km/125 mi; it is not just the distance that makes an early start a good idea. On the way there are several attractions, such as the scenically located temple of **Kelaniya**. Driving on via **Kurunegala** taking a detour to the rock fortress of **Yapahuwa** is worthwhile. It takes you back to the 13th century and is an attraction for its remote location in the jungle if for nothing else. There is not much time because the road to ❷****Anuradhapura**, the destination for this day, is narrow and busy. In the olden days Anuradhapura was the capital of Sri Lanka. Now it is a huge ruin that is still being uncovered with the financial support of UNESCO. There is plenty to be seen: after all, a total of 119 kings ruled here, of whom many left their architectural mark. One of them even had a nine-storey building erected (accommodation in Anuradhapura).

Day 3: Anur-
adhapura
– Giritale

Leaving Anuradhapura the route continues to ❸****Mihintale** (16 km / 10 mi), the »cradle of Buddhism« in Sri Lanka. The view from the platform on which the gleaming white dagoba rises is magnificent. The afternoon is earmarked for visiting ❹****Polonnaruwa**, the second capital of the Singhalese kingdom. The many ruins, which are around 100km/60mi from Mihintale, possess countless valuable details. Of course a visit to the world-famous rock sculptures in **Gal Vihara** are a must. The drive then continues for 85km/50mi in the evening to ❺**Giritale** (accommodation in Giritale).

Day 4:
Giritale
– Kandy

Getting an early start today is important because the day starts off with a visit to the unique ❻****rock fortress of Sigiriya**, approx. 43km/25mi from Giritale. King Kassyapa had it built to escape the revenge of his half-brother, which did not do him any good because he inexplicably left the fortress to face the battle. This virtual suicide is one of the biggest unsolved mysteries of Singhalese history. Also not to be missed on any account is an in-depth look at the »**cloud maidens of Sigiriya**«. The well-known ❼****cave temples of Dambulla**, approx. 20km/12mi from Sigiriya, are also a must. The main cave with its 66 statues of Buddha and the unique wall paintings from different centuries is particularly beautiful. Carrying on to Kandy approx. 72km/45mi away (the road runs through ever more lavish landscape into the higher parts of the island) there is the monastery of **Alu Vihara** (Matale) and the town itself can also be visited. Anyone who has the time should definitely look in on these historically interesting sites. The next accommodation stop is Kandy.

❽****Kandy**, the city in which the last king of a Singhalese kingdom reigned before he was forced to capitulate by the British in 1815, is rich in different kinds of attractions. The morning is best spent visiting the most important Buddhist shrine in Sri Lanka, namely the **Temple of the Tooth**. It was severely damaged in 1998 when it was bombed by the Tamil Tigers, the militant Tamil organization, but it

has long since been rebuilt. The attack cost the Tamils much of the sympathy they had hitherto enjoyed.

An afternoon activity could be visiting the wonderful **Botanical Gardens of Peradeniya** (Kandy). This magnificent park, which is surrounded on three sides by Sri Lanka's longest river, the Mahaweli Ganga, has a wealth of exotic plants and trees (accommodation in Kandy).

From Kandy it is around a three-quarter of an hour drive to Pinnawala (42km/25mi away), a town that at first glance seems fairly

Day 6: Kandy – Nuwara Eliya

The torsos of these ladies in the Sigiriya Rock Fortress seem to emerge from the clouds, hence the name »cloud maidens«

unassuming. However, it has a unique institution, namely the **9**✶✶ **Pinnawala Elephant Orphanage** (Kegalla). It is unique because the state acts as the financial sponsor and pays for the upkeep of any elephant regardless of age, which, for whatever reason, requires special protection. The entrance fee only covers a fraction of the costs. It should be considered that a grown elephant requires around 250 kg/550 lbs of food a day and an elephant calf is raised with 60 litres (16 US gallons) of milk a day.

The trip continues past tea plantations to **10**✶**Nuwara Eliya**, the highest town in Sri Lanka (approx. 100km/60mi). That is the reason why it was so popular with the British colonial rulers. The air here is clearer than in Colombo and the temperatures are nowhere near so high as they are in the lowlands. In the afternoon there should be enough time left to spot the traces of the British colonial rulers, which are still visible in many places (accommodation in Nuwara Eliya).

Carrying on towards the west coast via the A 7, it is possible to see many Tamil women working hard in their badly paid jobs as tea pickers on the vast **tea plantations**. Ignoring the turning to Hatton/ Dikoya, a pretty double village in the midst of magnificent landscape, visitors will arrive at a place right by **Kitulgala** (Avissawella) that is particularly interesting to cinema buff: this is where part of the film **The Bridge on the River Kwai** was filmed, since no suitable location could be found in Thailand, where the actual bridge stood. Unfortunately the set is no longer there. There is a guesthouse not far from the location and there is further accommodation in Avissawella (44km/27mi away).

Day 7:
Nuwara Eliya
– Avissawella

If the second accommodation option is chosen, the drive to the ruins of the former ⓫ **royal city of Sitavka** (Avissawella) on the final day of this trip is not too long. It is situated on a bend in the river of the same name and possessed Portuguese/Dutch fortifications. It is only another 50km/30mi to Colombo, the starting point of this round trip. The road to take is the A 4.

Day 8:
Kitulgala or
Avissawella
– Colombo

The Central Highlands

Tour 3

Start and Destination: Colombo   **Distance:** 1150 km/720mi
Duration: 4 or 5 days

The drive for this trip departs Colombo directly for the Central Highlands and the towns of Kandy and Nuwara Eliya. The focal point is less on visiting historically significant temple complexes and more on getting a good impression of the unique landscape of the island's interior.

Leave ❶ **★★Colombo** on the A 1 towards Kurunegala early in the morning. The first destination after around 11km/7mi is ❷ **Kelaniya**. It is home to the remarkable temple of **Raja Maha Vihara**. The wall paintings in the older part to the right of the main temple are particularly interesting. They depict scenes from the Jataka, the tales that describe Buddha's previous lives. The trip continues onwards to ❸ **Ambepussa** (52 km/33mi). Although there are no particularly noteworthy sights here, the landscape alone is interesting enough. **Kegalla**, one of the less significant capitals of the Singhalese kingdom, does not reveal much of its former glory anymore either. The actual attraction is a few kilometres to the north of Kegalla; it is the ❹ **★★Pinnawala Elephant Orphanage** (Kegalla, approx. 35km/22mi drive). Lucky visitors will be able to witness the baby elephants being fed, as there are always some calves around. Kandy is then reached in

Day 1:
Colombo
– Kandy

the evening after a further 60km/40mi. It was the final capital of the former kingdom (accommodation in Kandy).

Day 2:
Kandy –
Nuwara Eliya

Reserve the morning for visiting the impressive ❺**★★Temple of the Tooth** in Kandy. Thousands of believers assemble in front of what is by far the most significant Buddhist shrine in Sri Lanka every day to worship the Buddha relic in the magnificent reliquary that stands around 1m/3ft tall.

Leave Kandy via the A 1 southwestbound. Peradeniya with its famous **Botanical Gardens** (Kandy) is around 10km/6mi away. Only plan a short visit to the gardens on this round trip. Leave Peradeniya via the A 1 and carry on southbound on the A 5 after 15km/9mi. Passing Gampola, the Sacred City on the River (i.e. the Siripura Ganga, on which the pretty town stands) the road has already reached the **Central Highlands**, a fact made pretty obvious by the temperatures. This region is known for the cultivation of the best tea on the island. A short stop at the ❻**Ramboda Falls** should be seized upon to enjoy the unique landscape. From here it is another 55km/32mi to ❼**★Nuwara Eliya**, the »town in the clouds«, the destination for the second day (accommodation in Nuwara Eliya).

Day 3:
Nuwara Eliya
– Ratnapura

The drive on day 3 is around 150km/90mi. It departs Nuwara Eliya on the A 5 eastbound, then, from Ratnapura, it carries on southbound (approx. 135km/90mi). Near Haputale the road turns west again and

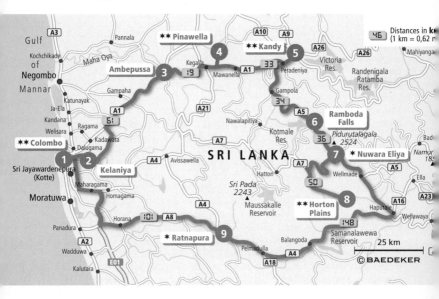

passes the ❽****Horton Plains**. From the valley this landscape is not much different from that of the rest of the Central Highlands at first glance. However, the plateau on which the Horton Plains are located forms an interesting change to everything else around. Nature lovers and hikers may want to plan an extra day here. Ratnapura is reached in the evening, which is the centre of prospecting for and trading in gemstones (accommodation in Ratnapura).

For those who choose to drive back from Ratnapura to visit the Horton Plains this tour will be extended by a day. It is also a good idea to stay an extra night in Ratnapura. It is only around 86km/55mi from Ratnapura to Colombo so there is plenty of time to take it easy on this day. One option would be to visit the gemstone museum in ❾*** Ratnapura**, which is definitely worthwhile. During the drive back to Colombo the changing landscape from the lush green of the mountains to the dry areas of the west coast is very striking.

Day 4 or day 5: Ratnapura – Colombo

Combination with Tour 3

Tour 4

Duration: 4 or 5 additional days

Distance: an additional 475km/300mi

This round trip is based on tour 3 described above for the first two days, but it also offers the chance to get to know the fauna of Sri Lanka in the famous Yala National Park.

Instead of driving from ❶***Nuwara Eliya** towards Ratnapura take the A 5 to ❷**Badulla**. The **Dunhinda Falls** deserve a brief visit before driving approx. 95 km/60mi southbound via the A 5 and then the A 16 to ❸**Ella**. Visiting the **rock sculptures of Buduruvagala** (Ella), at the centre of which is a 15m/50ft statue of Buddha carved from the rock; it is not to be missed. It was created either in the 4th century or, according to other sources, not until 500 years later. Leaving Ella the trip carries on via the A 23, which turns into the A 2 that goes to ❹**Tissamaharama** not far from Sri Lanka's southeast coast (approx. 90km/55mi; accommodation in Tissamaharama).

Day 3: Nuwara Eliya – Tissama-harama

❺****Yala National Park** is not far from Tissamaharama. It offers a good insight into Sri Lanka's diverse fauna. It is a good idea to start a trip to Yala National Park as early as possible, since the animals retreat to the cover of the bushes during the heat of the day. If Yala National Park is reached by 9am the probability of seeing even leopards in the large area is high. In addition the park is home to countless wild elephants, birds and reptiles. The afternoon can be used for vis-

Day 2: excursion

iting the **Maha Devale** in Kataragama. The temple looks as if it has survived the times unchanged (accommodation in Tissamaharama).

Day 3:
Tissamahara-
ma – Galle

The road from Tissamaharama to Galle runs along the south coast almost all the time, through **fishing villages** and small towns, where the odd worthwhile market is taking place (distance approx. 153km/96mi). Near Tagalle is the ❻**Blow Hole**, a gap in the rock through which the sea water, pushed here by waves, is forced into the air like water in a fountain. If there is time, definitely visit the outstanding beach of **Unawatuna** 73km/45mi away. It is considered not just one of the most beautiful in Sri Lanka, but said to be one of the seven most beautiful bathing beaches on Earth. In addition there is accommodation for all tastes and budgets here. Those who chose to continue however, could make ❼**Dondra Head**, the southern tip of Sri Lanka, the next day's destination. It is marked by a 64 m/210 ft **lighthouse**. ❽**Matara** is the next stop. From Matara it is only 42km/26mi to ❾**Galle**. Assuming that this city, which was so significant during Portuguese and Dutch times, is reached in the afternoon, a pleasant option would be to stroll through the **Fort** district. The witnesses to colonial architecture, such as some of the churches

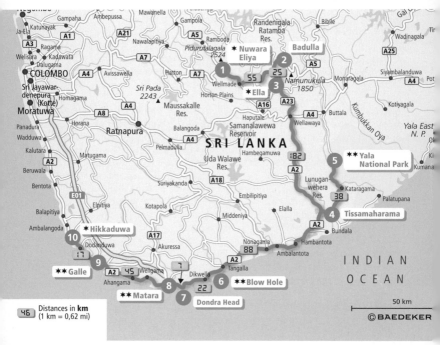

as well as the largely excellently preserved fortifications, are impressive (accommodation in Galle).

Along the southwest coast the A 2 makes its way to the lively tourist town of ⑩***Hikkaduwa**. It is only around 20km/12mi, so there is time to stop and relax on one of the **magnificent beaches** on the way.

Day 4: Hikkaduwa – Colombo

From Hikkaduwa to Colombo it is another 116km/60mi, which will take less than two hours on the new fast road. Given the time it is a good idea to find **accommodation in Hikkaduwa** or else in Bentota in order to be away from the noisy bustle of the city. This is also true for those who have booked or want to book a room in a hotel in Negombo north of Colombo for their remaining time in Sri Lanka. The drive from Hikkaduwa or Bentota to Negombo goes through Colombo, and so it will take up at least half a day.

SIGHTS FROM A TO Z

Jungle landscapes, tea plantations in the mountains and dream beaches aren't all Sri Lanka has to offer. An ancient culture has also left impressive traces.

** Adam's Peak (Sri Pada)

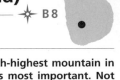

B 8

Province: Sabaragamuwa
Height at summit: 2243m/7359ft

Although Adam's Peak is only the fifth-highest mountain in Sri Lanka, it's regarded as the island's most important. Not only for Hindus, Buddhists and Muslims, but also for the country's Christian population, it is the top place for pilgrims; for nature-lovers standing on its summit and watching the sun rise it's an unforgettable experience.

Adam wept for 1000 years

The mountain probably owes its present name to a tradition attributed to the Arab explorer Ibn Battuta (Famous People). In one of his numerous travel accounts, he describes a holy mountain called Al Rohun, on which, following his expulsion from Paradise, Adam first set foot on earth and is said to have bemoaned his fate for no less than 1000 years. There is also a passage in the account of the Venetian ex-

Buddha is said to have left his footprint on the summit

Adam's Peak

GETTING THERE

By car: from Colombo to Dalhousie take the A4 to Avissawella, then take the A7 to Hatton (app. 127km/79mi) By train: from Colombo to Kandy, from where there are daily connections to Hatton. There are buses and taxis in Hatton.

By bus: there are no regular bus services to Dalhousie, just pilgrim buses. One alternative is to take a bus from Colombo to Maskeliya. There are several connections per day (journey time app. 6 hours); then continue by taxi.

WHERE TO STAY

There are countless guesthouses and pilgrim's hostels at very inexpensive prices in Dalhousie (such as the White House £). Another recommendable guesthouse is the Slightly Chilled (£, tel. 051 351 94 30, www.slightly-chilled.tv).

Insider Tip

Ceylon Tea Trails £ £ £ £
Reservations via Tea Trails Pvt. Ltd.
46/38 Nawam Mawatha
tel. 011 230 38 88
www.teatrails.com

The four exceptionally luxurious bungalows in the cottage style are located amid a magnificent landscape and were once the homes of wealthy tea-plantation owners. The distance between the individual plantations, which were set up between 1888 and 1923, is around 32km/20mi. There are 20 rooms in total with every comfort imaginable, not to mention stunning views of the magnificent mountain landscape and the nearby Adam's Peak. The restaurants here are among the best gastronomy Sri Lanka has to offer. 'All inclusive' is no less standard than the butler, who is always at the ready.

White Elephant Hotel £
tel. 051 350 73 77
www.hotelwhiteelephant.com
The best and most comfortable accommodation in Dalhousie has 15 large, clean rooms (no air conditioning!) with flawless service and a restaurant. There is a natural pool for swimming and anyone wanting a guide for the ascent of Adam's Peak can book one here.

plorer Marco Polo, who visited Sri Lanka in the 13th century, where he suggests that Adam lies buried on the mountain. While it is mainly Muslims who have adopted this tradition, some of Sri Lanka's Christians base their belief in the significance of the mountain on it. Others however say that St Thomas, one of the apostles, climbed the mountain during his missions to India and Persia and left a footprint on the summit.

Buddhists and Hindus alike regard Adam's Peak as a holy site, in their case as the mountain of the god Saman, one of the four guardian deities. But for Buddhists the holiness resides first and foremost in **Buddha's footprint** (Sri Pada), a depression 1.6m/5ft 3in long and

A mountain for every faith

75cm/2ft 6in wide, which the Buddha is said to have left on one of his three visits to Sri Lanka. The footprint is supposed to have been discovered by King Valagam Bahu in the 1st century AD.

Hindus too regard this depression as sacred, seeing in it a **footprint of their god Shiva**. They call Adam's Peak Shivanadi-padam. But ultimately they also give credence to the Buddhist interpretation, for in their eyes Buddha is an incarnation of the god Shiva.

CLIMBING ADAM'S PEAK

Two routes Of the two routes leading to Adam's Peak, the longer one winds its way up from the south, i.e. from the direction of Dalhousie. The other begins on the northern side near Maskeliya.

Whichever way is chosen, **no less than two days should be allowed** for the ascent. The path leading to the summit is some 6.5km/4mi in length, includes about 5,200 steps, and is extremely strenuous; especially in the hot and tropically humid season, you need to be physically fit. Good equipment (stout shoes or boots, sufficient drinking-water and warm clothing) is a must. At a comfortable rate of progress, the climb takes between three and four hours. When starting out from Dalhousie, the first day should be devoted to getting there. Stay in one of the guesthouses or in the nearby town of Dikoya (►Hatton Dikoya). The actual climb to the summit should be started around midnight, in order to not to miss the fantastic sight of the sunrise on the mountain. The route from the tea plantation in Dalhousie leads to the top of the mountain entirely via steps, so that no additional signposting is necessary. There are teahouses along the way serving drinks, and the route itself is lit by thousands of small lamps.

> **?** **MARCO POLO INSIGHT**
>
> *Not at the weekend!*
>
> Choose a weekday to climb Adam's Peak. At the weekends, the path to the summit can have a queue of pilgrims going back several kilometres and accommodation also tends to be overcrowded.

On the summit The summit is a 300sq m/360 sq yd densely built-up platform, on which the footprint (evidently of a left foot), with a wall around it, is enclosed within a small temple. In the 12th century King Parakrama Bahu I had a temple erected on the summit of Adam's Peak, dedicated to the Hindu god Saman. Later it was occupied by Buddhist monks, until King Raja SinhaI, who had converted to Brahmanism, restored it to the Brahmins in the 16th century. It was only two centuries later, under King Kirti Sri, who brought Buddhism back to Sri Lanka, that Buddhist monks moved in once more. The

Brahmin priests were however not expelled; they built themselves a smaller temple which is still extant. All the other buildings are fairly recent; they are not remarkable.

The **bells** which visitors can strike on reaching the summit have a symbolic significance for pilgrims: on their first ascent, they are permitted to strike one of them once, on their second visit twice, and so on. Following the sunrise, which is celebrated by the faithful with wild cheering, there is a splendid panoramic view from the summit (in good weather) extending across the highlands as far as Colombo.

** Ambalangoda

⎯⎯⎯⎯⎯⎯⎯⎯⎯⎯⎯⎯⎯ ✴ **B 9**

Region: Southwest coast
Province: Southern
Altitude: 5m/16ft
Population: app. 60,000

This town occupies a splendid location on the south-west coast of the island; one of its special highlights is a swimming-pool hewn out of a rock. Those seeking refuge from the crowds of tourists in Bentota or Hikkaduwa and looking for contact with the locals will like it here.

WHAT TO SEE IN AMBALANGODA

Ambalangoda is the home of Singhalese mask carving. Numerous workshops still produce masks based on traditional motifs, some of them thousands of years old. They are used for the various forms of Singhalese dance. The magnificent, colourful Kolam masks are carved for the popular dance theatre. Sanui (or Thovil) masks are used when exorcizing demons. Only three sorts of wood are permitted: sandalwood, kadura (a kind of mangrove) and the wood of the strychnine tree (Nux vomica). **Carved masks**

Ambalangoda is the birthplace and home of the famous Wijesooriya mask-carving family, who have been practising this craft for generations. They run a small museum located in the home of Wijesooriya's grandson, Ariyapala Gurunnanse. Here the history of the art of mask-carving and the significance of the various kinds of mask is explained in a lively and informative fashion. There is also a workshop in the building; a brochure is available at a small charge **Mask Museum**

❶ 426 Patabendimulla; daily, 8.30am – 5.30pm, admission free

Ambalangoda

GETTING THERE

By car: from Colombo (102km/63mi),
Bentota (24km/15mi), Hikkaduwa
(13km/8mi) and Galle (35km/22mi) via
the A2
By train: station on the Colombo–Matara route
By bus: there are regular connections
from the places mentioned above

WHERE TO STAY/EAT

Sri Lanka Ayurveda Garden
£ £ – £ £ £

95B Sea Beach Road
Patabendimulla, Ambalangoda
tel. 091 225 98 88
Nicely situated, traditional hotel with a
familiar atmosphere. Nine rooms and
one apartment as well as an Ayurveda
herb garden.

Heritance Hotel £ £ – £ £ £

Ahungalla tel. 091 555 50 00
www.heritancehotels.com/ahungalla
160 rooms, a restaurant with regional
and international cuisine, a bar, a pool
and all kinds of watersports. Not far
from Ambalangoda, the city of mask
carvers. This hotel is right on the sea as
well as on one of Sri Lanka's most
beautiful beaches. It is possible to book
this hotel as »all inclusive«, which
means (almost) what it says.

Piya Nivasa Guesthouse £

Galle Road, Akurala
(5km/3mi outside of Ambalangoda)
tel. 091 11 748 82 88
www.piya-nivasa-guesthouse-
ambalangoda-sri-lanka.lakpura.com
Nice guesthouse in the colonial style
with clean rooms and its own beach.
Six double rooms with breakfast for
less than EUR10.

The Sri Lanka Ayurveda Garden dates back to colonial times

Also in the centre of town is the Bandu Wijesuria Dance School, where **lowland masked dances** are performed from time to time. They originate from mythological stories and stand in contrast to the Sanni Yakuma Dances that are typical of this region. These dances serve exorcist purposes, driving out demons for example, and are generally only performed in secret locations to a local audience.

Bandu Wijesuria

5km/3mi from Ambalangoda in the direction of Hikkaduwa is Galagoda Temple, which houses Sri Lanka's **longest recumbent Buddha statue**, measuring some 50m/165ft. The exact length of the statue is not known, however, because it is considered blasphemous to measure it.

Galagoda Temple

At the southern exit to the town there is also one of the largest temples in Sri Lanka, the Sunandaramaya Mahavihara. A noteworthy feature is the arch over the entrance, which not only displays Hindu elements, but also murals dating from the 18th/19th centuries depicting scenes from the Buddha's previous lives. It therefore combines Hindu and Buddhist elements.

Sunandaramaya Mahavihara

★ Ampara

✦ E 7

Region: Southern section of the east coast
Province: Eastern
Altitude: app. 25m/270ft
Population: app. 60,000

Ampara, the provincial capital, will be encountered by visitors exploring the Gal-Oya National Park and by those who have chosen the broad, quiet beaches of the east coast for a holiday. The town is largely inhabited by Muslims.

Here, as throughout the province, the tsunami caused huge damage; more than 10,000 people, about one third of the population, were killed. Not far away one of five SOS Children's Villages was established, providing a home for traumatized children.

Many tsunami victims

The town in the Gal-Oya valley was founded as long ago as the 10th century, but almost nothing has been preserved from this period or the following centuries. What little there is can be seen in the small archaeological museum.

Practically no historic remains

Ampara is the centre of the Gal Oya Development Scheme, the largest such project on the island. It was started in 1950. One result is the

Development project

Ampara

GETTING THERE
By car: two routes from Colombo: via Kandy–Mahiyangana–Maha Oya (app. 270km/170mi) or via Ratnapura–Wellawya–Siyambalanduwa (app. 300km/185mi); the first route is recommended because it goes through a very attractive mountain landscape.

WHERE TO STAY
Monty Hotel £ – £ £
C 32, 1st Avenue
tel. 063 222 21 69
www.montyhotel.com
There are not many recommendable hotels in Ampara. This one is a positive exception. The ten rooms, some of them fairly new, are basic and the older rooms do not have air conditioning. The associated restaurant has a lovely terrace, while the kitchen also serves Western dishes.

WHERE TO EAT
Chinese & Western Food Court £ – £ £
Stores Road
tel. 063 222 22 15
Maybe the best restaurant in Ampara and definitely very popular with the locals. The best place to sit is the small, lovingly tended garden. The restaurant also has a few rooms, but they are very basic.

Senanayake Samudra, a **reservoir** covering 77sq km/30sq mi, forming the central feature of the Gal-Oya National Park and named after Don Stephen Senanayake, Sri Lanka's first prime minister. Exploration of this very attractive landscape generally starts from Juginiyagala, a town at the eastern end of the reservoir, about 16km/10mi from Ampara, to which it is linked by a good road.

AROUND AMPARA

Buddhist temple
Near Digayapi, some 10km/6mi east of Ampara between the town of Trakkamam and the coast, the ruins of a Buddhist temple were uncovered. It had been erected on a spot which according to legend had been visited by the Buddha in person.

Hamangala Caves/ Malayadi Temple
The Hamangala Caves, some 20km/12mi from Ampara, were already inhabited very long ago by, among others, the Vedda. Some of the caves contain inscriptions, while one has **ancient wall-paintings** by them. The caves are accessible by driving north-west along the A27, turning left between the 8th and 9th milestones, taking the road as far as Bandaraduwa, and then another 6km/4mi or so along a jungle track. The Malayadi Temple, also known as the Raja Maha Vihara, consists of several **once inhabited caves**, in one of which there are also Vedda murals.

⋆⋆ Anuradhapura

⟶ ⊹ **B 5**

Province: North Central
Altitude: app. 90m/300ft
Population: 56,000

Anuradhapura, one of the oldest and most interesting cities in Sri Lanka, lies in the island's Dry Zone. The present-day town of Anuradhapura consists of an area of ruins plus a new centre, which dates from the 20th century. The spectacular ruins of Anuradhapura have been declared a World Heritage Site by UNESCO.

The name of the town, Anuradhapura, was once thought to be derived from the Singhalese word »anuva«, which means ninety, and this was seen as an allusion to the city of the 90 kings. However, since there were actually 119 kings who ruled from Anuradhapura, this derivation is probably mistaken. It is more likely that the name of the town goes back to an aristocratic family by the name of Anuradha. According to other sources, the town was named after the star Anuradha, which embodies the god of light in Indian astrology.

City of the 90 kings?

Anuradhapura, today an imposing ruin, was the island's first capital and was the residence of kings for 13 centuries; it was one of the most important capitals of the Singhalese kingdom. It was here, (and in ▶Mihintale) that the first Buddhist shrines were erected, and here too that a classical artistic style developed. Permeated by the Buddhist idea, the buildings bear witness to the high degree of self-assurance felt by the young kingdom. The literary and religious culture centred on the monasteries and royal palace.

Royal capital

While the town-planning looks modern, it is around 2500 years old. Three reservoirs (wewa in Singhalese) constructed in the 1st century BC and a **sophisticated canal system** allowed the very dry land to be irrigated while at the same time providing drinking water for the inhabitants, who in the city's heyday must have numbered several hundred thousand.
In about 380 BC the settlement of Anuradhagama (gama=settlement) was raised by King Pandukabhaya to the status of capital of the Singhalese kingdom. He called it Anuradhapura (pura=town, city). The actual history of the city, however, only started with the reign of King Devanampiya Tissa (250–210 BC), who adopted and supported the doctrine of Buddhism as preached by the monk Mahinda. It was during this period that the first substantial building activity took place, though the first buildings consisted of simple dwellings for the popu-

Modern town-planning

lace and the ruler, while those in honour of Buddha were more monumental.

In 993 came the first disruption in the city's development, when it was occupied by the Chola invaders from southern India. However they also attacked the city of ▶Polonnaruwa, less than 100km/60mi away, which they made their capital, and it was from here that Anuradhapura was administered in the following period. In 1070 the former Prince of Ruhuna, King Vijaya Bahu I of Polonnaruwa, which he had already recaptured 15 years earlier, succeeded in snatching Anuradhapura too back from the Cholas. As Polonnaruwa occupied a more strategic location, he retained it as his capital, and confined the reconstruction of Anuradhapura to the restoration of the largely destroyed irrigation system and some Buddhist shrines.

A sleeping beauty Anuradhapura then fell into a Sleeping-Beauty-like slumber and over the centuries became overgrown by the surrounding jungle. Until the

Anuradhapura is considered a sacred place because of its Bodhi tree

beginning of the 19th century, all that was known of it was that a British civil servant, Ralph Backhaus, who came here by chance, gave an enthusiastic account of a magnificent ruined city in the north of the island. In about 1820 the British archaeologist H.P. Bell decided that these reports were worth investigating and discovered the city. It was 1890, however, before excavations began.

In 1980 UNESCO made the ruins of Anuradhapura a World Heritage Site, which is incredibly helpful for the excavations, which are by no means complete.

TOUR OF THE RUINS

We recommend the Tissa Wewa Resthouse on New Road as the starting point for the sightseeing tour recommended here. It was built by a British governor as a summer residence and is surrounded by an attractively laid-out park. The building has all the charm of the for- **Starting point**

Anuradhapura

GETTING THERE
By car: from Colombo on the A 1, 6, 10 or 28 (202km/125mi); from Puttalam on the A12 (app. 70km/43mi); from Polonnaruwa on the A 11 (app. 97km/60mi)
By train: station on the Colombo–Jaffna route
By bus: regular connections from the abovementioned places

WHERE TO STAY / EAT
❶ The Village £ £ – £ £ £
Habarana
tel. 066 227 00 47
www.johnkeellshotels.com
Ideally situated hotel, halfway between Anuradhapura and Polonnaruwa with 108 very comfortable rooms in the cottage style; restaurant, pool and bar.

❸ Palm Garden Village £ £ – £ £ £
Puttalam Road Pandulagema

tel. 02522 239 61
www.palmgardenvillage.com
The expansive, nicely designed complex with its large pool is impressive. The 50 rooms (of which 10 are suites) are located in small buildings. There is also a restaurant.

❷ Tissawewa Rest House £ – £ £
Old Town Anuradhapura
tel. 011 117 48 82 88
This pretty colonial-style Rest House is situated in amid a tropical garden and is not far from the ancient ruins of Anuradhapura. The 15 rooms are unfortunately a bit dated, but there are plans to renovate them. The veranda in front of the building with a view of the garden is also a bar; in the evenings, after dinner in the hotel's restaurant, it is a popular meeting place for guests.

The outdoor section of the museum includes urinating-stones decorated with reliefs; these originally stood in the forest monasteries to the west of Anuradhapura (Mon–Sun 8am–5pm, closed on holidays, admission charge).

** **The world's oldest tree**

Not far from the museum is the Sri Maha Bodhi, allegedly the world's oldest tree. It is said to have grown from a twig cut from the Indian bodhi tree (Ficus religiosa) beneath which Siddharta Gautama found enlightenment. After coming to Sri Lanka, legend has it that it was planted here in 230 BC by Sanghamitta, the sister of the Indian missionary Mahinda. The tree, which today, because of its size, has to be propped up, is **the destination of countless pilgrims** from the whole Buddhist world every day; they venerate it by making offerings (blossoms, food, incense sticks etc.). It is surrounded by a high wall erected in the 18th century, so that it is almost impossible to get any real idea of its actual size. The white façade of the entrance gate is decorated with numerous reliefs of Buddhist and Hindu deities and with floral elements. Before entering the sacred area, take a look at the finely carved moonstone flanked by the obligatory guardian steles.

? MARCO POLO INSIGHT

The shape of the dagobas

The shape of the dagobas on Sri Lanka is said to go back to Buddha. When his followers asked him what they should build in his honour after his death, he only answered: »build heaps of sand, like rice, that everybody needs.«

In the interior courtyard is a hall for devotions, surrounded by a number of shrines with statues of the Buddha. The terrace on which the bodhi tree stands was restored under Kirti Sri Raja Sinha, the last king of Kandy, in about 1800.

Lohapasada (bronze palace)

Among the most imposing ruins of Anuradhapura are the 1600 columns erected in rows of 40 which formerly bore the Lohapasada set up under King Duttha Gamani (161–137 BC). This was probably a nine-storey structure containing **more than 1000 rooms**, a masterpiece of secular Singhalese architecture at the time. Over the years it was destroyed and rebuilt on a number of occasions, most recently under King Parakrama Bahu I (AD 1153–1186). The first building is said to have been destroyed by fire just 15 years after its completion. According to tradition, there were only two similar buildings in the world: there is another in Bangkok, Thailand.

The Lohapasada probably got its name from a bronze roof, but the façades are also said to have been clad in copper plates. According to the Mahavamsa chronicle, the roof ridge and eaves were set with precious stones, silver ornaments and quartz crystals. In the great audience hall on the ground floor there was a richly carved throne, around which a thousand monks could gather. They lived in the palace, which was actually, then, a residential monastic building, in accordance with a certain order of rank: the simple monks lived in the lower storeys, the old monks and those regarded as holy on the upper floors.

The Lohapasada also includes the Ruwanweli Dagoba Ruwanweli Dagoba, which was likewise erected during the reign of King Duttha Gamani in thanks for the victory over the Tamil king Elara. Maybe, though, he also had it built as a sign of his personal remorse for the war, which cost many thousands of lives.

Ruwanweli Dagoba

The dagoba is **the oldest of the monumental structures of this kind in Sri Lanka**, measuring to no less than 90m/295ft to the tip of its golden pinnacle, which is said to have been a gift from Burma, and 91m/298ft in diameter at its base. Its shape was due to a desire of the king that the architect should build the dagoba so that it would look

The Ruwanweli dagoba originally had a droplet shape

like a drop falling on to water. In the succeeding period, more of these **drop-shaped dagobas** were constructed. The king himself is said not to have lived to see the completion of the dagoba. On his death-bed, though, his son covered the incomplete sections with cloth, in order to do his father one last favour. The terrace of the dagoba is surrounded by a wall decorated on its outer surface by 338 stucco elephants. Today, though, the original sculptural quality can only be made out with difficulty, as the sculptures have been restored several times over the centuries. It is striking that the elephants are all different. All four access routes lead across the square terrace to the altar, which is built against the side of the dagoba and is itself decorated with noteworthy **elephant friezes**. In the northern part of the terrace it is worth sparing a moment for the stones, some of them ornamented with attractive **reliefs**, which have come to light during the excavations. Their original locations are not yet known with any certainty. Leaving the dagoba area to the west, you will see a very attractive ancient bathing pool, with carefully carved stone steps leading down into it.

> **? MARCO ◍ POLO INSIGHT**
>
> *Moonstones*
>
> The semi-circular moonstones, decorated with ornaments, mark the transition from a profane to a sacred space. The moonstones are also semi-precious stones reminiscent of the light of the moon.

Thuparama Dagoba

Thuparama-Dagoba further to the north is the oldest dagoba in Sri Lanka. King Devanampiya Tissa had it built in the 3rd century BC. It was intended to house a sacred relic, a splinter of Buddha's collar bone, a gift from King Ashoka. Whether it ever did, is lost in the mists of history. The dagoba was also once in the »heap of rice« form, but numerous restorations gave it its present bell-like appearance. The base was constructed of four blocks of gneiss, while the pillars surrounding the dagoba in for concentric circles date from the 1st century AD and once supported a round timber roof. It is thought that this structure may have been the first vatadage in Sri Lanka; they became more frequent from the 7th century on. The road leading northwards from this dagoba is lined on the right by a few small dagobas, and on the left by the ruins of a Hindu temple.

Lankarama Dagoba

The road now branches: the left-hand fork leads to the ruins of the smaller Lankarama Dagoba built in the reign of King Vattagamani in the 1st century BC. The pillars, whose capitals are decorated with reliefs, probably once supported a roof.

Ratna Pasada (Jewel Palace)

Beneath the ruins, mainly huge stone pillars, of the Ratna Pasada, a 2nd-century building probably once belonging to the Abhayagiri

Insider Tip

monastery, there is what is probably the most beautiful guardian stele in Sri Lanka. It dates from the 8th and 9th centuries and is entirely in the classical style. 1.38m/4ft 6in in height, the stele depicts the snake king Naga with a pointed hood protected by the seven-headed Naga. In one hand he holds the Purnagheta, the vase of abundance, brimming over with magnificent lotus blossoms, in the other a blossoming lotus stalk: both are symbols of purity. On a pillar to the side kneels a guardian elephant. The foundation walls and some of the sizable supporting pillars are all that is left of the palace itself, which was destroyed by the Cholas.

The Queen's Pavilion was built at the end of the 3rd century and is famous for the most beautiful moonstone in Sri Lanka. As it was damaged several times in the past, it has been enclosed by an iron fence intended to prevent people stepping over the stone, which is supposed to symbolize the transition from the material to the spiritual world. Of the pavilion itself, though, nothing remains but a few stone pillars and surrounding walls.

Moonstone on the Queen's Pavilion

Measuring 115m/377ft in height overall, Abhayagiri Dagoba is the second-tallest in Sri Lanka. It was erected during the reign of King Vattagamani Abhaya at the end of the 1st century BC, while in the 3rd century AD it became the centre of the Mahayana sect. Faxian (around 337–422AD), a Buddhist pilgrim from China who visited Anuradhapura in 411, wrote in his »A Record of Buddhist Kingdoms« that this monastery was home to more than 5000 monks. The relic of the tooth that is now in Kandy was temporarily kept here as well. Over time the dagoba became overgrown with grass; its restoration has been going on for decades.

Abhayagiri Dagoba

One of the most famous Buddha statues in Sri Lanka is the 2m/6ft 6in tall Samadhi Buddha, a stone sculpture dating from the 4th century. The artist succeeded in using a minimum of means to achieve a maximum of expression. The face shows transcendental calm and the highest degree of internalization in equal measure. The nose however has had to be reconstructed, as it was hacked off by looters, probably in 1914, for its precious gems. There is now no trace of the original paint. There is an unadorned roof to protect the statue from the weather, but at certain times of the day it prevents the fascinating effects of the sunlight; the statue comes across best in the early morning.

Samadhi Buddha

Round about the 7th century, the two classically beautiful Kuttam Pokuna cisterns formed the bathing facilities of a monastery that presumably stood where today the ruins known as the Kaparama are to be found. A Buddhist university was possibly also attached to the

Kuttam Pokuna (pools)

monastery. The pools measure 42m/138ft x17m/56ft and 30m/98ft x17m/56ft respectively, and the water for them is brought here by a 6km/4mi subterranean pipe; it flows through a filter complex first into the larger and then into the smaller pool. Considering when this pipe, which was only discovered a few years ago, was designed and constructed, it can only be described as a really extraordinary engineering achievement. Both pools are clad with carefully shaped granite blocks arranged stepwise, the edges being decorated with a few reliefs, including for example a very beautiful Naga stone. The monks would have taken their baths not just to keep clean, but also at religious occasions.

Dalada Maligawa

Following the road southwards, you come to the ruins of the Dalada Maligawa, the Temple of the Tooth, which was built under King Sirimeghavana in the 4th century. It is said to have housed the tooth relic of the Buddha when it first arrived in Sri Lanka in AD 313; it is now in ►Kandy.

Jetavanarama Dagoba

With a height of 122m/400ft, Jetavanarama Dagoba Jetavanarama Dagoba was once the tallest building of its kind in Anuradhapura, but today it is only about 75m/246ft tall and was for a long time covered in dense greenery.

However a restoration process started a few years ago. It was built at the beginning of the 4th century in the reign of King Mahasena, who preferred Mahayana Buddhism, to which the Jetavana school belongs, to the austere teaching of Hinayana Buddhism. This was, incidentally, the only period in which Mahayana Buddhism played any major role in Sri Lanka.

Jetavana Museum

The Jetavana Museum is located nor far from Jetavanarama Dagoba, on Trincomalee Road. It exhibits countless artefacts found during the dagoba's excavation and restoration works. The bronze miniatures of Hindu deities, jewellery and coins from the reign of King Parakramubahu I are particularly remarkable.

❶ Daily 8am–5.30pm; admission charge

Ranamasu Uyana (Royal Gardens)

The Royal Gardens, which are also known as the »Park of the Golden Fish«, are situated close to the Tissa Wewa, but were formerly much more extensive than they are today. For example, it included artificial waterways, small lakes, bridges, pavilions and bathing facilities. The gardens were laid out as early as the 1st century BC and constantly enlarged thereafter. The two well preserved baths are among the finest examples of rock-building; the more northerly, whose basin was largely carved out of the rock, is the older of the two. It got its water via a canal from the Tissa Wewa. A noteworthy feature is the elephant frieze carved directly into the rock.

The ruin compound also contains three artificial lakes created 2500 years ago to irrigate the arid areas

The rock monastery of Isurumuniya Vihara is worth a visit if only for its unique reliefs, but its picturesque location on the Tissa Wewa is also noteworthy. The conical and spherical rocks are integrated into what used to be a more extensive complex, dating from the 3rd century, while the temple is even built into the cliff. All the buildings visible today are later in date, however; all that is left from the original period being the hermit's cave in the centre of the cliff.

Isurumuniya Vihara (rock monastery)

The baths on the right-hand side, which belonged to the monastery, are edged by coarsely fitting blocks of stone; the steps are of the same material. On the cliffs to either side of a deep cleft behind the bath are **attractive bas-reliefs depicting almost jaunty-looking**

elephants. On the way up the steps to the actual shrine, there is on the right-hand side a very fine relief of a »man with a horse«, which should not be overlooked. It probably dates from the 7th century. It depicts a man in a relaxed pose while the head of a horse appears from the background and touches the man's arm. The purpose and meaning of the portrait, which resembles those of the India Pallava style, are unknown. Maybe an artist simply gave free rein to his imagination. By the way, the main shrine no longer houses all the statues, some of them having been moved to a small museum right next door. Kept here also is **probably the most famous relief in this monastery**, which bears the title »The Lovers«. It is dated to the 5th or 6th century, and reveals a rare harmony in its depiction of a warrior with a woman. In the past it was thought to depict two deities, but the attributes, the sword and shield, point rather to a couple belonging to this world. On this topic there is also a legend in the Mahavamsa chronicle, according to which the couple are

The Isurumuniya Rock Temple has a picturesque location on Tissa Wewa

Prince Saliya, a son of King Duttha Gamani, and his wife Asoka-mala. She was actually the daughter of a blacksmith, whom the prince was only able to marry after renouncing all rights to the throne. But as it states in the Mahavamsa, nothing and nobody could separate them, as they had already been married to each other in a previous life. The princess was, it was said, reborn into a lower class because she had been disrespectful towards her mother.

SURROUNDINGS OF ANURADHAPURA

The western suburb of Anuradhapura was not considered a desirable area to live in. It was the location of cremation sites and cemeteries, and the local inhabitants were all from low castes. Even so, a community of strictly ascetic Pamsukulika monks (monks dressed in rags) settled here, possibly in protest at the worldly ideas of various city monasteries. They ate for example nothing but rice and the bitter oil of the margosaa tree, and sewed themselves robes from pieces of clothing which they found in the nearby morgue. They surrounded their precinct with high walls in order to protect themselves from the gaze of the curious. The buildings were without exception simple, but well-proportioned. Each building had a roofed hall and an open terrace, but the monks renounced sculptures and other decoration entirely. There was one exception, though: the urination stones. These were decorated with reliefs. When they did their business, they could see the magnificent buildings of the people who followed the Buddha's teachings less strictly, as it were. Towards the end of the 8th century, the order still had applicants and enjoyed a high reputation among the devout population thanks to its principles; it has now completely disappeared.

Western monasteries

The famous **excavation site** of Nillakgama lies some 45km/28mi from Anuradhapura in the direction of Maho. It is best accessed by car. An inscription on the western entrance gate, dating from the 8th or 9th century, indicates that the structure had the function of a bodhigara. It has still not been explained, however, who endowed it or what the place was called in Antiquity. In the late 19th century, under the supervision of H.P.C. Bell and Dr Paranavitana, the remains of an interesting monastic complex dating from the 8th to 10th centuries were uncovered. They include an almost completely preserved bodhighara with finely worked reliefs. **This sacred bodhi tree enclosure is the oldest yet found in Sri Lanka.** It consists of a square platform measuring 3.3m/4ft on each side, with the two opposite anterooms of a masonry wall. On this platform is another, smaller one measuring one metre (3ft 3in) on each side, on which the bodhi tree stood. On the outside of the masonry enclosure be-

**Nillakgama

tween two carefully carved cornices is an elephant frieze, with the individual animals separated by pilasters. A balustrade, convex towards the outside, whose underside in the vicinity of the entrance anterooms is decorated with geese, forms the top of the 2m/6ft 6in wall.

The moonstone in front of the two steps is undecorated, while the short balustrades are also simple, and lack the usual makara form. The anterooms on the other hand are decorated with elaborate reliefs: the motifs are a flute-playing dwarf and the snake king Muchalinda beneath the spread hood of the Naga, with the vase of abundance in his hand along with a blossoming twig. In addition, they show an archer mounted on a rearing horse, an unusual motif in Sri Lanka. In his hand he is holding some indefinable objects, and there is a kneeling figure at the horse's feet. A flat slab of stone forms the roof of the anteroom.

The 2m/6ft 6in high stone base of the inner platform is surrounded by a frieze with geese, cornices with lotus leaves, and an elephant frieze, the last being unusual in that some of the elephants are shown from the front, others from the side. The small courtyard is paved with carved stones of various sizes. There are flower altars on each side. 16 pillars, of which some are still extant, once supported the wooden roof.

Ruins of Ranjangane

About 30km/20mi south of Anuradhapura (on the A 28) are the ruins of Ranjangane. They are the remains of a large forest monastery, which was probably founded in the 6th century. These monks preferred to live in isolation in the solitude of the forest and also restricted themselves to buildings without any architectural or artistic elaboration. This architecture experienced its heyday in the 8th and 9th centuries. An interesting feature here is the vatadage, a round temple with a stupa beneath a wooden roof supported by several concentric circles of stone pillars.

Aukana

✳ C 5/6

Province: North Central
Altitude: app. 130m/425ft

Aukana is located near the Kalawewa reservoir. This reservoir as well as the nearby Balaluwewa reservoir were constructed in the context of an irrigation programme with a total of 18 reservoirs. The programme was initiated by King Dhatusena (AD 455–473) and was designed to supply Anuradhapura with drinking water.

Aukana

GETTING THERE
By car: from Anuradhapura on the A 9 to Kekirawa, from there app. 6 km/3.5mi northeastwards on the road to Talawa. Turn left in front of the railway tracks and drive along the Kalawewa reservoir for app. 5km/3mi, then turn right to Aukana (4km/2.5mi). The last section can be impassable during the monsoon season.

By train: the closest train station is in Kalawewa (on the Colombo –Trinco-malee route).

WHERE TO STAY
There is no recommendable accommodation in Aukana. Better options include Anuradhapura (48 km/30mi) and Dambulla (36 km/22mi).

WHAT TO SEE IN AUKANA

Rising out of the middle of the mountain jungle near Aukana is the monumental statue of a standing Buddha, approx. 14m/45ft high, which is regarded as a masterpiece of the Singhalese stonemason's art. It was carved out of a single rock and is one of the most important Buddhist shrines in Sri Lanka. The statue was probably made at the bidding of King Dhatusena. To be admired are its perfect proportions, the **transcendental effect of the face** and the working of the robe, which falls in regular folds, with the thick hem fold characteristic of the period, and held in the left hands in such a way that this end seems to float. The Buddha's right hand is raised in the gesture of blessing (asiva mudra). On his head is the flame of enlightenment (ketumala).

**Buddha Statue of Aukana

The small monastery next to the statue is no longer home to many monks. From here there is a waymarked path to caves in the cliff, which were occupied by Buddhist anchorite monks in the 3rd century, when the scratches on the rock were also made.

Monastic complex

SURROUNDINGS OF AUKANA

About 6km/4mi south of Aukana is Vijithapura, one of the oldest towns in Sri Lanka. It was founded as long ago as the 6th century BC and has a now derelict dagoba, in which the holy relic is said to be a jawbone of Buddha.

Vijithapura

12km/8mi to the west of Aukana, near Sasseruwa, there is a further Buddha statue, which is 12m/40ft tall and features the Buddha in the gesture of »according protection«. It was possibly made by a pupil of

Buddha Statue of Sasseruwa

the man who sculpted the one in Aukana. According to other sources, though, it was only made in the 8th or 9th century. There were
once a number of monasteries in the area, and more than 100 caves
inhabited by monks. These can however only by reached via rough
paths.

Avissawella

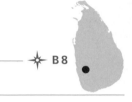

✳ **B 8**

Province: Western
Altitude: app. 85m/280ft

**Avissawella, surrounded by luxuriant tropical vegetation, is
located on the banks of the River Sitavka, and is a centre of
the rubber industry. Sitavka, as the city was formerly known,
was a royal residence in the 16th century and capital of one
of the Singhalese sub-kingdoms. During the Portuguese colonial period it was much fought over.**

History The name Sitavka is probably linked to Sita, the consort of Rama. According to the Ramayana, she was abducted by the demon king Ravana in India and kept hidden here. While this is one of the legends
of the Ramayana, it accords with the fact that Sitavka played am important part when the kingdom of Kotte was divided in three and
King Mayadunne set up his residence here. His son too, King Raja
SinhaI, who converted from Buddhism to Brahmanism, lived here
until his death in 1592. Both kings offered the Portuguese stout resistance, although the city changed hands several times. The Portuguese were followed by the Dutch, who also built a fortress.

WHAT TO SEE IN AVISSAWELLA

Old Sitavka Old Sitavka lies on a bend in the river of the same name. Only a few
ruins of the royal palace are still to be seen, and this goes for the Portuguese and Dutch fortresses too.

Royal grave To the left of Talduwa Road, near the police station, a stone marks the
burial place of King Raja Sinha I. It is the only grave of a Singhalese
king whose location is known for certain.

Shiva Temple Beneath the bridge, a path to the right of Ginigathena Road leads to
the temple of Berende Kovil, which is dedicated to Shiva. It was started by command of King Raja Sinha I, but for reasons unknown it was
never completed. Some of the stone sculptures are worthy of note.

Avissawella

GETTING THERE
By car: via the A 4 from Colombo (95 km/60mi)
By train: final stop of the train line from Colombo
By bus: good and regular bus connections from Colombo

RAFTING
The Kelani Ganga carries a lot of water and as such is one of the best rivers for rafting in Sri Lanka. One ideal place to get in the water is near the tea factory in Pattewata. The first few kilometres

are quite demanding. There are lots of places to get out further down the river as the road runs parallel to it.

WHERE TO STAY
Kitulgala Rest House £
Kitulgala tel. 036 875 28
www.kithulgala-rest-house-kithulgala-sri-lanka.lakpura.com
This guesthouse is situated in in the middle of stunning landscape, not far from where the film »The Bridge on the River Kwai« was filmed. Of the 19 rooms, 15 have no air conditioning.

SURROUNDINGS OF AVISSAWELLA

From Avissawella a road leads eastwards via Talduwa to the village of Kitulgala in a landscape dominated by dense forest. Kitugala achieved fame as the **location for the jungle scenes in the film *The Bridge on the River Kwai*** (1957). A bamboo bridge (35m/115ft high, 130m/425ft long, at the time the biggest bridge ever built for a film, was constructed over the Kelani River and blown up for the final scene. The real bridge, during the building of which tens of thousands of Allied POWs and forced labourers lost their lives, was however in Thailand.

Kitulgala

✴ Bandarawela

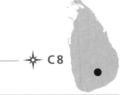

✳ C 8

Province: Uva
Altitude: app. 1250m/4100ft

Bandarawela is one of the centres of tea-growing in Sri Lanka. Its pleasant climate has made it a kind of health resort since colonial times.

WHAT TO SEE IN BANDARAWELA

Typical of the landscape around Bandarawela are the undulating hills and conical mountains, on which every square centimetre seems to

Landscape

be covered with tea plants. The climate also favours the growth of strawberries and other fruits, though.

Tea-factory viewing
In and around Bandarawela there are several tea factories, some of which are open to visitors (signs at the access roads). The guided tours provide interesting information about the local tea plantations and tea production, and about the difference between the individual varieties. They also include tea tastings, and of course you can buy the products.

A general guideline is that the higher the tea plantation, the better the quality of the tea. The highland tea, grown between 1200m/3900ft–2250m/7400ft, in particular is a treat for gourmets (►MARCO POLO Insight p.332).

SURROUNDINGS OF BANDARAWELA

Caves of Istripura
Some 21km/13mi north-west of Bandarawela is the Welimada Rest House, which is a good starting point for exploring the caves of Istripura to the north. The caves contain the longest underground passages in Sri Lanka; The name Istripura means »city of women«. It is said the caves were once a king's harem. The ruins of Fort MacDonald, built by the British, are nearby.

Dowa Temple
The scenically very attractive stretch northeastwards towards Badulla leads after 6.5km/4mi to the Dowa Temple, carved out of the rock. It is decorated with an 8m/26ft tall Buddhist statue, likewise carved from the rock. For reasons unknown, it was never completed, but probably dates from the 10th century and represents the bodhisattva Maitreya. A few smaller statues of Hindu deities and some fine murals, which have been carefully restored by monks, also deserve closer attention.

Drive over the Haputale Pass to Haputale
Particularly fine scenic views can be enjoyed on a drive across the 1600m/5300ft Haputale Pass, which leads through the nature conservation area of the same name. Some wild elephants still live in the dense jungle here.

Haputale itself is a **popular resort**. It lies at a height of about 1300m/4300ft and is built on a steep rocky ridge. On clear days the magnificent view stretches to the south coast of the island. At night even the light from the Hambantota lighthouse is visible. Down on the plain is the Uda Walawe National Park with the lake of the same name, one of Sri Lanka's largest reservoirs.

Excursion tip
Bandarawela is a good base from which to visit the scenically very attractive ►Horton Plains.

Bandarawela

GETTING THERE
By car: from Badulla on the A 16 (30 km/19mi), from Nuwara Eliya on the A 5 (50 km/31mi), from Colombo (183 km/114mi)
By train: station on the Kandy–Badulla route
By bus: good bus connections from Kandy and Nuwara Eliya.

SHOPPING
There are quite a few signposted tea factories in the highlands of Bandarawela where visitors can taste and buy the teas.

WHERE TO STAY
Orient Hotel £ £ £
12 Dharmapala Mawatha
tel. 057 222 24 07
www.orienthotelsl.com
A mid-range hotel that has been recommended for many years because of its 48 clean and tidy rooms and two suites, but especially because of its acceptable prices. The restaurant is also popular with the locals. There is also a

bar and a billiards room. The hotel also offers trips to the surrounding area, such as to a tea factory.

Bandarawela Hotel £ £
14, Welimada Road, Bandarawela
tel. 057 222 25 01
www.aitkenspencehotels.com
Sri Lanka's first mountain hotel was built in 1893 and has traditional charm. The 33 cosy rooms with plush and lace are furnished in the British colonial style.

Ayurvedic Resort – Hotel Blue Wings £ £
6th Milepost, Mirahawatta
(app. 9 km/5.5mi from Bandarawela)
www.afamhotelbw.com
Small ayurveda hotel certified by the Ministry of Health and set in a tranquil, idyllic location. Four standard and two premier rooms; also suitable for families (special therapies just for children!). The focus is on traditional Panchakharma treatments; ayurvedic cookery classes and individual trips are also on offer.

Red Lantern £ £   Insider Tip
34 Welimada Road
tel. 057 222 22 12
www.lankaholidays.com
In around 1890, the British governor had this place built as his residence. Today, it is a small, smart hotel. The number of guests is manageable because there are only five large rooms. The building is surrounded by a very well-tended garden and there is a good restaurant. There are also occasional barbecue evenings.

Batticaloa

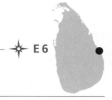

— ✳ E 6

Province: Eastern
Altitude: app. 1–8m (3–26ft)
Population: app. 100,000

Batticaloa, which lies half on a spit of land and half on an island in the north of a 54km/90mi long lagoon, is a town of picturesque charm, while excursions to the hinterland have much to offer in the way of exotic experiences. Tracking down the phenomenon of the »singing fishes« in the lagoon can turn into an adventure.

Lagoon location
The main attraction on the east coast of Sri Lanka lies in the wonderful long and almost empty beaches in the immediate and less immediate vicinity. The city's sheltered location on a lagoon largely protected it from the tsunami. However serious damage was caused by the flood waves in the nearby fishing villages, where hardly one stone was left upon another. The damage has now largely been repaired and some hotels and guesthouses have also reopened. Nothing stands in the way of developing the tourist infrastructure of this region, which was neglected for decades.

History
Tamils settled in the area around Batticaloa at an early date, calling the place Madakala puwa (»Marshy Lagoon«). Later Arab and Malay traders also settled. In 1602 the Dutch admiral Joris Spielbergen landed in Batticaloa, to be followed shortly afterwards by Admiral de Weert. He could however reach no agreement with King Vimela Dharma, who sought to expel the Portuguese colonial masters from the island with the help of the Dutch, and at a meal together there was a major diplomatic incident: when the king casually remarked that he had to get back to Kandy, as he could not leave the queen alone for so long, de Weert replied ambiguously that there must be enough men at court to entertain the queen, whereupon the king struck him dead.

In spite of this setback, an agreement was sealed in Kandy in 1612 with another Dutch admiral, de Boschouwer, which was aimed at removing the Portuguese and obliged the Dutch to take measures in this direction. In around 1620 the Portuguese managed to establish a small fort in Koddamunai (Tamil: »spit of land with the fort«), with which they hoped to ward off attacks by the Dutch. In 1636 the Dutch returned under Admiral Coster, however, and in just two years had driven out the Portuguese and taken the fort. Together with the town of Batticaloa, they handed it over to the kings of Kandy. By around 1660, though, the Dutch East India Company had recognized the strategic importance of Batticaloa, and so it suited them well that the kings of Kandy still owed them promised payments for the war: they took the town as a lien and built a fort here too. When in 1795 the British started occupying increasingly large swathes of Sri Lanka, the little fort at Batticaloa was unable to offer resistance for very long. It held out, in fact, for just three weeks.

It was during the period of British colonial rule that the road between Batticaloa and Kandy was built. The development of Batticaloa, however, did not keep up with that of Trincomalee 145km/90mi to the north, as the latter had a far better natural harbour. The modesty prosperity of the inhabitants today is primarily due to rich fisheries along with fruit and vegetable growing. The well connected location in regard to transport infrastructure also allowed steady growth. Thanks to the rebuilding of the railway with the help of Chinese money a few years ago, Batticaloa is once again connected to the Sri Lankan railway network.

WHAT TO SEE IN BATTICALOA

*Lagoon

The 54km/33mi long saltwater lagoon between Chenkaladi in the north and Kalmunai in the south can be explored by boat, and the scenery, with its notable diversity of bird species, is very attractive. In two places, near Batticaloa and near Kallar, the lagoon is connected to the open sea by narrow channels. A bridge (near Batticaloa) and a causeway (near Kallar) connect the long narrow island with the mainland.

Dutch fort

The Kallada bridge links the small island of Batticaloa with the spit of land where, directly on the lagoon, the Dutch built their fort in the 17th century. The massive outer walls, now much overgrown with grass, are well preserved. At each corner there was once a defensive tower armed with cannon.

Lady Manning Bridge

The Lady Manning Bridge is made of iron and one of the longest bridges in Sri Lanka, connecting the spit of land with the island; it carries the A 4 road leading to the south.

Hindu temples

As Batticaloa is largely inhabited by Tamils and most of the Moors still left in Sri Lanka, almost all the religious buildings are Hindu temples. They are attractive enough to look at, but without exception of fairly recent date and of no great art-historical importance.

Singing Fishes

The phenomenon of the »Singing Fishes« has long been known in Batticaloa, even finding mention in the Encyclopædia Britannica! If a paddle is dipped into the water on moonlit nights in calm weather,

Batticaloa

GETTING THERE
By car: from Colombo on the A 1 to Kandy, from there via the A 26 and later the A 5 to the east coast. Then turn right on to the A 15 (app. 309 km/192mi)
By train: final station of the Colombo route that goes via Polonnaruwa

WHERE TO STAY/EAT
Centara Passikudah Resort & Spa
£££–££££
App. 20 km/12 mi south of Batticaloa
tel. 011 247 23 97
www.centarahotelsresorts.com
A four-star resort that opened in April 2013 right on the beach of Passikaduah. It has all the comforts and conveniences a hotel with such a ranking should have. All of the 126 generously proportioned rooms have views of the sea, a place where water sports enthusiasts will surely have a good time. Four bars and restaurants create culinary pleasures. There is a separate pool for children as well as a Kids' Club.

Maalu Maalu Resort & Spa
£££–££££
Passekudah
Reservation in Colombo:
tel. 011 738 63 86
www.maalumaalu.com
Architecturally, the four-star hotel is based on a fishing village. It is located right on the beach of Passekudah and consists of two-storey chalets with a total of 40 rooms. The Ocean Suites with sea views share a pool.

Amethyst Resort Passikudah
££–£££
28 km/17 mi north of Batticaloa
tel. 065 567 60 03-5
www.amethystpassikudah.com
The 97 rooms, housed in several single-storey buildings, are supplemented by a few suites and beach chalets. There is a narrow lagoon between the reception building and the rooms. Swimming in the sea as well as in a freshwater pool with a separate kids' area. Good selection of water sports!

Bridge View Hotel £
No. 63/24 New Dutch Bar Road
tel. 065 222 37 23
www.hotelbridgeview.com
The lovingly tended garden surrounding the building is remarkable. The name, however, is deceptive, because the bridge in Batticaloa cannot be seen from any of the rooms. Nevertheless the Bridge View Hotel is one of the best addresses in town.

Co-Op Inn £
Trinco Road
tel. 065 226 13
Basic but clean and inexpensive rooms in the town centre. The restaurant serves outstanding curries!

Riviera Resort £
New Dutch Bar Road Kallady
tel. 065 222 21 65
www.riviera-online.com
Clean guesthouse, situated favourably on the lagoon with 15 lovingly furnished rooms, two family villas (partially without air conditioning) and a restaurant

WHERE TO EAT

RN Buffet & Take Away £

42 Covington Road
daily 11am – 2.30pm
This small, recommendable restaurant
is not easy to find. It is located on the
first floor above a grocery store. There
is a daily lunch buffet with six different
curries and other dishes.

Riviera Resort £ – ££

Dutch Bar Road (in the Riviera Resort)
tel. 065 222 21 64
Take some time for this restaurant
because all the dishes are freshly prepared. And that takes time. But it is
worth it because the curries
are excellent and the bill is
reasonable.

Insider Tip

Rest House £ – ££

Brayne Drive
tel. 065 222 78 82
Currently the best restaurant in Batticaloa; it is a good idea to book a table
early. The location in the old Dutch fort
is great and the views of this piece of
the town's history are a free bonus
while dining. The menu features local
and international dishes.

by holding your ear to the other end you will hear (perhaps) about
six different, very clear notes. There is still **no scientific explanation**
for the sounds, and no one has ever seen the fish. The »singing« may
perhaps emanate from the numerous molluscs in the waters here. The
assumption is that the noise is caused when the rise and fall of the
tides causes the water to flow through the empty shells. Others suggest that the noises may be produced by catfish, which are also very
numerous here. However, nobody has managed to deliver any proof
for this theory either.

SURROUNDINGS OF BATTICALOA

Sri Lanka's most beautiful beaches are located just 30km/20mi north **Passekudah,**
of Batticaloa, near Passekudah and Kalkudah. Since this region has **Kalkudah**
become safe for travellers again after the end of the civil war and the
removal of the tsunami damage, this piece of information has spread
among the worldwide surfer community in particular. While cultural and historical sites are few and far between in this Tamil part of
the island, the region boasts wide, golden, child-friendly, sandy
beaches; Kalkudah Bay Beach can have big waves, making it ideal for
surfing and body-boarding. The flat beaches are also perfect for a
holiday with children.

There are a few guesthouses along the coast whose modest but functional comforts are compensated for by the family atmosphere. In
Passekudah there are more upmarket hotels right on the beach, such
as the Centara Passikudah Resort & Spa and the Amethyst Resort,
with very comfortable rooms.

Bentota

——————————————— ✳ **A/B 9**

Province: Southern
Altitude: 2–5m (6–18ft)

A very attractive palm-lined beach was the main reason why in the 1980s the fishing village of Bentota was developed into a world-famous tourist centre. But Bentota has paid for its colourful beach life with a loss of local colour. However there are still some good restaurants here, serving excellent fish dishes.

History From 1644 to 1652 the Dutch/Portuguese border ran to the north of Bentota. The Dutch had advanced as far as here from the south, destroying the fort the Portuguese had built apart from one building, which they furnished as a Rest House for their officers. The British, who later replaced the Dutch as the colonial power, enjoyed coming to Bentota to recuperate in the much better climate if they wanted to escape the oppressive heat and humidity of the capital Colombo.

Lots of watersports When Sri Lanka's east coast was still suffering as a result of the civil war and was difficult to access, the region around Bentota and Hikkaduwa further to the south developed into watersports centres. The magnificent coral reefs were legendary; however, they have been partially plundered by unscrupulous divers.
The tsunami also left visible marks on the underwater world. Despite all this, this region is still considered a good destination for snorkellers and divers and many dive schools have adapted to accommodate the visitors. Anyone preferring to stay above the water could enjoy a tour in one of the glass-bottom boats run by many of the hotels.

WHAT TO SEE IN BENTOTA

*Beach The 4km/2.5mi long sandy beach is what people actually come to see in Bentota, although bathing can be dangerous during the monsoon season. There are also surfing and sailing opportunities.

Galapatha Raja Maha Vihara The Galapatha Raja Maha Vihara probably originated in the 2nd century BC and is said to have been built in the reign of King Duttha Gamani. Later, under King Parakrama BahuI, a relic is said to have been placed here, which is why the temple was for a long time an important pilgrimage centre. It is also claimed that there was an important Buddhist university here too, but there is no evidence for that.

At the full moon in November/December the colourful Perahera takes place in Bentota, which many people from the surrounding towns and villages attend.

Perahera

Rewarding excursions from Bentota include the mask-carving town of ►Ambalangoda and the popular bathing resort of ►Hikkaduwa further to the south. To the north lies the district administrative centre of ►Kalutara with an imposing dagoba.

Excursion tips

A never-ending sandy beach lines the hotels in Bentota

Bentota

GETTING THERE

By car: Colombo or Galle via the A 2 (79km/49mi and 70 km/43mi respectively)

By train: station on the Colombo – Matara route (several connections per day)

By bus: regular connections from the abovementioned towns (journey time in each case app. 90min.).

DIVING

Bentota is an interesting destination for divers and many dive schools have responded to that demand. The offshore coral gardens are very rich in fish and other marine life. This guide lists the two largest dive schools as representative of the many that exist

LSR Bentota Dive Center (CIS)

29B, de S. Jayasinghe Mawatha-Dehiwala
tel. 011 282 49 55
www.lsr-srilanka.com
Dive school with PADI training and equipment hire. Daily trips to interesting dive sites.

Sunshine Watersports Center

tel. 034 428 93 79
www.sunshinewatersports.net
Qualified beginners and advanced lessons in line with the internationally recognized PADI qualifications as well as daily trips to dive sites. This dive centre near Beruwela also offers windsurfing, wakeboarding, water skiing and jet skiing.

WHERE TO STAY

Club Bentota £ £ £ – £ £ £ £
Paradise Island, Aluthgama
tel. 034 227 51 67
www.clubbentota.com
For many years now it has been one of Bentota's best hotels. Situated between the Indian Ocean and a lagoon on a headland, it was designed in 1982 by the well-known South African architect John Drake. The only way to reach it from the mainland is by boat. The 146 rooms are very clean and comfortable. There are several bars, a large freshwater pool, a spa and a gym. The location on the sea makes this a good base for many water sports, including diving.

Saman Villas
£ £ £ – £ £ £ £
Aturuwella, Bentota
tel. 034 227 54 35
www.samanvilla.com
Just 26 villas in an outstanding location on a cliff right above the sea. Maybe the best address in Bentota and definitely one of the most expensive. Very attractive, comfortable interior; two restaurants, two bars, a large freshwater pool with a children's area, a spa, extensive range of excursions. The attentive service is universally praised.

Taj Exotica Bentot
£ £ £ – £ £ £ £
Kaikawala Induruwa
tel. 034 555 55 55
www.vivantabytaj.com
Recently (2013) renovated luxury accommodation owned by the Indian Taj hotel chain. The hotel has kept its lovely location above a headland and therefore on one of the best beaches for miles around. 162 rooms, several restaurants and bars, pool, spa, gym.

Avani Bentota Resort & Spa
££–£££
tel. 034 494 78 78
www.serendibleisure.com
The Avani is one of the more recent
hotels in Bentota. It has 14 standard
rooms, 46 superior rooms and 13 deluxe rooms as well as two suites. The
two restaurants serve both local specialities as well as international fare.
There are three bars to choose from in
the evenings and there is a spa offering
Ayurveda therapies. The two freshwater pools are also suitable for children.

Ceysands ££–£££
Aluthgama, Bentota
tel. 034 227 50 73
www.centarahotelsresorts.com
Hotel located on a headland between
the Bentota River and the sea that was
reopened in 2013 after a complete refurbishment. 166 very comfortable
rooms, restaurants and bars, large
pool, including for children, its own
beach, great spa and gym, water sports
centre and much more. The evening
dinner boat trips on the river are romantic.

Induruwa Beach Hotel ££–£££
Kaikawala Induruwa
tel. 034 33104
www.induruwabeachresort.com
Very nice hotel with good views and
comfortable rooms, all with sea views
(90 rooms plus 15 rooms for Ayurveda
guests). Nice garden with a generous
pool.

Zum Deutschen £–££
Thunniyara Watta 3/293
Bentota Warahena
tel. 077 414 24 36
www.urlaub-auf-sri-lanka.com
Pretty, well-tended complex, owned by
a German who emigrated to Sri Lanka
countless years ago and who has lots
of insider tips and will arrange individual round trips. The five rooms are basic
but comfortable. Even though the Indian Ocean is just a stone's throw
away, there is a large pool.

WHERE TO EAT
All the hotels in Bentota and the surrounding area have their own restaurants, which serve both local and international specialities; thanks to a lack of
alternatives, they are frequented by the
locals too. Nevertheless it is worth exploring the restaurants outside of the
hotels, such as the Amal on the road to
Galle with an acceptable choice of dishes at quite inexpensive prices (tel.
034 394 28 31). A further recommendable restaurant is the Singharajah, also
on the road to Galle (tel. 034 227 49 78).
Every day it serves a delicious buffet with
a large number of dishes (daily 7.30am –
10pm). Again on the road to Galle is the
hotel and restaurant Wunderbar (tel.
227 59 08) with its very good fish dishes.

Beruwala

✳ **A 9**

Province: Western
Altitude: app. 7m/25ft
Population: app. 33,000

The small fishing town of Beruwala, idyllically situated in a broadly curving bay, is probably the oldest Muslim settlement in Sri Lanka and a place of pilgrimage for all Moors.

Lively bathing resort The Muslims probably landed in this sheltered bay in around AD 800, but the first documented evidence of settlement by them dates from 1024. At that time the town was called Barberyn. Today Beruwala is a popular bathing resort with a few comfortable hotels by the beach. It's possible to observe the **toddy tappers** at their risky business on the ropes stretched between tall coconut palms. They use the palms as a source of the sap from which the spirit called arrack is made. This spirit is produced in an arrack distillery in Beruwala.

> ❗ MARCO ⊕ POLO TIP
>
> *When Ramadan is over ...*
>
> ... almost 60,000 Muslim pilgrims come to Beruwala to let loose and celebrate the end of the month of fasting. During this time there are markets and cultural events worth visiting.

WHAT TO SEE IN BERUWALA

Kachimalai Mosque Kachimalai Mosque (13th/14th century) still dominates the skyline of Beruwala with its slender minaret; it is **the oldest mosque in Sri Lanka**.
There is a modern mosque in China Fort, the quarter inhabited by wealthy Arab gem dealers. The tomb of a Muslim saint, whose stone sarcophagus is supposed to have been washed ashore, is the destination for many Sri Lankan Muslim pilgrims.

Gemstone workshops In Beruwala there are some workshops in which predominantly local stones are cut.

Islands There are a number of offshore islands with luxuriant vegetation and protected by a **coral reef**. This is however no less threatened than most of the others around Sri Lanka, as even strict prohibitions cannot stop the locals from plundering it.

Beruwala

GETTING THERE
By car: from Colombo or Galle via the A 2 (71/78mi and 72 km/79mi respectively)
By train: station on the Colombo – Matara route (several connections daily)
By bus: several connections from the abovementioned towns every day

WHERE TO STAY/EAT
Eden Resort und Spa £ £ – £ £ £
Kaluwamodera
tel. 034 227 60 75
www.eden-resort-spa-beruwela-sri-lanka.lakpura.com
After extensive refurbishment in 2013, this hotel, which does not just cater to Ayurveda guests, now has very comfortable rooms and an extensive selection of therapies. Generous pool area, restaurant, coffee shop, bar, lots of sporting activities.

Heritance Ayurveda Maha Gedara £ £ – £ £ £
Beruwela
tel. 117 48 82 88
www.heritancehotels.com
Another Sri Lankan building where Geoffrey Bawa, the island's best-known architect, has made his mark: clear lines in the architecture that blends in wonderfully in the existing surroundings. This mark remains despite a full refurbishment and a name change after his death in 2003. It was previously known as the Neptune Hotel. 64 individually furnished, comfortable rooms in four different categories. Ayurveda is offered in various packages, there is a lovely pool and a restaurant that also serves non-ayurvedic cuisine.

Lanka Princess £ £ – £ £ £
Kaluwamodara
tel. 034 227 67 18
www.lankaprincess.com
A much recommended hotel management: 110 rooms, restaurant, bar, pool.

Barberyn Reef Ayurveda Resort £ – £ £
Morgolla
tel. 034 227 60 36
www.barberynresorts.com
One of the best Ayurveda hotels with cosy rooms. Ayurveda cookery courses.

Bavarian Guesthouse £ – £ £
92 Barberyn Road
tel. 034 227 61 29
www.bavarianguesthouse.com
Seven rooms of which three have air conditioning, situated in a lovely garden. The rooms are very clean and since the two owners, Dennis and Judy Leard, speak English. It is a three-minute walk to the beach and there is also a freshwater pool. The hotel restaurant is known for its good German and Austrian cuisine; the owners also arrange trips.

Bundala National Park · Bundala Bird Sanctuary

—✳ **D 9**

Province: Southern
Altitude: app. 2m/6ft

For anyone with ornithological interests Bundala National Park with its Bird Sanctuary is an absolute must. There are no fewer than almost 200 bird species, some of them magnificently colourful, that come here to breed. Visiting between September and March, during the Sri Lankan winter, is the most eventful.

Meeting place for migratory birds During the winter, the national park, which opened in 2006 and covers an area of around 6.2sq km/2.4 sq mi, is a meeting place for migratory birds in particular. They arrive from the southern Asian mainland and prefer to spend the winter in the biotopes in one of the five coastal lagoons. It is also worth visiting during the rest of the year however, because the flora and fauna are particularly diverse during these wetter months.

Bundala National Park

GETTING THERE
By car or by taxi:
The park entrance is located 18km/11mi east of Hambantota or 30km/19mi east of Tissamaharama

Visitor centre
Daily 8am – 6pm
Admission fee: USD10, children up to the age of 12 pay half price, plus an USD8 service fee for the conservation authority. The vehicle costs a further 250Rs and visitors will also have to pay taxes.
There is a visitor centre at the main entrance to the national park, which contains a worthwhile exhibition of stuffed animals and sun-bleached bones of wild animals as well as some interest-

ing information panels. A 28km/17mi trail leads through the park; it is possible to drive it in one of the park administration's jeeps when accompanied by a knowledgeable local ranger.
Beware: for safety reasons there are only three clearly signposted locations in the national park where visitors are allowed to leave their vehicles!

WHERE TO STAY
There are two campsites that can be booked in the office of the Bundala Community Based Ecotourism Camping Council in Hambantota or by phone (071 830 70 81), bring your own tent! More solid accommodation can be found in Hambantota and Tissamaharama.

Bundala is one of Sri Lanka's most interesting national parks for other reasons too, although it gets far fewer visitors than Yala National Park, which is just a few kilometres away. The land dwellers are as diverse as the birds, from imposing saltwater crocodiles to many wild elephants and turtles that lay their eggs on the beach, allowing visitors to experience an exceptional species diversity.

Other animals

Chilaw

 A 6

Province: Western
Altitude: app. 5m/16ft
Population: app. 24,000

The bustling fishing port of Chilaw, one of the most important in the country, is situated at the northern end of a long lagoon on the west coast known as Chilaw Lake, which opens out into the sea some 2km/1.5mi further on. This is also the mouth of the Deduru Oya, marking the southern boundary of the hot dry zone of the island.

In the past Chilaw played an important role as the site of one of the larger Jesuit mission stations. This also explains why more than a third of the local population are Roman Catholics.

Jesuit missionary base

WHAT TO SEE IN CHILAW

The work of the fishermen and of the women and girls who carry fish around in baskets on their heads to the morning fish market can best be watched from the bridge connecting the town to a narrow spit of land to the west of Chilaw Lake.

Fish market

Near the sea is the large Catholic cathedral of St Mary, dating from the 19th century, which bears witness to the effectiveness of the Jesuit mission. Chilaw today is one of eight Catholic dioceses in Sri Lanka.

Catholic church

SURROUNDINGS OF CHILAW

Approx. 3km/2mi east of Chilaw, near the village of Munneswaram, is one of the oldest Hindu shrines on the island. The Munnesvaram Kovil is dedicated to the god Shiva and greatly venerated by the faith-

Hindu Temple

ful. Every year in August/September the entire region comes to life to celebrate for four weeks in accordance with Hindu rites. Hindus believe that the lingam, the phallic symbol, was given by Rama when he stopped here after his victory over King Ravana. In 1578 the Portuguese had the temple destroyed; the kovil was only rebuilt in 1753 under King Kirti Sri.

One interesting feature at the heart of the temple is a golden statue of Shiva's wife Parvati, draped in garlands. There are several processional floats in the left part of the main hall. They are dedicated to the main gods and are pulled through the streets during the festivities. By the way, men must strip to the waist before being allowed to enter the kovil.

Lake Tinapitiya   The road to Marawila, a town app. 24km/15mi to the south, passes Lake Tinapitiya. To the left, next to the temple of Taniwella Devale is the figure of a rearing horse. The story goes that a merchant's horse shied when its rider tried to pass the temple in a hurry without confirming his devotion to the gods. The merchant fell to the ground badly hurt, and swore to endow the temple with an image of his horse when he recovered.

Marawila   Marawila is one of the centres of Sri Lankan batik production. It is possible to buy **batiks** here more cheaply than in the tourist centres.

Chilaw

GETTING THERE
By car: from Colombo via the A 1 northbound (81 km/50mi)
By train: station on the Colombo–Puttalam route
By bus: good connections from Colombo (travel time app. 3 hrs).

WHERE TO STAY/EAT
Club Palm Bay Hotel
££–£££
Morogolla
tel. 034 227 60 39
Nice mid-range beach hotel with 140 comfortable rooms, a large pool and a good restaurant. Particularly recommendable for families!

Rico-Shadow-Guest House
£–££
Kammala North, Waikkala
tel. 077 734 08 61
www.rico-shadow.com
Very well-tended guesthouse with 20 cosy rooms; just a half-hour drive from the airport. The beach is also close and there are some attractions nearby. The restaurant serves local and international dishes; guests can also make use of Sri Lanka's largest pool for free in the neighbouring Hotel Dolphin.

** Colombo

A 8

Province: Western
Altitude: app. 1–5m/3–18ft
Population: 753,000

Even though the district of Sri Jayawardenepura has been the seat of the government and parliament since 1982, Colombo is still the island's de facto capital. Bustling and noisy today, it is an agglomeration of previously separate towns, each of which has retained its style and character.

The gulf between rich and poor becomes particularly clear after a visit to the Pettah and Cinnnamon Garden districts. While Pettah still has hovels where the misery hits you in the face, Cinnamon Garden is dominated by the villas of the wealthy. And while Pettah comes across as noisily oriental, the traffic in Cinnamon Garden proceeds along broad avenues past neatly tended gardens.

Deprivation and affluence

The favourable location on the island's west coast along with the fact that this particular coastal strip is fertile, certainly favoured Colombo's rise to become an **economic centre** of Sri Lanka. But it was never a royal city, the Singhalese rulers preferring places like Anuradhapura, Polonnaruwa and Kandy, maybe on account of the more pleasant climate. Since 1982 Colombo has no longer been the seat of the parliament, which is now based in Sri Jayawardanapura, an artificial city that was once called Kotte. A suburb of Colombo, it got its present name only when it became the administrative capital. Even so, Colombo is still the seat of numerous ministries and other government agencies.

Historical development

1344	First mention of the port
1505	The Portuguese make landfall and build a fort in 1518
1658	The Dutch conquer the city
1796	The British take over the city
1869	Colombo becomes an important trading port with the opening of the Suez Canal
20th century	Colombo becomes a city; Ceylon achieves independence from Great Britain in 1948; Sri Jayawardenepura becomes the administrative capital in 1982.

It is not known for certain **where the name Colombo comes from**. In the 5th century AD the Chinese traveller Faxian mentioned a small port, but failed to say what it was called. By around the 8th century, the harbour had attained some importance as a result of Arab traders settling here, the forebears of the Moors now living in Sri Lanka; they called in Calenbou. The Chinese merchant Wang Tai Yuan, who visited Colombo in about 1330, mentioned in his notes a town called Kao-lan-pu. It was only under the Portuguese that Colombo got its present name, maybe in memory of the explorer Christopher Columbus. Other versions trace it back to the Singhalese words Cola-amba (= leaf of the mango tree). The third theory is the simplest: the Singhalese always called the place Kolamba, which just means harbour.

The majority of Sri Lanka's foreign trade goes via Colombo docks

Colombo

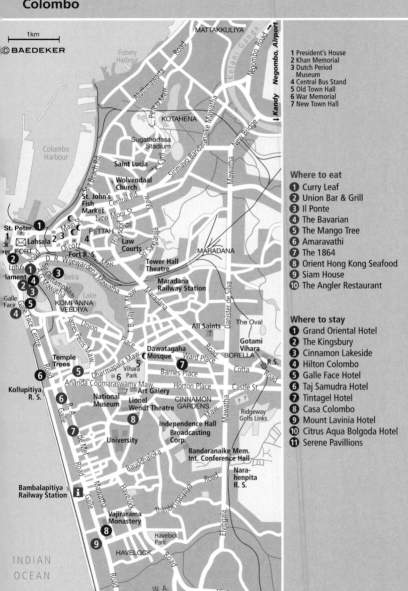

1 President's House
2 Khan Memorial
3 Dutch Period Museum
4 Central Bus Stand
5 Old Town Hall
6 War Memorial
7 New Town Hall

Where to eat
1 Curry Leaf
2 Union Bar & Grill
3 Il Ponte
4 The Bavarian
5 The Mango Tree
6 Amaravathi
7 The 1864
8 Orient Hong Kong Seafood
9 Siam House
10 The Angler Restaurant

Where to stay
1 Grand Oriental Hotel
2 The Kingsbury
3 Cinnamon Lakeside
4 Hilton Colombo
5 Galle Face Hotel
6 Taj Samudra Hotel
7 Tintagel Hotel
8 Casa Colombo
9 Mount Lavinia Hotel
10 Citrus Aqua Bolgoda Hotel
11 Serene Pavillions

Colombo

INFORMATION
Sri Lanka Tourist Board
80, Galle Road Colombo 3
tel. 011 243 70 55, 243 70 59
www.srilanka.travel
The Travel Information Centre (tel.
011 225 24 11) is located in the arrivals
hall of the Bandaranaike International
Airport; it is open 24 hours. Both offices stock a large number of brochures in
various languages.

EMERGENCY
Tourist police
Fort, Colombo 01
tel. 011 22 69 41 and 242 11 11

TRANSPORT
The best way of getting around in Colombo is to take a taxi or to rent a car
including driver.

Buses
The public buses tend to be hopelessly
overcrowded and are often confusing
to tourists who do not know the area.
Beware: skilled thieves often chance
their luck on these buses! The districts
of Fort and Pettah are easy to explore
on foot.

Taxis
Taxi signs and taximeters are not common in Colombo so negotiate a price
in advance. Taxis often wait at special
locations, such as on Galle Road or in
Sea Street in the Pettah. A trip should
cost around 40Rs per kilometre. Official
taxi companies can be identified by the
Radio Cab sign. These taxis are the
ones hotels will call for their guests.

Three Wheeler
These rattling three-wheeled modes of
transport make taximeters superfluous
since the journey price, generally app.
40Rs per kilometre, has to be negotiated before setting off. If the price
seems too much, just call the next
Three Wheeler. As a try-on, many drivers quote completely overpriced tourist
fees.

MARKETS
There is a large bazaar to the west of
Fort station that mainly sells souvenirs
and clothes. A (shopping) stroll
through the Pettah district is also
worthwhile. There is a Sunday market
underneath the aerial root trees in the
old fort.

SIGHTSEEING
Many visitors stay away from the capital, which can get quite hectic. That is
a shame because Colombo has some
nice attractions. They can be explored
on Wednesdays, Saturdays and Sundays from 8.30am during a four-hour
tour in a double-decker bus. The ticket
price includes something to drink as
well as snacks; the highlights are explained in English (tel. 077 759 99 63;
www.colombo-citytours.com).

SHOPPING
Odel Unlimited
Alexandra Place
Colombo 07
www.odel.lk
daily 10am – 8pm
Large shopping centre with lots of
shops (fashion, leather goods, jewellery, tea, ayurveda cosmetics, sporting

goods and much more), and factory outlets selling goods from European designers who have their clothes produced in Sri Lanka.

Paradise Road
213 Dharmapala Maw 61,
Ward Place Colombo 07
www.paradiseroadsl.com
Mon – Sat 10am – 7pm
One of the most recommendable addresses in Colombo. The rooms are filled with treasures: hand-painted porcelain, table décor made out of palm branches, ayurvedic oils, furniture fabrics from the bolt, or hand-crocheted pillowcases.

Elephant Walk
61, Ward Place
Colombo 7
Mon – Sat 9am – 8pm
This is one of the newer shopping paradises in Colombo. Home textiles, utility items for the kitchen and original souvenirs can all be found in this historic venue.

Victorian Charm Kalaya
No. 08 Palm Grove 116 Havelock Road, Colombo 03
Mon – Sat 10am – 7pm
A real treasure trove for quality crafts. The owner combines eastern and western textile production methods, such as hand-made lace, and also exquisite embroidery.

Hermitage Gallery Suriya Home Décor Store
28 Gower Street 61,
5th Lane Colombo 05
Mon – Sat 10am – 7pm
Chests, tables and other pretty pieces

of furniture are sold here as are old household goods, from birdcages to brass lamps and historical pictures.

Barefoot
tel. 011 258 01 14
704 Galle Road,
Colombo 03
www.barefootceylon.com
Mon – Sat 10am – 7pm
This shop in an old colonial villa belongs to the well-known designer Barbara Sansoni. She is known for her hand-woven fabrics in bright colours, which also get made into beautiful items of clothing.

Cottage Craft
40 Stratford Avenue,
Colombo 06
This place sells paper goods that are made out of elephant dung. The smell is removed from the dung in a special process, after which it undergoes further processing.

Sri Lanka Tea Board Shop **Insider Tip**
574 Galle Road,
Colombo 03
tel. 011 259 09 68
www.pureceylontea.com
Mon – Sat 10am – 6pm
Tea is one of Sri Lanka's most important exports, which is why it is difficult to get any of the best tea varieties on the island itself. But this shop stocks a good selection of high-quality tea specialities.

WHERE TO EAT
The Sri Lankan capital was for a long time not exactly a Mecca for gourmets. They were left with virtually no choice but to hotel restaurants, which of

course often had top chefs preparing local and international dishes. Things have changed for the better in recent years and the selection outside the hotels has become richer and more diverse.

❼ *The 1864*
£££–££££

2 Galle Road, Colombo 3
tel. 011 254 10 10
It is not just hotel guests who dine here at star-level. For that reason this restaurant in the Galle Face Hotel is also one of the most expensive in the capital.

❶ *Curry Leaf*
££–£££

200 Union Place (in the Hilton Hotel), Colombo 3
tel. 011 254 46 44
Probably the best restaurant in Colombo for outstanding curries. Lovely garden.

❷ *Union Bar & Grill*
££–£££

200 Union Place (in the Hilton Colombo), Colombo 2
tel. 011 534 46 59
Daily from noon–4pm this restaurant serves a rich lunch buffet that includes Sri Lankan cuisine; in the evening it mainly serves international fare.

❸ *Il Ponte*
£–££

2 Sir Chittampalam A. Gardener Mawatha, Colombo 3
tel. 011 254 46 44
This Italian restaurant is located in the Hilton Colombo. It is considered the best and most affordable Italian in the city.

❹ *The Bavarian*
£–££

11 Galle Face Court, Colombo 3
tel. 011 242 15 77
Anyone in the mood for hearty German cuisine will not just get typical Bavarian dishes here but also German beer from the barrel.

❺ *The Mango Tree*
£–££

82 Dharmapala Mawatha, Colombo 7
tel. 011 537 97 90
Anyone in the mood for northern Indian cuisine will enjoy this much recommended restaurant.

❻ *Amaravathi*
£–££

2 Mile Post Avenue, Colombo 3
tel. 011 257 74 18
This restaurant has specialized in southern Indian vegetarian cuisine.

❽ *Orient Hong Kong Seafood*
£–££

1 A Race Course, Colombo 7
tel. 011 269 90 07
This Cantonese restaurant in Colombo's Cinnamon Gardens is the top address for outstanding seafood.

❾ *Siam House*
£–££

17 Melbourne Avenue, Colombo 4
tel. 011 259 59 66
www.siamhouse.lk
The Siam House in Bambalapitiya serves outstanding Thai cuisine and is definitely recommended.

❿ *The Angler Restaurant* **£**

71, Hotel Road, Mount Lavinia
tel. 011 271 66 26

There are not many dishes on the menu, but all of them are prepared with ingredients bought fresh from the market that day.

WHERE TO STAY
❼ Tintagel Hotel
££££
65 Rosmead Place
tel. 011 460 21 21
www.tintagelcolombo.com
This boutique hotel near Viharamaha Park has just ten suites, but they are exquisitely furnished. The building was constructed in around 1930 and made the headlines in a sad event when the prime minister at the time, S. W. R. D. Bandaranaike, was shot on the terrace by a Buddhist monk in 1959. There are two restaurants, one swanky bar, a pool and a spa with a sauna.

❽ Casa Colombo
££££
231 Galle Road Col 4
tel. 011 452 01 30
www.casacolombo.com
Once home to a respected Indian merchant family, this hotel now houses twelve individual suites. The magnificent building was constructed in the colonial style with Moorish set pieces in the mid-18th century; despite being renovated several times, it has held on to its original character. The pool is an attraction in and of itself: it is pink and the guests can use glass loungers to relax on.

❿ Citrus Aqua Bolgoda Hotel
££££
Diggala Road (Ruskin Island near Panadura, south of Colombo)
tel. 077 364 14 80 (mobile)

www.citrusvacations.travel
A refuge for those tired of the city, wishing for a retreat from the hectic capital Colombo. The complex is located on a small island in Bolgoda Lake and consists of just three generous, detached villas that are furnished to a high standard. Every villa has its own small pool. The range of sporting activities on offer is extensive: there is tennis, squash, badminton and a gym.

❷ The Kingsbury
£££–££££
48 Janadhipathi Mawatha
tel. 011 242 12 21
www.thekingsburyhotel.com
The view of the Indian Ocean alone justifies the price for a stay here. The 229 rooms, all with sea views, are very comfortable.

❸ Cinnamon Lakeside
£££–££££
115 Sir Chittampalam A. Gardener Mawatha
(Fort district)
tel. 011 249 10 00
www.cinnamonhotels.com
This hotel on Beira Lake, which opened in 1982, is among the best places to stay in the city. 340 tasteful rooms, several restaurants (including one serving Thai cuisine and a sushi bar) are on offer. The pool is remarkably big and there is also a spa.

❹ Hilton Colombo
£££–££££
2, Sir Chittampalam A. Gardiner Mawatha
tel. 011 254 46 44, www.hilton.com
Centrally located hotel with a nice, big garden right on the promenade. The

384 rooms are furnished in the art deco style and are very comfortable. The generous pool is one of the best in Colombo.

❺ *Galle Face Hotel* £££-££££

2, Galle Road,
Colombo 3
tel. 011 254 10 10
www.gallefacehotel.com
This hotel, built in 1864, is located right on Colombo's main boulevard, Galle Road. It is a dignified hotel in the colonial style with a modern extension. The 127 rooms are spacious and exude the charm of bygone times. For five o'clock tea or for a sundowner guests meet on the terrace that faces the sea and that also has a pool. The Galle Face Hotel serves an opulent breakfast that is open to non-guests as well – daily 7am–10.30am.

❻ *Taj Samudra Hotel* £££-££££

25, Galle Face Center Road
tel. 011 244 66 22
www.tajhotels.com
The Taj Samudra is among the top addresses in Colombo. While the building, with the 300 rooms, is hidden in a beautiful garden; the top service does not need to hide. Guests are offered all the comforts and conveniences of a luxury hotel.

❾ *Mount Lavinia Hotel* £££-££££

100, Hotel Road, Mount Lavinia
tel. 011 271 17 11
www.mountlaviniahotel.com
Anyone not wanting to stay in Colombo proper will be well looked after in this traditional colonial-style establishment with its 200-year history. It has 226 rooms, 2 restaurants, a pool, a gym, a spa and shopping arcades. It is located near Galkissa on a cliff right by the sea and is one of Sri Lanka's most renowned yet affordable hotels. It has been named one of Asia's best hotels several times. The hotel also has a private beach.

⓫ *Serene Pavilions* £££-££££

No. 20 Upali Mawatha
tel. 038 229 68 90
www.serenepavilions.com
This hotel is located right by the sea around 32 km/20mi south of Colombo. There are twelve excellently equipped pavilions, including three with two bedrooms, as well as a large pool, a spa and a gym. The restaurant »The Pavilions« enjoys a good reputation thanks to its outstanding fish dishes. This hotel also offers ayurveda therapies.

❶ *Grand Oriental Hotel* ££-£££

2, York Street (by the harbour)
tel. 011 32 03 91
www.grandoriental.com
The location by the harbour meant that this colonial-style hotel became the go-to place for travellers arriving in Colombo by boat. One of the best-known guests to have stayed here is the German author Karl May, who stopped here during his trip to the orient in 1899. The 672 large rooms and two suites are a bit dated now but the Oriental is still a popular and inexpensive address.

Colombo has been known since Antiquity, for example to King Solomon and the kings of Sheba, through whom it achieved great wealth as a result of worldwide trade as long ago as the 1st century BC. The small harbour mentioned by Faxian developed to become an important entrepôt for the trade in pepper, cinnamon, gemstones, ivory and peacock feathers. lbn Battuta, the great Arab traveller (Famous People), described Calenbou, as he called the place, in the 14th century as the »most beautiful town on the island of Serendib«, but he is likely to have been referring to its commercial importance and cosmopolitan flair rather than its physical attractiveness as a city. In 1518 the **Portuguese**, with the consent of the kings of Kotte, built a massive fort to the south of Colombo in the vicinity of the harbour. It watched over the actual town, which consisted mostly of wooden huts but also included some prestigious administrative buildings. In 1656 the **Dutch** succeeded in taking the fort. They extended the fortifications and founded the residential quarters of Wolfendahl and Hulftsdurp. They also laid out numerous canals, including the one from Kalutara, south of Colombo, to Puttalam; 174km/108mi long. This period also saw the laying out of the Cinnamon Garden, today the best address in town.

In 1796 the **British** occupied Colombo and made the fort district the seat of their administration. The cinnamon gardens disappeared to make way for the colonial housing needs. In 1872 most of the fortifications were demolished. In 1822 Colombo replaced Galle as the most important port. In 1877 the British governor Sir William Gregory hd the open mooring developed into a sheltered harbour. Following independence, the Sri Lankan government and parliament moved into the buildings erected by the British. In 1950 a Commonwealth foreign ministers' conference was held in Colombo, at which the » Colombo Plan for Cooperative Economic Development in South and South-East Asia« was decided upon.

** FORT (DISTRICT)

Approximately triangular in shape, the Fort district could be termed the germ-cell of the present-day city of Colombo. It is bounded by

Colombo Fort

Harbour · Jayanthi Dagoba · Maritime Museum · Harbour · Old Dutch Cemetery/Khan Memorial · Indian · Conmis St. · Wharf Road · L. Bastion Rd. · Church Street · Gordon Garden · Garrison Church of St. Peter · Gem Museum · (Marine Drive) · Galle Bick Road · Flagstaff Street · Padrao Rock · Sir Baron D. B. · York Street · Jayatillaka Mw. · Railway Station · The Canal · Janadhitathi Medura · (Queen Street) · Mudalige Mw. · Lotus Road · Upper Chatham St. · Fort Mosque · Bristol St. · Duke St. · Chatiya · Fort Clock Tower · Lower · Central Telecom Office · Central Bank · Ceylinco House · York Street · Chatham Street · Expo Centre · Janadhigathi Mw. · L. Banku Mw. · Canal Row · Lotus Rd. · Lake House · World Trade Center · D. R. Wijew. Mw. · Road · Ocean · Lotus Road · Sir. Ch. A. Gardener Mw. · Presidential Secretariat · Finance Ministry · 200 m · © BAEDEKER · Kollupitiya, Bambalapitiya · Slave Island

the docks, Marine Drive, Lotus Road and York Street; the latter was a canal during the Dutch period, but was filled in by the British. Nor is there now anything else in Fort to recall the presence of the Dutch, as only a few remains can now be seen of the once massive fortifications that once enclosed the district. Even the streets have lost their Dutch names, and now have English ones. The remains of the fortifications can be found behind Queen's House, where a bulwark dominates the rocky coast – known to the Singhalese as Gal Bokka, Rock Belly, corrupted by the English into Galle Buck. The **lighthouse** where Chaiytya Road becomes Marine Drive was built on a rocky promontory, but is fairly modern.

At the end of Marine Drive is the Neo-classical Old Parliament Building, erected in the typical style of the colonial period. Since Sri Jayawardenepura City became the seat of parliament, this building has served as an administrative centre only.

Clock Tower

Diagonally opposite the Old Parliament Building, Janadhipathi Mawatha, formerly Queen's Street, leads to the centre of the district, which is characterized by the Clock Tower. It was actually built as a lighthouse in 1850, but because it became crowded in by tall buildings all around, it could no longer serve its purpose, and was consequently converted in 1952.

Further buildings

Going up the street to the north, we come to a white building in the colonial style on the left. It was once the residence of the British governor, but today is the **official residence of the prime minister**. The long building is another piece of colonial prestige architecture, the **General Post Office**, which is open round the clock. The residence is adjoined by an attractive park, which however is inaccessible for security reasons.

Streets with formerly magnificent houses

After crossing Sir Baron Jayatillake Mawatha (formerly Prince Street), we come to a building on the right which houses the Cabinet Offices. The street was largely built during the British colonial period, as still evidenced by numerous buildings. However time is visibly doing its destructive work. Sir Baron Jayatillake Mawatha now joins the broad York Street, conspicuous for the red building of Miller's department store with its roof balustrades, gables and turrets. Not far away is the state-owned Laksala department store with a large selection of craft objects along with gemstones and textiles. The Grand Oriental Hotel on the corner of York and Church Streets likewise proclaims the charm of bygone days, but the glamour imparted by such celebrated visitors as the writer Somerset Maugham has now largely faded.

Colombo Port Maritime Museum

Not far from Church Street is a building that dates back to 1676. It once served as a prison for the Dutch authorities but is now the Co-

Highlights Colombo

▶ **Fort**
The former Dutch fort is now a lively commercial quarter with lots of shops.
▶page 219

▶ **Pettah**
Lively bazaar quarter where visitors will encounter all kinds of jugglers and snake charmers.
▶page 221

▶ **Galle Face Green**
Popular place to come and relax right on the coast.
▶page 224

▶ **Cinnamon Garden**
Colombo's exclusive residential neighbourhood also has a huge park with old trees, which is a great place to take a break.
▶page 226

lombo Port Maritime Museum. The main entrance is on Chaitiya Road. The many exhibits illustrate the early days of Colombo's harbour more than 2000 years ago and reveal its development to become a significant trading post for goods of all kinds. The museum also documents the proven trade relationships with the Chinese, the Arabs, Indians and the Europeans, who were particularly interested in Sri Lanka's spices. The Dutch East India Company played a significant role here.

The exhibition also features historical events from even earlier times. Alongside many other models of ships there is one that the Arab globetrotter Ibn Battuta (▶Famous People) is said to have used to get to Sri Lanka. Another famous explorer, Marco Polo (▶Famous People), is also said to have visited Colombo. There are a few Dutch naval cannon outside the museum. Daily 10am–7pm, admission charge

Also on Church Street is the old Garrison Church of St Peter (19th century), which today houses the offices of the Mission to Seamen.

St Peter's Garrison Church

✴✴ PETTAH (DISTRICT)

The Pettah (Tamil: pettai, old town), which adjoins the Fort district to the east, used to be the quarter where the residential and business district of the Portuguese, and later of the Dutch. The traces of the latter are still visible in many places. Today the Pettah is the noisy, frenetic bazaar quarter of Colombo, where all manner of goods are available for very low prices if you know how to haggle. The Pettah is still home to many Moors, the descendants of the Arab seafarers, but also to members of all the other ethnic groups in Sri Lanka. During the 1983 unrest, the Pettah was the target of looters and arsonists, the

Traders' and market district

Moors being the main victims. The streets form an approximate grid pattern. **Each street is reserved for a particular class of goods**: metal wares in one, textiles in another, while currently spices, herbs and tea, for example, are only sold on the 5th Cross Road, and jewellery along the 2nd Cross Road.

Hindu Temple The 2nd Cross Road is also the location of one of the most important Hindu temples in Colombo. It is dedicated to the goddess Kali, the consort of Shiva. Its façade is decorated, perhaps too richly, with figures from the Hindu pantheon. Inside, the cruel and bloodthirsty, but courageous goddess is depicted by a statue; as usual she has a tiger skin around her black body, and is depicted with a necklet of human skulls, while in her hands she holds a sword and stick, a noose, and a man's head. Kali, the Black One, symbolizes all-consuming time.

On Sea Street, the street of goldsmiths, which leads uphill, there are three imaginatively decorated Hindu temples dating from the early 19th century, known respectively as the Ganeshan, the New Kathiresan and the Old Kathiresan Temples. The latter is dedicated to Skanda, the god of war. Every July it is the scene of a colourful ceremony in honour of the god.

Jami Ul-Afar Jumma Mosque The Jami Ul-Afar Jumma Mosque (1908) in 2nd Cross Road is also known as the Great Mosque; the decorative use of red and white bricks gives it a magical appearance. The architectural elements, too, such as the domed clock-tower and the slender minarets, the seemingly »twisted« pillars, the pilasters and the gables, all exercise an incomparable charm.

Dutch Period Museum This museum, set up with the support of the Dutch government, is housed in a 17th-century building. It provides an insight into the history of Sri Lanka during the Dutch colonial period. One interesting exhibit is a portrait of the Dutch general Gerard Hulft, who died during the siege of the Portuguese fort on 10 April 1656. Unfortunately, the building, which has served many different purposes over time (first as the residence of the Dutch governor, later as a military hospital, a boarding school and most recently a post office), comes across as somewhat unkempt, but it still possesses a certain charm.

❶ Tue–Sat 9am–5pm, closed on holidays, admission charge

HULFTSDORP

Former Dutch residential quarter To the east of the Pettah lies the formerly Dutch Hulftsdorp, a residential and legal district named after the Dutch governor Gerard Pieterszoon Hulft. Beyond the Anglican church of All Saints, a 19th-century building, is the Supreme Court, built in the Dutch colonial style, and imposing with its colonnades. Along the narrow, hilly Hulftsdorp Street and in its side alleys there are still a few typically Dutch houses, albeit pretty dilapidated.

The Dutch Reformed Wolfendahl Church, built in 1749 in the quarter of the same name, is the oldest Christian church in Colombo still extant. It stands on the foundations of the Portuguese church of Aqua de Lupo. With its cruciform plan, the massive building dominates a hilltop, from which there is a **fine view** of the docks and the old parts of Colombo. Some of the attractive tombstones, decorated with reliefs, of Dutch governors and colonial officials and their families are older than the church; they were transferred here from the old Dutch cemetery in Gordons Garden in the Fort quarter. Noteworthy features inside the church are the pulpit, the pews and the registers.

Wolfendahl Church

! Insider

Dining with a view **Tip**

MARCO ⊕ POLO TIP

Anyone dining in the Restaurant Harbour Room in the Grand Oriental Hotel will have a great view of the goings-on in the harbour and by the sea. But it is necessary to book a table a few days in advance. (tel. 011 232 03 20).

NORTH OF THE PETTAH

This district to the north of the Pettah is still largely inhabited by Christians; Kotahena, an 18th-century mission station, is home to many descendants of mixed marriages between Portuguese and Singhalese, known as Burghers. Some of the many churches in this district are worth a visit.

Burgher district

The splendid Roman Catholic St Lucia's Cathedral is the largest Christian church in Sri Lanka. The building with its nave and two aisles was built in the Romanesque Revival style between 1873 and 1910. It can hold an impressive 5000 worshippers. There is a magnificent dome on the cathedral, which is accompanied by a further four smaller ones. The gravestones of some French bishops inside the church, which itself has a plain interior, are worth taking in. Also take a look at the modern-looking clock on the outside of the church. Its movement is around 20m/65ft from the clock faces. St Lucia is today the seat of the bishop. The ensemble also includes a Benedictine monastery and a boys' college.

Churches

The Anglican Christ Church was endowed in 1845 by the first Anglican bishop Dr James Chapman. The local residents still call the church by its old name of Stone Church.

Christ Church

in commerce and the colonial administration, while its terrace was often termed the »most beautiful East of Suez«. Even today some of the magic of this venerable establishment can still be felt, even though the shine has faded somewhat.

Other sights　The street that branches off in front of the Galle Face Hotel to the city centre leads past the Holiday Inn, whose architecture is based on the Islamic style, to the interesting 19th-century **Christ Church**. Galle Road runs parallel to the coast through the districts of Kollupitiya, part of which is **enlivened by street markets**, Bambalapitiya, Wellawatta and leads eventually to **Mount Lavinia**, a popular bathing resort since time immemorial. This street is also the location of several other hotels in the luxury class along with a number of embassies.

> **!** MARCO ● POLO TIP
>
> *Lunch with cricket*　**Insider Tip**
>
> At lunchtime, a predominantly young audience meets in the Cricket Club in the hip Kollupitiya quarter to enjoy the light cuisine and watch cricket matches from all around the world on the five televisions (34 Queens Road).

The Scots Presbyterian **church of St Andrew** is a Gothic-revival building dating from 1842. Among its characteristic features are the crenellated vestibule and the towers, which resemble castles. Two buildings in the best English colonial style are the **United States Embassy** and the **Prime Minister's Residence** in the middle of a magnificent park with frangipani trees.

** CINNAMON GARDEN

The upmarket district of Colombo　The streets named Dharmapala Mawatha and Ananada Kumaraswamy Mawatha, which branches off the former, now lead to the suburb of Cinnamon Garden, **Colombo's leafiest neighbourhood**. The British chose it as their preferred residential district, and today it is home mostly to wealthy Singhalese. Their attractive houses are largely hidden behind tall trees, ornamental shrubs and bushes. This opulent district got its name from the fact that there were once extensive cinnamon and other spice plantations here.

Viharamaha-devi Park　The heart of Cinnamon Garden is Viharamahadevi Park, which until 1958 was called Victoria Park. Its present name derives from the mother of King Dhutta Gamani, who liberated the city of Anuradhapura from Tamil rule in the 2nd century; there is a statue commemorating her in the park. At the northwestern end, opposite the Town Hall, is a fine statue of a seated Buddha, at the southwestern end a memorial to those killed in the two world wars. The park today is a **popular recreation area** for the people of Colombo, particularly at the weekends. At its north-east corner is the imposing **Town Hall**, whose dome is reminiscent of that of the Capitol in Washington. Also impressive is the massive portico with attractive decoration on the capitals of the pillars.

The modern Bandaranaike Memorial Conference Hall, an hexagonal structure, was built in 1973 as a gift to Sri Lanka from the People's Republic of China. It bears the name of the assassinated Prime Minister Solomon Bandaranaike (▶Famous People), who is memorialized in a small museum. It contains numerous mementoes and documents relating to the prime minister's life.

Bandaranaike Memorial Conference Hall

❶ Tue–Sat 9am–5pm; admission charge

The shining white, stately building which houses the National Museum of Colombo stands in the middle of an attractively laid-out park. The park and the building reflect the grace and dignity of the Victorian colonial style. The architectural elements and the façade with its three pediments and projecting portico radiate an impressive harmony. The museum was built between 1873 and 1877 at the instigation of the Royal Asiatic Society under the auspices of the British governor Sir William Gregory.

National Museum

On the ground floor there are various artefacts from the former capitals of Anuradhapura and Polonnaruwa that were discovered during digs. The large collection of sculptures from this period is most interesting; one of the outstanding items in that collection is a very nice, limestone Buddha with a harmonious feel. It is attributed to the Toluvila complex (app. 300–500 AD). There is an extraordinarily attractive marble standing Buddha from the 6th/7th century and there are also lots of Hindu deities. One room features set pieces of sacred architecture, which are indispensable in Sri Lanka's temple buuildings, such as moonstones. The various forms of the dagobas so typical of Sri Lankan Buddhism are also shown and explained.

Another room houses several bronze statues from the Polonnaruwa period (12th century), including a dancing Krishna, the eighth form of the god Shiva as shepherd god. Also on the ground floor, a one-hour multimedia presentation explains Sri Lanka's history. Further exhibition rooms on the ground floor are dedicated to ancient coins. Those from Rome are particularly interesting. They are proof of the trading relationships that existed between the continents even in ancient times. Another interesting item is a throne that a Dutch governor gave Vimala Dharma Surya II, who was the king of Kandy from 1687 to 1707.

The upper floor houses an exhibition of paintings that was only compiled and made accessible to the public a few years ago. The watercolours by the painter and composer Andrew Nicholl (1804–1886) from Northern Ireland depict motifs of Sri Lankan life; the paintings give an overview of the work of an artist renowned in his day. Nicholl spent some years at the Royal College in Colombo.

❶ Daily except holidays 9am – 6.30pm, admission charge

SURROUNDINGS OF COLOMBO

Dehiwala

Dehiwala forms a pair of twin towns together with Mount Lavinia, and is separated from Colombo's southernmost district, Wellawatte, by the Dehiwala Canal. The first street to the right after the traffic island leads to the Buddhist temple of Sri Subnadarama, whose interior walls are decorated with attractive paintings. It also houses the figure of a recumbent Buddha, whose sapphire eyes gleam in the light of an oil-lamp.

In Dehiwala the **Zoological Garden of Colombo** is also worth a visit, not only because of its large and varied collection of animals, but also because of its attractive grounds, with their many trees, shrubs and flowers. Near the entrance various species of parrot live in large aviaries; next comes a zone with all manner of deer, and then the section for beasts of prey such as lions, Bengal tigers, pumas, leopards, jaguars and bears. The aquarium has a particularly diverse stock. A further enclosure is home to crocodiles and snakes. There are also areas that are home to sea lions, turtles, monkeys, storks, kingfishers and many other animals. The zoo is famed as **one of the best in Asia**. Its beginnings go back to the eldest son of the German modern zoo pioneer Carl Hagenbeck, Carl Gottfried Wilhelm Heinrich Hagenbeck. He travelled to Sri Lanka several times in search of wild animals for his famous zoon in Hamburg.

❶ Daily 8.30am–6pm, admission charge.

Dutch Canal

The exceptionally straight 120km/75mi Dutch Canal that runs northwards from Colombo to Puttalam is a masterpiece of hydraulic engineering. The canal was built by the Dutch more than 300 years ago, primarily to transport cinnamon. However, it has almost lost its role as a commercial shipping route. The section between Colombo and Negombo is quite lovely and is popular with leisure boaters. Such tours are put on by the Muthurajawela Boat Center, but they can also be booked through some hotels in Colombo. Highlights of the two-hour trip include many waterfowl, as well as the odd crocodile.

Muthurajawela Boat Center: Pamunugama Road 2/14 in Delathura (app. 15 km/9mi north of Negombo), tel. 031 22725

Mount Lavinia

Some 3km/2mi south of Dehiwala is the famous seaside resort of Mount Lavinia, which can be reached by train or bus from Colombo. In 1819, on a cliff overlooking the sea, the British governor Sir Thomas Maitland had a **large, splendid residence** built, albeit only for weekend use. However his successor, Sir Edward Barnes (governor from 1824 to 1831) was instructed by the Colonial Office in London to sell it again, because it had been built without government permission. Later the residence was converted into the Mount Lavinia Hotel, still a first-class establishment. From its terrace there is a view far out to sea and down to the kilometres of palm-lined beach. During the monsoon period there are high waves and strong undercurrents, which make bathing dangerous.

The name of the hotel does not go back to some woman called Lavinia, but rather to the plant of that name, or possibly to the Singhalese word Lihiniya-gala, which means bird-cliff. The Singhalese, who visit Mount Lavinia mainly at weekends, still call the place, which used to be a fishing village, by its old name of Gakkissa.

Romantic destination: Mount Lavinia

** **Dambulla**

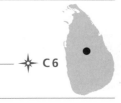

—————————— ✳ C 6

Province: Central Province
Altitude: app. 175m/575ft

Dambulla, a small town on the road between Matale and An-ura-dhapura, is best known for the five caves with numerous Buddha statues and some incredibly unique wall and ceiling paintings, which are among the most beautiful things ever produced by Singhalese artists. The town itself has nothing worth seeing as such, but the large daily market on Matale Road is worth a visit.

CAVE TEMPLES OF DAMBULLA

History Probably one or two of the caves of Dambulla were already holy plac-es in prehistoric times. In the 1st century BC they were taken over by Buddhist monks. In 102 BC King Vatta Gamani Abhaya, also known as Valagam Bahu, hid here when he was driven out of Anuradhapura by the Tamils; not until 85 BC did he succeed in regaining his king-dom. Out of gratitude to the monks who had offered him shelter, he transformed the caves into magnificent temples, making them a **des-tination for pilgrims**, and also founded a monastery. King Vijaya BahuI (1055–1110) had the decoration of the caves restored, and in part redesigned. For this purpose he provided funds for several sculptures and donated land. It is also known that King Nissanka Malla (1187–1196) donated further statues. And finally the rulers of the Kandy kingdom, Senerat (1605–1635) and Kirti Sri Raja Sinha (1747–1778) were also involved in the further re-design of the caves.

Temple museum There is a museum at the car park by the caves of Dambulla that ex-hibits replicas of some of the artworks from the caves. The explana-tions are in English, allowing visitors to gain a good overview of the magnificent, centuries-long period of artistic creation.
❶ Daily, 7.30am–4.30pm, admission charge

Ascent to the temple The black granite cliff, Dambula-gala, is climbed via its east side. The ascent leads first along a simple track, and then up about 250 steps cut into the rock. From the top platform, there is a fine view of the jungle landscape with its many reservoirs, while on clear days, the imposing cliffs of Sigiriya are visible in the distance. In the temple forecourt an inscription in memory of King Nissanka Malla can be seen directly to the right. The entrances to the caves are located be-neath the projecting cliff wall, and are marked by open structures

Dambulla

GETTING THERE

By car: from Kandy via the A 9 (72 km/45mi); from Anuradhapura via the A 13 and A 9 (108 km/67mi), from Kurunegala via the A 6 (55 km/34mi)
By train: the closest station is Habarana (26 km/16mi) on the Colombo – Trincomalee route.
By bus: good bus connections from Kandy and Kurunegala

WHERE TO STAY

Amaya Lake
£ £ £ – £ £ £ £
app. 10 km/6mi northeast of Dambulla
tel. 066 446 15 00
www.amayaresorts.com
A nice hotel in the middle of a large park. The 95 rooms and suites are decorated with Sri Lankan handicrafts. Three restaurants serve local and international cuisine, there is a bar in the evenings. The spa has 14 treatment rooms.

Heritance Kandalama
£ £ £ – £ £ £ £
On the banks of Lake Kandalama (app. 20 min. from Dambulla)
tel. 066 555 50 00
www.heritancehotels.com
The architect Geoffrey Bawa, who is famous on Sri Lanka, got his talented hands involved in this project. The 152 rooms all have a very pleasing interior. The views from some of the rooms of Lake Kandalama is impressively beautiful. There are two restaurants to choose from. Apart from the obligatory trip to the caves of Dambulla, the hotel offers an extensive programme that covers almost everything, from riding elephants to trekking and mountain biking.

Amaya Lake Dambulla £ £ – £ £ £
Kandalama, Dambulla
tel. 066 446 81 00
www.amayaresorts.com
Enjoying a picturesque location by a lake, this hotel has 92 rooms and a large sports programme to offer.

Culture Club
£ £ – £ £ £
tel. 066 223 18 22
www.connaissanceceylon.com
www.ecotourism-culturaltourism.com
This hotel is located in a lovely park not far from the famous rock temples. 92 very comfortable rooms and two restaurants.

Gimanhala Hotel £ £
Anuradhapura Road
tel. 066 228 48 64
gimanhala@hotmail.com
A small hotel with 17 rooms (air conditioning), a restaurant and a bar, located at the northern end of Dambulla. The pool can also be used by non-guests for a fee.

Dambulla Guest House £
Kandy Road
tel. 066 228 47 99
www.ceylonhotels.lk
Since its renovation, this guest house has become a small, cosy hotel. The service is attentive, while the restaurant serves tasty local and international fare. In the evenings guests meet in the bar that faces the street.

** *Cave Temples of Dambulla*

It is well known that the ways to paradise are hard; to get to the wonderful cave temples, visitors have to climb a high, free-standing rock on top of which the Dambulla monastery stands. The hard work is rewarded with breath-taking views across the green plain, framed by hills and the five lavishly decorated temples, whose oldest artworks date back to the pre-Christian era, the newest from the 20th century.

ⓘ Daily 8am – 5pm

❶ Devaraja-lena

The first cave contains a 14 m/46ft statue of a recumbent Buddha who is just about to cross into Nirvana was cut straight from the rock. His favourite pupil, Ananda, is sitting in front of him. The wall and ceiling frescoes, partially restored, date back to the 1st century BC.

❷ Magharaja-lena

The second rock temple is 60m/197ft long, 30m/98ft wide and up to 15m/49ft high, making it not just the largest but also the most beautiful rock temple and also the one with the most precious treasures.

❸ Maha Alut Viharaya

The Buddha statues in the third cave largely date from the 18th century. They include the main cult icon, which depicts Buddha under the Makara arch, as well as a statue of the last Kandy king Sri Kirti Raja Sinha. Here too the walls are lavishly covered with bright frescoes; they depict Buddhas and bodhisattvas in various sizes and poses as well as with different skin colours. They are made out of marble, sandalwood and ebony to achieve that effect.

❹ Pacchima Viharaya (not in the picture)

The small, fourth cave contains five statues in the folksy Kandy style. The small dagoba allegedly once contained the crown jewels of the wife of King Valagamba.

❺ Devana Alut Viharaya (not in the picture)

The most recent of the five caves has a recumbent Buddha as well as several characters of the Hindu pantheon dating from more recent times. The frescoes date from the late Kandy period.

Museum

The monastery contains a small museum that explains how palm leaves are made and much more.

The magnificent recumbent Buddha in the second cave of Dambulla

built on to the cliff; the gable above the main entrance is shaped like a dagoba. The first three caves are the oldest, and in part date back to the 1st century BC; the other two caves are no older than the 18th century.

First cave temple
The first cave bears the name Devaraja-lena (cave of the gods) and contains the 14m/50ft long recumbent figure of a Buddha, carved out of the rock and adorned with fine gold ornamentation. Sitting in front of him is his favourite pupil Ananda.

Second cave temple
The second cave temple, known as Maharaja-lena (cave of the great kings), is **beyond doubt the most beautiful**: 66 juxtaposed Buddha statues of various dates surround a small dagoba. Some of the statues are carved out of the rock. They were once gilded, but today they are simply painted gold. The Buddhas, in the Kandy style, can be recognized by the red stole over the left shoulder and the red hem of their garment. Near to the more westerly of the two entrances is the statue of King Vatta Gamani Abnaya, and opposite him the statues of Vishnu and Rama.

The large standing Buddha statue is surrounded by murals, whose theme is the temptation of Buddha by Mara the seducer: Mara, having been defeated by Buddha, is seen falling from his black elephant, with his army of snakes, demons and mythical beasts around him. Other paintings on the ceiling depict **episodes from Buddha's life**: the attack on Mara's army for example, while the elephant on which Mara sits indicates its submission to Buddha. Further scenes show the start of Siddharta Gautama's path to becoming the founder of a religion, preceded by some scenes of life at the parental court: he proves his mastery of the bow in the palace courtyard; he sets out to practise his use of weapons – his servants are carrying a sword and a discus, among other things – and finally his departure from the palace on his horse Kantaka.

Behind the statues at the end of the cave is a **frieze** depicting scenes from the battle of King Duttha Gamani against the Tamil ruler Elara. In the second half of the 2nd century BC Elara ruled the city of Anuradhapura. In paintings, some of them containing a multitude of figures, come across as very colourful and display compositional idiosyncrasies. These, along with the faces, have given rise to the idea that the artists may have been influenced by the Moghul paintings of the Deccan in India, or possibly even came from there.

Next to the entrance is a small **dagoba**, surrounded by seated Buddhas. Some of them are sitting on cobra plinths, symbolizing the snake-god.

There is one spot in the cave where water drips incessantly from the ceiling. It is caught in a stone basin and is used for ritual ablutions. The constant source does not dry up even in the dry months, and is supposed to have given the place its name: »Dambulla« means »water« in Pali. According to legend, the **secret spring** is part of a subterranean river which is said to flow uphill.

The wow factor of the third cave, Maha Alut Viharaya (great new temple), is its size; it is up to 10m/33ft high. It likewise contains numerous standing and sitting Buddhas, most of them dating from the 18th century. They include the **main cult image**, which shows Buddha beneath the Makara arch, along with a statue of King Kirti Sri Raja Sinha (reigned 1747–1780). Two of the likenesses were carved straight from the rock, which was technically demanding for those times. Here too the walls have a superabundance of murals; they show Buddhas and bodhisattvas of various sizes and in various attitudes, and with different skin colours.

Third cave temple

The small fourth cave (Pacchima Viharaya, western cave) contains five statues and attractive, some of them inexpertly restored, wall paintings. The fifth cave (Devana Alut Viharaya, second new temple) is the most recent; along with a recumbent, relatively modern Buddha, it has figures from the Hindu pantheon. A noteworthy feature is the statue of Devata Bandara, a local deity. The paintings date back to the late Kandy period and were restored in the 1920s.

Fourth and fifth cave temples

Dedigama

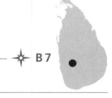

✧ **B 7**

Province: Sabaragamuwa
Altitude: app. 83m/272ft

Dedigama, located in the foothills of the gentle Sabaragamuwa highlands, is important mainly because one of the most glorious of the rulers of the Singhalese kingdom, Parakrama Bahul, was born here. He emerged as victor from the battles of the princes for the kingship. In the 14th century, Dedigama became the residence of King Parakrama Bahu V, who ruled over one of the island's three independent kingdoms from here.

WHAT TO SEE IN DEDIGAMA

The Mahavamsa chronicle reports that King Parakrama Bahu I had a massive dagoba erected at the exact place where he first saw the light of day. However it was only recently that Dedigama could be positively identified as this site. The dagoba called Kota Vihara was

Punkhagama (dagoba)

Dedigama

GETTING THERE
By car: from Colombo via the A 1 until just after Ambepussa, then turn right (68 km/42mi). From Kandy via the A 1 until a few kilometres after Nelundeniya, then turn left (50 km/31mi)
By train: the closest train station is Alawwa (11 km/7mi away)

By bus: good connections from Colombo and Kandy.

WHERE TO STAY
There is no recommendable accommodation in Dedigama. The proximity to Kandy makes it advisable to look for accommodation there and visit Dedigama as part of a day trip.

elaborately restored in the early 1980s. It is in the splendour of the Polonnaruwa style and has **relic chambers**. Some of the contents are to be seen in the small nearby archaeological museum, among them a very beautiful bronze oil-lamp decorated with dancing figures and an elephant. The museum also has some Buddha statues and other finds from the immediate vicinity.

Kumarankanda Raja Maha Vihara   Some 5km/3mi further south, in the strictly isolated forest hermitage of Salgala, Buddhist monks lead an ascetic life of meditation. The monastery has a long tradition, but was re-occupied only in 1931.

* Ella

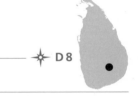

✦ D 8

Province: Uva
Altitude: 1012m/3320ft

Ella lies in the enchanting jungle landscape of the Uva plateau with its caves, gorges and waterfalls. In many places, there are wonderful panoramas of the varied landscape. The town is a suitable base for walking as well as interesting drives, for example through the Ella Gap.

WHAT TO SEE IN ELLA

Legendary view   From the Ella Rest House there are perhaps the most fantastic views that Sri Lanka has to offer, ranging across the amazing landscape all the way to the sea about 100km/60mi away. The large cave, now filled with water, in front of the Rest House is where the demon king Ravana is said to have kept Sita, the consort of Prince Rama, captive and hidden. In the Neolithic period, the cave was probably inhabited, as simple tools, mainly of quartz, of the Balangoda culture have been found in other caves in the vicinity.

SURROUNDINGS OF ELLA

The Dowa Temple, app. 6km/4mi south of Ella, is worth a visit. There are some steps leading into the interior of the temple, which is completely carved out of the rock. The wall paintings have been very carefully restored by the monks in recent years. Also worthy of note are the statues of various Hindu deities and an 8.1m/27ft tall image which probably dates from the 10th century and is said to represent the bodhisattva Maitreya.   **Dowa Temple**

Ella

GETTING THERE
By car: from Bandarawela on the A 16 (12 km/7.5mi); from Badulla on the A 16 (18 km/11mi)
By train: station on the route between Colombo and Badulla
By bus: good connections from Bandarawela and Badulla

WHERE TO STAY/EAT
Grand Ella Motel £ £ – £ £ £
Wellawaya Road
tel. 057 222 86 55
www.ceylonhotels.lk
Even just the drive there takes you through a fascinating mountain landscape, past paddy fields and tea plantations. Ever since its renovation the motel has been a three-star establishment.

Ella Adventure Park £ £ – £ £ £
app. 10 km/6mi to the south of Ella on the road to Wellawaya
tel. 057 228 72 63
www.ellaadventurepark.com
This hotel almost offers campfire ro-

mance in a landscape that is one of Sri Lanka's most beautiful. Stay in one of the nine pretty rooms, or in a tree house.

Insider Tip
Mountain Heavens £ £
On the road between Bandarawela and Wellawaya
tel. 057 492 57 57
www.mountainheavensella.com
Maybe the nicest hotel in Ella, and definitely one with fantastic views. Large windows give guests a magnificent view of the surrounding mountains. The restaurant serves both local specialities and international dishes.

Waterfall Homestay £ – £ £
tel. 057 567 69 33
www.waterfalls-guesthouse-ella.com
The view of the Ravana Falls is stunning, especially during the rainy season when the water plummets down in powerful cascades. The owners from Australia look after their few guests very well. The three rooms are comfortable and tastefully decorated.

Waterfalls 6km/4mi south-east of Ella a road leading downhill to Wellawaya passes the foaming **Ravana Falls**. A further 13km/9mi west of Wellawaya are the majestic **Diyaluma Falls**, whose water plunges about 175m/575ft. This is the highest waterfall in Sri Lanka.

Rock statues of Buduruvagala In the middle of the jungle near Buduruvagala is a group of important rock statues, carved according to some sources in the 8th or 9th century AD, according to others, though, as early as the 4th century BC. They can be accessed from Wellawaya (app. 7km/4mi) via the Tissamaharama Road leading south, then turn right and continue for 4km/2.5mi along the unmetalled road. The centrepiece of the relief statues carved out of the rock is a 15m/50ft tall standing Buddha in the gesture of fearlessness (abhaya-mudra). He is flanked by two groups of three, whose 7.3m/24ft tall centre figures each represent a bodhisattva (an enlightened being). The one on the left, probably the bodhisattva Avalokitesvara, which symbolizes universal compassion. Artistically it is the best of the seven. Alongside him in graceful tribhanga pose is the goddess Tara, holding a vase with a lotus in her hand. The figure on the other side probably represents Sudhana Kumara, the companion of Avalokitesvara. The bodhisattva on the right may be Vajrapani, a »guardian of the doctrine«, who holds the Vajra (lightning, thunderbolt), but may represent the bodhisattva Maitreya. Legend has it that it is Upatissa, a son of King Silakala (523–535). **This king was the first in Sri Lanka to forbid the killing of animals, in accordance with Buddhist teaching. The two other figures have not been identified.

❶ Daily 9am–5pm, admission 300Rs

Archaeological museum **Wellawaya** has an Archaeological Museum that exhibits several interesting fragments of Buddha statues that have an original connection to the statues of Buduruvagala.

❶ Wed–Mon 8.30–5pm, admission free

** Galle

✳ B 9

Province: Southern
Altitude: 7m/25ft
Population: 91,000

Visitors to Galle might be forgiven for thinking they were back in the 17th century – that is how well the buildings of the Dutch colonial period have been preserved. The main reason for their good state of repair may well be that when the British took the town in 1798, not a shot was fired. Today Galle is a UNESCO World Heritage Site.

As a natural harbour, Galle was of great strategic importance for the Arabs and Chinese at an early date, and later also for the colonial powers. Today Galle is **Sri Lanka's seventh-biggest city**, and is home to many Muslims and Christians, alongside the Buddhists, who form by far the largest faith group. The city is known too for its industry, primarily cement production and fisheries and tuna in particular. Galle is, in addition, a **craft centre**; its lace-making is well-known. In the hinterland are a few tea, rubber and coconut plantations. The harbour is mainly employed exporting tea all over the world.

Industrial location

The Fort district has a striking layout

Worst tsunami damage
Galle was the scene of some of the worst damage caused by the tsunami of 26 December 2004. While the massive fort by the harbour withstood the wave, more than 1000 people were killed in the bus station behind it within a few minutes.

Name of the city
The name Galle derives from the Singhalese word Gala (cliff, mountain, but also place to rest). The Dutch incidentally confused Gala with the Latin gallus (cockerel), an error which explains the cockerel on the coat-of-arms of the **Dutch East India company**. The Arabs, who probably ran a trading dock in Galle as long ago as the 9th century, called the city Kalahl.

14th century	First mention of the harbour in Galle
1505	The Portuguese land in Galle and build a fort in 1589.
1640	The Dutch take Galle, destroy the fort and build one of their own in 1663.
1796	The British take Galle without a fight.
1815	Galle's position as the most important harbour on the south-west coast is lost to Colombo.

History
Galle could be the place mentioned in the Bible as **Tarsis**, which King Solomon only knew from hearsay, but from where he got gemstones, silk and spices. The Chinese and Arabs conducted much of their trade via Galle, their goods being shipped from here as far afield as Genoa and Venice. In the 9th century Galle seems to have been a significant Arab trade settlement. In 1505 Portuguese ships trying to capture Arab spice ships coming from Sumatra or the Malay peninsula chanced upon Galle when they were driven into the harbour by a storm. They soon departed, on to return in 1518 with the intention of getting a foothold on the island. The first Portuguese trading settlement and a small church date from 1543; in 1587 the Singhalese king was forced to hand over the entire town to the Portuguese, who built a fort they called Santa Cruz. Within a short time they had built a rampart and three bastions, and fortified the harbour.

After the Dutch under General Coster had landed with twelve ships at the future Sun Bastion in Galle harbour in 1640, they only needed 2000 men to take the city. In 1663 they surrounded the headland with fortifications, which were greatly reinforced under the Dutch governor Petrus Vuysr (1728–29). In addition the Dutch built kitchens, administrative buildings and houses. In 1796 the Dutch governor Dieterich Thomas Fretzsz handed over the Galle garrison keys to the British major general, Lachlan Macquarie without a fight.

The further development of the harbour suffered from the fact that offshore coral reefs made access much harder in stormy weather. As a result the British chose Colombo as their main port and developed that instead. The harbour in Galle became more and more insignificant.

Galle

GETTING THERE
By car: from Colombo, Kalutara and Hikkaduwa on the A 2 (from Colombo 115 km/71mi); from Matara on the A 2 (45 km/28mi)
By train: station on the stretch from Colombo to Matara
By bus: good bus connections from Colombo and all the other towns cited above

SIGHTSEEING
It is easy to explore Galle on foot. The wide wall around the fort, which is partially overgrown with grass, is a good landmark. A walk takes a bit more than an hour, but can easily be extended to two hours by taking the same route back to the starting point. It starts at the main gate in the northern part and ends at Triton Bastion.

SHOPPING
There are many street vendors in the Fort district selling hand-made lace tablecloths and wood carvings for inexpensive prices. There are also countless shops in Galle that have specialized in antique furniture and in shipping it reliably to Europe.

MARKETS
Markets take place every morning in Galle, such as in Main Street and especially the fruit and vegetable market, the Dutch Market. This is also a good places to get original spice mixes at inexpensive prices.

SOUVENIRS
Laksala
74, Sea Street
www.laksala.lk
daily 9am – 7pm
One good place to shop for souvenirs is in the state-run Laksala branch in Galle. It is not possible to barter here; the prices are fixed.

SHOPPING CENTRES
Outside the fort is the Selaka Shopping Complex, a large department store with lots of shops and some small restaurants. Right next door is a Cargills store, a supermarket with snack bars that also has a pharmacy.

ANTIQUES
Olanda Antiques
30 Leyn Ban Street
www.olandafurniture.com
daily 9am – 6pm
Anyone in search of antiques will definitely find something in Olanda. The building also houses a cosy café.

TEXTILES
Barefoot
49 Pedlar Street
daily 9am – 7pm
Barefoot sells pretty textiles made in Sri Lanka.

LACE
Shoba Display Gallery
67 Pedlar Street
www.shobafashion.org
daily 9am – 6pm
Anyone wanting to watch how beautiful lace is made is at the right place here. This dying art is practised by women who work for fixed wages at the Shoba Life to Hands Women's Co-operative Society. There is a café here

as well, which is open every day from September to May from 7.30am – 10pm.

WHERE TO STAY/EAT

❶ *Amangalla*
£ £ £ £
Church Street
tel. 091 223 33 88
www.amanresorts.com
Stylish accommodation in the Dutch Fort: the Amangalla is located in the former New Oriental Hotel. It is one of the island's most expensive hotels. Double rooms start at £600 per night.

❸ *The Fort Printers*
£ £ £ £
39, Pedlar Street
tel. 091 224 79 77
www.thefortprinters.com
Following the trend of converting old buildings into modern hotels, this establishment was set up in the Dutch fort. It has only five stylish rooms.

❹ *The Fortress*
£ £ £ £
Matara Road, Kogolla Beach,
PO Box 126
tel. 091 438 94 00
www.thefortress.lk
A luxury option near Galle with all the creature comforts. The architecture is inspired by the Dutch forts. There are elaborately designed gardens and water landscapes behind the walls.

❷ *Galle Fort Hotel*
£ £ £ – £ £ £ £
28, Church Street
Galle Fort
tel. 091 223 28 70

www.galleforthotel.com
New hotel in the 300-year-old listed building of an old-established merchant family. Individual atmosphere, outstanding and yet inexpensive restaurant, which is open to non-guests too.

❺ *Light House*
£ £ £ – £ £ £ £
Dadella
(at the northern end of town)
tel. 091 222 37 44
www.jetwinghotels.com
The top address in Galle. Even just the stairs leading up to the reception are impressive. 60 very comfortable rooms, all with sea views and top quality gastronomy as well as a pool and a private beach.

❻ *Closenberg*
£ £ £ – £ £ £ £
11, Closenberg Road
Magalle
tel. 091 222 43 13
www.closenberghotel.com
Legendary building dating from 1860, situated on a headland and surrounded by a lovely garden. The 20 rooms and suites have been furnished with many lovely colonial-style antiques.

❼ *The Lady Hill*
£ £
29, Upper Dickson Road
tel. 091 224 43 22
www.ladyhills.com

Insider Tip

The rooftop bar is probably the place with the best view of Galle and the sea. The 15 rooms are friendly and comfortable.

TOUR OF THE FORT DISTRICT

The Fort district, the old Dutch town centre, is located on a small **Old Dutch** peninsula and is separated from the Kaluwella district by the old **town centre** Dutch Parana Ela canal, and from the Dharmapala Park district (formerly Victoria Park) and the Pettah to the east of the canal on the harbour bay by a stretch of grass known as the Esplanade. The Butterfly Bridge, dating from Dutch times, and the Main Street connect Fort and Pettah with Kaluwella. The fort still contains 400 extant colonial buildings. 240 of them are owned by locals, 100 are occupied by public authorities and the rest are in the hands of foreigners who tend to develop them into luxury homes. However, because of their World Heritage Site status, there are strict regulations that have to be adhered to when renovating them.

The ramparts of the fortifications, a **popular promenade**, follow the line of the shore and on the landward side separate the peninsula from the hinterland. Their length is about 4km/2.5mi, including the second rampart, which the Dutch built to reinforce the first. The ramparts have eleven bastions, of which the Star, Moon and Sun Bastions secured the fort to the landward side.

The Fort is entered today by the New Gate constructed by the British **New Gate** in 1873. They also built the Clock Tower. The Moon Bastion on the Esplanade stands on the remains of the Portuguese fort, the Conceyçao, while the Star Bastion stands on the remains of the St Antonia fort, also built by the Portuguese. To the west are the Aeolus, Clippenburg, Neptune – on which the signal station once stood – and Triton bastions, built in around 1730. On the cliffs known as Vlagge Klipp and Flag Rock at the southern tip there were once a further Portuguese bastion and a lighthouse.

The new lighthouse stands on Point Utrecht Bastion, while nearby **Bastions** looms the former Powder Tower with an inscription that records that it was completed in 1782. The next bastions are Autors Bastion and Akersloot Bastion, named after General Coster's birthplace. During the Dutch colonial period there is said to have been an underground passage between Akersloot and Zwart Bastion (Black Bastion, today a police station). Zwart Bastion is probably the oldest of all the fortifications; the remains of the Portuguese Santa Cruz fort, dating from 1580, can still be seen. Here incoming ships used to be inspected and let into the harbour through a grid, which still exists.

From 1669 and 1873, the old gate formed the only entrance to the city. The relief on the outside of the gate shows the coat-of-arms of King George III of Great Britain (reigned 1760–1820), while that on the inside shows that of the Dutch East India Company, flanked by two lions, surmounted by a cockerel, and below, the date 1669 in Ro-

!

Jewellery, antiques, handicrafts

The Historical Museum in one of the fort's oldest buildings (1618) is worth a visit. It has an interesting, eclectic collection of antiques and handicrafts (Leyn Baan Street 31, Tue – Sun 9am – 6pm).

man numerals. The Sun Bastion was built in 1667 and forms the northern boundary of the harbour. Between it and Zwart Bastion there used to be two more forts, Vismark Bastion diagonally opposite the New Oriental Hotel, which is now the luxury Amangalla Hotel, and Commandment Bastion. The street names are English translations of the Dutch names. Any walk through the district will pass former Dutch administrative buildings, one Dutch and two English churches, a Buddhist temple and the former residences of wealthy English merchants, built in the typical Dutch style.

Government House The old Government House near the old gate (Queen's House), today the headquarters of Walker, Son & Co., was once the residence of the Dutch governor of Galle, and then of the British administrator. The stone plaque above the entrance features a cockerel and the date 1683.

Churches Of the old Dutch church of 1640 nothing now remains. The present **Dutch church** in Church Street, completed in 1755, was endowed by Gertuyda Adriana de Grand in gratitude for having given birth to a daughter after years of childless marriage. The church has two fine Baroque gables. The floor inside, paved with grave slabs, is worth seeing. Opposite the church is an bell-tower (1701). Somewhat further along Church Street is the Anglican All Saints' Church, built in 1871, with epitaphs from British colonial days. Further still are the Arab College, and, near the seafront, the mosque. In Light House Street is the Methodist church, dating from 1894, while at the intersection of Rampatt/ Great Modera Baystreet is the Sri Sudharmalaya Buddhist temple.

Galle National Museum Galle's National Museum is located in Church Street near the main gate to the fort. It is housed in an old building dating back to the Dutch period and displays a curious mix of exhibits. It is nonetheless worth a visit. The collection includes traditional wooden masks.
❶ Tue–Sat, 9am–5pm, admission charge

Dutch Period Museum This museum, also known as the Historical Mansion, is an absolute must for anyone visiting Galle. But this museum too has a tendency to be deliciously jumbled in its collection, which consists of all kinds of interesting and curious objects. The museum, which was opened in 1992, was founded by a committed gem trader and collector called H.M.H.A. Gaffar. Over the course of more than 40 years of collecting, he acquired everything he could get his hands on: Chinese porcelain

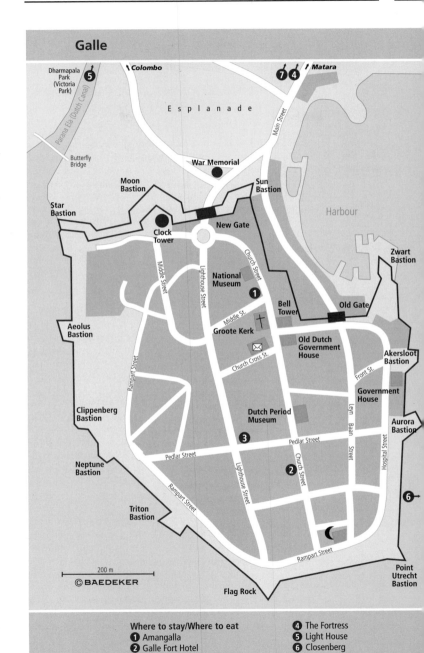

Galle

Dharmapala Park (Victoria Park)

Parang Ela (Dutch Canal)

Butterfly Bridge

Colombo

E s p l a n a d e

Matara

Main Street

War Memorial

Moon Bastion

Sun Bastion

Star Bastion

Harbour

Clock Tower

New Gate

Middle Street

Zwart Bastion

Lighthouse Street

National Museum

Church Street

Aeolus Bastion

Bell Tower

Old Gate

Middle St.

Groote Kerk

Rampart Street

Church Cross St.

Old Dutch Government House

Akersloot Bastion

Front St.

Government House

Clippenberg Bastion

Dutch Period Museum

Leyn Baan Street

Aurora Bastion

Pedlar Street

Pedlar Street

Neptune Bastion

Church Street

Lighthouse Street

Hospital Street

Pedlar Street

Rampart Street

Triton Bastion

200 m

© BAEDEKER

Rampart Street

Flag Rock

Point Utrecht Bastion

Where to stay/Where to eat
1 Amangalla
2 Galle Fort Hotel
3 The Fort Printers
4 The Fortress
5 Light House
6 Closenberg
7 The Lady Hill

recovered from shipwrecks, tiles of Dutch provenance, old typewriters, antique furniture and much more. The building, which was originally the residence of the Dutch governor, dates back to 1860 and a few years ago was carefully restored, in part using original Dutch designs. The small shop sells souvenirs at quite inexpensive prices.

❶ 31–39 Leyn Baan Street, Fort: Sat–Tue, 9am–6pm, Fri noon–2pm, admission free

National Maritime Museum This very worthwhile museum, totally destroyed by the tsunami and re-opened in 2010 with Dutch support, is located on the ground floor of a former warehouse near the Old Gate. It too has been recently carefully restored; ever since it has provided an interesting overview of the history of seafaring on Sri Lanka and in Galle in particular. The museum was designed with educational criteria in mind and since it has a lot of hands-on exhibits, it is **particularly suitable for a visit with children**. One of the especially impressive exhibits is a 13m/43ft whale skeleton mounted on the roof.

❶ Tue–Sat 9am–5pm, admission 300 rs

OTHER SIGHTS

Kaluwella (district) North-west of the Fort, on the other side of Dharmapala Park, is the district of Kaluwella (black town), the **native quarter** – as opposed to Fort, the white, or European, quarter. Right by the grounds of the Town Hall on Calvary Hill is the Roman Catholic cathedral of St Mary, built in 1874.

Pettah To the east of the harbour is the Pettah, the **bazaar quarter** of Galle. With a bit of luck you might find some pretty craft items. In the Kerkhof, a Dutch cemetery near the market, are the graves of Dutch officials and officers. The gate bears the inscription »Memento mori« (»Remember You Will Die«) and the date 1786. From this date this cemetery presumably replaced the two older ones inside the Fort.

SURROUNDINGS OF GALLE

Kogalla At the milestone with the inscription 83, south of Galle, a road turns off the left towards the Kathaluwa Temple, about 3km/2mi further on. Its interior walls are covered with paintings by four 18th-century artists. They depict, arranged in friezes, scenes from the Jataka, the various lives of Buddha, dancers, and a group of musicians dressed in Western costumes. The style is provincial, and the depiction of the human figures somewhat clumsy. The plants and animals are by con-

Intact residential quarter that dates back to the Dutch period

trast more lively. What is remarkable, though, is the artists' delight in story-telling and the relatively subtle coloration.

Typical of this region is surf-angling, which can be seen on the way from Ahangama, a few kilometres to the east of Kogalla. The fishermen sit on pillars about 5m/17ft high driven into the sea-bed. From there they cast their lines. As serious attempts to catch anything are only made in the early morning, or maybe in the evening just about, any anglers who can be observed in the daytime or who sit around on the shore are doing it for the tourists, in other words they are hoping for a tip.

Surf-angling

Gal Oya National Park

✦ D–E 7

Province: Eastern/Uva
Altitude: 7–30m/25–100ft

Gal Oya National Park is 256sq km/100sq mi in extent, making it Sri Lanka's fourth-largest. The hilly landscape, dominated by high grass and trees, is criss-crossed by waterways, while the horizon is marked by the bizarre outlines of rocks and mountains.

Vedda homeland

The area has always been considered the tribal homeland of the Vedda, of whom there are still a few hundred living here. However, only very few of them still live in the traditional manner as hunters and gatherers because that tends to lead to conflicts with the farmers and national park administration.

The National Park is one result of the damming of the Gal Oya to create the huge Lake Senanayake, Sri Lanka's largest lake, natural or artificial. It was the focus of an ambitious development project which has brought the region a certain prosperity. Since the end of the civil war, access to the park is unrestricted.

WHAT TO SEE IN GAL OYA NATIONAL PARK

Senanayake Dam

The Senanayake Dam, built with American support, is 1200m/1300yd long and 90m/300ft high. Its construction created the lake of the same name, some 90sq km/35sq mi in area; it commemorates the first Prime Minister of Sri Lanka, then called Ceylon, Don Stephen Senanayake. The whole project includes a number of other, albeit much smaller, reservoirs, among them the Ekgal Aru, the Jayanthi Wewa and the Namal Oya Wewa, along with some rivers and canals in the valley of the Gal Oya. The economic development gave rise to a few small factories on the fringe of the National Park. Additional inhabitants were also enticed into the area because of the economic activity.

Nature conservation area

The main entrance to the nature conservation area is a few kilometres to the west of ▶Ampara, where Jeeps can be hired. Like all of Sri Lanka's national parks, it may only be explored on land by Jeep in the company of a ranger, while **leaving the vehicle within the park is strictly forbidden**. However it is also possible to explore the park by boat; information about this is available at the main entrance.

The Gal Oya National Park is primarily the home of numerous wild elephants, but there are also deer, including the white-spotted chital, a few leopards and, allegedly, some bears, which are, it must be said, rarely seen. The banks of the waterways are a paradise for numerous birds. Among them is the toucan, easily recognizable by its oversized bill. Occasionally crocodiles can also be seen.

Vedda caves

Inside and outside the National Park there are a few caves which were originally occupied by the Vedda. For example in the Danigala mountains at a height of more than 610m/2000ft and near Makara, which is also a good place to observe wild elephants. Ratugala, 32km/20mi north of Inginiyagala, is home to a small **tribe of Vedda**, who live in the jungle in fairly primitive conditions. In Gonagala there are some

Gal Oya National Park

GETTING THERE
By car: from Colombo via Kandy and Mahiyangana – Maha Oya – Ampara – Inginiyangala
(app. 290 km/180mi) or via Ratnapura – Wellawaya – Siyambalanduwa – Inginiyala
(app. 320 km/200mi)

Visiting times: unlimited
Park entrance and office of the wildlife protection authority: in Ingiyaniyala at the southern side of the protected area, app. 22 km/14mi west of Ampara
Admission fee: app. USD10

WHERE TO STAY
There are some state-run, basic chalets that are functionally equipped and there is also a campsite.

Mahoora Luxury Tented Safari Camp £££–££££
Near the park entrance
tel. 077 772 15 06
www.mahoora.lk
No hotel, no bungalows, but tents with varying degrees of comfort. An ideal starting point for ranger-accompanied trips through Gal Oya National Park. The restaurant serves authentic Singhalese fare; the bar and the camp fire are two popular meeting spots in the evening.

caves with rock paintings, which presumably date from the 3rd or 8th century, the remains of a dagoba and a moonstone.

On the south-east edge of the National Park is the rocky summit of the 558m/1830ft mountain known as Westminster Abbey, from where there is a magnificent view. It was given its unusual name by British seafarers, who, sailing along the coast, were reminded of the silhouette of the church in London. At the foot of the rock is another Vedda cave.

Westminster Abbey (mountain)

Giritale

✷ C 5/6

Province: North Central
Altitude: app. 105m/340ft

One of Sri Lanka's oldest reservoirs, which was restored at the start of the 20th century, forms the focus of one of the most interesting nature conservation areas on the island. The landscape is extraordinarily attractive, with jungle alternating with open grassland. Thanks to Giritale's favourable transport links, it is a good starting point for visiting the ruins of Polonnaruwa and the rock fort of Sigiriya.

Giritale

GETTING THERE

By car: from Habarana to Minneriya
(20 km/12mi), from there onwards to
Giritale (12 km/7.5mi); from Polon-
naruwa to Giritale (12 km/7.5mi)
By train: stations on the Gal Oya – Bat-
ticaloa line are Minneriya and Hingu-
rakgoda (both app. 6 km/3.5mi from
Giritale).
By bus: good connections from
Habarana, Polonnaruwa and Minneriya

WHERE TO STAY
The Deer Park Hotel £££–££££
tel. 027 224 62 72
www.deerparksrilanka.com
77 very comfortable cottages, pool and
spa. Some of the rooms have lovely
views of Minneriya Reservoir.

Giritale Hotel ££–£££
tel. 027 224 63 11
www.giritalehotel.com
The hotel, which has 42 rooms, provides plenty of comforts and lovely
views of the reservoir. A renovation is
being planned in the near future. Till
then, at least, the prices are moderate.

The Royal Lotus Hotel ££–£££
tel. 027 224 63 16
www.royal-lotus-hotel-giritale-sri-lanka.
lakpura.com
Comfortable hotel with 54 inviting
rooms and attentive service. The best
options are the chalets with the particularly good interiors. The view of the
lake is remarkable. In the afternoons it
is possible to watch wild elephants
from the terrace.

WHAT TO SEE IN GIRITALE

Minneriya reservoir The Minneriya reservoir with an area of app. 1800 hectares or 4500 acres was created in AD 275 by King Maha Sena, taking its water from the Elahera canal dating from a century earlier. In 1903 the reservoir was renovated, having silted up considerably, and connected by a 140km/90mi extension of the Elahera canal to the Kandul and Kantale reservoirs further to the north.

Giritale reservoir The small Giritale reservoir, built in the 7th century, is also connected to the canal network; like the other reservoirs, it too provides for adequate irrigation for the local agriculture.

Giritale Minneriya Sanctuary Impenetrable jungle and open grasslands characterize the Giritale Minneriya Sanctuary a few kilometres from Giritale. It is home to not only more than 150 wild elephants, but also leopards, which are how-ever rarely seen. There is a better chance of observing the diverse lo-cal birdlife. No fewer than 39 species have been counted on a single walk through the sanctuary, including the white-throated kingfisher, various paddybirds, the Sri Lankan brown fish-owl, the Indian oriole and the koel, a grey-spotted cuckoo species. A **boat trip on the Minneriya reservoir** is a good idea, as it will provide a sighting of a large number of birds. On the edge of the sanctuary there are a few sizable teak plantations planted by the government as part of the re-afforestation programme.

Hambantota

✦ **D 9**

Province: Southern
Altitude: 7m/25ft
Population: 12,000

The town is a centre for obtaining sea-salt and a lively fishing port. It is located in the dry zone of the south coast on a splendidly curving bay. Typical of the region are the undemanding palmyra palms which have been planted in an attempt to secure the shifting dunes.

In addition to the Singhalese, this place is home to many Malays, who are adherents of Islam. They are said to have given the place its name: hambans (little boat) and tota (harbour) are words in Malay. Hambantota is also a good starting point for trips through the ►Yala National Park.

Tsunami damage

Hambantota was not merely damaged by the tsunami: almost the whole place was washed away over a length of a kilometre by a flood wave up to 12m/39ft high. At the Sunday market alone, which was in progress at the time, more than 5,000 people lost their lives in the space of just a few minutes. The Hambantota region became a model for speedy and unbureaucratic reconstruction. As a result, most of the signs of the disaster have now been removed.

In spring 2013 a second international airport, the Mattala Rajapaksa International Airport, was opened near Hambantota – the other being in Colombo – and it is even large enough to accommodate long-haul flights. Once complete, it aims to process around five million passengers a year. Flights to and from Europe are however not yet possible. Environmentalists have criticized this airport for its questionable proximity to the national parks. A further prestige project is the Mahinda Rajapaksa International Stadium, which was opened in 2009 and named after the incumbent prime minister, who was born here. This stadium, which officially belongs to the Sri Lankan army, hosts international cricket matches. It can hold almost 60,000 spectators.

A new dock with four terminals has been built with Chinese funds. It cost around 6 billion US dollars and opened in 2010.

Hatton · Dikoya

GETTING THERE
By car: from Colombo via Avissawella on the A 7 (135 km/443mi); from Nu-wara Eliya on the A 7 (48 km/157mi); from Kandy on the A 5 to Ginigathena, then on the A 7 (72 km/236mi)
By train: the station of this twin town is located on the highlands route
By bus: good bus connections from all the abovementioned towns

WHERE TO STAY
Castlereigh Holiday Bungalow
£ – £ £
tel. 051 222 36 88
www.castlereigh.net
This guesthouse with its five rooms is situated in the magnificent mountain landscape. The rooms are well looked after and clean and there is a restaurant.

WHAT TO SEE IN HATTON AND DIKOYA

Landscape   The landscape around Hatton is a sight in itself: rolling hills, on which it doesn't just look as if every square metre is covered in tea-bushes, dense green forests and the backdrop of magnificent mountains. A visit is recommended especially between December and March, when there is hardly any rain and the air is pleasantly fresh.

Tea factories   A visit to a tea factory is an interesting experience, usually taking about half an hour. During this time visitors will find out a great deal about the processing of the leaves and about the different varieties. Among the properties than can be visited are the Mount Vernon Estate and Court Lodge Estate near Dambulla and Talawakelle, and the Tea Research Institute in St Combs Estate; **no booking necessary**. In most tea factories the tour ends with a freshly brewed cup of tea. Even so, visitors should remember the poor conditions in which the countless tea-pluckers live and work. Their work is hard, while their pay is very low.

✳ Hikkaduwa

✳ B 9

Province: Southern
Altitude: 5–36m/18–130ft

Hikkaduwa is a bathing resort famous for its beautiful beaches, located on the southwest coast of Sri Lanka. Its famous coral reefs however have been seriously damaged by both human and environmental influences. Even so, Hikkaduwa has lost little of its popularity, and the hospitality of the inhabitants continues to be its greatest capital.

Hikkaduwa was also badly hit by the tsunami and almost all the ho- **After the**
tels along the coast were seriously damaged. All have since reopened, **tsunami**
however, and the proprietors have made the best of the situation by
upgrading their rooms. In the low season, Hikkaduwa looks almost
deserted, but even at this time bathing is possible in some places.

WHAT TO SEE IN HIKKADUWA

Although the coral gardens near the coast have been placed under **Coral reefs**
protection as the Hikkaduwa Coral Sanctuary, they are no longer the
preferred goal of divers and snorkellers. However the variety of the
marine life is still considerable. One great way to spot numerous fish
species, molluscs etc. is by going on a **trip in a glass-bottomed
boat**. Beyond the coral banks there are also large fish such as barra-
cuda and Moray eels, as well as turtles. The worldwide phenomenon
of coral bleach has not spared the coral reefs of Hikkaduwa either.
Much that was spared by both disasters mentioned above was destroyed by careless divers and snorkelers. Nevertheless, Hikkaduwa
is still a popular destination for underwater sports enthusiasts, and
wreck divers in particular. There are more than 20 shipwrecks on
the sea floor close to the coast. Some of them make good diving even
for beginners. They include the Earl of Shaftesbury, a four-masted
British vessel with a steel hull, which sank in 1893, or the steam-
powered Conch, which ran aground on rocks ten years later. Another attractive destination is the Lord Nelson, a cargo ship that capsized
during a severe storm in 2000 and is now also on the sea floor.

The landscape around Hikkaduwa is not only marked by wide and **Landscape**
fairly well looked after beaches, but also by a hinterland covered by a
broad variety of vegetation. To the north of the town centre there is
a large lagoon, with boat trips on offer.

Some 2km/1.5mi from Hikkaduwa bus station is Sinigama Vihara **Sinigama**
temple. The only way to reach it is via a wooden walkway. It is one of **Vihara**
two temples in Sri Lanka where people who have been robbed pray
for the return of their property. In the temple there is a special oil
which can be ignited at home, whereupon the thief will be beset by
disease, accident or some other unpleasant fate. In order to avoid
worse, he then gives himself up.

SURROUNDINGS OF HIKKADUWA

The present Buddhist temple of Purana Totagama Raja Maha Vihara **Telwatta**
in Telwatta, a small town to the north of Hikkaduwa, was built in

Hikkaduwa's beauty under water

1805, but goes back to an earlier foundation. At the start of the 15th century this was the home of Sri Lanka's most famous poet Sri Ranula, before King Parakrama BahuII summoned him to his court in Kotte. The Makara arch at the entrance is regarded as one of the most beautiful of the Kandy period. The figure of the god Amora with arrows tipped with flowers is unusual. This motif from European art seems to have come here if anything by chance. The murals inside depict scenes from the life of the Buddha.

Dodanduwa The fishing village of Dodanduwa is picturesquely located on the magnificent Lake Ratgama, formed by the Ratgama Oya, on which there are a number of luxuriantly vegetated islets. Lots of cinnamon bushes grow in the immediate surroundings. The villagers are known for their strict Buddhism.

The temple of **Kumarankanda Raja Maha Vihara** in the middle of the village has some very fine murals and a footprint of the Buddha. Also of note are various statues of gods.

About 1km/1100yd further on stands the **temple of Sailabima Aramaya**, reached by a long stone staircase. The murals tell of Buddha's birth and depict other scenes from his various lives (Jakata). This was the site of Sri Lanka's first school for the sons of Buddhist laymen, as well as a college for the monastic community.

Hikkaduwa

GETTING THERE
By car: from Colombo on the A 2 (110 km/68mi); from Galle on the A 2 (19 km/12mi).
By train: station on the train line from Colombo to Matara
By bus: good bus connections from Colombo and from Galle

BEACHES
The beaches of Hikkaduwa are considered the best for surfing in Sri Lanka. Surfers from all around the world come here between November and April; the more skilled surf at the southern end of the coral reef. Some shops hire out boards. The water is also good for swimming, but this is not a place to get away from the crowds.

MARKET
A large Sunday Market supplied by farmers from the surrounding area is held on Sundays above the station.

WHERE TO EAT
There are countless good restaurants in and around Hikkaduwa. Most of them can be found on the main road by the beach. During the low season, between May to October, many of the restaurants are closed.

Restaurant Refresh £ £ – £ £ £
384, Galle Road
tel. 091 227 81 78 10
Large menu, lots of fresh fish straight from the sea. Good atmosphere, but therefore a bit pricier than average.

Spaghetti & Co. £ £ – £ £ £
Galle Road

tel. 077 697 32 99
Daily 6am – 11pm
Not the only Italian but the best in Hikkaduwa. Excellent pasta and pizza, but expensive

Abbas Restaurant £ – £ £
7, Waulagoda Road
tel. 091 227 71 10
Railway fans will enjoy this place because the tracks go right by the restaurant. But it serves the best steaks in town as well as good coffee. And there are not that many trains.

WHERE TO STAY
Amaya Coral Rock
£ £ £ – £ £ £ £
340, Galle Road
tel. 091 227 70 21
www.amayacoralrock.com
The Coral Rock is one of the best addresses in town. It has 64 tastefully furnished rooms. The meals are served either à la carte or as a buffet. There is a kids' club for children during the day.

Chaaya Tranz £ £ £ – £ £ £ £
390, Galle Road
tel. 091 227 73 87
www.chaayahotels.com
Under its old name, Coral Gardens, this hotel on the sea was one of the less expensive hotels in Hikkaduwa. After it was taken over by John Keells Holdings and was expanded to 150 rooms, the hippie atmosphere disappeared, even though the sobriquet Tranz is still a little reminiscent of the old days, referring to the music and dance style that only exists here in Hikkaduwa. The culinary offerings include six restaurants,

coffee shops, bars and a lounge. The pool lies high above the sea and is also suitable for children.

Citrus Hikkaduwa ££ – £££

400, Galle Road
tel. 091 556 00 01-5
www.citrusleisure.com
Every one of the 40 modern rooms has unobstructed views of the sea as well as remarkable interior design. Furthermore there is one large freshwater pool and an extensive selection of sports and spa services. There are two bars that open in the evenings.

Coral Sands Hotel ££ – £££

326, Galle Road
tel. 091 227 75 13, 227 74 36
www.coralsandshotel.com
Modernized hotel right on the beach with 82 rooms, a restaurant, bar, two pools and a choice of water sports.

The Plantation Villa Hotel ££ – £££

Wattalaya Watta, Nehinna, Dodangoda
tel. 011 257 42 70-1
ww.srimalplantation.com
Anyone wishing to get away from the hustle and bustle of Hikkaduwa will like this small hotel in the hinterland. Recommendable restaurant; regular cookery courses.

Ayurveda-Centrum Lawrence Hill Paradise ££ – £££

47, Waulagoda Middle Road
tel. 091 227 75 44
www.ayurvedakurlaub.de
13 rooms, ayurveda restaurant, pool. The hotel with its 13 rooms is located in a lovely, large garden on a hill above Hikkaduwa. It is exclusively for ayurveda guests. All the treatments are included in the price.

Kallabongo Lake Resort ££

22/8K Field View, Baddegama Road, Nalagasdeniya
tel. 091 438 32 34
www.kallabongo.com
Somewhat further inland, situated right on a lagoon. Ten of the 15 attractively furnished rooms have air conditioning, while the others have a ceiling fan. There is a large pool in which guests can cool down. The restaurant's menu features local and international dishes.

Sri Lanka Beach House £ – ££

Booking in Europe:
tel. +49 40 229 78 04,
in Sri Lanka: tel. 077 640 43 73
www.srilankabeachhouse.de (site languages include English)
On his property near Dodanduwa Nimal Chandana lets a spacious house with very tastefully furnished rooms. The house, which is right on the sea, also has a freshwater pool. Nimal's wife will cook for guests on request. An ideal accommodation option for families!

Mambo Beach Guest House £ – ££

434/4 Galle Road
tel. 091 227 55 09, www.mambos.lk
Since this guesthouse's restaurant opens at 7am, it is a central meeting place for hungry surfers. But they tend to be quite undemanding as long as the waves are big enough. The best rooms in the two categories have air conditioning. The restaurant is also frequented by diners who are not staying at the hotel. The Saturday parties on the beach are legendary.

Castlereigh Holiday Bungalow £
tel. 051 222 36 88
www.castlereigh.net
Set amid the magnificent mountain landscape and countless tea bushes, this guesthouse has a mere five rooms and was built as far back as 1927. There is a restaurant serving local and international dishes. A good way to explore the surrounding area is by mountain bike or on foot.

Polgasduwa (island)

The island of Polgasduwa in Lake Ratgama, which is served by boats from the lakeside, has become quite famous. In 1911, a 33-year-old German by the name of Anton Gneth – his monastic name was Nyanantiloka, and later he was honoured with the name of Mahathara, i. e. Eldest – founded **a Buddhist monastery**. He and the other German monks were deported during World War I and not allowed to return until 1926. By then the little monastery was in ruins and everything had to be rebuilt. Gneth, or rather Nyanantiloka, made a name for himself as the author of numerous commentaries and as the translator of parts of the Pali canon, including the Visuddhi Magga (Path of Purity) and Anguttara Nikaya (Discourses of the Buddha). He spent the last four years of his life with his pupil Nyanaponika in the latter's forest cell near Kandy, dying in Colombo in 1957 in the wake of an operation; he was honoured with a state funeral.

MARCO POLO TIP

Walking on the only path   **Insider Tip**

The monastery on Polgasduwa only accepts male visitors who will spend a few days learning Buddha's teachings. The island can only be visited with a written invitation (tel. 011 492 03 04). There are four Spartan guest rooms.

Excursions

Within easy reach of Hikkaduwa by bus or train there are a number of worthwhile excursion destinations, e. g. ▶Galle and further south ▶Matara or ▶Kalutara and ▶Ambalangoda to the north.

** **Horton Plains**

✦ C 8

Province: Central
Altitude: app. 2150m/7000ft

The lonesome highlands of Horton Plains –Sri Lanka's most elevated plateau – are covered with grass and scrub, and are a popular destination for ramblers, as well as being a particularly pleasant place to stay in the hot months. The area takes its name from Sir R.W. Horton, who was the British governor of Ceylon from 1831 to 1837.

Horton Plains

GETTING THERE

By car: from the west via Talawakelle (A 7), Agrapatana and Diyagama Estate; from the north via Nuwara Eliya or Hakgala. From Colombo the Horton Plains are app. 170 km/105mi away. By train: the closest train stations are in Pattipola and Ohiya (both app. 11 km/7mi away).

Visiting times: unlimited
Park entrance: 29km/18mi south of Nuwara Eliya
Entry fee: USD17 plus taxes

WHERE TO STAY

Mahoora Luxury Tented Safari Camp £££ – ££££
Near the park entrance
tel. 077 772 15 06, www.mahoora.lk
There are no hotels within the Horton Plains, but there is a tent village with accommodation of various categories. It is the ideal starting place for ranger-accompanied trips through Gal Oya National Park. Restaurant with Singhalese cuisine, meet at the bar or the camp fire in the evenings. If that does not appeal, there is accommodation in Nuwara Eliya.

There are lots of refreshing waterfalls on the Horton Plains

The Horton Plains have been a conservation area since 1969 and were made a National Park in 1988 in order to protect the last remaining tropical cloud forests as well as the fauna with its app. 40 leopards and sambar deer. In 2010 they were put on UNESCO's World Heritage List. The locals call the Horton Plains Maha Eliya, which means something like »open plain«.

Meaning and name

Thotupola Kanda has an elevation of 2359m/7740ft, making it Sri Lanka's third-highest mountain. It also marks the northern boundary of the Horton Plains. An ascent will take around two hours. The country's second-highest mountain, Kirigalpota (2389m/7838ft) in the western part of the national park is also climbable.

Mountains

Three of Sri Lanka's largest rivers rise on the Horton Plains: the Mahaweli Ganga, the Kelani Ganga and the Walawe Ganga. Their sources are the result of an average of 5000mm/200in of precipitation per year. No other place in Sri Lanka is wetter.

The flora of the Horton Plains isn't exactly diverse. They are dominated by grasses, tree ferns and rhododendrons. The tall quina trees, which can be recognized by their umbrella-like tree tops, are typical of this wetland.

Plants

The fauna is not exactly varied at this altitude either. There are some endemic bird species, however, such as the Sri Lanka whistling thrush, the Sri Lanka scaly thrush and the Sri Lankan junglefowl (Sri Lanka's national bird). It is a rare event to spot a leopard. Sambar deer sightings are much more common. One very special and threatened animal is the **red slender loris** (Lat. Loris tardigradus nycticeboides), which only grows to about 25cm/10in and only lives on the Horton Plains. It is a nocturnal primate that was once considered extinct. It was rediscovered by experts from London's Zoological Society in 2010; by spending more than 200 hours lying in wait, they even managed to get photographs.

A hike across the Horton Plains is one of the most memorable experiences that Sri Lanka has to offer the nature-lover. Hikers should set out early, because at this time of day there are still good views over the pristine landscape and bizarre vegetation; by 11am – especially at World's End – there are often dense fog banks. It must be said that the fauna at this altitude is not particularly diverse, consisting at best of a few species of birds.

Rambling on Horton Plains

The Horton Plains is criss-crossed by a **well signposted network of footpaths**, which ramblers are not allowed to leave. Stout footwear is needed, the paths are slippery! To get there, an off-road vehicle is advisable, but these can be hired in all of the nearby centres. There is an admission charge for the National Park itself. This is also a good place to hire a knowledgeable guide (recommended!).

World's End A walk across the undulating grasslands and areas with subtropical vegetation leads to **two viewpoints**, Big World's End and Little World's End. At the former, the cliff wall drops almost 1000m/3300ft steeply into the valley, and the latter is also impressive, though here the drop is only (!) 600m/2000ft.

Baker's Falls A magnificent but sweaty 30-minute walk leads from the park entrance to Baker's Falls, a wild and romantic waterfall with large tree ferns and rhododendrons growing around the pool at the bottom.

Jaffna

✦ A/B 2

Province: Northern
Altitude: 2–7m/7–25ft
Population: 79,000

Even in the past, the Jaffna peninsula saw few visitors. With the outbreak of the civil war in 1983, the tourist trade, such as it was, collapsed. Now that the confrontations between the Tamil and Singhalese population have ended, a tentative increase in tourism is tangible, even though in view of the significant destruction it will still be several years before anything like normalcy returns.

Marked by destruction Almost all the native Singhalese have been driven out and their houses burned down. The town of Jaffna will certainly be marked for years to come by the destruction caused by the ethnic conflict. However, the continuity of the Dravidian culture with its roots in south India had already been broken when the colonial masters destroyed the old temples and palace buildings.

Barren landscape Even so, the landscape of the peninsula offers a surprisingly marked contrast with the rest of the country. It is barren, and dominated by undemanding vegetation. The irrigation of the agricultural areas is not effected through reservoirs and canals, as it is just a few dozen kilometres further south, but by the use of wells. Nonetheless, numerous small fields bear witness to the hard work of the local people, who have succeeded, in spite of all the obstacles nature has placed in their way, in getting the soil to bring forth some fruit at least. The people, small and very dark-skinned Tamils, have been settled here since time immemorial; they are hospitable and friendly. Most of them –following the expulsion of the Singhalese, there are now only about 60,000 inhabitants – live packed together in Jaffna town, and are adherents of Hinduism.

People gather at the temple dedicated to the god of war, Skanda, for the Nallur Festival

Not much is known about the historical development of this part of the island. It is likely that in the first half of the 13th century a Tamil adventurer, maybe a king's son, from southern India set up a principality on the Jaffna peninsula, whose capital was called Nallur. Marco Polo, who visited this city in 1292, reports that the principality was ruled by a king named Sandernaz, who owed tribute to no other king. The Rajavali chronicle reports that in the 14th century, King Arya Chakravarti was the most powerful ruler in Ceylon, because the two other kings, Vikrama Bahu II in Gampola and Alakeshvara in Rayigama, paid tribute to him. When King Alakeshvara, who had established a new, heavily fortified royal city in Kotte, not far from Colombo, refused to pay, Arya Chakravarti marched south. He took Chilaw, Negombo and Colombo, but was repulsed from Kotte, thus bringing to an end the payment of tribute to the ruler in the north. In the first half of the 15th century, the kingdom of Arya Chakravarti in Jaffna was subordinated to the powerful Vijayanagara kingdom in southern India. In about 1450 the Singhalese king Parakrama Bahu IV succeeded in reconquering the north of Ceylon and united it with his own kingdom. He enfeoffed the victorious general Prince Sapumal with the peninsula. In 1477 Arya Chakravarti invaded Jaffna once more, however, and prised it away from the Singhalese kingdom, which was in any case falling apart.

History

Until 1619 the rulers of Jaffna held out against the Portuguese, but they were forced to surrender after the last of them was executed in 1621. In 1658 rule passed from the Portuguese to the Dutch, and in 1796 to the British. During the whole period of colonial rule, Jaffna was a target of intolerant missionary efforts. The Portuguese introduced Roman Catholicism, but the Catholics in their turn fell victim to the Dutch, who sought to establish their own Reformed Church.

Jaffna

GETTING THERE

By car: from Colombo via Anuradhapura (A 6, A 10, A 28, A 20), continue on the A 14 to Mannar and from there on the A 32 to Jaffna. There are several check points in this route.

By train: there currently is no rail connection from Colombo to Jaffna. But the plan is to have it repaired in the not so distant future.

By bus: regular bus connections to Jaffna run by private companies, e.g. from Colombo; the journey time is a good 10 hours and the distance app. 400 km/250mi. The buses, which are fitted with air conditioning, tend to travel overnight. The central bus station is in Hospital Road.

SHOPPING

Jaffna is definitely no city for shopping (yet). But the daily market in Hospital Road is a good place to look for souvenirs. Hats, bags and cutlery made out of the wood and leaves of the Palmyra palm. These can also be purchased in the Sri Lanka Palmyrah Development Board (129 K. K. S. Road; Mon – Fri 9am – 5pm, Sat until 1.30pm). Everyday utility items can be bought in the Lanka Sathosa Super Market (140 Kasthuriya Road; daily 8.30am – 6.30pm).

WHERE TO STAY

Even though the civil war ended a few years ago now, the hotel situation is still quite unsatisfactory. There is some accommodation where the often quite basic standards are made up for by the friendliness and attentiveness of the owners and the staff.

Expo Pavillion
£ £ – £ £ £
40 Kandy Road
tel. 021 222 37 90
Those who care about a smart ambience, will like this boutique hotel. There are seven tastefully decorated rooms with air conditioning and the hotel restaurant is known for its down-to-earth cuisine.

Tilko Jaffna City Hotel
£ £
70/6 K. K. S. Road
tel. 021 222 59 69
www.cityhoteljaffna.com
Currently the best accommodation in Jaffna, with 40 spacious rooms in a modern building. The penthouse with its lovely view of the town is a good option. The restaurant serves tasty local and international fare and is very popular with tourists and locals alike.

Blue Haven £ – £ £

70 Racca Road
tel. 021 222 99 58
www.bluehavenjaffna.com
Having just nine rooms, it is more of a
guesthouse than a hotel, but there is
air conditioning in every category. It is
situated somewhat outside of the town
centre, so it is a suitable place to relax
and to enjoy trips to the surrounding
area. The restaurant serves the food
typical of north of the country and
there is also a pool.

Green Grass Hotel £ – £ £

33 Aseervatham Lane/Hospital Road
tel. 021 222 43 85
www.jaffnagreengrass.com
Centrally located hotel with 30 adequate rooms. The main building is currently being extended by a further
floor. The restaurant, which has a terrace, serves local cuisine and there is
also a rooftop bar. There is a covered
pool in the pretty garden.

New Bastian Hotel £ – £ £

11 Kandy Road
tel. 021 222 73 74
www.bastianhotel.com
This somewhat outdated hotel is particularly popular with business people
who have come to Jaffna for work. It
has twelve rooms with and six rooms
without air conditioning. Attentive service makes up for the basic nature of
the rooms. The restaurant serves good
Tamil and international cuisine.

WHERE TO EAT

Things are not as good as they could
be in Jaffna when it comes to food either. It is best to rely on the hotel restaurants or go to the town centre.

Cosy Restaurant £ – £ £

15 Sirampiyadi Lane off Stanley Road
Those who enjoy the spicy cuisine of
the Indian subcontinent will enjoy this
place. This restaurant is considered the
best Indian in Jaffna; the tandoori oven
is very typical. The chicken tikka is a
must.

Rolex Restaurant £ – £ £

340 Hospital Road
This small restaurant has a daily very
recommendable, tasty buffet with
plenty of dishes typical of the region.
The many local diners appreciate it too.

Malayan Cafe £

36 – 38 Grand Bazaar
This restaurant is right across from the
big market in Jaffna. It is almost an institution. The vegetarian rice dishes are
outstanding. They are served on banana leaves.

Mangos £

Nallalaxmy Avenue
359 Temple Road
This restaurant serves Tamil fully vegetarian fare. The tables are often taken
by large local families. The plentiful
curry and rice buffet, served at lunch, is
this restaurant's speciality, but so too
are the flatbreads made of rice and
black lentil flour and served with onions, green chillis and grated coconut.

New Rest House £

19 Somasutharam Road
A simply furnished small restaurant,
but one that serves tasty food. The
outstanding curry dishes are at the
heart of the menu.

A Torn Country

Since the Sri Lankan civil war is officially a thing of the past for some years already, it has a firm place in the island's history. Ethnic conflicts between Buddhist Singhalese and Hindu Tamils were the focal point of the fierce battles that went on for years and were sometimes fought as an underground war

▶ **Conflicting parties**

Government of Sri Lanka
Dominated by (Buddhist) Singhalese

CONFLICT

Liberation Tigers of Tamil Eelam (LTTE)
Union of radical (Hindu) Sri Lankan Tamils, strongest rebel political and military force

CONFLICT

CONFLICT

Janathā Vimukthi Peramuna (JVP)
The communist party fights for a socialist Sri Lanka without cooperation with the LTTE.

Indian Peace Keeping Forces (IPKF)
The Indian forces with a UN mandate was supposed to prevent the conflict from crossing over to the southern Indian state of Tamil Nadu.

▶ **Stations of a conflict**

After conquering Ceylon the British establish an administration dominated by Tamils and bring in Tamils workers from southern India. The conflict that smouldered in southern India for centuries crossed over to Ceylon.

Ceylon becomes independent.

Sinhala (Singhalese) becomes the official language through the Official Language Act.

Ceylon is renamed Sri Lanka. Sinhala is the only official language and Buddhism is the preferred religion. Tamils are increasingly discriminated against.

23 July 1983
Presumable cause of the c war is an atta on a military base in the north of the island.

Establishment of the LTTE

| 1815/40 | 1948 | 1956 | 1972 | 1976 | 1983 |

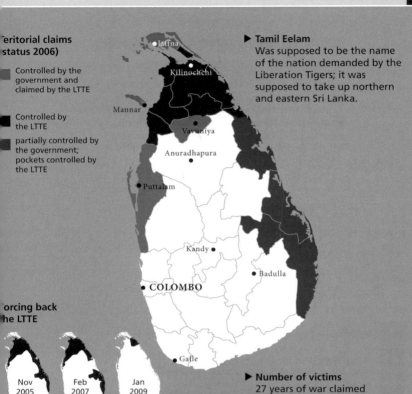

Territorial claims
(status 2006)

Controlled by the government and claimed by the LTTE

Controlled by the LTTE

partially controlled by the government; pockets controlled by the LTTE

▶ Tamil Eelam
Was supposed to be the name of the nation demanded by the Liberation Tigers; it was supposed to take up northern and eastern Sri Lanka.

Forcing back the LTTE

Nov 2005   Feb 2007   Jan 2009

©BAEDEKER

▶ Number of victims
27 years of war claimed an estimated 80,000 to 100,000 lives

India sends the Indian Peace Keeping Force (IPKF) to Sri Lanka.

After bloody, unsuccessful battles with the LTTE the Indian troops leave Sri Lanka.

The prime minister of Sri Lanka, Ranasinghe Premadasa, is killed in a suicide attack by the LTTE.

The last of the cities controlled by the LTTE, Jaffna, is taken by the Sri Lankan army in January.

16 May 2009
President Mahinda Rajapaksa declares that the LTTE is »completely defeated« and the civil war is officially over.

1990   2000   2010

Point Pedro Point Pedro is located around 33km/21mi northeast of Jaffna. It is the northernmost inhabited point of the island. It is worth visiting for its interesting and diverse landscape which, now that the military conflicts have ended, is being used again for agricultural purposes such as growing rice and tobacco. On route, along the AB 20, there are **several Hindu temples** such as the Pillayar Kovil and the Kovil Sri Selvachchannithi. Point Pedro itself is a small fishing port that is at its busiest during the morning. It can be seen very well from a lighthouse. When the weather is good, it is possible to see India across the Palk Strait.

Islands Palk Strait, which separates Sri Lanka from the Indian subcontinent, has a number of smaller and somewhat larger islands. Three of them, **Karaitivu, Kayts and Punkudutivu**, are connected to Sri Lanka via causeways. The second is also the largest. It is worth visiting the Catholic St James Church, which was built in 1716. The island of Karaitivu has a lovely beach, which is quite the inviting place to go for a dip. The island to the west of Jaffna is called **Nainativu**. The island is particularly significant for Sri Lanka's Buddhist population because Buddha himself is said to have come here to assuage the argument between the snake king Naga and his nephew. **Delft Island**, to the northwest of Jaffna, still has the remains of a Dutch fort as well as those of a derelict Buddhist temple.

Kalutara

✳ **A 8**

Province: Western
Altitude: 3m/10ft
Population: 38,000

Kalutara lies on both sides of the mouth of the Kalu Ganga, which is 300m/330yd wide at this point. A bridge connects the two halves of the town, which is a centre of the rubber trade and home to basket and mat weavers.

History In 1042, the south-Indian prince Vikrama Pandya, who ruled the Ruhuna kingdom, moved his seat of government to Kalutara, as he feared attack by the Chola kings, who at this time ruled in Polonnaruwa. But just one year later he was murdered by a prince from northern India, who then established himself as ruler of the Ruhuna kingdom. In the early 13th century, many people moved from the heartland of the kingdom to the south and southwest. In order to secure them a living, King Parakrama Bahu II had coconut palms planted on the coast. In 1655 the town fell to the Dutch. They built a fort, extended and strengthened the fortifications already built by the

Kalutara

GETTING THERE
By car: from Colombo on the A 2 or on a route through the country's interior via Bandagarama (52 km/32mi); from Bentota on the A 2 (22 km/13.5mi)
By train: station on the Colombo–Matara route
By bus: good bus connections from Colombo and from the seaside resorts further south

WHERE TO STAY/EAT
Avani Kalutara Resort £ £ – £ £ £
St. Sebastian's Road,
Katukurunda Kalutara
tel. 034 428 08 01
www.avanihotels.com
A new hotel was built in the spot where the well-known Kani Lanka Resort once stood. Some of the old buildings have been incorporated into the new hotel. Geoffrey Bawa, a highly esteemed architect in Sri Lanka, was responsible for designing this accommodation in a timeless, modern style. The 75 rooms are very comfortable. There are two restaurants, three bars, a generous pool and a fitness suite.

Lily Beach Hotel £
123/12 De Abrew Drive Kalutara North
tel. 034 222 21 59
lilyrest@sltnet.lk
Five rooms, some of which have wonderful views of the sea. The owners are known for their delicious Sri Lankan cookery (speciality: seafood, especially the lobster!) Good value for money.

AYURVEDA HOTEL　Insider Tip
Siddhalepa Ayurveda Health Resort £ £ £ – £ £ £ £
861, Samanthara Road, Wadduwa
tel. 038 229 69 67
www.ayurvedaresort.com
A strict ayurveda retreat does not have to mean guests have to go without all creature comforts during their stay. This resort, around 12km/7mi to the northwest of Kalutara, has air conditioning, flat-screen TVs and coffee makers, but still values sticking to the ayurveda programme, which is put together by experienced ayurveda doctors. The chalets are located in a lovingly designed garden, in which the herbs for the treatments also grow. Generous pool.

Portuguese, and turned Kalutara into an important trading centre. 1797 saw the arrival of the British, who, preferring Colombo, did not enlarge Kalutara any further.

WHAT TO SEE IN KALUTARA

The striking landmark of the town is the (admittedly relatively modern) dagoba. It differs from the traditional dagoba in that its interior is hollow, and can be accessed. Opposite the dagoba is the little temple complex of Gangatilake Vihara. The buildings are also relatively modern and from the point of view of cultural history, of little sig-　**Dagoba** nificance. On the roadside is a small shrine, where Buddhist motorists stop to make an offering of a few coins to ensure a safe onward journey.

Surroundings of Kalutara   The hinterland of Kalutara has extensive **rubber tree plantations** for the harvest of natural rubber. 31km/20mi to the east of the town is the Rubber Research Institute, specializing in new methods of production.

★★ Kandy

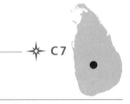

✦ C 7

Province: Central
Altitude: 490–504m/1600–1650ft
Population: app. 125,000

Kandy, the »most beautiful city in the land« and the heart of Sri Lanka, lies in undulating, forested hill country. The pride of the city is the Temple of the Tooth, but the idyllic lake in the middle of town and the world-famous Botanical Garden are also something to write home about.

Intellectual and religious centre   Kandy is very conscious of the historic role which it played as the last capital of the Singhalese kingdom and seat of the last Singhalese king, Raja Sinha II. Today the town is the intellectual and religious centre of Sri Lanka, a result not least of the fact that Buddhists, Hindus, Moors and Christians all co-exist here. The university, founded in 1835, is the country's largest by far. The inhabitants of Kandy like to see themselves as Sri Lanka's elite, as the very description »**Kandyans**« indicates. The name Kandy, incidentally, is short for »Kanda uda pas rata«, which means »kingdom in the mountains«.

15th century	Viceroy Vikramabahu makes Kandy his capital and builds a palace
16th/17th centuries	The Kingdom of Kandy is the centre of resistance to the Portuguese invaders
1636	Protection contract with the Dutch against the Portuguese
1760–1766	Battle against the Dutch »protector«
1815	The British take over colonial rule in Kandy; the Singhalese kingdom comes to an end

History of the city   Kandy was long protected from the colonial invaders not only by the hills, marshes and the mighty Mahaweli Ganga, which forms a loop to the north of the city, but also by the climate, which is conducive to

Highlights Kandy

► **Kiri Muhuda**
An evening boat trip on Kandy Lake is romantic.
►page 276

► **Dalada Maligawa**
The Temple of the Sacred Tooth is the most significant Buddhist temple on Sri Lanka.
►page 282

► **Botanical Gardens of Peradeniya**
An incredibly lavish, colourful natural landscape
►page 279

► **Hunas Falls**
An impressively beautiful water world near Kandy.
►page 295

malaria. Until 1815, when the British finally succeeded in taking possession of the city, Kandy was the last residue of the Singhalese kingdom.

As temple inscriptions in the area prove, the Kandy region was already settled in the 5th century. It was only at the end of the 15th century, however, that the viceroy Vikrama Bahu (1447–1511), hitherto resident in Gampoha, in his search for a secure location, made this then insignificant place his **capital** and had a palace built. During this period the central royal house was based in Kotte, not far from Colombo.

In 1518 the Portuguese started their conquest of the island. But while the king of Kotte joined forces with the Portuguese in the hope of gaining political advantage, a powerful **resistance movement**, formed under his brother Mayadunne, the king in Sitavka, which was carried on by his son, the future King Raja Sinha I (1582–1592). Kandy was ruled at this time by a prince named Karalliyadde Bandara, who was defeated by Raja Sinha I in 1582, and forced to flee with his daughter Dona Catherina to Trincomalee. But Raja Sinha I was unable to hold Kandy, and in 1588 he was deposed. In 1592, with the help of the Portuguese, the Singhalese Don Juan, who had converted to Christianity, became king of Kandy. But his conversion was short-lived as he immediately announced his return to Buddhism, taking the name Vimela Dharma Suriya I. This was seen by the Portuguese as a provocation, and in revenge they occupied Kandy briefly, looting it in the process. Dharma Suriya I soon succeeded, however, in defeating the Portuguese occupa-

? **MARCO POLO INSIGHT**   *The Big City*

Kandy has always had several Singhalese names, one of which is Maha Nuwara (Big City). It was called Kanda uda pas rata (kingdom in the mountains); the Portuguese turned that into Candia. The city got its current name during the British colonial period.

tion forces left behind in the city, whereupon he continued to rule undisturbed until 1604. The reign of his successor King Raja Sinha II (1605–1687) was also dominated by conflict with the colonists. In 1606 he formed an alliance with the Dutch, who had landed in Sri Lanka, with a view to expelling the Portuguese. The Dutch for their part had no intention of helping the king, as soon became clear. They used the non-payment of alleged war debts as an excuse to take a number of coastal towns, from which they had previously expelled the Portuguese, as a lien. In other areas too there were continual disputes, especially in respect of the cinnamon trade and the introduction of a new system of taxation, but ultimately the lords of Kandy always came out on top.

From 1739 Kandy was ruled by the Tamil Nayakkar dynasty, whose kings however were for the most part not Hindus, but Buddhists. Under Sri Vijaya Raja Sinha (1739–1747) the Christians were expelled from Kandy. The most important ruler was Kirti Sri Raja Sinha (1747–1778), who initiated a movement of religious renewal, leading his kingdom into a cultural heyday. In spite of treaty obligations to the Dutch, he entered into secret negotiations with the British with the aim of expelling the Dutch from Sri Lanka. The British however were not interested in making concessions, and in 1795 began to conquer the island for themselves, declaring it a crown colony in 1802. Only the kingdom of Kandy managed to escape their clutches, at least until 1815. It took three military campaigns after 1802 to secure the final British victory. The king was captured and taken to south India, where he died in 1832. In the Convention of Kandy (1815) the last remains of the kingdom were also declared a crown colony, and Colombo became the capital. Until independence in 1948, however, Kandy remained the centre of the anti-colonial resistance.

Resistance to the colonial government

WHAT TO SEE IN KANDY

The long artificial lake which gives Kandy much of its charm was created between 1810 and 1812 in the reign of the last king of Kandy from a modest pond which had been maintained as a home for the sacred terrapins. The masonry embankment was commissioned by the British governor in 1875 on the occasion of a visit by the Prince of Wales; it resembles the decorative walls of the Temple of the Tooth. On the lakeside, not far from the entrance to the temple precinct, stands a pretty pavilion, which once served the royal dynasty. Today it houses a public library and the tourist information office. There are

Kiri Muhuda (lake)

Kandy, the island's third-oldest city, is considered the most beautiful of the old royal cities

Kandy

INFORMATION
Sri Lanka Tourism Promotion Bureau
Kandy City Centre, L 2 – 3, Level 2
Dalada Veediya, Kandy
tel. 081 222 26 61
www.srilanka.travel/quickinfo
www.kandycity.org
Daily 8.30am – 5pm

GETTING THERE
By car: from Colombo on the A 1 (116 km/72mi); from Kurunegala on the A 10 (45 km/28mi); from Dambulla on the A 9 (12 km/7mi) and from Nuwara Eliya on the A 5 (76 km/47mi)
By train: the closest train station is Peradeniya on the Colombo–Matale route.
By bus: good bus connections from all the abovementioned towns

SHOPPING
In addition to the obligatory bric-a-brac, Kandy is also good place to buy high-quality carvings and locally produced furniture as well as wonderful batik fabrics. These items can be found in many small shops in the centre, such as in the streets and alleys to the north of Dalada Veediya. Junoid's – The Saree Gallery (17 – 19 Yatinuwara) is recommendable because of the wide selection, as is the Kandy branch of the state-owned Laksala chain (05, Sangaraja Mawatha,
tel. 081 222 20 87, www.laksala.lk). This place also sells high-quality souvenirs, but it is not possible to barter here as the prices are fixed. In Rarapihilla Mawatha to the south of Kandy Lake there is shop after shop . Good ones for fine fabrics for example are Senani Silks Factory (30 Rajapihilla Mawatha) and Gunnatilake Batiks (173A Rajapihilla Mawatha). Traditional wood carvings and mahogany furniture is available next door at Rajanima Craft. The Kandyan Art Association & Cultural Centre (Sangharaja Mawatha) is known for its nice handicrafts, made out of brass for example. Kandy's big market that is held every day near the station in S. W. R. D. Bandaranaike Mawatha is also a treasure trove for the odd memento, but especially for spices and spice mixes. Tea from Sri Lanka is available in many places but the selection cannot be beaten at Mlesna in Kandy City Center (5, Dalada Veediya).

TIME FOR MEDITATION
Around Kandy there are several ways of using a stay in Sri Lanka to look inwards. But come with a certain earnestness because meditation is not easy. Well-known establishments include the Nilambe Meditation Centre (tel. 081 222 54 71, www.nilambe.net, around 20 km/12mi south of Kandy), and the Lewella Meditation Centre (160 Dharmashoka Mawatha, tel. 081 492 18 14). Further information about Buddhism is available in Britain from The Buddhist Society, 58 Eccleston Square, London, SW1V 1PH, Tel: 020 7834 5858, Fax: 020 7975 5238, Email: info@thebuddhistsociety.org

WHERE TO STAY
During the great Perahera in July/August it is important to book accommodation in Kandy in a timely fashion. Otherwise everything will be booked out and the prices will be much more expensive.

❽ *Chaaya Citadel Kandy* £££–££££
124, Srimath Kada Ratwatte Mawatha
tel. 081 223 43 65
www.chaayahotels.com
This modern hotel was built right above the powerful Mahaweli Ganga. All of the 121 rooms have lovely views of the river. The rooms in three categories have elevated levels of comfort. The hotel has a pool and a small selection of sports. The reception will also organize excursions.

❸ *Mahaweli Reach Hotel* £££–££££
35, P. B. A. Weerakoon Mawatha
tel. 081 447 27 27, www.mahaweli.com
This hotel, located outside of the centre above the Mahaweli Ganga, does not just have 112 very tasteful and comfortable rooms, it also has a pretty garden with a big pool. The spa treatments follow ayurvedic principles; anyone wishing to get active can do so on the tennis court (with equipment hire).

❹ *Rangala House* £££–££££
928 Bobebila Road, Makuldeniya
tel. 081 240 02 94
www.rangalahouse.com
In recent years more and more boutique hotels have opened in Sri Lanka. Quite a number of them are located in buildings that were once used commercially. The Rangala House, around an hour's drive from Kandy, is one such. It once belonged to the owner of a tea plantation. Today it is testament to the former owner's good taste. There are only three double rooms and they are all filled with lots of antiques.

❶ *Hotel Suisse* ££–£££
30, Sangaraja Mawatha

tel. 081 223 30 24
www.hotelsuisse.lk
The striking 19th century building on the banks of Kandy Lake was once used by Lord Louis Mountbatten, the British commander, as the headquarters of the troops stationed in southeast Asia. Today it has aged somewhat, but the efforts of the friendly members of staff make up for the occasional disadvantage. Some of the 94 rooms and six suites are reminiscent of the colonial times. The hostel restaurant is one of the best in Kandy.

❷ *Kandy House* ££–£££
Amunugama Walauwa
tel. 081 492 13 94
www.thekandyhouse.com
Kandy House is a sophisticated mix of hotel and guesthouse, because the number of rooms, eight, speaks of an individual place to stay that is housed in an old manor from the year 1804. It is surrounded by a beautiful garden, which also has a pool.

❺ *Hill Top Hotel* ££–£££
200/21 Bahirawakanda
tel. 081 222 41 62
www.aitkenspencehotels.com
This hotel is recommendable if only for its situation in the magnificent mountain landscape! Most of the 73 rooms have views of the valley and Kandy.

❼ *Swiss Residence* ££–£££
23, Bahirawakanda
tel. 081 220 46 46
www.swissresidence.lk
40 rooms in two categories as well as a Royal Suite. Restaurant, bar, a cosy pub and a nice pool. The very clean rooms are furnished in the colonial style and offer a lot of comfort.

⑨ *Amaya Hill* ££ – £££

Heerassagala, Peradeniya
tel. 081 447 40 22
www.amayaresorts.com
This pretty hotel with its 99 rooms, which have great views of the surrounding mountains, is located somewhat outside of Kandy's centre.

⑤ *Blue Haven Guesthouse* £ – ££

30/2 Poorna Lane, Asgiriya **Insider Tip**
tel. 081 222 96 17
www.bluehavenguesthouse.com
An insider tip for a comfortable yet affordable accommodation option in Kandy: the ten rooms (some without air conditioning) are individually furnished. The building is situated above the centre and can be reached easily on foot. There are rental bikes.

WHERE TO EAT
⑤ *Helga's Folly* £££

32, Frederick E. de Silva Mawatha
tel. 081 223 45 71
www.helgasfolly.com
Do not miss this: Helga's Jolly is an institution in Kandy that does not just focus on the intake of food. Rather, it's about the delicious smorgasbord of historic and modern-day items just waiting to be looked at.

④ *History R.* ££ – £££

27A Anagarika Dharmapala Mawatha
tel. 081 447 06 42
This restaurant offers a small history lesson of Kandy because the walls are hung with photographs from bygone times. The menu is also good. Fish dishes are a speciality here.

② *Flower Song* ££ – £££

137 Kotugodelle Veediya
This restaurant, considered the best »Chinese« in Kandy, even serves Peking duck. It offers large, yet inexpensive portions.

③ *Paiva's Restaurant* £ – ££

37 Yatinuwara Veediya
The cuisine of the Indian subcontinent, which can be quite spicy at times, is cultivated here. The various curries are particularly tasty.

① *Rams* £ – ££

11, D. S. Senanayake Vedeeiya
Maybe the best Indian in Kandy. The selection of curries is impressive, but anyone who prefers it less spicy should tell the waiter in advance.

Market Hall On no account should a visit to the Market Hall at the western end of Dalada Vidiya be missed, as it has a **larger range of fruits** (►MARCO POLO Insight p.136) on offer than anywhere else in Kandy. The best time to go is the morning.

National Museum of Kandy The museum occupies that part of the former royal palace that was reserved to the queen and was opened to the public in 1942. The collection consists of 5000 objects, including jewellery, textiles, weapons, pottery, ritual objects and ivory carvings dating from the 17th to the 19th century.

● Sun–Thu 9am–5pm; admission charge

✷✷ DALADA MALIGAWA (TEMPLE OF THE TOOTH)

The history of Kandy is – like that of all the royal cities in Sri Lanka – closely linked to the history of the holy tooth relic, which has gathered its fair share of legends. After the solemn cremation of the Buddha's remains in Kushinagara (northern India) in 483 BC a number of unburnt fragments of bone, including a collarbone, were found in the ashes, and also four teeth. One of the teeth went to the king of Kalinga in southern India, where it was venerated for 800 years. When the Buddhist faith disappeared from India, the relic was at risk of being stolen by Hindu kings and possibly destroyed. One legend has it that the tooth had resisted all attempts by the Panda king to destroy it, and was even raised on a lotus blossom back to the surface of a pond into which it had been thrown. The Buddhist nun Hemamala, daughter of King Guhasiwa, brought the Tooth – concealed in her hair – to Sri Lanka in AD 313. King Sirimeghavana had a special temple built for it in his palace precinct, and in the succeeding years the Tooth was taken annually in a solemn procession to the Abhayagiri monastery, where it could be venerated by all the faithful.

The Sacred Tooth

> ! MARCO POLO TIP
>
> *To Kandy by rail* Insider Tip
>
> The train journey to Kandy and onwards to Badulla is spectacular. The 180km/112mi climbs 2000m/6560ft and winds its way along several hairpin bends and no fewer than 47 mountain tunnels. The best views are to be had in the end carriage.

In the political turmoil of the late 10th century, when Anuradhapura had to be abandoned as capital, **the great migration of the relic** began, although it continued to enjoy the particular attention of the kings. Finally its possession came to be the most important bargaining point for any claimant to the throne. It initially passed through the principality of Ruhuna (in the south of the island), and then, among other places, Kotmale, the Beligala rocks, Dambadeniya and eventually to Yapahuwa, where it was stolen and taken back to India by the Pandyas, who had stormed the fortress towards the end of the 13th century. By clever negotiation, King Parakrama Bahu II managed to get the Tooth back, however, and he had it taken to Polonnaruwa. After that it was in Kurunegala and in Gampola, where allegedly it was kidnapped and taken to China, like the Singhalese king himself. King Alakesvara is said to have got it back again, and it can be proved to have been present at the coronation of Parakrama Bahu VI in Rayigama in 1412.

From there, the Tooth was taken to the new capital of Kotte, where it fell into the hands of the Portuguese at the end of the 16th century. They are said to have taken it to their Indian colony of Goa and destroyed it. In order to legitimize himself as king to the people, however, Vimela Dharma SuriyaI, who seized power in Kandy in 1592, needed the Holy Tooth. So he spread a rumour that the Portuguese had only destroyed a copy, and that he possessed the original. The people decided to believe the king. Since then, the Tooth in Kandy has been regarded as the holiest Buddhist relic in Sri Lanka.

Opening times The Temple is accessible all day long, but the shrine, a two-storey wooden structure in the inner courtyard, is only opened for the religious ceremonies (puja) at 5.30am, 9.30am and 6.30pm. These occasions are announced by loud gong-beats and drum-rolls.

Temple complex The Dalada Maligawa, the »Temple of the Tooth«, stands within the former palace precinct. Nothing now remains of the earliest buildings put up to house the holy relic. The oldest extant part is the inner building, which dates from the reign of King Kirti Sri Raja Sinha (1747–1778). The present appearance of the whole complex dates from 1803 under the last king of Kandy, Sri Vikrama Raja Sinha (1798–1815), who had the conduits laid out and ordered the construction, using European architectural forms, of the massive entrance pavilion, the decorative exterior walls and the dominant octagonal front building with its ambulatory. Visitors enter the temple complex from Palace Square, having passed through a number of **security checks** introduced since the attack. A first noteworthy feature is the staircase with its five steps, two of which are flanked by elephant reliefs carved in the exterior walls. They come from the palace of King Sri Vira Marendra Sinha (1707–1739) in Kundalase and reflect, in their expressiveness and rich decor, the typical sculptural style of the Kandy period. The two decorative columns above the reliefs are gifts from Burma.

The semicircular, richly ornamented **moonstone** is workmanlike, but does not match the quality of the moonstone in Anuradhapura. Another moonstone only appears to follow the patterns, thus for example the lions and wild geese do not face the central point, the lotus, but are looking at the approaching beholder. In the moat, which is crossed by means of a stone bridge, live **terrapins, regarded as sacred**. A relief opposite the temple gate depicts the goddess Lakshmi with two elephants. Also worthy of note are a few gates and doorposts on the lower floor richly decorated with sculpted reliefs. They show male and female guardians, a Makara gatearch, the wheel of teaching set in motion by the Buddha, lions, lotus blossoms, and much more besides.

Attack on the temple

On 26 January 1998 a member of the Tamil Tigers detonated 250kg of explosives in front of the temple complex. This attack shook the whole country. Eight people lost their lives and the temple complex also suffered serious damage, much to everyone's dismay.

The temple complex of the Sacred Tooth is idyllically situated by the lake

In the interior courtyard stands the actual shrine, which is also the oldest part of the temple. It is a two-storey, richly decorated building, built entirely of wood. The columns and rafters have carvings of extraordinary beauty. A staircase leads to the upper storey, from which a corridor leads to a door studded with silver and decorated with mother-of-pearl and ivory inlays. Behind the door is the holy of holies, the Tooth. The reliquary consists of seven dagoba-shaped golden containers or karanduwas fitting into one another, and studded with pearls and precious stones.

The final and most precious container, the last, is of ivory, and holds the sacred relic, the Holy Tooth, which is 5cm/2in long and 1.5cm/0.7in in diameter. It is, however, only displayed at special ceremonies that take place every four years. Apart from the **original relic**, which lies on a lotus blossom, it is also possible to see a replica which is taken on procession through Kandy once a year at the Esala Perahera, a solemn festival lasting several days. The seven containers are lockable, the keys being in the possession of the high priests of the Malwatte and Asgiriya monasteries, who also take it in turns to officiate at the religious ceremonies in the temple.

**Dalada Maligawa

The Temple of the Tooth in Kandy guards the island's most valuable treasure, one of Buddha's canine teeth. The relic has been moved several times over the centuries, but now it captivates the followers of the enlightened Buddha in the temple in Kandy. Every year in July/August, during the eleven-day Perahera of Kandy, it is carried through the town on a magnificently decorated elephant.

ⓘ Shrine: 5.30am, 9.30am and 6.30pm

➊ Moat

Visitors to the temple will cross a stone bridge that spans a moat in which there are lots of fish and turtles. The moat goes back to Kandy's last king, Sri Vikrama Rajasinha (reigned 1798 – 1815).

➋ Architecture

The foundations for the current building started to be laid in 1706. Its kinked, tiled roof is a typical element of »Kandy architecture«. The octagonal, tower-like extension was added in the early 19th century. It was built so that the sacred tooth could be presented to the people from its balustrade. Today it houses a library with valuable palm-leaf manuscripts.

➌ Devotion chamber

There is a devotion chamber on the ground floor with lots of Buddha statues donated by Buddhists from all around the world.

➍ Chamber of the relic

The 1m/3ft shrine in the shape of a dagoba, in which the relic is kept, is located on the first floor, the Udamale, behind a door adorned in ivory that is opened to the sound of drums during times of worship. The shrine contains six further containers, one inside the other, that are all decorated with gemstones. The final container houses the venerated relic, Gautama Buddha's top right canine.

Mountains of flowers pile up in the Temple of the Tooth thanks to the sacrificial offers of the faithful.

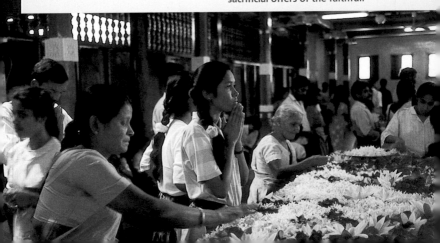

Flag
he Templ

Octagon The way to the Octagon leads past a room containing several statues of the Buddha dating from various eras. The Octagon itself was erected for the royal family; a throne used to stand here, from which the ruler could watch the Perahera and present the relic. By means of a trapdoor the king could get into a tunnel that led directly to his pleasure palace on the islet in Lake Kandy.

Sermon Hall The three-storey Sermon Hall, an impressive structure richly decorated with sculptures, which also served as a residential building for the monks, rounds off the temple complex to the east. On the second floor is a museum; among the exhibits is a wooden model of the Temple of the Tooth and a copy of the Buddha's footprint on Adam's Peak. Smaller buildings to the side link the Sermon Hall to the Halls of Veneration.

Audience Hall To the east of these is the former Audience Hall of the kings of Kandy, which stands on a tiered plinth. It was started as early as 1784, but not finished until the reign of the last king. The carvings on the columns and rafters are worth seeing; they were only completed under British rule in 1820. In 1815 the Convention (in reality more a surrender) between the Kingdom of Kandy and the British was signed here, declaring the last Singhalese kingdom on the island to be a British colony. Today the hall houses the Kandy supreme court.

Hall of Columns To the north, the temple precinct is adjoined by the Hall of Columns, erected in 1803. The rafters are extravagantly decorated with carvings, in particular flower motifs.

Archaeological Museum Further to the north are the remains of the old royal palace, which in colonial times was the residence of the deputy governor in Kandy. Today it houses an archaeological museum. The collection includes mainly items from the Kandy period.
❶ Sat–Thu 9am–5pm; admission charge

National Museum The graceful building to the south of the Audience Hall, built to Dutch plans in 1765, now houses the National Museum of Kandy. The collection is worth seeing, and includes the golden crown of King Raja SinhaII, precious ivory and wood carvings, ritual oil lamps, lifesize wooden figures with the typical Kandy costume, and palm-leaf manuscripts. Also worthy of note are the engravings with views of 19th-century Kandy, and maps of Ceylon.
❶ Tue–Sat 9am–5pm;

Natha Devale (temple) To the north-west of the Temple of the Tooth is the 14th-century Natha Devale, the city's oldest religious building. Here the rulers of the Singhalese kingdom were presented with the sword, the sign of their office. The Hindu goddess Natha is, incidentally, the city's patron. The most noteworthy feature inside the Devale is the sculpture of a recumbent Buddha.

The British Garrison Cemetery, a reminder of the British colonial period, is located on a side street of Anagarika Darmapala Mawatha. **British Garrison Cemetery** After it was closed in 1822, it was for many years at risk of becoming overgrown and thereby of falling into oblivion, until a citizens' initiative was set up to restore the **historic burial ground**. In 1998 the complex was reopened; of the original 450 graves 163 can still be seen. Famous people were laid to rest in many of them. However, there are also the graves of simple British soldiers.

❶ Mon–Sat, 8am–5pm, free admission, donation requested

> **? MARCO ⊕ POLO INSIGHT**
>
> *Elephants in the temple*
>
> There are no more than 3500 elephants still living wild in Sri Lanka, and around 300 are used as working elephants. Since it is considered a good deed to lend or give elephants to monasteries for their processions, the Temple of the Tooth alone has twelve of them.

Not far from the Natha Devale is the Pattini Devale, a temple dedicated to the goddess Pattini, a deity of Mahayana Buddhism. She **Pattini Devale** embodies purity and helps to protect man and beast alike from epidemics and other diseases. There are very few depictions of her on the island, another being in the National Museum in ▶Colombo. It was King Gaja Bahu (112–134) who introduced the Pattini cult to Sri Lanka, staging an annual festival in honour of the goddess, in order to guarantee rain and thus prosperity in the kingdom.

In the north of the Pattini Devale is the Wel Bodhiya, a large Bodhi **Bodhi tree** tree that is surrounded by a wall. It was planted by King Narendra Simha in the 18th century and is said to be derived from the tree in Anuradhapura, which is considered the oldest tree in the world.

It must be **pretty unique worldwide** to find a nature reserve in the **Udawattakele Sanctuary** middle of a city. But there is one in Kandy, where immediately above the Temple of the Tooth there is the Udawattakele Sanctuary, originally a royal hunting ground. Some of the footpaths through the sanctuary still bear the names of the wives of British governors and senior colonial officials. There are many different birds, butterflies and monkeys to be seen here.

Under the aegis of King Sri Vikrama Rajasimha, who, based in **Royal Palace Park** Kandy, ruled from 1798 to 1815, the Royal Palace Garden was set up to the south of Kandy Lake. It is worth visiting for the **great views of the town and lake** alone. The entrance is in Rajapihilla Mawatha; the admission charge is currently 100Rs.

❶ Daily 8.30am–4.30pm

SURROUNDINGS OF KANDY

**Peradeniya Botanical Garden   The Peradeniya Botanical Garden is one of the most beautiful and comprehensive in south or south-east Asia. Almost every species of Asian tropical plant of this continent is to be found here, as well as some from the temperate zones. The garden, 80 hectares/200 acres in extent, is surrounded on three sides by the River Mahaweli Ganga, whose bed here is horseshoe-shaped.

The history of the garden goes back to 1371, when King Vikrama Bahu II had a palace built here in the midst of a pleasure garden. King Kirti Sri Raja Sinha (1747–1781) made it his royal garden, and his successor Raja SinhaII also had a residence here.

Today's Botanical Garden was set up in 1821 by the Englishman **Alexander Moon**, and it was opened to the public in 1824. Moon, though, died the following year, and for years the garden was neglected, until it was re-instated and enlarged by George Gardner in 1844. The worldwide fame enjoyed by the Botanical Garden today, however, is largely due to G.H.K. Thwaites, the director of the Garden from 1849 to 1857, who further enlarged it and added a large number of tropical plants.

Even before entering, visitors will be met on the right by a row of Amherstia nobilis from Burma and the Malayan peninsula, also known as the **»Queen of Flowering Trees«**. On the other side are two fine Rambong rubber trees from Assam, which were planted in 1914. On the triangular lawn opposite the entrance is a splendid mahogany and on either side of the entrance is a royal poinciana or Flame of the Forest from Madagascar.

Next to the entrance is the **Spice Garden** with an almost-180-year-old nutmeg tree, as well as cinnamon trees, ginger, cardamom, cloves, vanilla and pepper. Following Lake Drive, visitors will come to the Cajuput rubber tree, and then the Upas tree from Java, whose bark contains a poison that was used for arrows or blowpipe darts. Not far on is the Burmese giant bamboo, the world's tallest bamboo: it reaches a height of 40m/140ft and a diameter of 24cm/10in.

Turning left into South Drive, the next feature is the lake, covered in **water lilies and lotus blossoms** and set in gently undulating landscape. On its banks grow various water plants, including papyrus from Egypt.

The hill path to the left crosses the **Palm Garden** with betel-nut or areka palms, whose fruit and leaves are rolled up and chewed in

Botanical Garden

Summer house

Mahaweli Ganga

River Drive

River Drive

Mahaweli Ganga

19

Thwaites Memorial

17

Great

Circle

9

14

16

13

18

15   11   12

10

Gardners
Memorial

2

3,4

1

Entrance

5

8

6

Kandy

5

7

Colombo

©BAEDEKER

1 Main Entrance
2 Spice Garden
3 Hibiscus bushes
4 Giant bamboo
5 Palm tree garden
6 Herb garden
7 Study garden
8 Pine grove
9 Herbarium,
plant museum
10 Succulents house
11 Orchid house
12 Orchid greenhouses
13 Java almond trees
14 Palm avenue
15 Flower garden
16 Tropical ferns
17 Aqai palm avenue
18 Cook's pine avenue
19 King palm avenue

many parts of Asia on account of their mildly intoxicating effect. Further on are kitul or toddy palms, whose nectar is used to make the arrack which is very popular on the island. In addition there are specimens of the aqai, royal and sealing-wax palms, as well as the native Sri Lankan nibong palm. To the left of the path are three talipot palms, at 25m/85ft the tallest of all palm species. Their huge fan-shaped leaves are used to create palm-leaf manuscripts (olas). There follows a further **Herb Garden** with medicinal herbs, and then a study garden with an experimental breeding station.

Following Lake Drive, the visitor will see various trees native to Sri Lanka (Ceylon screw pine, sandalwood tree, mahogany). From the corner of River Drive/Jonville Drive there is a fine view over the large lawn with Gannoruwa Hill in the background. The focus is a particularly beautiful specimen, planted in 1861, of Ficus benjamina with a magnificently spreading crown. To the north of the lawn there is a **herbarium**. Where Jonville Drive meets Monument Road, there is a specimen of the famous Coco de Mer, which otherwise only grows on the Seychelles. The road from the lake to the north leads to the **orchid house** with numerous splendid specimens from all over the world. Continuing along River Drive northwards, you will come to the avenue of açaí palms, which were planted in 1905, followed by an interesting arboretum. There are numerous specimens of native trees and shrubs in front of the suspension bridge over the Mahaweli Ganga. The return route to the starting point passes an avenue of stone pines named after Thomas Cook, and the avenue of royal palms.

❶ Daily 8am–7pm; small admission fee

Gadaladeniya Vihara

The monastery of Gadaladeniya is about 6km/4mi to the west of Peradeniya. It was built as long ago as 1344 on a low rock ridge. Architecturally, the Vihara is a combination of a Buddhist image building and a Hindu devale: the main shrine has a hall and another building with a secondary temple in front of it. The way the cornices on the latter and on the main building are structured shows strong Dravidian influences. The secondary temple has a dagoba-like top to its roof, while the main shrine has an octagonal sikhara. Once past the pillar lined entrance, visitors will see the bronze statue of a standing Buddha inside. The complex includes a further temple, the Vijayotpaya. It has a cruciform ground-plan, and niches occupied with Buddha figures. Here a Burmese influence is evident. Memorial trees The part of the garden commemorating prominent visitors to Sri Lanka is worthy of note. Each has had a tree planted in his or her honour, with a sign at its foot giving the name of the person and the species of tree.

Hantane Tea Factory (Tea Museum,

Just 5km/3mi to the southwest of Kandy, in Hatane, there is an interesting museum in the old Hatane Tea Factory that does a good job explaining the history of tea growing on the island using lots of historical documents and equipment used for tea production. The museum's main focus, however, is on the man who set up the first commercial tea plantation in 1867, namely the Scotsman James Taylor. The museum also has a restaurant with a lovely view of the mountains around Kandy (►MARCO POLO Insight p.332).

❶ Daily 8.15am–4.45pm, admission 400Rs

About 2km/1.5mi south of Gadaladeniya is the monastery of Lankatilaka, which was also built during the Gampola period in the 14th century. Inscriptions in the ancient Singhalese language report on the building of the temple, whose construction, reminiscent of the Burmese architecture of Pagan and its **exposed location on a rounded rock** make it one of the most beautiful examples of Sri Lankan architecture. 172 steps carved into the rock lead up to the building, but the strenuous climb is rewarded by a splendid view over the rice fields and the wooded hilly countryside. The rectangular central shrine is surrounded by a building with halls projecting at each of the points of the compass, producing a cross-shaped ground-plan. The façade is very finely structured with cornices, projections and recesses, and decorated with attractive elephant statues. The building was originally of four storeys, but when the two top ones collapsed, they were replaced by a tiled roof supported by solid timber rafters.

*Lankatilaka Vihara

Inside there is a colossal statue of a seated Buddha, flanked by two further Buddha figures. Characteristic of the time when they were carved – the 14th century – are the folds of the garments, falling in regular wavy lines. The painting at the rear imitates architecture, while to either side there are paintings of lions and mythical beasts. Also worthy of attention are the walls and ceiling of the anteroom; their attractive paintings were subject to major restoration during the Kandy period.

To the south of the Lankatilaka Vihara is the Embekke Devale, the third temple from the Gampola period; it too dates from the 14th century and is dedicated to the Hindu god of war Skanda. It differs from the previous temples in having **highly elaborate wood carvings**, which were enjoying a heyday at the this period. The open hall of the drummers (Dig-Ge) is particularly attractive, its 32 wooden pillars and also the rafters being full of highly varied carvings. Among other things, one can recognize wild geese, a double-headed eagle, wrestlers, dancers, soldiers and further statues, in graceful, flowing movement. Another noteworthy feature is the structure of the rafters, designed to achieve an optical effect. The 26 struts unfold from a single point towards visitors as they enter. This building was probably once used, at least some of the time, as the audience chamber of the kings of Gampoha; it is thought that it was brought here by one of the Kandy kings and restored.

**Embekke Devale

The white building of the Lankatilaka Monastery can
be seen from afar

KANDY HIGHLANDS

Gampola   Gampola, the »holy city on the river« (Siripura Ganga), is an attractive place in the Kandy Highlands around 20km/12mi from Kandy itself, with pretty houses and gardens along either side of the Mahaweli Ganga. As the **rulers' residence** and artistic centre during its heyday, Gampola enjoyed a few years of splendour. In 1344 King Ghuvanaike Bahu IV (1341–1351) moved the capital of his realm here, while his brother, King Parakrama Bahu V, resided in in ▶Dedigama. Vikrama Bahu III (1357–1374), and also Alakeshvara, king of Rayigama and Kotte, was required to pay tribute to the king of Jaffna. The next king in Gampola, Bhuvanaike Bahu V, succeeded in annihilating the forces of the king of Jaffna at the battle of ▶Matale. There are two versions of what happened next: according to one, Vira Bahu II ascended the throne in 1391 or 1392, while according to the other seven regents ruled successively until 1412. The sixth of these was Vira Alakeshvara, who in 1399 was forced to flee to India, but later returned and made himself king. In 1411 he and his family were captured by the Chinese general Cheng Ho and taken to China. There his trail went cold. Cheng Ho had put in Sri Lanka with some of his ships on his second expedition, according at least to Chinese chronicles, in order to take the Holy Tooth to China. Of the palace and temples of the kings who resided here, **there are only a few sparse remains**. A good impression of the buildings of this period can be got from the Lankatilaka Vihara and the temple of Gadaladeniya (►Kandy). Gampola is home to many Muslims and Hindus apart from the Buddhists. A Hindu temple in the centre is worth seeing, with its high roof covered with hundreds of statues of Hindu deities.

4km/2mi south of Gampola on the road to Nawalapitiya is the **Niyamgapaya Vihara**, whose stepped base with figurative sculptures and attractively carved door jambs date from the Gampola period. The superstructure was added later, however.

The pleasantly cool climate, the beauty of the gently undulating landscape and the comfortable Hunas Falls Hotel, situated in a picturesque location on a hillside in the middle of a garden fill of flowers, are the **major attractions of this region**. The water from the Hunas Falls collects in a small lake next to the hotel, where one can also fish for trout. Even non-residents should take the opportunity to stroll through the pretty gardens – including a kitchen garden with herbs and fruit.

In the surroundings you will also find cinnamon, cardamom, nutmeg, clove and tea plantations, while to the east are the Matale mountains with their highest peak, the 1862m/6109ft Knuckles massif.

Hunas Falls

Hanguranketa (28km/18mi from Kandy), in the 17th century the place of refuge for the Singhalese king Raja SinhaII, also lies in the enchanted Kandy Highlands near the deep Great Valley. In the surroundings maize, vegetables and above all tobacco are grown, as well as rice on elaborately laid-out terraces. It was around Hanguranketa, incidentally, that the first coffee bushes on Sri Lanka were planted.

An uprising in Kandy forced King Raja Sinha II to flee the capital in 1864 and hand over the throne to his son, still a minor. He sought shelter in Hanguranketa, and when he was able to return to Kandy once more, he had a kind of summer palace built in the place of his exile, and it was here that he spent most of his time from then on. Even so, it is said, he was very suspicious of all his compatriots, but even more so of strangers who tried to approach him. So by night he had drums beaten and trumpets blown in order to show people that he was on his guard. He himself would wander through the palace in disguise, watching his bodyguards, in case there were a traitor among them. He occupied the inhabitants of the town by getting them to

Hanguranketa

Kandy is surrounded by hills. Atop one of them is a colossal Buddha statue that is visible from miles around

divide a large hill in two, and to build a canal and embankments, in order to fill the valley with water. He scared off Europeans with wild animals, which he kept in the garden. In his book **»A Historical Relation of Ceylon«**, the Englishman Robert Knox, who was his prisoner at the time, provides a lively description of life at court. During the fighting with the British and the uprising of 1817, the town was badly damaged.

The **Buddhist temple** in the city was built in 1830. Typical of the post-Kandy era is the moonstone. decorated with floral elements, unusual by contrast is the stupa. In one room of the Vihara various ritual brass lamps can be seen; these have donated by the faithful. The library contains one of the most comprehensive collections of palm-leaf manuscripts (olas) anywhere. Wall paintings depict the Perahera, the great festive procession in Kandy, in which the monks from this monastery also take part.

Not far from the Buddhist temple is a **Hindu shrine** dedicated to the god Vishnu, which would be unremarkable but for two costly cloths from the 17th century. These were donated by King Raja SinhaII. They depict scenes from his battle against the Portuguese, which he won. On one picture a regiment of Moors mounted on camels can be seen, the only such picture in Sri Lanka. If you ask a monk nicely, he will be pleased to show you the cloths.

One important feature is a 17th-century **door-frame** carved out of a single rock, with finely worked relief sculptures, that was taken from the former royal palace. The motifs are bird-like mythical creatures and ornamental foliage, a crowned female figure, makaras and a band of lotus blossoms. The entrance is guarded by lions and stags. In 1885 a large stash of jewels was discovered here.

The two Hindu temples dedicated to the god Vishnu and the goddess Pattini were built during the Kandy period. Apart from the usual decorations, there is nothing much to see.

The monastery of Alu Vihara (▶Matale), famous not least because of its history, is also worth a visit. Also easily accessible from Kandy is the Pinawela elephant orphanage (▶Kegalle). A journey through the magnificent mountain landscape leads to the ▶Hunnas Falls.

Other places to go

Kataragama

✳ **D 9**

Province: Uva
Altitude: app. 16m/60ft

Kataragama, the most sacred place on the island for Hindus, lies at the foot of Kataragama Peak (424m/1391ft) and on the crystal-clear Menik Ganga, the »river of jewels«, and next to the Yala National Park. At the full moon at the end of July or beginning of August, thousands of pilgrims visit what is otherwise a dreamy place for the feast of Esala Perahera, filling it with life.

The history of the place goes back to the 3rd century BC. This is said to have been the headquarters of the Kshatriya warrior caste invited by King Devanampiya Tissa to Anuradhapura to plant a cutting of the Bodhi. In 181 BC, King Duttha Gamani, before moving from his principality if Ruhuna to Anuradhapura, is said to have visited the temple in Kataragama in order ask the war-god Skanda to liberate the town from the Chola.

History

According to the legend, Skanda, the second son of Shiva and Parvati, who lived on the mountain of the gods, Kailasa, in Tibet, heard of the beauty of the chief's daughter Valamma, and decided that she must be his. Disguised as a beggar, he confessed his love to her on the Menik Ganga, and asked her to marry him. Valamma, though, was outraged, and rejected him. Then Skanda's brother Ganesha appeared in the form of a wild elephant, and scared the girl so much that she fell into the arms of the alleged rescuer, and said yes after all. Skanda then transformed himself into a shining hero and took her to Kataragama Peak.

Kataragama

GETTING THERE
By car: from Colombo via Ratnapura and Timbolketiya, from here either on the southern route (A 18) via Ambalantota and Tissamaharama or on the northern route from Tissamaharama (app. 290km/180mi). From Tissamaharama it is around 16km/10mi.
By train: The closest train station is in Matara (the terminal station of the Colombo line); from there, there are bus connections (travel time app. 4 hours)

WHERE TO STAY
There are not many recommendable options in Kataragama; all accommodation will be fully booked long in advance during the days before and during the Perahera. The many rest houses for pilgrims make do without almost all the conventional hotel standards. As a result, we recommend finding a place to stay in Tissamaharama during the Perahera and visiting Kataragama as part of a day trip.

Rosen Renaissance Hotel ££ – £££
tel. 047 360 30-2
www.kataragama.org/rosen-hotel.htm
Four-star hotel set in a stunning landscape not far from Kataragama centre. The 52 rooms are all invitingly furnished and decorated.

Mandara Rosen Hotel ££ – £££
57 Detagamuwa, Tissa Road
tel. 047 223 60 30
www.mandarahotels.com
A new hotel situated somewhat outside of Kataragama. It is considered the best hotel in town. The 50 rooms and two suites are very comfortable. There is also a restaurant, a pool, including for children, a spa and a gym. The pool has a novelty feature: underwater loudspeakers.

Esala Perahera of Kataragama

Every year, on the occasion of the full moon that takes place at the end of July or the beginning of August, thousands of Hindus, Muslims and Buddhists gather in Kataragama to take part in the rites and processions of the well-known Esala Perahera. **The festivities last for nine days**, getting more lively all the time, before culminating magnificently on the last night. All the ceremonies begin with a ritual bath in the Menik Ganga. After various ritual acts, the actual procession begins, with richly decorated elephants, one of which carries the reliquary. This procession is repeated every evening, becoming noisier and more magnificent all the time. An interesting event takes place on the last evening, when the faithful flagellate themselves or fall into a trance and walk barefoot over glowing embers.

Apart from the thousands of believers who take part in the Perahera, there is a group that starts the festival 45 days earlier. Their journey, known as Pada Yatra, begins at the foot of the Jaffna Peninsula in the far north of the island, in the spot where Buddha is said to have set foot on Sri Lankan soil for the first time. They go on a pilgrimage via

The Esala Perahera is magnificent and colourful

Trincomalee, Batticaloa and through Yala National Park all the way to Kataragame. Their deep devotion and readiness to make sacrifices is honoured particularly highly after their arrival in the famous place of pilgrimage, which is why they are at the heart of the Perahera festivities.

WHAT TO SEE IN KATARAGAMA

The holiest temple in Kataragama, the Maha Devale, is a white, square and rather unassuming building. It stands at the end of a large palace on the banks of the Menik Ganga, surrounded by a wall decorated with elephants and peacocks, the latter being the creature on which Skanda rides, in a park-like compound. Since the precinct has been declared a »Sacred Zone«, snack bars and the like have had to move out. The only stalls are those selling offerings. The entrance gate is decorated with carvings. The interior of the shrine is surprisingly plain, without even

Maha Devale

?

Skanda or Kataragama?

The god of war, Skanda, is called Kataragama by Buddhists. Since all Hindus also worship Buddha, they turn to him with requests and venerate the town of Kataragama. In addition they believe that Buddha meditated here during his third visit to Sri Lanka.

a picture of the god. In the sanctuary, to which only the priests have access, is a container whose contents, maybe a relic, are unknown. Flowers and fruits are presented to it, and the oil-lamps have been kept alight since time immemorial. Clearly nothing has ever been changed here, as underscored by the timelessness of this holy place. The temple comes to life during the daily prayer sessions at 4.30am, 10.30am and 6.30pm, when believers gather before the shrine of their chief god. Their prayers produce a haunting atmosphere.

Next to the Maha Devale, other sights include the Ganesha temple dedicated to the elephant god, and a shrine dedicated to Vishnu, each of which holds a statue of Buddha, Vishnu and Skanda. At the other end of the square is the no less plain mosque and the graves of two Muslim saints. The older of the two is the destination for a pilgrimage by Sri Lanka's Muslims, because it contains the mortal remains of **Jabbar Ali Sha**, a pious man who lived in Kataragama at the end of the 19th century. The Kiri Vihara (milk dagoba), a large, bluish-white structure, dates back to the 3rd century BC, though it was renovated in the 1980s and given a crystal pinnacle with a gold setting. Buddhist pilgrims make offerings of flowers and coconuts here, before moving on to the Maha Devale.

To the right in front of the dagoba is a **small archaeological museum** that exhibits some items used in Hindu and Buddhist rites. There are also some attractive statues. The bodhi tree nearby is said to have been planted by King Devanampiya Tissa in person; it is allegedly more than 2200 years old. Near the tree is the little Pattini temple, where women pray for fertility.

Museum: daily, 8.30am–6pm, free admission, donation requested

Kegalle

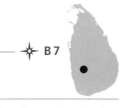

✦ **B 7**

Province: Sabaragamuwa
› **Altitude:** 124m/407ft
Population: 18,000

Kegalle, a bustling town in the middle of a productive rice-growing region, is situated at the foot of the rugged Hill Country around Kandy, which is covered in lavish vegetation. In addition to rice there are also tea and rubber plantations here. The famous elephant orphanage is nearby.

Kegalle

GETTING THERE

By car: from Colombo on the A 1 (77 km/48mi); from Kandy on the A 1 (39 km/24mi)

By train: the closest train stations are Polghawela and Rambukkana (both app. 12 km/7mi away).

By bus: good bus connections from Colombo and Kandy

WHERE TO STAY

There are two hotels near the elephant orphanage, but in light of the fairly basic amenities, they are above average with regard to price. Hence it is better to visit the establishment as part of a day trip, from Colombo or Kandy for example.

Elephant View £ £ – £ £ £

tel. 035 226 52 92

16 well furnished rooms with air-conditioning. A pleasant atmosphere and a restaurant. Views of elephants bathing in the river from here.

Elephant Park £ £ – £ £ £

tel. 035 226 61 71
www.pinnalanda.com

This smart hotel, which has 12 air-conditioned rooms and is particularly popular with tourists, also has good views of the river. The hotel restaurant (tel. 035 226 52 97) serves regional and international fare.

✶✶ ELEPHANT ORPHANAGE IN PINNAWALLA

The internationally famous Elephant Orphanage in Pinnawala is government-funded, **making it unique in the world**. This place, not far from the Maha Oya riverbank, is home to around 70 elephants of all ages, which for whatever reason are enjoying special protection by humans (►MARCO POLO Insight p.300).

Every tour operator and many taxi drivers offer trips to Pinnawala. It is a good idea to negotiate a fee before embarking on the journey. An appropriate price from Kandy would be app. 3500Rs.

Visiting times

The best time to visit the orphanage is when the few-month-old elephants are given the bottle. This has to be done five times a day, but only the feeding times of 9.15am, 1.15pm and 4.15pm are open to visitors. The bath in Maha Oya is also an event (daily 10am–noon and 2pm–8pm)

Beligela

A few kilometres west of Kegalle is Beligela, the former residence of King Parakrama Bahu's cousin and feudal vassal Prince Gajabahu II (1132–1153), who defeated the king in their battle for power and probably also killed him. Nothing is left of Gajabahu's palace. All that has remained is the temple, which was expanded and beautified by later kings. Of the good stonework, a finely worked moonstone is particularly remarkable.

Well Protected Little Giants

Not even a century ago, when there were still around 12,000 wild elephants in Sri Lanka, it was no problem for even injured animals to survive. Even if the mother was unavailable, the herd looked after the offspring.

That changed when humans set about taking possession of the wild elephants' places of refuge. Forests were logged, roads were built. These often cut through the elephants' routes, routes they had known and travelled for centuries. A further reason was ruthless poaching and a desire for the precious ivory, which was particularly prominent among the colonial rulers. Is the elephant orphanage in Pinnawala just a way to quiet a bad conscience? Or is it merely a welcome way of bringing in some tourists? It is probably a bit of both, but it should be noted that the government really does seem to worry about the continued existence of these likable animals.

Feeding

It is just after nine o'clock in the morning. The elephant keepers are dissolving particularly nourishing milk powder in large vats filled with water. As if it could not wait, a small elephant nudges the keeper gently to the side with its trunk. It is not long before the expensive special feed has been prepared and the little elephants can be fed. It is the second meal of the day already because they already got around eight litres of baby milk earlier. For dessert the little elephants gets a fat bundle of fresh, green sugar cane stalks and a few

leaves. That is expensive, the keeper says, but it is paid for by the state, which covers the majority of the deficit, but on the other hand also makes sure through advertising that Pinnawala is part of every tourist agenda. The locals make good money from selling T-shirts with elephant prints and stools covered in elephant skin. The larger elephants can look after themselves. A grown bull eats around 250kg per day. Here, in the elephant orphanage, they are served their food almost ready to eat and because there is nothing nearby that the elephants like to eat, it has to be brought in especially by lorry.

Bathing

Until that happens there is time for a refreshing bath. One by one the animals head down to the river. There is a mahout next to every elephant. The mahout is the driver, the only and most important reference person in the life of a tamed elephant. Every now and then he will use a hook to gently pull is charge in the desired direction, which the elephant will do without complaint. A short while later the elephants can be seen rolling around in the muddy brown water of the Maha Oya, visibly enjoying themselves and in no way irritated by the dozens of

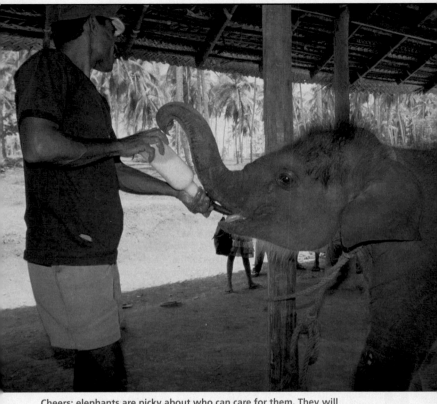

Cheers: elephants are picky about who can care for them. They will only take a bottle from their personal mahout.

cameras, while their mahouts scrub their skin.

Working?

In this regard they have it better than the 200 elephants that have been roped in to work in agriculture and forestry on Sri Lanka. They are particularly indispensable in the thick jungle, where they are able to drag teak tree trunks that weigh several tons.

The elephants in Pinnawala do not have to do any tiring work. Since they cannot just be released into the wild again, where their fellow elephants would not accept them anymore, they will spend their whole lives in the orphanage. But some of them will be allowed to do a very pleasant job: serving as a magnificent parade elephant at the great Perahera in Kandy.

Temple
interior
The **main room** to the right is the oldest part of the temple. The other rooms were added much more recently. It houses the 13m/42ft figure of a recumbent Buddha. The wall paintings reveal a clear European influence in their vitality as well as in the coloration and luminosity. Between the pictures, which mainly depict scenes from the Jataka, there are dancers, musicians and flower motifs. One of these pictures deserves special attention, because it shows the nun Hemamala bringing Buddha's sacred tooth to Sri Lanka – according to legend she hid it in her hair. The ceiling of the main room is painted in interesting geometrical patterns.

Bodhi tree
One important feature outside is the magnificent bodhi tree, which stands on a structured terrace. Throughout the day Buddhists can be seen here walking around the terrace with containers filled with water with which they sprinkle the tree while they mutter prayers. The pools in front of the main entrance of the temple, in which **ritual cleansing** takes place, were only built recently.

Buddhist
university
The remaining buildings in the temple grounds are part of the Buddhist university that was founded in 1958. It is known by the name Vidyalankara and developed from a school, founded by Buddhist monks, for the reforming and deepening of Buddha's teachings.

Kurunegala

—✳— **B 7**

Province: North
Western: Altitude 85m/279ft
Population: 30,000

The rugged rocks on the outskirts of Kurunegala, including the 330m/1083ft »Elephant Rock«, the idyllic Batalagoda Reservoir and several cultural attractions in the surrounding area make this town particularly appealing.

History
Between 1293 and 1326, during the reigns of kings Bhuvanaika BahuII and Parakrama BahuIV, who felt the capital of ▶Polonnaruwa had become too unsafe as it was constantly being threatened by the Tamils, Kurunegala was the capital of the Singhalese kingdom. The kings built a palace and a temple for the sacred tooth relic here (▶Kandy). It was also during this period that Marco Polo (▶Famous People) visited the city.
After the death of King Vijaya Bahu V his sons argued about who should ascend the throne. The usurper Vasthimi Kumareya, whose mother was a Muslim concubine, was the first to seize the throne,

Kurunegala

GETTING THERE
By car: from Colombo on the A1 to
Ambepussa, then on the A6 (133km);
from Kandy on the A10 (42km)
By train: station on the Colombo–Jaff-
na line
By bus: good bus connections from
Colombo and Kandy

WHERE TO STAY/EAT
Diya Dahara Hotel £ £
7, Northlake Road
tel. 037 222 34 52

The best rooms are in the hotel's newly
built section. The seven rooms are
comfortable but quite expensive.
Many have sea views. The restaurant is
recommended.

The Ranthaliya Resthouse £
South Lake Road
tel. 037 222 22 98
This guesthouse is basic and only offers
modest levels of comforts. But the
rooms are clean and the good restaurant serves tasty local dishes.

while the younger rightful son retreated to the country. After some
time he was sought out, however, since his brother showed excessive
favouritism towards the Muslim subjects. After his coronation he
moved to Dambadeniya with the justification that Kurunegala had
been desecrated by a half-Muslim king. Kurunegala subsequently lost
its importance.
Today Kurunegala is the capital of Northwest province, with good
traffic connections, lying on the railweay from Colombo to the north
of the country.

WHAT TO SEE IN KURUNEGALA

Nothing remains of the royal residence and the temple. They probably **Town on the**
once stood on the site of the present-day market, which always has a **lake**
large variety of different fruits on offer. Many jewellers' shops with
engraved goods line the streets. The very pretty Lake Batalagoda with
its countless water lilies all around the edge was probably created by
King Bhuvanaike Bahu II as a water reservoir; on its western shore is
a pretty rest house which has been extended into a small hotel.

Above the town are some very strangely shaped rocks named after **Rocks of**
animals: Elephant Rock (Etagala) and Tortoise Rock (Ibbagala) for **Kurunegala**
example; Elephant Rock is the highest at 330m/1083ft. In addition
there are Goat Rock and Crocodile Rock as well as several other
smaller ones. The views of the densely forested mountain landscape
and the reservoir are particularly stunning from Elephant Rock and
Tortoise Rock, where Ibbagala Vihara is a **worthwhile destination**

as it has some Buddha statues and a highly venerated footprint of Buddha to offer.

AROUND KURUNEGALA

Silver Temple

Around 20km/12mi northeast of Kurunegala there is a temple, situated on a rocky outcrop, known as Silver Temple; 200 steps lead up to it. King Duttha Gamani is said to have founded it in around 100 BC out of gratitude for the vein of silver he discovered here. The current buildings date from the 18th century when King Kirti Sri Raja Sinha had the monastery refurbished. It is known for its extensive collection of old palmleaf manuscripts kept in the library. The richly carved doors decorated with ivory inlays are also remarkable. The motifs have been taken from the world of mythology: in addition to tendrils and lotus blossoms there are a dancing-girl and lions as well as a vase of abundance, from whose foliage female deities appear. **The works are of exceptional refinement**. A peculiarity is the altar, which was a gift from a Dutch governor. The Delft tiles that adorn the altar depict Christian scenes.

Arankale (hermitage)

Around 23km/14mi north of Kurunegala is the hermitage of Arankale, an interesting ruin in a beautiful, tranquil forest. Access it via Ibbagamuwa, turn left behind the town towards Kumbukwewa, when the road forks take the left-hand road. At the start of the 1st century the sage Maliydeva retreated here with his monks. The complex can be accessed via a cobbled **meditation path** lined by high metrosideros trees. The path arrives at a **meditation circle** surrounded by tall, carved stones. Stone columns lying around are the only visible remains of the monastic complex, which was probably built in the 6th century. Believers from the villages place their food donations for the monks on the tables made of carved stone that stand in a nearby clearing.

Dambadeniya

Dambadeniya is around 30km/18mi from Kurunegala. For a few years, during the confusions of the Chola rule in the 13th century, the town was considered the Singhalese capital during the resistance to the Tamils in the actual capital of Polonnaruwa. Vijaya Bahu III, the nominal king from 1232 to 1236, based himself in Dambadeniya, but it was only his son who managed to liberate Polonnaruwa again. The town later fell once more into insignificance. Some ruins survive of the period when Dambadeniya was the capital, but they are hard to verify.

Sri Wijaya Sundarama Raja Maha Vihara

Parts of the Sri Wijaya Sundarama Raja Maha Vihara temple, which is protected by a large rock, date back to the 13th century. The unusual shape of the dagoba is also striking. It bears a rectangular roof and also possesses an atrium. The guard stones flanking the staircase up to the statue house are also unusual; they depict scenes from the Jataka, the stories of Buddha's past lives. The left-hand one shows a seated Buddha at the centre, above and below him battle scenes, while the right-hand one also depicts battle scenes and an elephant which is evidently stamping on the victims. The atrium to the image gallery is adorned by a pretty roof in the Kandyan style, whose fan-like timberwork deserves particular attention. The exterior and interior walls of the upper floor, which is reached via a narrow stairway, are decorated with good wall paintings – those on the external walls were not completed. On the right-hand wall is a depiction of Vishnu clad in a Buddhist robe; he is leading a number of worshipping monks.

The large image gallery from more recent times houses the statue of a recumbent Buddha. Opposite the entrance a path goes through paddy fields to a rock on which a citadel once stood.

Mahiyangana (Alutnuvara)
✦ C–D 7

Province: Uva
Altitude: approx. 223m/732ft

The now quite small town whose dagoba becomes the destination of many Buddhist pilgrims once a year during the September full moon is situated in magnificent scenery on Mahaweli Ganga at the foot of the Central Highlands.

Mahiyangana was inhabited long before the time of Christ and in the 17th century it was still a flourishing town, not least because several European missions reached Kandy from Batticaloa via the Mahawli Ganga, which is navigable as far as Mahiyangana. There are still some Vedda settlements around Mahiyangana; the Vedda are Sri Lanka's aboriginal inhabitants. They enjoy special government protection, which is also why they cannot be visited.

History

★★ MAHIYANGANA DABOBA

The chronicle of the Mahavamsa, which is filled with many a legend, reports that Buddha visited a town called Mahanaga – or Maha Nagara, which means »big town« – nine months after his enlightenment in order to convince the Yakshas, Sri Lanka's legendary daemonic aboriginal inhabitants who gathered here from time to time, of his teachings. He is said to have achieved this by performing several **miracles**. The most impressive event, as recorded by the chronicle, is

Surrounded by park-like landscape

Mahiyangana

GETTING THERE

By car: from Kandy on the A 26 (74 km/46mi), from Badulla on the A8 to Waywatta, from there on the A 26 to Mahiyangana
By train: from Colombo to Kandy (several connections per day), from there onwards by bus or with a rental vehicle
By bus: daily bus connections from Kandy, Batticaloa and Badulla

WHERE TO STAY

The closest accommodation is in "Kandy; there is hardly any recommendable accommodation in Mahiyangana itself.

Insider Tip

The Nest £ – £ £

45 Paiyathalawa Road
tel. 077 619 95 11 (mobile)
www.nest-srilanka.com
Family-run guesthouse with five rooms, some of them with air-conditioning (for an additional charge). It is located 2km/1mi east of Mahiyangana at kilometre-marker 75. The guesthouse owner also runs tours such as to the jungle in the surrounding area and to the Veddas. It is also possible to opt for open-air camping in the jungle. The owner has all the equipment necessary for this. The restaurant serves outstanding local dishes. Most of the ingredients are home-grown.

that Buddha flew off through the air after his sermon. According to the historical tradition it was Mahanaga, a brother of King Devanampiya Tissa (250–210 BC) and founder of Magama, the old capital of the kingdom of Ruhuna and now an abandoned place in the dense jungle, who had the dagoba built. A curl of hair dedicated by the enlightened one to the Yakshas was the first relic of this dagoba. The lock was placed in a gem-encrusted urn and was the reason why the dagoba was built. To this day it is one of the most important Buddhist places of worship in Sri Lanka.

Temple complex
To get to the dagoba there are two options; either via the 2000 steps of the pilgrim's path or via a narrow road. The dagoba's 2.2m/7 ft door surround is adorned with Buddhist symbols such as suns, lotus blossoms and hares; these depictions refer to a story in the Jataka in which Buddha's previous lives, of which there are more than 500, are described. The moonstone is decorated with a band of elephants and horses as well as a closed lotus bud.

Reliquary chamber
During restoration works in the early 1950s a reliquary chamber with a square floor plan was uncovered; it was probably only built during the restoration of the 11th century. The niches at the cardinal points of the four walls house one or more likenesses of Buddha in the Indian Amaravati or Pala style. The stone, box-shaped container in the middle of the room, which has an edge length of 1.22m/4ft and a

height of only 1.1m/3ft 6 in, contained two relics, small dagobas made of copper with a golden tip as well as coins and flowers made of gold leaf. Four bronze figures of people on horseback, armed with sword and shield, accompanied by a woman stood as if on guard at the sides of the stone container. The other objects in the chamber (including iron tridents as a symbol of Shiva, golden banners, copper containers and lamps, bowls with coins as well as precious stones) were set up symmetrically around the stone container. The walls were covered with paintings of which only fragments survive. These were carefully removed and, just like the other objects, taken to the national museum of ▶Anuradhapura.

Matale

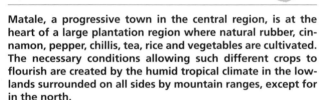

✳ **C 7**

Province: Central
Altitude: approx. 360m/1180ft
Population: 37,000

Matale, a progressive town in the central region, is at the heart of a large plantation region where natural rubber, cinnamon, pepper, chillis, tea, rice and vegetables are cultivated. The necessary conditions allowing such different crops to flourish are created by the humid tropical climate in the lowlands surrounded on all sides by mountain ranges, except for in the north.

WHAT TO SEE IN MATALE

Above Saxton Park at the centre of Matale are the remains of Fort Macdowall. It was built by the British at the start of the 19th century during the war against the kings of Kandy.

Fort Macdowall

The Hindu temple situated on the main road through Matale, Sri Muthumariamman Thevasthaman, is a must-see for its lavish, colourful statues, but it is unremarkable as an example of sacred architecture.

Hindu temple

✳✳ ALUVIHARA (ROCK TEMPLE)

Situated in a rugged rocky landscape, Aluvihara is one of the most significant sites for Buddhism in Sri Lanka. Even though not much remains from the monastery's great heyday it is still worth visiting for

Historically significant

Dagobas

Dagobas evolved from Indian stupas. The first structures of this kind appeared on Sri Lanka in the 2nd cent. BC. The term comes from Sanskrit and means as much as »piling up« or »gathering«. A dagoba often holds a relic or serves as a symbolic monument to Buddha. Believers always circle around them clockwise, which is considered to have a positive effect on the next life.

▶ **Origins**
The term »stupa« is common in India. In Sri Lanka these reliquaries are called dagoba, in Mongolia suburghan, in Burma and Tibet chorten, in Thailand chedi and in China pagoda.

Pagoda

Stupas

▶ **Varieties of forms**
The dome makes up most of the dagoba and is the place where the relic is kept. The most common shape is the bell shape.

Name	Ruwanweli	Jetavana	Thūpārāma
Construction date	161–137 BC	AD269–296	about 149 B
Height	91.4m/298ft	70.7m/233ft	36.6m/120ft
Diameter of dome	90.8m/300ft	102m/336ft	18m/59.4ft

Forms of dagobas

Dagobas were copied from Indian models.
In the course of time Sri Lanka developed its own forms..

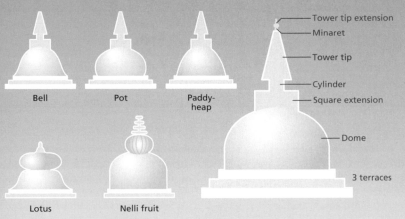

Bell

Pot

Paddy-
heap

Lotus

Nelli fruit

Tower tip extension
Minaret
Tower tip
Cylinder
Square extension
Dome
3 terraces

©BAEDEKER

► **Meditation system**
Dagobas reflect the
form of the sitting
Buddha.

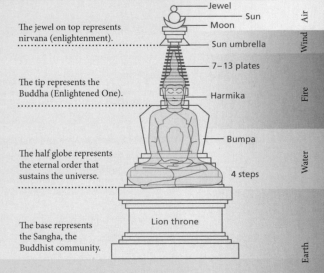

The jewel on top represents
nirvana (enlightenment).

The tip represents the
Buddha (Enlightened One).

The half globe represents
the eternal order that
sustains the universe.

The base represents
the Sangha, the
Buddhist community.

Jewel
Sun
Moon
Sun umbrella
7–13 plates
Harmika
Bumpa
4 steps
Lion throne

Air
Wind
Fire
Water
Earth

Mahiyangana
about 300 BC
19.2m/63ft

Matale

GETTING THERE

By car: from Matale (3 km/2mi), from Kandy on the A 9 (26 km/16mi), from Dambulla on the A 9 (48 km/30mi), from Kurunegala via Kandy (51 km/32mi), via Ibbagamuwa (43 km/27mi)

By train: Matale is the terminal station on the train line from Kandy; take a taxi to the complex from here.

By bus: many direct connections per day from Kandy

WHERE TO STAY

Clover Grange
££
95 Kings Street
tel. 066 223 11 44
Cosy hotel with a restaurant in the middle of some stunning landscape

and surrounded by a lovely garden. The six rooms are furnished well, in line with the price, but they do not have air conditioning. The building itself is more than 100 years old; a few years ago it was renovated, while remaining true to its style.

Ancoombra Holiday Bungalow
££££

Insider Tip

392 Main Street
tel. 066 222 4254
mobile 077 234 9080
www.meezans.com
A recommended guesthouse with only four well-furnished colonial style rooms. Located very nice amidst a breathtaking landscape close to a tea plantation. Fine meals are prepared on request.

the famous rock temple alone. The ability of the Singhalese to incorporate buildings harmoniously into the landscape also becomes remarkably clear here.

The monastery was founded by Wattagamini Abhaya in the 1st century BC. There are two stone staircases with around 50 steps each leading up to it from the road. It is almost jammed in between splintered granite rocks; the **best overview of the entire complex** can be had by climbing a further steep slope and looking down from the dagoba above the actual temple.

Beside the lower dagoba is a hall carved out of the rock containing paintings and statues depicting the enlightened one in the typical poses (meditating, teaching and resting). Other caves contain the monks' living quarters. King Walagam Bahu is said to have stayed in one of the caves. He fled the capital Anuradhapura from the Tamils in around 103 BC.

The rock temple of Aluvihara obtained its great significance in 80 BC when around 500 Buddhist monks from all around the world met here to write down Buddha's teachings, which had previously been handed down orally, on palm leaves (olas). This is when the canon of scriptures known as Tripitaka (= three baskets) was written down in

The Aluvihara has a picturesque situation among a group of rocks

Pali, the sacred language of Buddhism. In these three baskets, Vinayapitaka, Suttapitaka and Abhidammapitaka, Buddha's teachings have been summarized. Together with the comments written down by the monks they are still used as the guideline for recitations. In a small museum nearby monks demonstrate the art of writing on palm leaves. The fact that they are true masters of this art benefits them now because during the war between the British and the kings of Kandy in 1646 a large number of the valuable manuscripts were destroyed. The reconstruction work is still going on. To this day new insights of the Buddhist religion from all around the world are written down in this traditional manner.

AROUND MATALE

Hunas Falls
Around 15km/9mi east of Matale are the Hunas Falls (►Kandy), set in beautiful mountainous landscape.

Nalanda
Nalanda (23km/14mi from Matale) is still in the area dominated by the extensive plantations that begin north of Kandy. The crops culti-

vated here include cocoa, rubber, vegetables and rice. Beyond this are is a mountain region still partially covered in dense jungle. In the first half of the 12th century Nalanda was briefly the residence of the Ruhuna princes and later King Parakrama Bahu I, who went to battle from here against Gaja Bahu III from Polonnaruwa. However, he was only able to rule after his death in 1153.

Nalanda The Nalanda Gedige around 1km/0.6mi east of the town is one of the
Gedige earliest stone buildings in Sri Lanka. It is dated to the 8th or 9th century. The architectural style and the still extant sculptures reveal it to have been alternately a Buddhist and a Brahman temple; its monks followed Mahayana Buddhism. The shape of the temple with its arched roof and horseshoe-shaped gable that was certainly taken over from Hindu models strongly exhibits the influence of the southern Indian architecture of the Pallava period (approx. 625–800). Other details such as the stair design with moonstone and the Makara balustrade as well as the dancing dwarfs come from the Buddhist architectural canon. **Remarkable sculptures** were found in the temple and the surrounding area. Now they are exhibited in the temple. Amongst them are a guard stone with a snake temple under the seven-headed shield of Naga, a four-armed Ganesha as well as several small sculptures in erotic positions. This latter kind of sculpture is mainly found in southern India.

❶ 8am – 6pm. The admission charge to the temple is included in the collective ticket for the Cultural Triangle.

> ! **MARCO ◉ POLO TIP**
>
> *Spice gardens* **Insider Tip**
>
> There are many spice gardens in Matale, along the road to Kandy for example; they are worth visiting. See how spices are grown and processed. And of course it is also possible to buy spices here.

Nalanda The way to Wahakotte, 15km/9mi north of the town, goes past the
Wewa picturesquely situated Nalanda Wewa, one of Sri Lanka's many arti-
(reservoir) ficial lakes. On its shores many different bird species can be seen.

Elahera Canal To get to Ataragollawa, 21km/13mi from Nalanda, take the A9, then turn right. Situated amongst ruins is the relatively well preserved 12m/40 ft statue of a recumbent Buddha from the 9th/10th century. Near Elahera, 8km/5mi further east, there were once high-yielding gemstone mines, which have, however, been exhausted. The Elahera Canal, created by Vasabha (67–111), the first ruler of the Lambakanna dynasty, was initially and incredible 50km/30mi long but in the 6th century it was lengthened by 100km/60mi and formed a significant part of the complex irrigation system that also includes Amban Ganga and the reservoirs of Minneriya and Giritale.

Matara

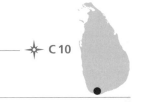

✳ **C 10**

Province: Southern
Altitude: 7m/23ft
Population: 43,000

Matara is situated on a wide bay in the island's far south. This is where Nilwala Ganga, coming from the mountains, flows into the sea and this is also where the railway line from Colombo ends. The hinterland was once a large spice garden. Today visitors will only find cinnamon and tea plantations as well as citronella fields. The town is somewhat remote and so it has maintained some of its charm from days gone by.

Between 1518 and 1656 the Portuguese occupied Matara several times, but it was only the Dutch who built two forts between 1656 and 1796. When the Kandyan king Kirti Sri Raja Sinha (1747–1781)   **History**

Matara

GETTING THERE
By car: from Galle on the A 2 (41 km/25mi); from Hambantota on the A 2 (70 km/43mi)
By train: terminal station on the train line from Colombo
By bus: good connections from Galle

WHERE TO STAY/EAT
Kingdom Ayurveda
£££
Walgampokun, Kottegoda (Dickwella)
The focal point of this very smart hotel on the Indian Ocean is ayurveda. The hotel has deliberately chosen not to install air-conditioning because according to the ayurvedic teachings, the body is to adapt to the ambient temperatures. The eight rooms in the colonial-style building are all attractive.

Turtle Eco Beach
££ – £££
Beach Road, Batala Watta
tel. 041 222 33 77
www.turtleecobeach.com
A hotel furnished wholly with ecological principles in mind. Located right on a wide sandy beach. The 18 rooms are spread over five buildings. The Olive Ridley restaurant serves local fare as well as seafood.

Mandara Resort Marissa
££ – £££
West of Matara
tel. 041 225 39 93
www.mandararesort.com
This new hotel has 20 rooms; it is right on a wide sandy beach. The rooms in the Superior category are the best. They have their own pool. The restaurant serves outstanding local food as well as international fare.

tried to seize power over some of the Dutch territory, the Dutch retaliated by stopping salt deliveries to Kandy. The king reacted by moving south with his troops and conquering Matara. However, in 1765, after the Dutch had entered Kandy, he had to withdraw his troops again and make peace with them as well as hand over the entire southern strip of coastline to them.

** DUTCH FORT

The star-shaped fort complex was built by the Dutch governor van Eck in 1763. The monumental entrance gate bears his name as well as the Dutch coat of arms and the year 1770, the year of its completion. The fort now houses a **small museum** whose collection is a smorgasbord of items that cannot necessarily be connected to Matara. However, the many aerial photographs of Sri Lanka's archaeological excavation sites are noteworthy. The buildings within the larger fort near the coast are now used by the government and administration because Matara is the district capital. Not far away is the obligatory clock tower dating back to the Dutch period. A causeway connects the mainland to the small island of Chula Lanka, whose now abandoned monastery was founded by a Thai monk.

AROUND MATARA

*Polhena beach

Just over a kilometre west of Matara is one of Sri Lanka's nicest swimming beaches: the small bay of Polhena. Offshore there are nice, but partially plundered coral reefs.

Dondra Head

Not far from here is Dondra Head, **the southernmost point of the island of Sri Lanka**. There is a lighthouse here that stands 52m/171ft, making it the tallest in Sri Lanka. The structure with its octagonal footprint was built by the British colonial powers in 1889. The light from its dome can been seen from up to 28 nautical miles away. The somewhat laborious climb is rewarded by splendid views of the Indian Ocean.

Dondra itself is an important place of pilgrimage for Hindus and Buddhists. The Vishnu Devale and the Buddhist Devinuvara Temple, both in the town centre, are worth visiting. According to the Ramayana Chronicle, this is where Prince Rama found and rescued his wife Sita, who had been taken by the demon king Ravana. Skanda, the god of war who is highly venerated on Sri Lanka, is also said to have made landfall near Dondra. Every year in July/August a **Perahera** is held in Dondra. It continues for ten days and is attended by thousands of pilgrims.

Medirigiriya

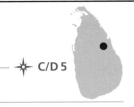

✳ **C/D 5**

Province: Northern Central
Altitude: 155m/509ft

Medirigiriya, now a fairly forlorn place situated in the middle of some magnificent landscape not far from Polonnaruwa, possessed a significant temple from very early on. The well preserved ruins have great significance for the artistic development in Sri Lanka.

✳✳ VATADAGE OF MEDIRIGIRIYA

As is reported in the Mahavamsa chronicle, Kanittha Tissa (approx. 164–192) had a Uposatha hall built in Mandalagiri Vihara, as the place was called at the time. In the second half of the 7th century King Agabodhi began building the Vatadage (round temple). According to an inscription a hospital was added to the monastery complex in the 9th century. At this time a number of villages in the surrounding area were also part of the monastic complex. King Nissanka Malla had the Vatadage restored at the end of the 12th century; he also commissioned four statues of sitting Buddhas, which face the four staircases.

Complex

As in ▶Anuradhapura the temple complex of Medirigiriya fell into ruin over time. It was only in 1934 that archaeologists from Colombo started paying attention to the complex, which by then was completely overgrown by the jungle. It was not until 1941 that restoration work began, which was completed in 1955.

Alongside the Vatadage of Polonnaruwa the one in Medirigiriya is **the most significant example of this temple type in Sri Lanka**. It stands on a granite rock that has steps leading up it.

Medirigiriya

GETTING THERE

By car: from Polonnaruwa on the A 11 to Giritale, then turn right towards Hingurakgoda, then head north (app. 30 km/19mi)

By train: from Polonnaruwa to Hingurakgoda, from there continue by taxi

WHERE TO STAY

Unfortunately there is no recommendable accommodation in Medirigiriya and the surrounding area. It is better to continue to "Polonnaruwa.

»Vatadage« means »round temple«

Dagoba At the centre of the round temple is a dagoba with a diameter of approx. 8m/27 ft; at its core it is around 800 years older than the rest of the structure. At the four cardinal points, opposite the entrances, are the statues of Buddha, but only the eastern one is in its pristine state. The other three statues were put together from remains that were found within the complex. However, the facial features and postures are still very impressive.

On the terrace laid out on irregularly worked granite and limestone blocks stand octagonal stone pillars with remarkably beautiful capitals. They are arranged in three concentric circles and vary in height: the 16 pillars of the innermost circle have a height of 5.18m/17ft, the 20 of the second circle 4.88m/16ft and the 32 of the outer circle only 2.74m/9ft; they are incorporated in a surrounding balustrade. Between the second and third circles of pillars was a brick wall with openings at the four cardinal points; apart from a few remains in the southwest it has disappeared. It and the columns once supported the wooden roof.

The gallery terrace is paved with granite slabs. The 5.20m/17ft pedestal is made of brick and stands on a natural rock   .

The entrance to the Vatadage is in the north. Visitors walk through a 2.75m/9ft gate to get to the 27 steps that lead up to an almost square platform. The moonstones in front of the four stairways leading up to the temple proper are unadorned.

the foundations of a number of square stone pillars without capitals still survive of the statue house to the northwest of the Vatadage, as do three colossal statues of standing Buddhas. The pedestal of the bodhi tree enclosure, richly adorned with lion reliefs, was made towards the end of the Anuradhapura period (during the 10th century). Amongst the remains of the hospital a vat carved from a monolith is of note. It was probably made in the 9th or 10th century and was most likely used to store cooked rice until it was time to hand it out to the monks and patients.

Statue house, bodhi tree

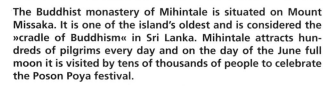

** Mihintale

✳ C 5

Province: Northern Central
Altitude: approx. 309m/1014ft

The Buddhist monastery of Mihintale is situated on Mount Missaka. It is one of the island's oldest and is considered the »cradle of Buddhism« in Sri Lanka. Mihintale attracts hundreds of pilgrims every day and on the day of the June full moon it is visited by tens of thousands of people to celebrate the Poson Poya festival.

The monastery of Mihintale owes its construction to the monk Mahinda, who was sent out by King Ashoka to spread the teachings of the enlightened Buddha in Sri Lanka. He found a keen listener in King Devanampiya Tissa, who soon declared Buddhism the state religion. That was in 250 BC, shortly after the king had ascended the throne. Mahinda, the son of the Indian king Ashoka (ruled 268–253BC), who had himself ordained a monk, had been sent to Sri Lanka after the third Buddhist council in Pataliputra in India (c. 253 BC), along with four fellow believers, to spread the teachings of the enlightened Buddha. He lived for a long time as a hermit in Mihintale, proclaiming Buddha's teachings. He also founded a Sangha, one of the first Buddhist communities. King Tissa had a large monastery and dagobas for several relics built on the hill near Mahinda's hermitage. Despite the confusions of the centuries Mihintale never fell into oblivion. All of the rulers were interested in preserving the buildings and renovating them when necessary.

History

MONASTERY COMPLEX OF MIHINTALE

From the town of Mihintale the A9 goes to the ruins of the monastery complex. To the left of the road are the remains of the old hospital,

Old hospital

Mihintale

GETTING THERE
By car: from Anuradhapura, A 9 (15 km/9mi); from Kandy on the A 9 (138 km/86mi)
By bus: good connections from Anuradhapura and Kandy

WHERE TO STAY
There is currently only one modest guesthouse in Mihintale; however, it is not far to "Giritale with its recommendable hotels.

whose foundations and pillars still allow visitors to make out the individual rooms. The **practical arrangement** of the wards is remarkable. They were easy to reach from an interior hallway. The stone tub that was carved from a granite block was presumably used for healing baths and the big millstone for grinding medicinal herbs.

Indikatuseya and Katuseya Dagobas
Somewhat further along on the same side of the road are the ruins of the Indikatuseya and Katuseya Dagobas from the 8th century. The base of the dagobas is impressive. It consists of a rounded ledge of carved stone. Its configuration is also remarkable. The stairway up to the stumps of a few pillars, all that remains of a building, is decorated by attractive guard stones.

Remains of a vatadage
Shortly before starting the climb up the stone stairs, notice the remains of a temple on the left-hand side. It resembles the Mahasena palace in Anuradhapura in its composition, but here it has the shape of a round structure, which is reminiscent of the vatadage temple type.

Stairway
The **monumental stairway** on the top of the hill presumably dates back to the monastery's founding days. It was carved out of the granite rocks and consists of four flights with a total of 1840 steps, which are lined by magnificently flowering frangipani trees.

Kantaka Chaitya Dagoba
From the first landing a narrower stairway leads up to a plateau on which the **Kantaka Chaitya Dagoba** rises up. It was named after the horse on which Buddha is said to have left the parental court and forsworn the lavish lifestyle. According to the legend, the horse died of grief. The dagoba was probably built in the 2nd century BC and was around 30m/100ft tall; today it is in ruins. The circumference of its well preserved base is 130m/426 ft; its three parts are typical of the early Singhalese dagobas. The four vahalkadas (altars) with very nice sculptural ornamentation, largely from the 1st century AD, are quite striking. They boast finely chiselled edges, friezes consisting of elephants, wild geese and extremely lively depictions of dwarfs. The left

stele of the eastern vahalkada has ornaments of plants, an elephant, a peacock with its young and a vase of abundance with two birds. On the stone altar in front of the vahalkadas offerings were made during ritual acts. On the right side of the eastern Vahalkada is the torso of a female figure, on the southern one the relief sculpture of the snake king Muchalinda in human form. They are very unusual because they are believed to be the **earliest pieces of sculpture in Sri Lanka.**

In the area around Kantaka Chaitya there are **more than 60 living-caves** in the rocks and under rocky slopes. They were inhabited during the time of the first community of monks in the 3rd century BC. Some still have visible inscriptions in the Brahmi script.

Returning to the main stairs and climbing up higher visitors will reach the second section of the stairs and the **remains of a monastery** that was probably built in the 9th century. The remains of an aqueduct, supported by high stone pillars, are of interest, as is a large and a smaller stone basin, which was presumably used to store donated food, but possibly also to store herbs for making medicines. The ruins of a large building, probably the image gallery, include two vertical monoliths, probably from the 10th century. They bear inscriptions providing insight about the rules in place at the time: »Nobody who has taken life may live near this hill.« Other inscriptions explain the instructions for taking care of the sick as well as the tasks of the temple servants.

A path to the right of the main stairs goes to the lion pond (Sinha Pokuna) with **one of Sri Lanka's most attractive animal sculptures**. It depicts a lion through whose mouth the water once flowed into the pool. The finely chiselled pool surrounding is classically austere: a frieze on the outside with very attractive reliefs of animals and dancers and in the upper surround individual reliefs of figures.

Sinha Pokuna (lion pond)

Mihintale

↑ *Mihintale*

100 m

© BAEDEKER

Mahinda's bed

Ambasthala Dagoba

Monastery

Sila Rock

Giribandhu Dagoba

Anuradhapura

Stone pools

Maha Seya Dagoba

Naga Pokuna

Refectory

Kantaka Chaitya Dagoba

Sinha Pokuna

Kaludiya Pokuna ↑

At Dagoba

View from the top of Sila Rock

Naga Pokuna (snake pond) Continue up the main stairs, which now start becoming narrower. At some point a path turns off to the right and climbs up steeply to Naga Pokuna (snake pond). The pool is almost 40m/130 ft long and has been carved from the rock. The bas relief of a five-headed naga that has been carved into the rock is quite impressive.

Ambasthala Dagoba The main stairs now lead to Ambasthala Dagoba (mango tree dagoba) surrounded by high coconut palms; it was built in the first quarter of the 1st century AD. The reliquary chamber within contains some of the mortal remains of the monk Mahinda. Of the complex, built in the style of a vatadage, most of the pillars arranged in two concentric circles still survive and some of them have lovely capitals. A modern building with an octagonal floor plan to the south of the dagoba marks the spot where Mahinda and the king first met.

Mahinda's bed Opposite the entrance to the Ambastala Dagoba a path leads down to the spot known as Mahinda's bed. It is a cave with a carved, flat stone on which the monk is said to have slept and meditated.

Sila Rock Up steep steps carved into the rock visitors will get to Sila Rock, from where there is **a magnificent view** of the jungle, Mahakandarawa Wewa (a reservoir) and Anuradhapura in the west.

Mahinda Vihara On the opposite hill to the left of the small pond is the small rock temple of Mahinda Vihara, which contains a modern depiction of the encounter between the monk and the king.

The peak of Mount Missaka is adorned by the gleaming-white 21m/69ft Maha Seya Dagoba from the 10th century, which is visible far and wide. It has the typically Sri Lankan bubble shape. One of its relics is a hair from Buddha's head. The nearby Hindu temple is consecrated to Shiva, Parvati and Ganesha.

Maha Seya Dagoba

Monaragala

✦ **D 8**

Province: Uva
Altitude: approx. 74m/243ft

Monaragala is situated in the fertile lowlands of Kumbukkan Oya, which irrigates the paddy fields and allows countless rubber trees to flourish. To the north the foothills of the Uva's mountains rise up and to the south the jungle becomes denser.

While the town itself does not have any sights of its own to offer it is a good base for visiting several ruins in the area.

SURROUNDINGS OF MONARAGALA

Only a few kilometres east of the town is Galebadda, a fortified former residence of the kings of Ruhuna. It was probably built during the first half of the 12th century. The ruins allow the floor plan of the complex to be made out quite clearly; the actual palace was located within the walled citadel along with some other buildings. The citadel only had one entrance. A high wall secured the complex. Queen Sugala of Ruhua, who resisted the new king Parakrama Bahu I of Polonnaruwa, was in possession of the sacred tooth relic, the kingdom's emblem. When Parakrama Bahu I came to Udundora the queen had fled, but his troops still managed to find her and take possession of the relic.

Galebadda

Near Maligavila, 15km/9mi south of Monaragala, are the ruins of Dambegoda Vihara. It possesses a colossal statue of Buddha, which is now lying on the ground. It was originally 12m/39ft tall and 3m/10ft wide at the shoulders, and presumably once stood in a large image gallery made of brick, but none of this survives. The corresponding lotus-shaped pedestal with a 4m/13ft diameter, a moonstone composed of several pieces and a guard stele with the relief of a Naga king in the elegant Tribhanga pose are further remarkable features. It is thought all of these works were made in the 6th or 7th century.

Dambegoda Vihara

Monoragala

GETTING THERE
By car: from Wellawaya on the A 4
(34 km/21mi); from Hambantota on
the A 2 to Wellawaya, then turn right
on to the A 4 to Monaragala
By bus: good connections from
Hambantota

WHERE TO STAY
Kumbuk River £ £ £
tel. 077 293 08 74
www.kumbukriver.com

One of the most original hotels on Sri
Lanka. Chalets for up to 114 guests
have been built on a 16ha/40acre compound. One of the buildings has two
storeys, is 12m/39ft long and is in the
shape of an elephant. Various exploration paths have been created in the
landscape. There is also a programme
of excursions with surfing trips to
Arugam and outings to Yala National
Park.

Caves in the area The area south of the road between Wellawaya and Monaragla is rich in caves and many of them were likely to have been **inhabited in prehistoric times**. The large cave of Budugalge was a sacred Buddhist site and contains several interesting sculptures of Buddha, including a fairly large recumbent Buddha. To get to the cave turn south in Kumbukkana near Buttala, then drive approx. 8km/5mi further. From here it is a walk of around 1.5km/1mi. A long stone stairway leads up to the cave.

Negombo

⊹ A 7

Province: Western
Altitude: 5m/16ft
Population: 123,000

Negombo, one of the most important fishing ports on the west coast, is among the best-known seaside resorts in Sri Lanka. It is so appealing because of its geographical location at the end of a lagoon with countless little islands and pretty bays.

History Negombo is currently the island's fifth-largest town. It was founded by Arab traders. In the 16th century the Portuguese created a centre of their cinnamon trade here and fortified the town. In around the middle of the 17th century the Dutch took over Negombo and built a canal, which, together with the southern section, connects Colombo with Chilaw and Puttalam. It is still in use today. In 1796 the British occupied the town, which the Dutch had abandoned, and demolished many of the fortifications.

WHAT TO SEE IN NEGOMBO

The old town centre with its narrow, winding streets is now a **lively shopping district** with a large fruit and vegetable market under a huge banyan tree.

*Town Centre

The lively, very authentic fish market in Negombo is definitely worth a visit. It opens in the early hours of the morning and continues until 11am. Sometimes it can be a challenge for sensitive noses. Everything caught in the sea at night using the region's typical outrigger boats, the oruvas, is sold here. There is also worthwhile fishing in the lagoon of Negombo. Here too there is a daily fish market that starts at about 6am. It is held at the end of a bridge across the lagoon.

*Fish markets

Only the eastern main gate with the year 1678 at the southern end of Main Street and parts of two bastions still survive of the fortifications from the time the Dutch were here.

Dutch fort

In the old town of Negombo there are a large number of Catholic churches, some of which have beautifully ornamented façades. There is an old Dutch church near the canal, which dates back to the Dutch period; the steep roof that comes down low to the ground and the small belfry that acts as a ridge turret are characteristic features.
For a long time Negombo was a centre of Jesuit missionary activity and even today the majority of the inhabitants are Roman Catholics. That is one reason why a **Passiontide play, unique in Sri Lanka**, is performed here, or, more specifically in Duwa near Negombo. The celebrations come to a climax with a re-enacted Way of the Cross, a puppet theatre and of course a large market.

Catholic churches

The canal, built during the Dutch period, is used by padda boats to transport vegetables, fruit, coconuts and other goods, even today. The canal, which once had a length of around 120km/75mi and connected Colombo with Puttalam, played an important role at the start of the 19th century as a way of supplying the people with food. Taking a tranquil **trip in a padda boat** is highly recommended. Several of the boat owners offer them.
Muthurajawela Boat Center,:2/14 Pamunugama Road, Delathura

Dutch canal

This small museum is dedicated to Walisinghe Harischandra, a national hero who lived in Sri Lanka in the 19th century. His achievements consisted of him showing the people of Sri Lanka the value of

Walisinghe Harischandra Museum

cated on three different levels. Some have eaves up to 15m/49ft high with carved mouldings below. One of the inscriptions presumably dates back to the 3rd century BC when the temple caves were founded. From the top of the rock the wonderful view is reward enough for the somewhat laborious climb up a trail and the rocky, worn steps.

Tomb of Solomon Bandaranaike On the A1 towards Nittambuwa, just a few kilometres beyond Yakkala on the left-hand side is the tomb of Solomon Bandaranaike (▶Famous People), who was assassinated in 1959; it is a classically beautiful complex. The area belonged to his father, a senior official under British colonial rule. He built a comfortable house in the English colonial style here. The tomb itself is situated under a magnificent white fig tree.

✶✶ Nuwara Eliya

✦ C 8

Province: Central
Altitude: approx. 1880m/6170ft–2000m/6570ft
Population: approx. 26,000

Nuwara Eliya, the »city above the clouds«, is situated in the middle of the mountains of Uva, in a hollow formed by Sri Lanka's three highest mountains. As a result of its mild climate Sri Lanka's highest town is a popular place of refuge from the hot and humid southwest during the hot season. Temperatures here rarely exceed 25 °C/77 °F and the air is dry and fresh.

Very British The town clearly bears the signature of the British, who fashioned the houses and gardens according to their ideas: large lawns, golf courses and villas in the country-house style that were usually inhabited by tea planters at the time. Tea plantations still dominate the appearance of the fantastic mountain landscape all around. In the town the English flair and the atmosphere of a spa in the mountains still survive today.

History In the Indian epic Ramayana, the mountains around Nuwara Eliya play a role as one of the residences of the giant king Ravana. He is said to have abducted the princess Sita, the wife of the hero Rama, to this place. The town's history becomes more tangible and verifiable during the time of the British, who started coming here to hunt in around 1820 – preferably elephants and leopards; almost exclusively by giving chase – and in around 1825 they set up a rest home for their officers. The British governor Sir Edward Barnes had the first surfaced road built in 1828, and in 1846 Sir Samuel Baker built many

Nuwara Eliya

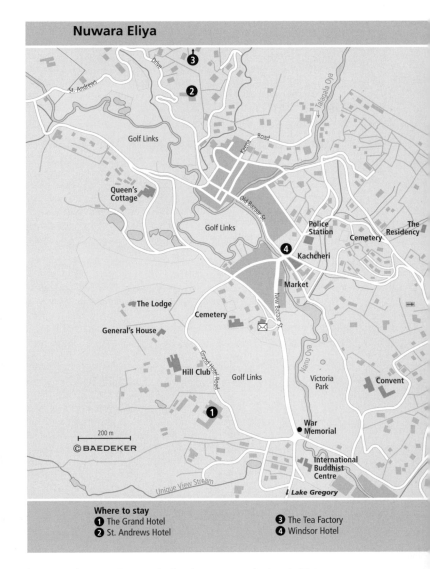

St. Andrews Drive

Golf Links

Queen's
Cottage

Golf Links

Keena Road

Old Bazaar St.

Talagala Oya

Police
Station

Cemetery

The
Residency

4 Kachcheri

Market

The Lodge

Cemetery

General's House

Grand Hotel Road

Hill Club

Golf Links

New Bazaar St.

Manu Oya

Victoria
Park

Convent

1

200 m

© BAEDEKER

**War
Memorial**

**International
Buddhist
Centre**

Unique View Stream

↓ Lake Gregory

Where to stay
1 The Grand Hotel
2 St. Andrews Hotel

3 The Tea Factory
4 Windsor Hotel

houses in the town. In 1875 the first horse race took place in Nuwara Eliya. Horse racing was prohibited when the British left, but these days it is allowed again; however, betting is still not permitted. In 1889 an 18-hole golf course was added.

Nuwara Eliya was also always important to Sri Lanka from an economic perspective. After the coffee bushes became infested by coffee rust, the Scotsman James Taylor began with the first experiments to naturalize tea from Assam in India in the mountains of Sri Lanka in 1867. He was successful, because to this day **the best tea in Sri Lanka is grown here**; it is known as Broken Orange Pekoe, a highland tea (▶MARCO POLO Insight p.332).

WHAT TO SEE IN NUWARA ELIYA

Townscape
Some of the buildings enlivening the parks and gardens are of the purest and most beautiful British colonial style. The post office with a pretty clock tower, the Anglican Holy Trinity Church and the war memorial are all of note. Victoria Park with its large lawn and tall trees, the Nanu Oya river and the idyllically situated ponds are all good places to go for walks.

*Grand Hotel
What is now the Grand Hotel, a spacious timber-framed country house, was built by Governor Barnes to be his home. The building has lost some of its former glory, which also attracted celebrities. Nevertheless it is one of the top addresses in Nuwara Eliya. Heavy red

Fog is no rarity in the mountains of Nuwara Eliya

curtains and massive leather suites in the communal areas, as well as magnificent chandeliers hanging from the ceilings are still an expression of the supposedly English way of life.

The Hill Club, a further symbol of the English way of life, was founded in 1876 by a British plantation owner called Waring, who employed 15,000 workers on his 20ha/50 acre plantation. The seventh generation of Warings handed the plantations and the Hill Club over to a successor in 1972. Although he is from Sri Lanka he made sure that the British atmosphere has stayed alive until today. The attractive stone building with timber framing was built in the Tudor style and is, strictly speaking, only open to members. However, visitors are

Hill Club

Nuwara Eliya

GETTING THERE

By car: from Colombo via Kotte, Kaduwela, Hanwella, Avissawella, Hatton (180 km/112mi); from Kandy via Gampola, Pussellawa and Ramboda (77 km/48mi); from Badulla on the A 5 (56 km/35mi)
By train: the closest train station is located in Nanu Oya on the Colombo–Badulla line (8 km/5mi away).
By bus: good bus connections from Colombo, Kandy and Badulla

WHERE TO STAY/EAT
❸ *The Tea Factory* £ £ £ – £ £ £ £
Kandapola, tel. 052 222 96 00
www.aitkenspenceholidays.com
This wonderful hotel with 57 rooms was set up in a tea factory that was built in around 1930. The fantastic views of Sri Lanka's mountains alone are reason enough to stay at this hotel. During its transformation a large part of the tea factory's technical equipment was left in place and for good reason because the hotel still has a tea plantation today.

❶ *The Grand Hotel* £ £ £
tel. 052 222 28 81-7

www.tangerinehotels.com
A very British establishment, even down to the afternoon tea: for visitors wanting to explore the legacy of the British colonial rule on Sri Lanka, the Grand Hotel with its 156 rooms is the number one choice. The more recent extension is both timeless and modern.

Insider Tip

❷ *St. Andrews Hotel* £ £ £
10, St. Andrews Drive
tel. 052 222 30 31
www.jetwinghotels.com
This Tudor style manor house has a British atmosphere; the former lustre has faded somewhat. Enjoy a tea in the lovely garden in the afternoon or a martini by the open fire in the evening. Sleep under heavy canopies. The 18-hole golf course is just a few metres away.

❹ *Windsor Hotel* £ £ £
2, Bandaranayaka Mawatha
tel. 052 222 25 54
www.windsorhotellk.com
Colonial-style hotel with 50 comfortable rooms, a restaurant, bar and a lot of atmosphere.

A Delicious Drink

Tea is Sri Lanka's major export commodity. It is the fourth largest producer, but the world's third largest exporter. About 330,000 tons of tea are produced annually, with a value of US$ 1.5 billion. The varieties that are grown high up in the central mountains, for example around Nuwara Eliya, have the best aroma.

▶ **The tea plant**
The Chinese tea bush **Camellia sinensis** and the **Assamese Camellia** assamica are considered to be the original tea plants. A **hybrid plant** that was cross-bred from these two is now the basis of almost all tea plants. The variety of teas comes solely from climatic conditions and the way the tea leaves are processed. Thus tea from Sri Lanka is generally described as being tart and strong in taste, reminiscent of citrus fruit

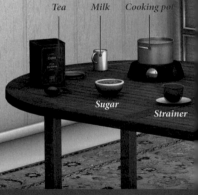

Tea *Milk* *Cooking pot*

▶ **Traditional Sri Lankan preparation**
Tea is simmered lightly in a pot with milk and sugar for up to ten minutes. Then it is strained into a teapot through a very fine strainer. This forms a sweet contrast to the tart, strong Ceylon tea.

Sugar *Strainer*

▶ **The largest tea exporting countries**

■ Kenya ■ China ■ Sri Lanka

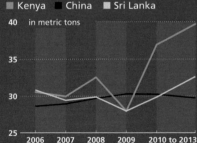

in metric tons

40
35
30
25

2006 2007 2008 2009 2010 to 2013

▶ **Customer countries for Sri Lankan tea**
in million kg (2011)

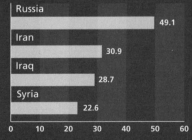

Country	million kg
Russia	49.1
Iran	30.9
Iraq	28.7
Syria	22.6

0 10 20 30 40 50 60

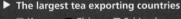

Quality standard
Only authentic Ceylon tea, which was grown and packaged on Sri Lanka, may bear the seal of quality with the lion.

Proper storage
So that tea does not take on any other flavours or aromas it should be stored in a cool, dry and dark place in a wooden, ceramic or non-rusting metal container.

▶ growing regions
The best tea comes from the higher locations in Sri Lanka like Dambulla and Uva. The tea from the Nuwara Eliya region gets its unique taste from the cypresses and mint plants that grow in the area.

▶ Effects
Tea is often processed into black tea and has more caffeine than coffee; the level is reduced because tea is made with more water than coffee is. The flavonoids in tea expand the blood vessels and thus promote blood circulation. Tea also contains vitamins and minerals and it strengthens the body's immune system.

©BAEDEKER

Tea classifications
Grades and sizes of leaves are classified

LEAF TEAS

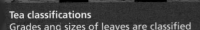

Whole leafs   **Broken leafs**

> Traditional tea consumption
> Hardly any mixed teas
> Individual taste in each harvest

SMALL LEAFED TEAS

Fannings   **Dust**

> Used for tea bags
> Frequent use of additives
> Varieties are mixed to keep taste constant

welcome, as long they are appropriately dressed in a jacket and tie from 7pm onwards. There are said to be members who also rent out their rooms to guests during their absence. Just enquire at the reception or send an email at www.hillclubsrilanka.net.

AROUND NUWARA ELIYA

**Mountains and tea plantations
Nuwara Eliya is an **excellent base for trips** to Sri Lanka's unique mountain landscape. The work on the tea plantations can be observed just a few kilometres out of town and many of the tea factories are open to visitors. One particularly worthwhile stop-off is the Labokellie Tea Estate, which is halfway between Kandy and Nuwara Eliya (www.mackwoodstea.com).

*Hakgala Sanctuary Botanical Gardens
Take the A5 to Hakgala Botanical Garden, situated around 10km southeast of Nuwara Eliya. It is one of three botanical gardens in Sri Lanka. The grounds go back to a coffee plantation; it was subsequently used to grow cinchona trees to obtain quinine against malaria and tea was also grown here. In 1861 William Nock created a model garden in which he experimented with plants from temperate climates. This allowed a wonderful park landscape with lotus ponds, old trees and an orchid house to develop over the years. From the summer house at an altitude of 1646m/5400ft there is a magnificent view over the mountains to the peaks of Namunkula.

Right beside the botanical garden is Hakgala Nature Reserve, which is still home to a few specimens of the rare big Purple-faced leaf monkey.

❶ Daily 8am–5pm, admission charge

Drive from Nuwara Eliya to Kandy
A drive from Nuwara Eliya to ►Kandy is one of the most scenic experiences in Sri Lanka. The road leaves the town and climbs steeply to Ramboda Pass at 1996m/6549ft, passing the falls of the same name, which plummet from 100m/330ft.

** Polonnaruwa

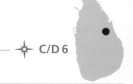

✳ C/D 6

Province: North Central
Altitude: approx. 110m/360ft

Polonnaruwa, for a long time protected by dense jungle, was the second capital of the Singhalese kingdom. One of the most outstanding rulers, Parakrama Bahu I (1153–1186) shaped its appearance with magnificent buildings, bringing about a significant style of Singhalese art.

AD 993	The administration is moved from Anuradhapura to Polonnaruwa.
1055	Polonnaruwa is made the capital.
1153–1186	Under the reign of King Parakrama Bahu I the town experienced a golden age.
1196–1215	Constant decline owing to quarrels over the succession; destruction of Polonnaruwa
19th century	The city is rediscovered by archaeologists and in 1935 opened up to visitors.

It is not entirely clear when the site of present-day Polonnaruwa was first settled; there are indications that people were here in the 4th century AD, but maybe earlier. The further history of Polonnaruwa is inseparable from that of ▶Anuradhapura. When the Cholas attacked and sacked the city in 993, and lodged themselves deep inside Singhalese territory, they designated it as their capital. Until 1073 they ruled Sri Lanka from here, the island having become no more than a province of their powerful south Indian kingdom. It was only King Vijaya Bahu I, a prince of the Ruhuna kingdom which had established itself in the south of the island, who managed to reconquer Anuradhapura and drive the Chola from Sri Lanka. But he too retained Polonnaruwa as his capital. Various kings reigned here until 1235, one of the most important being Parakrama BahuI, who as-   **History**

Polonnaruwa's town centre is located on Lake Parakrama Samudra

Polonnaruwa

GETTING THERE
By car: from Dambulla on the A 6 to Habarana, then on the A 11 (68 km/42mi); from Anuradhapura on the A 13 to Marandankawala, then on the A 11 (101 km/63mi)
By train: good connections from Dambulla and Habarana
By bus: several good connections from the abovementioned towns several times a day

WHERE TO STAY
❶ *The Village* £ £ – £ £ £
Habarana
tel. 066 227 00 47
www.johnkeellshotels.com
Ideally located between Anuradhapura and Polonnaruwa. 106 comfortable cottage-style rooms, as well as a restaurant and a pool

❹ *Hotel Sudu Araliya* £ £ – £ £ £
New Town
tel. 027 222 54 06
www.hotelsuduaraliya.com
Lovely hotel located right on Lake Parakrama Samudra. 104 very spacious rooms and a friendly ambience. Apart from a large pool there is a spa, a gym and a bike rental facility. The restaurant serves local and international dishes. There are also boat trips on the lake.

This hotel is within easy reach of three national parks (Minneriya, Kaudulla and Wasgamuwa).

❷ *Devi Tourist Home* £
Lake View Watte, New Town Road
tel. 027 222 31 81
This privately-run guesthouse, just under a kilometre from the town centre, is worth a recommendation. The five rooms are suitably comfortable, very clean, and yet inexpensive. The garden is lovely. There is a bike rental facility – this is a great way to explore the ruins.

❸ *Samudra Guest House* £
Habarana Road
tel. 027 222 28 17
No air-conditioning, cold water for washing but attentive and always friendly service. The rooms are adequately furnished. The owner organizes trips and also has some bicycles.

WHERE TO EAT
❶ *ACME Transit Hotel* £ **Insider Tip**
90, Polonnaruwa Road
tel. 066 700 16
If you need a break on the journey between Anuradhapura and Polonnaruwa, why not take it at this little restaurant. Outstanding Sri Lankan cuisine, pretty garden.

cended the throne in 1153 and is still regarded as the unifier of the kingdom. He was followed by King Nissanka Malla, before the Kalinga prince Magha attacked with a strong Malay army and subdued the Singhalese kingdom. A number of sub-kingdoms formed in revolt against these foreign rulers.
While King Parakrama Bahu II succeed once more in regaining and reuniting much of the kingdom, his residence was in ►Kurunegala (Dambadeniya) to the south. It was the first in a series of capitals, in

Highlights Polonnaruwa

▶ **Palace of Parakrama Bahu I**
Colossal structure that once contained 1000 magnificently furnished rooms.
▶page 339

▶ **Gal Pota (Stone Book)**
The heroic deeds of a king captured in stone
▶page 342

▶ **Rankot Vihara**
The largest dagoba in Polonnaruwa
▶page 350

▶ **Gal Vihara Rock Temple**
The four monumental statues in the former monastic complex are masterpieces of Sri Lankan sculpture.
▶page 346

an age today referred to as the Period of Short-lived Kingdoms. Polonnaruwa stepped into the limelight once again when King Parakrama Bahu III took over the government, but his successor moved their capital to the south; the city fell into oblivion and was overgrown by the jungle.

It was only in 1890 that public attention was aroused by reports of British colonial officials concerning the remains of a magnificent city in the jungle. A few years later excavations started, and in 1935 visitors were allowed on the site for the first time. For some years now UNESCO has contributed financially to the archaeological work, which is far from complete. Even so, the ruined city was declared a World Heritage Site in 1982.

WHAT TO SEE IN POLONNARUWA

Most of the sights in Polonnaruwa can be accessed by good roads, some of which are suitable for cars. The ruins are not so extensive as those of Anuradhapura, but it is still worth exploring them with a vehicle. Because of the continuing excavations temporary road closures are always a possibility, and new finds may not yet be accessible.

Roads

OUTSIDE THE TOWN WALLS

The fortified centre of town is situated on the eastern shore of the 18 sq km/7 sq mi Parakrama Samudra artificial lake. It is named after King Parakrama Bahu I, who had it made in order to heighten the yield of the paddy fields of the surrounding area by irrigating them with the lake's water. After Polonnaruwa's decline the lake also silted up. It was only enlarged in the previous century and is now fulfilling

**Parakrama
Samudra
(lake)**

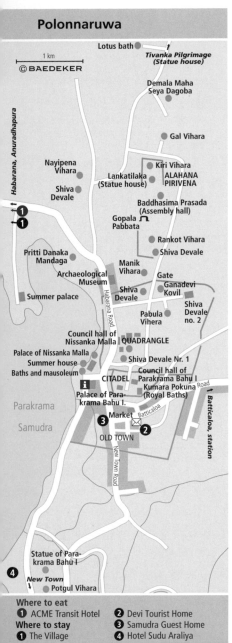

Polonnaruwa

1 km

© BAEDEKER

Habarana, Anuradhapura

Lotus bath
Tivanka Pilgrimage
(Statue house)
Demala Maha
Seya Dagoba
Gal Vihara
Nayipena
Vihara
Kiri Vihara
ALAHANA
PIRIVENA
Lankatilaka
(Statue house)
Shiva
Devale
Baddhasima Prasada
(Assembly hall)
Gopala
Pabbata
Rankot Vihara
Shiva Devale
Pritti Danaka
Mandaga
Manik
Vihara
Archaeological
Museum
Gate
Ganadevi
Kovil
Shiva
Devale
Summer palace
Pabula
Vihera
Shiva
Devale
no. 2
Council hall of
Nissanka Malla
QUADRANGLE
Palace of Nissanka Malla
Summer house
Shiva Devale Nr. 1
Baths and mausoleum
Council hall of
Parakrama Bahu I
CITADEL
Kumara Pokuna
(Royal Baths)
Palace of Para-
krama Bahu I.
Habarana Road
Batticaloa Road
Batticaloa, station
Parakrama
Samudra
Market
Batticaloa
New Town Road
OLD TOWN
Statue of Para-
krama Bahu I
New Town
Potgul Vihara

Where to eat
1 ACME Transit Hotel
2 Devi Tourist Home
Where to stay
1 The Village
3 Samudra Guest Home
4 Hotel Sudu Araliya

its original function again. There were once two summerhouses, or secondary palaces, on Parakrama Samudra, which could only be reached by boat when the lake was filled with water. Now a walkway leads to the one closer to the main palace. However, only a few broken pillars still remain.

At the western end of the dam that borders the reservoir is a **statue** carved from the rock that may be a depiction of **King Parakrama Bahu I**, but possibly someone else. The sculpture's contented facial expression is if anything evidence of the former assumption, because the king truly could be satisfied with the agricultural success his reservoir effected. To protect the statue from the weather it has unfortunately been covered in an unattractive sheet metal roof.

In the south, outside of the former town walls, is **Potgul Vihara**, a monastery in which the holy scriptures were kept. It presumably dates back to the time before Parakrama Bahu; surviving ruins include a mandapa (prayer pavilion) and a round building with a circumference of 48m/52yd on a rectangular base. According to an inscription it was built upon the request of Chandravati, the second wife of Parakrama BahuI. It is likely that dagobas once stood at the four corners. In front of the round building in the east is a small hall and this is also where the only recognizable entrance is. In front of the 4.5m/15ft bricks walls are façades that still have faint traces of artistic paintings. Next to the two long sides of the platform as well as on the east side there are still remains of two similar structures, which are all reminiscent of the temple architecture of Cambodia.

Just a few metres away the remains of the old town wall can be made out. At one point it was 5m/16ft thick and equally high. Not far from here is the former palace of King Nissanka Malla, probably a very modest two-storey building with thick brick walls. According to the historical facts the king had this palace built in a great hurry in just seven months since it could not be expected of him to have to live in the residence of a predecessor. At the same time as the palace Nissanka Malla had a council hall built, an elongated, rectangular pillared hall that is accessed by a few steps in the northeast. Some of the pillars have now fallen over, but they used to support a wooden roof. The pillars, square at the bottom and octagonal in the middle with simple, square capitals, are monolithic. At the bases of many pillars the names of ministers as well as other dignitaries have been recorded. According to an inscription a 1.8m/6ft stone lion, the kingdom's symbol, once bore the king's throne. The sculpture's design shows abstract tendencies, but the animal seems both dignified and fearsome.

Palace of King Nissanka Malla

TOWN CENTRE

The town's fortifications probably date back to the year 1037, but were significantly developed later on under Parakrama Bahu I. The wall complex consisted of three rings and had 14 entrance gates. The place grounds encompassed an area of around 10ha/25 acres and were surrounded by a high wall as well as, in some places, by moats. The main entrance is in the north.

Urban fortifications

The palace grounds and the main courtyard in the east are surrounded by a gallery. The palace of King Parakrama Bahu I itself, a massive brick structure, had a square floor plan of 46m/50yd by 46m/50yd. It contained a spacious atrium (31m/34yd x 13m/14yd) whose ceiling was once supported by wooden columns whose stone pedestals still survive. Adjoining the atrium were two further halls with remarkably thick walls. A gallery surrounding the building was divided into 40 rooms that were inter-connected and open to the outside. In the south a staircase leads up to the upper floors; according to the chronicle Culavamsa, there are supposed to have been seven of them. The beginnings of two storeys can still be made out on the high, magnificent ruins. The Culavamsa says the palace possessed more than 1000 magnificently furnished rooms.

**Palace of King Parakrama Bahu I

Somewhat further to the east of the palace is the council hall, a building with nicely designed features and a square floor plan. It too was

*Council hall

Polonnaruwa Quadrangle

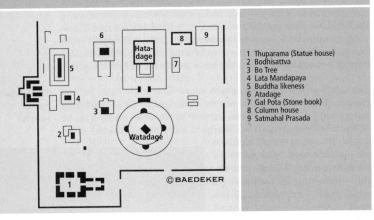

1 Thuparama (Statue house)
2 Bodhisattva
3 Bo Tree
4 Lata Mandapaya
5 Buddha likeness
6 Atadage
7 Gal Pota (Stone book)
8 Column house
9 Satmahal Prasada

theless seems the most probable. The niches of the individual »storeys« were once filled with statues of Buddha, of which some are still partially extant. On one side a small staircase leads up to a chamber which may have housed a relic in the past.

**Gal Pota (Stone Book) Not very far away is Gol Pota, the »Stone Book«. It is an 8m/27 ft long, 1.25m/4 ft wide and 60cm/24 in high monolith, which, according to a section of the extensive inscription, was brought here from Mihintale or Sigiriya. In 72 lines divided into three fields, King Nissanka Malla describes his achievements for the kingdom and for Buddhism as well as his building activities. On the stone's front end is a remarkable relief sculpture depicting Lakshmi the goddess of good fortune between two elephants who form a vase of abundance with their trunks. The group is framed by wild geese.

Gatekeeper's huts On the Quadrangle's east and west sides there are stone structures that may have served as gatekeeper's huts.

*Hatadage Nissanka Malla had the Hatadage (also known as Daladage) built for the sacred tooth relic. It was surrounded by a high brick wall. Its shape, with its step-like construction, resembles the old temples at Angkor Wat. And there is a reason for that: the Singhalese had the temple built in honour of the allied Cambodian soldiers. Hatadage means »house of the 60 relics«, but also »the house built in 60 days«. Daladage means »house of the tooth relic«. The wall forms a rectangle measuring approx. 36m/39 yd by 27.5m/30 yd; the entrance is on the south side. The atrium in the north bears inscriptions in which the king once again boasts about his deeds and achievements. A staircase leads up to the upper, wooden storey, in which the tooth relic was once housed. In front of the entrance is a moonstone, whose shape resembles a semi-oval, but whose visual depictions seem somewhat mannered. In the interior of the cella, between stone pillars, there are three statues of a standing Buddha on nicely designed lotus pedestals.

Atadage means »**house of the eight relics**«. This building was con-
structed during the reign of King Vijaya Bahu I in the second half of the 11th century and served as a model for the above-mentioned Hatadage built by King Nassanka Malla. It too consisted of several storeys, or certainly at least two. Here too the second storey was reserved for the tooth relic. Many stone images richly ornamented with reliefs still survive; one of the motifs is the vase of abundance, from which a liana is growing, forming medallions that contain figurative scenes. Also of note are the door frames adorned with reliefs and the very nice statue of a standing Buddha.

Atadage

Not far away is Nissanka Malla Mandapa, a place of worship for the sacred tooth relic surrounded by a simple stone wall. The eight stone pillars modelled on budding lotus stems are highly graceful. They appear to simply grow out of the terrace; the capitals form a lotus bud. At their centre is a miniature dagoba with an frieze of worshippers on the pedestal. The shrine was built under King Nissanka Malla and is evidence of a pleasure in ornamentation that enjoyed a heyday in his time. There was a large amount of extravagant construction during his reign.

Mandapa (place of worship)

OUTSIDE THE QUADRANGLE

Leave the Quadrangle in the north and turn eastwards. This is the location of the Pabulu Vihara (coral shrine), a kind of stepped dagoba donated by a wife of Parakrama BahuI. It has been kept very simple, though unfortunately it is dilapidated, and stands on a terrace. The complex was surrounded by a stone wall (prakara). Steps lead up to the first and second circular terrace. A carved rock was probably used as a flower altar.
Around the dagoba there are six small stone huts that house statues of Buddha and bodhisattvas; some of them appear to have come from Anuradhapura. In one of the statue huts the brick core of the sculpture of a recumbent Buddha can still be made out.

Pabulu Vihara (coral shrine)

*Shiva Devale (Hindu temple) The Shiva Devale is the only monument that can be placed with certainty in the **time of Chola rule** in Polonnaruwa. It is really very modest, built entirely of stone and still in quite a good state. The good condition of the small temple is probably due to the fact that it was made from natural stone. The proportions are elegant and harmonious, the structure austere. At the entrance there are two sculptures of the bull Nandi, Shiva's vehicle, which are remarkable. In its interior is a lingam, the symbol of Shiva, the god of fertility. An inscription reveals the temple's old name (Vanavan Madevi Isvarmudaiyar).

Vishnu Devale (Hindu temple) Not far from the fortified town's north gate are the ruins of Vishnu Devale, which dates back to the 13th century. Only the substructure made from carved stones is still extant, the structure above that was presumably made of bricks is, by contrast, severely weathered. It houses a statue of Vishnu in a bad state of repair.

Opposite are the ruins of the Ganadevi Kovil that once housed a lingam.

*Archaeological Museum This archaeological museum really is one of the most worthwhile museums in Sri Lanka. The rooms are structured by themes that focus on the various sections of the city: the citadel, the outer city, the monastery complex, the Quadrangle and the surrounding areas. The bronze figures, which have been given their own room, are particularly noteworthy. They depict Hindu deities. Some of the buildings of the ruined city that cannot be, or have not yet been, reconstructed are shown as models, giving insight into their former appearance.

❶ Daily 9am–6pm, admission charge

Manik Vihara Outside of the town's fortifications near the north gate is the Manik Vihara, a brick dagoba with a high rectangular terrace made of bricks. The platform is surrounded by a remarkably well preserved lion frieze. The animals are depicted from the front on terracotta slabs in such an **exaggeratedly terrifying manner** that they almost seem like caricatures. One of two nice stone stairs flanked by guard stones leads up to the terrace; a door frame put together from carved stones is also still extant.

Shiva Devale (Hindu temple) Along the northbound road on the left-hand side is a further Shiva Divale. Its ruins were restored in the 1980s by the Archaeological Department. The temple consists of an atrium and a cella as well as a two-part side room in the same order. The main cella contains a round yoni and the lower part of a lingam, while the cella of the adjoining building contains a brick pedestal for a statue that is no longer present. The door posts at the entrance to the cella reveal that the door was not even full height. A round stone on which the door must have turned has been reinstated.

The Rankot Vihara (also known as Ruvanveli Dagoba) has a height of 55m/180 ft and a diameter of 56m/185 ft, making it **the largest complete dagoba in Polonnaruwa**. The massive structure is surrounded by several statue houses and was only restored a few years ago. The many inscriptions reveal the dagoba was built by King Nissanka Malla. It is remarkable that limestone mortar was applied in layers at intervals of of approx. 3m/10 ft; this was probably done to balance out irregularities in the structure. On the lotus frieze on the lower terrace there are traces of earlier painting. At the entrance to the temple complex is a stone seat whose inscription states that Nissanka Malla oversaw the building works from here.

**Rankot Vihara (Ruvanveli Dagoba)

The Gopalabatta, a flat rock to the east of the road, has four caves on its eastern side that were, according to a Brahmi inscription, already inhabited by reclusive monks in the 5th century. During the Polonnaruwa period they were probably part of a monastery. In one of the caves the remains of a Buddha statue were found; it was therefore possibly once an image gallery.

Gopalabatta rock

The complex known as Alahana Parivena (cremation monastery) has an assembly hall for monks (Baddhasima Prasada), a statue house (Lankatilaka) and the Kiri Vihara (milk dagoba) as well as a cremation site for the deceased members of the royal family and the monks. It is likely that he mounds dotted around the area all contain small dagobas with the ashes of members of the royal family. Excavations have also uncovered the foundations walls of the monks' quarters. At the upper end of the complex are two caves containing magnificent Buddha statues.

Alahana Parivena

The ruin of the Lankatilaka is quite remarkable. It was once used as a statue house. It contains the torso of a Buddha statue that must have once been around 13m/43ft tall; it is quite striking. The richly structured façade is also interesting, giving beholders the feeling it is part of a multi-storey building, but this is an illusion because the interior is actually relatively small, not least because of the incredible thickness of the walls. Opposite the entrance to the Lankatilaka are the stone pillars of a mandapa, decorated with lotus blossoms, in which drummers and other musicians come together for the ceremonies.

Lankatilaka (statue house)

The Kiri Vihara, also called the milk dagoba after the gleaming white plaster made of crushed shells, was presumably donated by Suhadda, one of Parakrama Bahu I's wives. The simple 24m/80 ft structure in classical form is adorned with mouldings on the base and thus seems light and elegant. By the way, the dagoba has never been renovated: when it was freed from the invading jungle the bluish-white plaster was almost completely intact.

* Kiri Vihara

** GAL VIHARA ROCK TEMPLE

Black Rock Following the road further northwards, visitors will find the most significant attraction of Polonnaruwa, the Gal Vihara rock temple. Its actual name is Uttarama, but the term »Black Rock« is also customary. In the chronicle Culavamsa it is written that this temple was commissioned by King Parakrama Bahu I.

The four monumental Buddha statues carved from the rock that are now outside were most likely once housed in three statue houses of which only fragments of the walls remain. They are amongst the **masterpieces of Singhalese stonemasonry**. The largest statue is the recumbent Buddha, measuring 14.1m/46ft. The staggered feet indicate that this is a statue of the enlightened one who has entered Nirvana. The facial expression is clearly detached, the body is relaxed and yet the head and body have maintained their archaically charismatic force. Using the most basic means the sculptor achieved the **highest effect**; by using curving lines (such as on the waist and hips) or by making the creases in the gown wavy he softened the statue's austerity. The meaning of the 6.93m/23 ft statue next to its head still has not been determined with certainty. It is possible the statue is of Ananda, Buddha's favourite disciple, because he was present when the enlightened one entered Nirvana. However, Ananda is usually depicted standing at Buddha's feet, and so it could be that it is Mahinda, the monk who brought Buddhism to Sri Lanka. But he was not present at Buddha's death. The posture with folded arms and the hands lying on the upper arms is quite unusual and completely outside the usual iconographic framework. Many art historians consider this statue as **the artistically most valuable** of the four.

A grotto carved out of the rock contains a 1.5m/5 ft statue of a sitting Buddha whose high throne is adorned with lion reliefs, pilasters and flower ornaments. The statue, enclosed at the back by a makara arch, gets its quality from its simplicity. The fourth statue, a statue of Buddha meditating, is around 5m/16ft in height and is leaning against a rock wall richly adorned with makara arches. The artist placed a kind of halo around Buddha's head and the throne is decorated with a lion frieze.

Demala Maha Seya Dagoba King Parakrama Bahu I had the Demala Maha Seya Dagoba, the Great Tamil Dagoba, built, presumably by Tamils who had been captured and brought to Sri Lanka during his military campaigns in southern India. It may have been designed to be the formidable dagoba of Polonnaruwa, a suggestion supported by the magnificent base measuring 165m/180yd in diameter. It is uncertain what it may have looked like because everything that can be seen today dates back to more recent times, although older parts were incorporated.

The Gal Vihara is famous for its unique Buddha statues

Lotus bath

Somewhat further north on the left-hand side of the road is the lotus bath, made of finely carved stone in the shape of a lotus blossom. The application of the symbolic shape of the lotus to baths is **typical of the pleasure in ornamentation** peculiar to the Polonnaruwa period. It is thought that there must have once been seven other baths like it in the surrounding area. The complex once belonged to the Jetavana monastery founded under Parakrama Bahu I.

* Tivanka Pilimage (statue house)

The Tivanka Pilimage, the statue house of the Jetavane monastery, is the northernmost building of the historical Polonnaruwa. It got its name from a likeness known as a tivanka, the image of a standing Buddha, for which it was built by Parakrama Bahu I. The brick building with its powerful walls is still somewhat larger than Lankatilaka and the façades are more richly adorned with stucco reliefs. There was once a passageway in the wall of the front hall that leads up to the upper storeys. The entire building shows very strong southern Indian influences.

However, the statue house is famous for its **remains of wall paintings**, which unfortunately only survive in fragments, but probably once covered all the walls. They presumably date back to the late 12th/early 13th century and, using the format of continuous narrative, they depict scenes from the life of Buddha and scenes from the Jataka, Buddha's past lives. In most images the graphic aspect is foremost but some also try to bring across mood and atmosphere.

The 8m/26ft statue of a standing Buddha in the interior is impressive. It is, however, missing its head, which weathered and fell off over the years.

Pottuvil

GETTING THERE

By car: from Colombo on the A 2 to Panadura, further on the A 8 to Ratnapura, from there on the A 4 to Pottuvil (app. 322 km/200mi)
By train: from Colombo all the way to the terminal station Matara, from there continue by bus to Wellawaya; however, the bus only goes to Pottuvil twice a day from here.

WHERE TO STAY

There is no recommendable accommodation in Pottuvil. Most people want to carry on to Arugam Bay right away anyway. The rooms there do not tend to have air conditioning. The location on the sea creates a cool breeze, which can be supplemented by the ceiling fan if need be.

Siam View Beach Hotel £ £
Arugam Bay
tel. 077 320 02 01, www.arugam.com
The manager of this hotel knows how to make her establishment a place of refuge for guests from all around the world. All five attractively decorated and yet inexpensive rooms, and the apartment, have air conditioning. After the evening meal, where guests are served authentic Thai dishes, guests retire to the beach bar to enjoy a sundowner.

Hideaway £ £
Arugam Bay, tel. 063 224 82 59
www.hideawayarugambabay.com
This resort is not right on the beach, but not far away from it either. It has five rooms, seven cabanas and one recommended restaurant serving good local cuisine. A pleasant atmosphere and attentive service.

Palm Groove Holiday Inn £ £
Arugam Bay, tel. 063 224 84 57
www.palmgrooveholidayinn.com
This guesthouse is a little dated, and in spite of its name, it has nothing to do with the internationally renowned hotel chain. Three of the 16 rooms do not have air conditioning, but they are a little cheaper to reflect this.

Tri Star Beach Hotel £ £
Arugam Bay
tel. 063 224 84 04
www.tristarbeachhotel.com
This hotel is structured into two parts that are separated from each other by a through road. The chalets in the attractive garden have a good level of comfort; opposite there are a further 20 rooms. Almost all of them have air conditioning. One special feature here is that this hotel currently has the only pool in Arugam Bay.

Tsunami Beach Hotel £ – £ £
Arugam Bay, tel. 063 492 33 73
www.thearugambayhotel.com
The owner gave this guesthouse its name at a time when hardly anyone knew what a tsunami was and what destructive forces it could unleash. The ten well-furnished, clean rooms are housed in bungalows. One of them is right on the beach, which is why it is often fully booked. The restaurant is very popular because the chef cares greatly about using only the freshest ingredients.

Gecko Guest House & Restaurant £ – £ £
Arugam Bay
tel. 063 224 82 12

www.geckoarugambay.com
This guesthouse, owned by the British-Sri Lankan couple Ramesh and Liz, has six cabanas. They both care greatly about a smart but not excessively luxurious interior. They all have a terrace with sea views.

The Danish Villa £ – ££
Arugam Bay
tel. 077 695 79 36
www.thedanishvilla.com
Apart from the well-kept rooms in the main building, there is also a bungalow in the garden that can accommodate up to twelve guests. As the name suggests, the hotel is run by a Dane. It is a

mere 100 metres to the sea and the surf points.

Stardust Beach Hotel £ – ££ *Insider Tip*
Arugam Bay, tel. 063 224 81 91
www.arugambay.com
Very attractive, well-kept guesthouse, also under Danish management – and a popular option for surfers from all around the world. The accommodation varies in size. 14 rooms in a two-storey building as well as six wooden chalets. The restaurant's menu is remarkably extensive. The daily barbecue dinner is considered a speciality. The hotel prides itself on having the largest wine cellar on the east coast.

Panama is located a few kilometres from Arugam Bay; it is a small village whose predominantly Singhalese population enjoy visitors. This is where the surfaced road to Yala National Park ends, so that the people here still lead a more basic way of life. Near the village there are some sandbanks in the narrow rivers that are visited by many smaller and larger crocodiles which come here to soak up the sun, in the afternoon especially.
A further three kilometres west of Panama visitors will find a small lake with fascinating, colourful bird life.

Panama (village)

There are other national parks that can be accessed easily from Pottuvil, such as Yala National Park East to the south, or, somewhat further away in the interior, Gal Oya National Park.

Further national parks

Puttalam

✳ A 5

Province: North Western
Altitude: 3m–8m/10ft–33ft
Population: 41,000

Puttalam is situated in Sri Lanka's northwest on a wide lagoon that stretches north for around 60km/37 mi and finds its way to the open sea through Dutch Bay, which is dotted with several large islands.

Puttalam

GETTING THERE
By car: from Colombo on the A 3 (134 km/83mi); from Anuradhapura on the A 12 (79 km/49mi); from Kurunegala on the A 10 (88 km/55mi)
By train: currently the terminal station of the Colombo–Jaffna route
By bus: good connections from the abovementioned towns

TOURS
Sunway Holidays
25, Kimbulapitiya Road, Negombo
tel. 031 223 82 82 oder 531 25 55
www.sunwayholidays.lk
The organizer offers good tours to Willpattu National Park with a subsequent overnight stay in basic accommodation.

WHERE TO STAY
There is some accommodation in Willpattu National Park, but most only has functional levels of comfort.

Mahoora Tent Camp £ £ – £ £ £
tel. 077 772 15 06, in Colombo
011 583 08 33
www.mahoora.lk
It is possible to stay in comfortable tents or in timber huts. Only the best of the four categories has electricity – everything is tailored to being as close to nature as possible. Particularly recommended for families since all the facilities are child-friendly. Mahoora runs similar accommodation in other national parks.

Preshamel Safari Hotel £
(on the A 12 from Puttalam to Anuradhapura)
tel. 025 225 76 99
The drive from the hotel to the park entrance is one hour. There are five basic rooms (one with air conditioning) and a small restaurant that serves local cuisine. The hotel organizes day trips to the national park.

Leopard Den Hotel £
7 km from the national park entrance
tel. 077 347 62 88
www.wilpattunationalpark.com
Eight basic rooms and four newer, better ones with air conditioning. It is just fifteen minutes by car to the park entrance. Upon request it is possible to book accompanied tours with picnics. The restaurant serves local curries as well as international cuisine.

Christian pilgrimage destination Many of the town's inhabitants are Christians: the Catholic church of St Anne on the headland that protects the lagoon is an important pilgrimage destination for all Christians in Sri Lanka. The main economic activities here are fishing and obtaining salt from the seawater. In earlier days Arabian seafarers and merchants used this place as a base for their activities. Pearl fishing is also of significance. The dead-straight 120km/75mi Dutch Canal, which starts in the capital Colombo and which was built under Dutch rule, ends in Puttalam. These days, however, it is of no economic significance anymore.

WHAT TO SEE IN PUTTALAM

Puttalam is a typical fishing town and one of the island's most important. It is interesting to watch the bustling fishermen at the harbour, in the market hall, where the catch is auctioned off, and in the streets lined by stalls selling dried fish.

Shaped by fishing

The salt fields salt fields reach as far as Palavi, 6 km/4 mi south of Puttalam. More than a fifth of Sri Lanka's salt requirements are obtained here from sea water that is evaporated by the sun, leaving the salt behind.

Salt fields

The approx. 60km/37 mi headland opposite Puttalam, which separates the lagoon from the sea, is particularly attractive. It is covered in sand dunes and coconut palms.

Attractive headland

AROUND PUTTALAM

Near Talawila, approx. 24km/15mi northwest of Puttalam on the abovementioned headland, is St Anne's, a large church which is the destination of many pilgrims every year on 26 July. The church itself does not have any particular features of interest.

* Talawila

The town of Kalpitiya further north on the lagoon is inhabited by Moors, the descendants of the Arab seafarers. In medieval times it was an important port. The Portuguese built a fort at this strategically favourable location, which was later expanded by the Dutch. It is in a good state of repair, as is a church dating from the Dutch period.

Kalpitiya

About 33km/20mi north of Puttalam is one of the entrances to Wilpattu National Park; with an area of around 1317sq km/508 sq mi, it is **Sri Lanka's largest national park**. During the civil war it was a hotspot of military confrontation between the LTTE and the Singhalese military, which is why it was not open to the public. It was only in 2005 that the national park was opened to visitors again. The numbers are still remarkable. It is home to **Sri Lanka's largest leopard population** as well as to many other animals (elephants, bears, monkeys etc.). However, during the civil war many animals looked for new territories. The villus, large water pans filled by rain water that dry out completely during dry spells, are typical of the landscape here. There are more than 40 small and large villus in the park; they fill up with water during the monsoon period, when they attract a particularly large number of animals.

Wilpattu National Park

❶ Entrance near Hunuwilagaya. Admission fee US$15 (children up to 12 pay half price) plus a service fee for the nature conservation authority. Entrance with your own vehicle 300Rs.

** **Ratnapura**

── ✦ B 8

Province: Sabaragamuwa
Altitude: 86m/282ft
Population: 47,000

Ratnapura, the »city of gems«, is surrounded by mountains and is itself situated on hills in the wet, hot and humid valley of Kalu Ganga. It is also the capital of Sabaragamuwa Province. The name of the province is keeping the town's legendary name alive (Saba-ragama=village of the barbarians). Ratnapura is an ideal base for climbing ►Adam's Peak, Sri Lanka's most sacred mountain.

Gemstone Mecca
The pressure Adam's Peak puts on the rocks around Ratnapura has caused gemstones to form. Even the Greeks, Arabs and Chinese appreciated Ratnapura's wealth in gemstones more than 2000 years ago. These days the town and the surrounding area are inhabited by many Thais and Chinese working in the jewellery trade. It is not known when this town at the base of the highlands was founded; it already existed during the time of King Parakrama Bahu I (1153–1186), who promoted the search for gemstones here. During the Kandy period collecting gemstones was reserved for the kings. Now the state controls this enterprise.

WHAT TO SEE IN RATNAPURA

Fort
There are still some remains of the British Fort. From here and from other locations in the town there is a very good view of Sri Lanka's sacred mountain, Adam's Peak, which is only around 30km/20mi away.

Maha Saman Devale
Outside of town, above Kalu Ganga, is the Maha Saman Devale temple, which is visited by Hindu and Buddhist pilgrims every year. The temple is consecrated to the god Saman, the protector of the region but also of the gemstone dealers. The Devale represents the town's wealth; it is venerated equally by Hindus and Buddhists. The temple district is surrounded by a wall. In the forecourt are the remains of a Portuguese church from the 16th century. The archway leading into the temple complex also has Portuguese elements. In July/Aug an impressive Perahera takes place here, which lasts several days.

* Gemstone Mines of Ratnapura
The area rich in gems, the Ratnapura Trench, encompasses an area of approx. 8000ha/19,800 acres between the rivers Kalu Ganga and Am-

ban Ganga. The gravel layer that formed during the post-glacial period was later covered by a layer of silt. Gemstone mines are particularly numerous near the eastbound road to Pelmadulla, so it is possible to observe the hard physical work from close up. The search for gemstones (►MARCO POLO Insight p. 356) takes place under the control of government inspectors, but every worker is given a »bonus« when a valuable find is made. They are also allowed to keep every gem they find in an area declared to have been exhausted. Trading with gemstones was mainly in the hands of the Moors, except during the colonial period. The Moors once again own many of the jewellery shops that are thick on the ground here.

Ratnapura's National Museum was founded in 1946 and contains a small but good collection of gems and precious stones. Boards explain the history of gemstone mining and the museum also has a model of a gem mine as well as different finds from the town's history.

National Museum of Ratnapura

● Colombo Road, Sat–Thu 9am–5pm, admission charge

Ratnapura

GETTING THERE
By car: from Colombo on the A 4 via Avissawella (102 km/63mi), then onwards on the A 8 (98 km/91mi); from Hambantota on the A 2 to Nonagama, then on the A 18 (130 km/80mi); from Wellawaya on the A 4 (120 km/75mi)
By train: station on the Colombo–Opanayake line
By bus: good connections from the abovementioned towns

WHERE TO EAT
There are some restaurants serving Sri Lankan cuisine in the town centre around the clock tower.

Jade Restaurant £
Senanayake Road
Inexpensive, authentic Chinese and Thai food

WHERE TO STAY
Rainforest Edge £ £ – £ £ £
Balawatukanda, Waddagala

tel. 045 225 59 12
www.rainforestedge.com
This hotel was built on a hill at the edge of the Sinharaja Rain Forest, making sure the building suited its natural surroundings. It possesses lovely rooms with glorious views of the rainforest as well as an Ayurveda centre.

Rain Forest Lodge Deniyaya £ £
Temple Road, Deniyaya
tel. 041 492 04 44
www.rainforestlodge-srilanka.de
Guesthouse with just three rooms, in a wonderful setting in the midst of impressive landscape.

Ratnaloka Tour Inn £ – £ £
Kosagala, Kahandama
tel. 045 223 00 17
www.ratnaloka.com
Somewhat outside of town; good interior and pool. Most of the 53 rooms have wonderful views of the landscape.

City of Gems

All around Ratnapura there are many holes in the fields. At first glance they are difficult to spot, not least because most of them are covered in a roof of rice straw. And then there are the rivers of the surrounding area that flow down from the nearby mountains, carrying sand and stones with them. What will one day adorn elegant fingers is found under the ground and in the rivers: sapphires, rubies, aquamarines and topazes. However, there are no diamonds on Sri Lanka.

It is hard physical work to obtain what is so sought after all around the world, says Ahmed. Ahmed is a Moor, a descendant of the Arab merchants who arrived in Sri Lanka in the 8th century. Soon after their arrival they discovered gems at the foot of Adam's Peak. Ratnapura has been considered the city of gems ever since. Nowhere else on the island is the search for gems more fruitful than here. There are only two ways on Sri Lanka to get rich quick, or fairly quick: either by searching for gemstones or by trading in them. Ahmed has opted for the latter because it is by far the easier option – except in the case of discoveries that create a stir such as **the legendary »Blue Bell of Asia«**, which weighed an impressive 400 carats and was not meant for just anyone. Just anyone would not have been able to afford it, and so it was bought by the British royal family..

Hard Work

The methods of obtaining gemstones have remained unchanged since olden days. First a special pick-axe and spade are used to dig a square hole that is then extended to a shaft of up to 15m/50ft. When the hole is deep enough a scantily clad worker, either hanging on a rope or on a small wooden platform, is lowered and then digs a horizontal gallery. Using small spades the workers scrape to-

Cutting the gems

gether the clay earth by the light of candles or petroleum lamps. The candles do more than just provide light. They are also indicators of the air's oxygen content. Whatever the workers scratch off from the gallery walls deep below ground is tipped into a flat woven basket that is then transported back along the gallery and lifted out of the hole with ropes.

The Payoff

The workers above are already waiting for the basket and its contents. They carry it to the side, and one worker picks up a hose while the other switches on the diesel generator. The water gushes into the basket under very high pressure, getting smaller and sometimes larger stones out of the earth. With an expert eye and routine movement one of the workers separates the worthless stones from the precious ones. Often all they find are small moonstones or aquama-rines. Anything that looks as if it may be valuable is taken to Ratnapura. Here the buyers come into play. They assess the stones' quality and calculate a price, which is frequently arbitrary. There are no uniform prices, which is why many do not agree to the first price they hear..

Export and Processing

Every year gemstones worth around 65 million US dollars are exported from Sri Lanka to countries around the world. This is the official figure. It is hard to say what leaves the island by less regulated routes. This does happen of course, even though prospecting is

The gems are washed out in flat baskets

under state control. A large proportion of the gems goes to countries that have expertise in manufacturing jewellery, such as Thailand, where gems from Sri Lanka are sought-after raw materials for tasteful items in line with Western tastes. However, the government in Colombo has spent years trying to establish jewellery making on the island itself. Young, talented people are sent overseas to learn the art of the correct cut and suitable mount. But they also acquire knowledge and techniques that are actually frowned upon: sapphires that only have a low purity grade are heated in a special process, giving them a bluish hue that does not exist in nature. Such stones are popular, even though they lose their blue tint again after a few years. Of course there are also some talented jewellers on the island who have set up shop on their own initiative. They often market their creative work directly to tourists and also make items to order.

Sinharaja Rain Forest Reserve The drive from Pelmadulla in a southwesterly direction is very attractive. The road makes its way through the last surviving area of tropical rainforest, which seems almost pristine. As part of the Sinharaja Rain Forest Reserve it is not just under protection, it is also a UNESCO World Heritage Site. Strictly speaking this approx. 130sq km/50sq mi area may only be accessed by scientists, but some hotels offer **guided tours on the only trail that goes through the national park. The rainforest is home to many animal species as well as several endemic bird species.

** Sigiriya

C 6

Province: Central
Altitude of the fort: 363m/1190ft

The mighty rock of Sigiriya rises up 200m/984 ft from a plain surrounded by forests and lakes. As if the sight of it alone were not fascinating enough, the rock also has a (now derelict) fort on its summit plateau as well as the most famous wall paintings in Sri Lanka, the »cloud maidens of Sigiriya«, in a gallery beside the fort. The entire complex is now a UNESCO World Heritage Site.

Lion's Mouth The name Sigiriya developed in the 5th century during the reign of King Kaayapa: »giri« means mouth or also rock, »sinha« or »singha« means lion and refers to the front of a lion that has been carved from the rock and through whose mouth is the base of the stairs leading up to the peak. In the past they were nothing but small steps carved into the rock.

Stronghold The Culavamsa chronicle contains a legend concerning King Kassyapa I, who moved his seat of government here in the 5th century. It takes place around the rock of Sigiriya, but particularly around the fort on its summit plateau. He was the elder of two sons of King Datthu Sena (459–477); his mother was one of the king's concubines who came from a lower-class background, while Mogallana, the younger brother, was born to the king's main wife and queen. Upon the instigation of Migara, the army general and Datthu Sena's son-in-law, Kassyapa, imprisoned his father in the year 477, seizing the throne, while Mogallana fled to India. Meanwhile Migara was skilled at convincing Kassyapa that his father possessed great treasures that were not intended for him but for his brother Mogallana. As a result Kassyapa had his father tortured to find out the treasure's location. Duttha Sena finally led his son and Migara to Kala Reservoir, jumped

in, bathed and said: »This, friends, is all the treasure I have!« Kassyapa was so angry about this that he decided to kill his father. He had
him shackled naked and walled up alive.

Kassyapa I now began to fear the revenge of his brother, who had fled
to India, and so he moved from Anuradhapura to the rock of Sigiriya
after having a powerful stronghold built there. Mogallana indeed returned with a great army in 495. For reasons that remain inexplicable
to this day, Kassyapa left his fort and offered battle. However, when it
was became obvious he was defeated he used a knife to take his own
life. Mogallana became king in Anuradhapura. He handed over the
rock fort of Sigiriya to his priests. It soon fell into oblivion however,
and was only rediscovered in 1811 by the British major, H. Forbes. In
1894 restoration works got under way.

The rock of Sigiriya contains caves that were already inhabited very
much earlier in around the 2nd century BC, probably by reclusive
monks.

On the east and west sides of the base of the rock there are two rectangular spaces covering an area of approx. 40ha/100 acres, which are
surrounded by a wall and a moat. The western section is fortified by
two further walls with moats.

*** Royal
Gardens**

The main entrance is to the west, and on entering visitors will first get
to the extensive Royal Gardens, which are laid out in such a manner
that the axis points straight at the rock. The landscape designer(s)
incorporated the existing boulders into their plans. There are two
ponds respectively on either side of the path, each surrounded by a

The way to the rock fort goes through extensive gardens

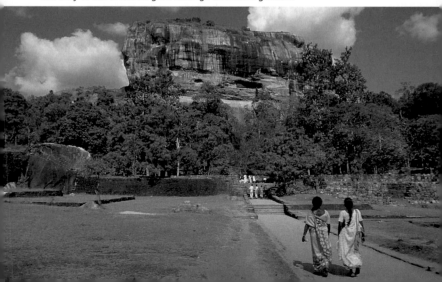

Sigiriya

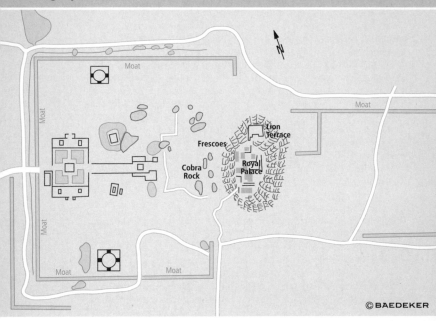

rectangular brick wall. The water was brought here from the lake via underground pipes. Between mounds surrounded by oval moats on which the remnants of some buildings can be made out, the path leads to an octagonal pond surrounded by a brick wall. The rock in the pond has indentations above the water's surface; these indentations were probably used to place oil lamps in.

**Rock Fort of Sigiriya A number of large rocks form a natural boundary between the Royal Gardens and the inner complex; they also form the first of several terraces at different heights on the main rock. Here too the remains of past construction can be made out in some places but their purpose is still being puzzled over today.

Rock caves The rocks of the western terrace house a total of 23 caves. Seven of them bear Brahmi inscriptions from the 2nd century BC–2nd century AD in their interior. It emerges from them that the caves served religious purposes, presumably as homes for the monks, long before Kassyapa had his palace built here. Some other caves on the other hand contain paintings of unknown provenance with depictions of

Sigiriya

GETTING THERE
By car: from Dambulla on the A 6 to Inamaluwa, then turn right (19 km/12mi); from Polonnaruwa on the A 11 to Habarana, then turn left and after around 4 km/2.5mi turn left again and after a further 4 km/2.5mi turn left yet again (55 km/33mi); from Anuradhapura on the A 13 to Maradankadawala, then turn left on to the A 11 to Habarana (see above) By train: the closest train station is in Habarana (19 km/12mi).

WHERE TO STAY
Aliya Resort & Spa £ £ £ – £ £ £ £
Sigiriya
Reservation in Colombo:
tel. 011 738 63 86
www.aliyaresort.com
This hotel opened in 2013. It has a timeless, modern style with 76 rooms and two suites in two-storey buildings. It is also possible to stay in one of the 18 luxury tents with a living space of almost 100sq m/1080sq ft.

Cinnamon Lodge Habarana £ £ £ – £ £ £ £
near Habarana
tel. 066 227 00 11

www.cinnamonhotels.com
This very nice five-star hotel is located in the middle of the Cultural Triangle. That makes it the perfect base for cultural tours. The hotel has 137 tasteful rooms, two restaurants, a pool and a bar.

Insider Tip

Hotel Eden Garden £ £ – £ £ £
Inamaluwa-Sigiriya Road
tel. 066 228 6635
www.edengardenlk.com
Centrally located hotel popular with tourist groups. 40 rooms with air conditioning. Ideal starting point for day trips to Dambulla, Sigiriya, Anuradhapura, Kurunegala and Polonnaruwa. The building is surrounded by a lovely garden and there is also a large, child-friendly pool.

Sigiriya Village £ £ – £ £ £
Reservation in Colombo:
tel. 011 238 16 44 and 238 16 45
www.sigiriyavillage.com
Nicely situated hotel with view of the rock of Sigiriya. 120 rooms in the cottage style, restaurant and pool.

women dating from Kassyapa's reign. Since the exploration of the entire complex is still ongoing, there is currently no interpretation for this.

On the first terrace the remains of a dagoba can still be made out. The Deranyagala cave, named after the palaeontologist Dr Paul Deraniyagala, on the terrace above also contains clearly recognizable paintings. In the northwest of this cave the narrow paths led to a brick staircase that was only discovered in 1958 and allowed the rock to be ascended from the west. Further routes up the rock can be found in the north and south. However, the southern route could not be re-

** *Sigiriya Rock Fort*

A bizarre rock made of gneiss rises up in the middle of the jungle. Together with the associated luxurious gardens, it was once a royal paradise. There is nothing comparable architecturally speaking. It conjures up thoughts of the wonders of the world. The magnificent artistic feat can still be recognized in the remains.

❶ 8am – 5pm

❶ Water garden

It is still possible to imagine the splendour and exquisite beauty when looking at the many remains of the ponds, pavilions, fountains and pools. They were all supplied by an ingenious system of canals. The four L-shaped pools once surrounded a pavilion. The pools themselves were probably used for bathing because they had smooth walls and steps.

❷ Stone garden

This area is ornamented by pretty stones. Winding paths also lead to the Cobra Hood Cave, the Preaching Rock and to an old monastic complex with a dagoba and a Bodhi tree.

❸ Terraced garden

The stone garden leads to the terraced garden. There are several terraces one above another here, all connected by brick staircases. They lead to the rock's entrance area, the Lion Gate.

❹ Lion Gate

Today it is merely the huge paws that are testament to the colossal loin that once covered the rock's entire façade.

❺ Royal palace on the summit plateau

The complex and layout of the 1.2 ha/3acre palace are still clearly visible. The inner palace can be found in the west, the outer one in the east. The palace gardens were located in the south. They were arranged around a rock pool that was used to store water.

❻ Sigiriya Wewa reservoir

Old inscriptions have revealed that this lake used to possess clear water covered in colourful water lilies. It fed the features in the water garden via an ingenious underwater pipe system, which had control flaps, circular pipeline and dirt traps. The water was collected via channels carved into the rock, which took up the water as it ran off.

A breather on the way up to the summit plateau

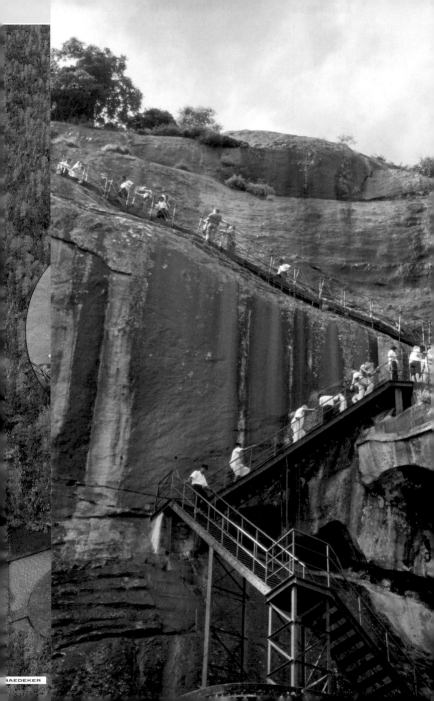

stored anymore and a portion of it was therefore replaced by a new staircase.

Cobra's Rock This staircase goes up to Cobra's Rock, which bears this name because of its astonishing resemblance to an upright cobra. Under a stone rain gutter at the entrance to a cave there is a Brahmi inscription from the 2nd century BC that reads: »The Cave of Chief Naguli«. Inside it are the remnants of wall paintings (including floral motifs).

Cistern Rock The path leads up to Cistern Rock, which got its name because of its shape, which is broken in two. The fallen section contains a throne carved into the rock as well as further seating. The terrace presumably had **Sri Lanka's first audience chamber**. A cave below the rock contains the remnants of some wall paintings.

Mirror Gallery The main access to the peak is a 145m/159 yd gallery that runs along the west side of the rock at a height of 15m/50ft. The first 19m/21yd form what is known as the Mirror Gallery, because the paintings that were once on the rock wall used to be reflected on the smooth surface of the ochre wall opposite. This wall is covered with many, still **well preserved inscriptions** (graffiti) that were carved by visitors between the 7th and 12th centuries with metal styli. Around 700 of them have been translated and published by the Singhalese archaeologist Paranavitana; some poetically praise the beauty of the women in the paintings, others the uniqueness of the royal palace on the rock of Sigiriya as well as the achievements of its builder.

Wall paintings The gallery with **Sri Lanka's most famous wall paintings was once not just protected by a projecting rock wall but additionally by a wooden roof. This is the only explanation of how these pictures have survived the centuries. An iron spiral staircase that was in a London underground station until the 1930s and then brought here leads up to the paintings 12m/39ft above the Mirror Gallery. The paintings depict **19 women of the utmost grace and perfection**; only fragments survive of another. Some archaeologists are of the opinion there must have been quite a lot more paintings, a hypothesis that is strengthened by further paint residue in other locations. Even though none of them have been restored, those that visitors can see depict some fair-skinned women (presumably mistresses) as well as some dark-skinned women (»gold-skinned«, as they are called in the graffiti), who presumably represent servants. At first glance they appear to be bare-breasted, but upon closer inspection a thin top can be made out, and the dark-skinned maidens are also wearing a rudimentary brassiere. Almost all of them are holding flowers in their slender, expressive hands. One dark-skinned maiden is serving petals and fruit, while another is holding what appears to be a jewellery box. The head-dresses of all of the maidens are particularly ornate. It is interesting that the girls can only be seen from the hips up, while the lower part of their bodies disappear in the implied clouds, which has earned them their common name **»Cloud Maidens of Sigiriya«**. Maybe they are not human but mythical creatures. The paintings are not frescoes in the proper sense. They were made using natural pigments to produce red, yellow, green, white and black, which were then applied to the rock surface that had been pre-treated with three layers. Their lines are

The graceful »Cloud Maidens«

very masterful, but of course the name of the artist who created them is unknown. Although in many of the details the paintings show a resemblance to the paintings in the famous caves of Ajanta in the modern state of Maharashtra in India, they still differ in significant ways and demonstrate a certain originality in Sri Lanka's art.

From the mirror gallery a path leads along the rock to the Lion Plateau. Between the magnificent paws carved from the rock a staircase secured by brick walls and then an iron staircase lead up to the summit plateau. It helps to have a good head for heights. It is also advisable to climb up to the summit plateau in the early morning because there are hornets' nests on the rock walls below the stairs and at times their inhabitants can react with irritation.

Climbing up to the summit plateau

Up on the summit visitors will now reach the citadel that was once surrounded by a wall that in turn appeared to be a continuation of the rock. Below the main rock, from which the view of the lush landscape and Sigiriya Wewa (reservoir) is magnificent, there are some impressive boulders in the northern section that contain further caves. The largest is around 12m/13yd long and contains the remains of a brick wall. Carry on northwards through the two boulders to get to a black rock whose surface is covered in many square holes. It is likely they once contained wooden columns that supported a further roof. Three wide seats, one above the other, are carved into the rock. Maybe King Kassyapa once sat on the uppermost one as he saw his half-brother's army that ultimately brought about his death, albeit indirectly.

Ruins on the royal palace

The significance of the buildings that once stood on the summit plateau has not yet been solved with absolute certainty. In any case, only their foundation walls remain and it requires a fair amount of imagination to interpret their former purpose. However, the masterful achievement of those who built the fort is quite evident; it must be borne in mind that all the construction materials had to be brought up to the summit plateau. After descending, why not visit the Archaeological Museum to the south of the town wall? It has Buddha statues, guard steles and the limestone statue of a queen.

Tangalla

✦ C 9

Province: Southern
Altitude: 5 m/16ft

Tangalla was valued as a seaport by the Dutch and the British alike. It is situated in the very arid zone of the island's south. The beautiful, palm-lined bathing beaches with their fine sand are very well known.

WHAT TO SEE IN TANGALLA AND AROUND

Reconstruction

Until the tsunami hit, several houses from the Dutch colonial power had survived, but the town was largely flooded. Reconstructions works have progressed a long way because this is one of the state's model projects for the reconstructions. All the hotels have reopened.

**Blow Hole (crevice)

Between Tangalla and Dickwella there is a very special phenomenon, the Blow Hole. What lay behind this very rare natural phenomenon was unknown for a long time. After intensive research the probable cause has been determined, namely a pressure difference between a closed cave system and the surrounding area. The air is blown out or sucked in through a hole on the surface. The Blow Hole in Sri Lanka is best observed during the monsoon period when there is more water in the underground cave system, causing it to be forced out when the swell is right.

To get to the Blow Hole turn off the A2 at milestone 117 into a narrow track to the sea and follow the signs.

Mulkirigala Rock

Around 16km/10mi north of Tangalla is the 91m/300ft black rock known as Mulkirigala (access from Wiraketiya or Beliatta). It contains several caves that were used as homes by monks. A cave temple with several statues of Buddha, including the sculpture of a 10.5m/ 35ft re-

Tangalla

GETTING THERE
By car: from Galle on the A 2 (75 km/47mi); from Hambantota on the A 2 (43 km/27mi)
By train: the closest train station is in Matara (termination station of the Colombo line)
By bus: good connections from Galle, Matara and Hambantota

WHERE TO STAY/EAT
Amanwella
££££
Bodhi Mawatha, Wella Wathuara Godellawela, Tangalle
tel. 047 224 13 33
www.amanwella.com
Even restrained luxury has its price: one night in this new resort strats at £700. It has more than 30 purist suites with every creature comfort imaginable. The location right on the sea is breathtakingly beautiful. There is also a 47m/154ft freshwater pool. The restaurant serves Asian and Mediterranean fare. The fishing village of Tangalla is just a few minutes away and it is not far to other sights either.

Tangalla Bay Hotel £££ – ££££
Hambantota Road, Pallikkuduwa
tel. 047 224 03 46
www.tangallabayhotel.com
This 1971 hotel, built on a slope on a headland almost seems like a ship. It does not look like much from the outside, but behind the façade there are twelve deluxe and 22 standard rooms, all of which have unobstructed views of the sea.

Sandy's Beach Cabanas ££ – £££
Tangalla
tel. 077 776 225 009
www.sandycabana.com
Very well-kept hotel with 14 rooms right on the beach in the cabana style. They have been built using largely natural materials. Air conditioning is unnecessary here because there is a constant fresh breeze coming from the sea. The garden is also lovely. It has a freshwater pool. Although there is no spa, it is possible to get a relaxing massage here.

Eva Lanka
££ – £££
Tangalla
tel. 047 224 09 40-1
www.eva.lk
23 cottage-style rooms with a very tasteful interior, a pool and a stunning beach! The owner is Italian and even though he does not cook himself, the food served is always delicious.

Coppenrath House & Ristorante
££ – £££
60/A Vijaya Road, Madaketiya, Tangalla
tel. 047 224 19 41
sachithjknw1@yahoo.com
This guesthouse is situated on the picturesque Medaketiya Beach. The unusual bathrooms have a jacuzzi and all the rooms have balconies with sea views. The restaurant also serves tasty Italian dishes because the son is a chef in Italy. During the season it is possible to hire surfboards and body boards for free. From time to time dolphins visit the beach.

cumbent Buddha, was built during the reign of King Duttha Gamanai (161–137 BC). The wall paintings in the Pihala Vihara date back to the 19th century; they recount episodes from Buddha's past lives in a naïve narrative manner. The monastery, one of the oldest in Sri Lanka, houses an extensive collection of books and manuscripts. In 1826 parts of the Mahavamsa chronicle, which was written in Pali, were found.

Tissamaharama

✦ **D 9**

Province: Southern
Altitude: 30m/98ft

Tissamaharama, as the capital of the former kingdom of Ruhuna, has a rich past. However, many treasures in the expansive area of ruins still have not been uncovered. The nearby Yala National Park is a paradise for animals, such as elephants, leopards, bears, buffalos, crocodile and deer. As a result it attracts many thousands of visitors. A further nature reserve that is somewhat further away is the Weerawile Tissa Bird Sanctuary. It is worth visiting for anyone particularly interested in Sri Lanka's birds.

History Mahanaga, one of King Devanampiya Tissa's (260–210 BC) younger brothers, is thought to be the town's founder. He called it Mahagam or Magama. Mahanaga had to flee from the capital Anuradhapura because the queen, who was very popular with the people, was out to kill him. During this time the Kshattriya dynasty, who had presumably come here from India and were members of the warrior caste of the same name, ruled the region from Kataragama, 16km/10 mi further north. Between them and Mahanaga there were bellicose confrontations initially, but later they made a peace that was subsequently sealed by marriage.

Later Kavana Tissa, one of Mahanaga's great-grandsons, married the daughter of the ruler of Kelaniya and added more territory to the kingdom of Ruhuna. As a result the kings of Ruhuna controlled the entire south of the island. At this time the Tamils who had come from southern India were already governing in Anuradhapura under King Elara (approx. 204–161 BC). Prince Duttha Gamani of Ruhuna, one of King Tissa's sons, gathered an army, moved to Anuradhapura with it and killed Elara in a duel. After his victory he ascended the throne and governed from 161–137 BC as a splendid king in Anuradhapura. During the subsequent period the Singhalese kings often sought refuge in the kingdom of Ruhuna to act against invaders from southern India. One of them was King Vijaya BahuI, who managed to oust the

Tissamaharama

GETTING THERE
By car: from Hambantota on the A 2 to Wirawila, then turn right and after around 6 km/3.5mi turn right again (29 km/18mi); from Wellawaya on the A 2, when the road forks at Wirawala Reservoir, bear left (62 km/38.5mi)
By plane: the closest international airport is in Hambantota; there are currently three flights a week.

WHERE TO STAY
Taprospa Resort £ £ – £ £ £
15, Courts Road, Tissamaharama
tel. 047 223 72 87, www.taprospa.com
This hotel is situated on the banks of Tissa Lake. It has 15 spacious rooms with air conditioning. There is also a pool. Three national parks (Yala, Bundula and Udawalawa) are all within easy reach.

Lake Wind Hotel £ £ – £ £ £
Punchi Agurugoda
tel. 047 223 96 87
www.tissalakewind.com
New terraced hotel right on the banks of Tissa Lake with tasteful rooms and air-conditioning. Guests can also use a pool above the riverbank. The restaurant serves local and international cuisine. This is a good starting point for safari trips to the abovementioned national parks.

Tissa Inn Guest House, Restaurant and Bar £ £
Wellawaya Road
tel. 047 223 72 33, www.tissainn.lk
Almost a hotel, but officially a guesthouse. It has a dozen pretty rooms with air conditioning or fan. The restaurant is universally praised for its cuisine.

Chola rulers from the island in 1070. However, some of the kings of Ruhuna also turned against the kings of the north, mainly to secure their area of influence in the south. Tissamaharama played an important role for a good 2000 years of the island's history, but then the town lost much of its importance.

WHAT TO SEE IN TISSAMAHARAMA

The ingenious irrigation system is quite remarkable. It was created by the early rulers of Ruhuna. It consists of several reservoirs (wewas) fed by the nearby rivers Kirindi Oya and Menik Ganga. This system transformed the originally bare region, which did though have fertile soils, into a **flourishing landscape**. It made it possible to grow rice on a large scale, helping the kings to become very rich. The system fell into ruin or silted up over the years and was only repaired in the 20th century. Since then people have been settling here again. **Irrigation system**

Several magnificent monolithic pillars still remain of the old royal palace on a hill to the east of town. They probably supported a multi- **Old royal palace** storey building, maybe made of wood. The building is likely to have been constructed in the 2nd century.

Yatala Dagoba The Yatala Dagoba was built in the 2nd century BC. The attached monastic complex contains inscriptions dating back to the time before Christ as well as to the 7th and 8th centuries. During restoration works significant finds were discovered, such as the head of a Buddha statue made of limestone, the sculpture of a standing Buddha as well as a statue that probably depicts King Kavanna Tissa. The statue of a Buddha with crossed arms is quite remarkable; such a pose is quite unusual in Sri Lanka. A further feature of note is the 80cm/31in stele with a depiction of seven male figures who have not been identified. The figure in the middle is standing under three parasols, making it likely that this is a depiction of a ruler and his retinue.

Chandagiri Vihara To the south of town the ruins of Chandagiri Vihara with inscriptions on a large octagonal stone that presumably date back to the period between the 1st century BC and the 1st century AD.

Tissamaharama Vihara The Chandagiri Vihara, founded in around 160BC under King Kakavanna Tissa, always used to be a meeting place at the start of the rainy season for all monks living south of Mahaweli Ganga. They meditated here and sought instruction from the monastery's resident monks. According to the chronicle, 363 monk's cells existed here in the 9th century. The dagoba, which was also built during the time the monastery was founded, is, at 60m/197ft, probably the tallest that ever existed in the kingdom of Ruhuna.

Ruins on the road to Kirinda The road to Kirina, a fishing port 13km/8 mi south of Tissamaharama, is lined by ancient ruins, most of which are still awaiting restoration. Kirinda was once a significant port for Tissamaharama.

Trincomalee

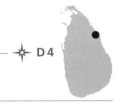

✦ **D 4**

Province: Eastern
Altitude: 8m/26ft
Population: approx. 115,000

Trincomalee, because of its sheltered location, has been a preferred location of trade and industry for many centuries. A large harbour, one of the world's most beautiful natural harbours, played a major role in this. The city in the northeast of Sri Lanka has also played a role in tourism, less because of any particular sites than because of the magnificent beaches.

Trincomalee

GETTING THERE
By car: from Colombo on the A 1 via Ambepussa and Kurunegala, continue on the new Kandy-Jaffna Highway (272 km/169mi, driving time app. 6 hrs.)
By train: from Colombo via Kurunegala, Dambulla and Habarana (app. 7 hrs.)
By bus: from Colombo via Maho and Galoya (app. 8 hrs.)

WHERE TO STAY
Club Oceanic £ £ – £ £ £
Uppuveli, app. 12 km/7mi from Trincomalee

tel. 026 223 07
www.johnkeellshotels.com
Renovated hotel with 56 rooms on a long, wide sandy beach. Many water sports opportunities. Especially suitable for families.

Pigeon Island Beach Resort
£ £ – £ £ £
tel. 026 738 83 80-3
www.pigeonislandresort.com
This hotel is situated on the lovely sandy beach at Nilaveli. The hotel has 30 comfortable rooms, eight suites, one good restaurant and a bar.

Peninsula

Trincomalee is situated on a very elongated peninsula that is hardly wider than a kilometre. Towards the northeast a headland projects into the open sea. This was the location of Fort Frederick. The actual city is situated on both sides for about 2km/1mi. There are several small islands just off the coast, such as Pigeon Island, which has **a very attractive coral reef**. Not far from Trincomalee near Mutur the Mahaweli Ganga, Sri Lanka's longest river, flows into the Indian Ocean after flowing across country for 332km/206mi.

Tamil character

According to estimates, the town of Trincomalee is home to around 115,000 people and recently, to Singhalese people again too. The vast majority of the population, though, is made up of Tamils and Moors. In and around Trinco, as the city is usually called, the tsunami caused severe damage and thousands of people were killed or injured and tens of thousands of families were rendered homeless.

History

Little is known about the early history of the city, which is called Go-kanna in the chronicle of Mahavamsa. Tamils from India settled here more than 2000 years ago. They called the town Thirukonamalai (sacred sun hill). Ptolemy mentioned Trincomalee as the »harbour of Helios«; Egyptian and Greek seafarers had told him about it. King Dhutta Sena (276–303), it is recorded in the chronicle, had all the Hindu temples in Gokanna destroyed. In the 8th century Muslim settlers arrived. In 1592 King Vimela Dharma SuriyaI fled Kandy to escape the Portuguese and came here. In order to expel the Portuguese from the island, King Senerat allowed the Dutch in 1612 to build a fort in Kottiyar, near Trincomalee; however, it was taken by the Portuguese shortly after it was completed. In the years that followed, this area was fought over by the French, Dutch and British. The British under General James Stuart finally managed to take Fort Frederick in 1795. To protect the entrance to the inner harbour they built the less well fortified Fort Ostenburg. From the 19th century until Sri Lanka's independence, Trincomalee was used by the British as a naval port from which they controlled the Indian Ocean. In 1905 the fortifications of Fort Frederick were razed to the ground and in 1942 a Japanese aerial attack on the British fleet destroyed the little that was left.

The harbour of Trincomalee had its heyday in the 17th and 18th centuries when sailing ships were still crossing the oceans. After Colombo harbour was developed, Trincomalee increasingly lost its importance.

Pigeon Island near Trincomalee, a paradise

WHAT TO SEE IN TRINCOMALEE

There are several Hindu temples in Trincomalee; however, they all **Temples**
date back to more recent times, which is why they are of little art-
historical value. On Dockyard Road Kadakarai Temple and Mu-
dugayan Kovil are still worth visiting because of their extensively
ornamented entrance towers.

The Thiru Koneswaram Kovil is one of the worthwhile temples in **Thiru Kones-**
Trincomalee, although the original 1622 buildings were destroyed by **waram Kovil**
the Portuguese, so that today's buildings are quite modern. The remains of the old buildings can still be spotted lying in the sea. The
best place for doing this is called Lover's Leap. According to tradition
the young Dutch woman Francina van Rhede threw herself off the
cliffs here in 1687 as a result of a broken heart, but naturally she survived the fall. The Hindu temple stands on Swami Rock, which rises
130m/427ft from the sea, is one of the most sacred of its kind on Sri
Lanka. The daily **Puja times** are 7am, 11.30am and 6pm, at which
point the faithful gather. In the Kovil is a lingam (symbol of Shiva,
the god of fertility) that was thrown into the sea by the Portuguese
and discovered by divers by accident. They also recovered it.

The fort of Trincomalee on the town's north side was built by the Por- **Fort**
tuguese. Some of the stones they used came from the Hindu temple
that was destroyed here, which was considered sacrilegious by the
Hindus. The Portuguese extended the fort in 1656. Since 1803 the
fort has had its name in honour of the then Duke of York. Even
thought it is still used by the Singhalese military, it can be visited with
almost no restrictions. Within the fort is the former residence of the
Duke of Wellington, who came here in 1792 to recover from an ill-
ness he had caught during a military campaign against Tipu Sultan
in southern India. There is a magnificent old bodhi tree in the garden. The **tame deer and stags** belong to the Koneswaram Temple
on Swami Rock at the end of the headland the fort stands on.

AROUND TRINCOMALEE

Only around ten minutes by boat from Trincomalee or Nilaveli is the **Pigeon Island**
small coral island of Pigeon Island. Every imaginable water sport can
be indulged in here, but the colourful coral reef makes diving and
snorkelling particularly interesting.

Near the small town of Kanniyai, a few miles northwest of Trinco- **Hot springs**
malee on the A12, there are seven hot springs whose creation is as- **near Kanniyai**
sociated with a legend from the Ramayana.

✶ Uda Walawe National Park

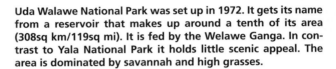

✳ C 9

Province: Sabaragamuwa / Uva
Area: central southern part of the island

Uda Walawe National Park was set up in 1972. It gets its name from a reservoir that makes up around a tenth of its area (308sq km/119sq mi). It is fed by the Welawe Ganga. In contrast to Yala National Park it holds little scenic appeal. The area is dominated by savannah and high grasses.

Wild elephants

And yet it's worth visiting this national park, since there is virtually no other place in Sri Lanka where there are such large herds of wild elephants. Up to 600 of them can be observed daily as they bathe in the reservoir. The best time for this is 6.30am–10am and in the late afternoon 4pm–6.30pm. The elephants enjoy special protection: the national park was fenced in to prevent them from wandering off.

Other animals that can be observed from a Jeep here include Sambar deer, wild water buffalo, crocodiles and foxes. With a bit of luck visitors might even spot a leopard. The national park is known as a popular place for migratory birds that overwinter here between November and April. The protected area is also home to around 30 species of snake, including the Sri Lankan krait.

Elephant orphanage

Around 5km/3mi to the south of the park entrance is a state-funded institution that was opened in 1995. Wounded and orphaned elephants are nursed back to health here. It is protected by the Department of Wildlife Conservation. The animals are fed three times a day at 9am, 3pm and 6pm. Anyone wishing to watch can do this for free.

Uda Walawe National Park

GETTING THERE
The entrance to the national park is at the 11th milepost on the National Road A 18 near Timbolketiya.

ADMISSION
USD15
(children up to the age of 12 pay half)

WHERE TO STAY
There is some accommodation not far from the park; the Task Safari Camp with 27 pretty cabanas is recommended www.srilankansafari.com,
tel. 011 486 22 25

★★ Una/Unawatuna

━━━━━━━━━━━━━━━━━ ✦ B 9 / 10

Province: Southern
Altitude: 2m–13m/6.5ft–42.5ft

The beach of Unawatuna, which has been popular with backpackers and package tourists since the 1970s (and with the Dutch military and merchants even before that) gets its popularity from its proximity to rich port of ▶Galle, which has many historical attractions on offer.

Another reason is that, over the years, Unawatuna provided an alternative to the increasingly hectic seaside town of Hikkaduwa. Unawatuna is a small, modest place with not much to see. But its sickle-shaped beach measuring 2km/1mi in length is seen as one of Sri Lanka's most beautiful and one of the seven most beautiful on Earth. It is particularly well suited to a holiday with children. Some hotels also try to attract visitors with special services for kids.
The tsunami on 26 December 2004 was hardly able to change anything about that, despite causing serious damage. Just a few days later reconstruction work on the largely destroyed accommodation began. It has to be noted (with disapproval) that some particularly enterprising hotel owners built their new hotels so close to the sands as to breach the limits set by the government. Should the latter get serious, some of the (strictly speaking) illegal buildings may have to be pulled down.

Beaches

> **! MARCO⊕POLO TIP**
>
> *Beach parties* **Insider Tip**
>
> The main days for parties in Unawatuna are Friday and Saturday. The beach is the focal point. The music blasts out of massive loudspeakers. The cocktail bars on the beach are a bit quieter. and spaced apart.

A different problem has always been the removal of refuse left by visitors; there is still a lot of work to be done here. And then there is noticeable erosion that has made the beach visibly narrower, especially in the west.
The beach of Unawatuna also became famous because of its magnificent offshore coral reefs, which continue to fascinate snorkelers and divers alike. Naturally there are a large number of dive schools that also put on training courses. The selection of water sports could not be more diverse, ranging from high-seas fishing to windsurfing.

WHAT TO SEE IN AND AROUND UNAWATUNA

While there is nothing cultural in Unawatura other than a small daily market, it is worth strolling through the fishing port, which is at its

Fishing port

Enjoy Unawatuna

GETTING THERE

By train: although Unawatuna has a small station, it is better to take the train to Galle and continue from there by taxi.

By bus: there are several good bus connections per day between Galle and Unawatuna (15 mins.).

By car: from Galle it is just 4km/2.5mi to Unawatuna along the coast on Matara Road or the A 2; from Colombo it is 125 km/78mi, to Kogalla 12 km/7mi and to Weligama 23 km/14mi.

WHERE TO EAT

There are lots of restaurants along the beach that have adapted to tourist tastes and requirements. Almost every menu here features spaghetti bolognaise (e.g. at what is probably the best Italian place here, Dream House, tel. 091 438 15 41 or in the Tataruga, tel. 091 492 71 16). Anyone looking for something different will enjoy the delicious fish and seafood dishes in the relatively expensive The Rock restaurant (tel. 091 224 62 88). Vegetarian fare can be found in several recommended restaurants, such as the South Ceylon (tel. 091 698 64 92).

WHERE TO STAY
Full Moon Resort £ £ – £ £ £
Yakddehimulla Road

Almost too beautiful to be true: Unawatuna Beach

tel. 091 223 00 91
www.fullmoonresortunawatuna.com
Maybe the most stylish hotel in
Unawatuna; the Italian owner has given
it its special mark. The 17 very comfortable, generously proportioned rooms are
surrounded by a pretty garden. Some
rooms don't have air conditioning, however. Instead, there are fans to provide
fresh air. The hotel restaurant is right on
the water.

Secret Garden Villa £ – £ £
Unawatuna Beach
tel. 091 224 18 57
www.secretgardenunawatuna.com
Cottage-style hotel that has been
around since the 1990s. It was founded
by a Swiss woman. What is special
about this hotel, which is surrounded by

a lovingly tended tropical garden, is particularly popular with guests who wish
to practise yoga under expert instruction.

Rathna Guest House £
Matara Road
tel. 091 493 34 05
www.rathna-guesthouse.com
More a family-run business than a hotel,
a fact largely ensured by the owner with
the loving nickname Mama Push-   **Insider**
pa. The two-storey cabana right   **Tip**
on the beach is particularly nice.
Together with her four children Mama
Pushpa provides a pleasant holiday atmosphere, offering everything from fishing to windsurfing (including for beginners) to complement visitors' stays.

busiest in the mornings. There are two interesting attractions nearby,
however. They should definitely be visited to take a break from lazy
days on the beach.

The oversized, bright white dagoba of the Wella Devale is quite a   **Wella Devale**
striking reference point in Unawatuna. The climb up the mountain
at the western end of the bay on which the dagoba stands is certainly
rather laborious, but the reward is the magnificent view of the landscape and the beach.

Rhumassala Kanda, which is known for its rare herbs, rises just a few   **Rhumassala**
kilometres from the beach. According to the Hindu Ramayana epic,   **Kanda**
it is from here that the monkey god Hanuman was set to the Himalayas by Rama to collect certain medicinal herbs for his wounded
brother Lakshmana and bring them back here. The legend continues
that Hanuman forgot the names of the medicinal herbs on the way
back, whereupon without further ado he just brought the whole
mountain and all the herbs growing on it.

Another very lovely beach is located between Unawatuna and Galle.   **Jungle Beach**
It is not yet so overrun and yet it has almost everything that you need
for relaxing days by the sea. The best way to get to Jungle Beach is on
a Three Wheeler.

Midigama Beach Around 10km/6mi to the southeast of Kogalla, near the small town of Midigama is **one of the best destinations for surfers. The most popular surf spots are called Plantation and Coconut. A third one is known as Ram's Point and is named after Ramyadava Gunasekara, or »Ram« for short, who has owned a small, inexpensive guesthouse with fifteen very basic, but clean rooms here for many years (tel. 041 225 26 39, rams-surfingbeach@gmail.com). The beaches are suitable for beginners as well as more advanced surfers. Allegedly the best surfing wave of Sri Lanka can be found right in front of Ram's Surfing Beach Guest House. Surfboards can be hired.

Weligama

B 10

Province: Southern
Altitude: 5m/16ft

The small fishing village of Weligama – the name means »village in the sand« – possessed an important seaport for many centuries but it lost its significance at the latest when the port facilities in Colombo were extended.

The construction of a road to shorten the distance between Galle and Matara has also cost the town much of its original charm. Nevertheless there are still some nicely situated beaches with tall coconut palm trees and fine sand here. According to legend, the first coconut to be washed ashore in Sri Lanka arrived on the island near Weligama. Coconut palms and their nuts have been the island's economic backbone for many years. They are still used intensively today.

WHAT TO SEE IN WELIGAMA

Bay The 3.5km/2mi bay framed by red laterite rock resembles the landscape of Galle and was also used as a seaport. Today only fishing boats come here. There are two **small islands** in the bay, Taprobane (Greek: copper island; one of the names the entire island of Sri Lanka held in earlier times) and Parei Duwa (pigeon island). Taprobane is only 1ha/2.5acres in size and was once in the possession of the French Comte de Nouny, who had a magnificent villa and a tropical garden set up here. The house was later inhabited by the American author and composer Paul Bowles; now it is an elegant hotel.

Statue of King Kustha Raja Near to the railway crossing is the Hindu Natha Devale with a colossal relief sculpture; it is believed to have been made either in the 6th

Weligama

GETTING THERE

By car: from Galle on the A 2 (26 km/16mi); from Matara on the A 2 (16 km/10mi)

By train: station on the Colombo–Matara line

By bus: good bus connections from Galle and Matara

WHERE TO STAY

Taprobane Island £ £ £ £

tel. 091 438 02 75

www.taprobaneisland.com

Situated on a small island. Very smart accommodation with 13 rooms of varying price categories: the most expensive are the luxurious beach houses. But it is also possible to rent the entire island …

Palace Mirissa £ £ £ – £ £ £ £

Coparamulla, Mirissa

tel. 041 225 13 03

www.palacemirissa.com

Maybe Mirissa's best resort. 13 very comfortable chalets situated on a hillside with lovely views of the beach and sea. Half-board is obligatory here.

There is a large pool that is also suitable for children. Arugam Bay, a hotspot for surfers, is just a few kilometres away.

Bay Beach Hotel Weligama £ £ – £ £ £

Kapparatota

tel. 041 225 02 01

www.baybeachhotel.com

Mid-range hotel with 60 sufficiently comfortable rooms. Nice pool and private beach as well as a PADI diving school.

Paradise Beach Club £ £

Mirissa

tel. 041 225 12 06

www.paradisemirissa.com

This resort was one of the very first on this beach. The team ensuring the cleanliness of the 42 rooms and the cosy atmosphere are correspondingly experienced. The restaurant is known for its excellent seafood dishes. Why not enjoy a sundowner in the beach bar. The pool is also suitable for children, which is why many locals come here for their holidays.

or the 11th century. It is located in a niche in the rock wall and was worked from the stone. It has not yet been determined whether the magnificently clad figure wearing a crown and a bracelet is the bodhisattva Avalokitesvara or the bodhisattva Samantabhadra (the god Saman). The legend says Kushta Raja, the leper king, came to Weligama to cure his sickness by drinking the juice of the royal palm for three months.

One of Sri Lanka's most beautiful beaches can be found near Weligama, around 10km/6mi to the west of Matara near the small town of Mirissa. It was once considered an insider tip among backpackers, but now it is popular with all tourists, especially since countless small hotels and bungalows have been built.

*Mirissa

** Yala National Park (Ruhuna National Park)

D–E8/9

Province: Uva
Area: South Coast

Yala National Park was founded as a reserve in 1900; it is the best-known of Sri Lanka's national parks, even though it may not necessarily be home to the most species. Nevertheless is it well worth visiting, since many other parks in the north and east only have limited access for visitors because of nature conservation reasons.

Only partially accessible

Yala National Park covers an area of approx. 1300sq km/500 sq mi and is structured into a western and eastern section. The latter has been given Strict Nature Reserve status and may only be visited with special permission.

Yala National Park is home to more than 400 bird species. The waders can be observed on a large number of its lakes.

Despite the sparse vegetation typical of Sri Lanka's south, Yala National Park is a refuge for all kinds of animals. Wild elephants live here just as peacefully as crocodiles, sambar and chital deer, flamingos, peacocks, tortoises, buffaloes, jackals, leopards and allegedly also some sloth bears. The flora resembles a savannah: low bushes, only few trees and shallow lakes with mangroves. The dead trees that can be found in some of the lakes are quite impressive, making ideal resting places for the many representatives of the local bird world. From November to April these birds are joined by many bird species from India and western Asia, which come here to overwinter.

Flora and fauna

There is an information centre at the park entrance near Palatupana, which houses a **worthwhile exhibition** on the flora and fauna of Yala National Park.

Information centre

❶ Daily 8am–5pm

On its southeastern side the park borders on the sea. The strip of coastline is even more attractive because of its **lovely sandy beach**. It is one of the few places where rangers give visitors permission to leave the vehicle and go swimming. A drive through the park is best early in the morning or in the afternoon because most animals try to escape the noonday sun, making them harder to find.

Bathing possible

Yala National Park

GETTING THERE
By car: from Hambantota on the A 2 to Tissamaharama, from there continue by Jeep to the main entrance
By train: the closest train station is in Matara (terminal station of the southbound Colombo line); then continue by bus or taxi

TOURS
The park is open every day 6am–6pm. The main entrance is Palaputana Gate, which can be found around 20km/12mi to the east of Tissamaharama. There are always drivers offering their services here. The park can only be entered by vehicles accompanied by a ranger. Entering the park in private vehicles is prohibited. It is also forbidden to leave the vehicle, unless the

ranger gives permission in certain locations. Visitors will have to pay an admission charge as well as a fee for the vehicle and a fee for the ranger.

WHERE TO STAY
Yala Safari Game Lodge £ £
P. O. Box 1, Tissamaharama
tel. 047 380 15
The comfortable Yala Village Resort is by far the best hotel on the edge of Yala National Park. It hires out Jeeps and licensed guides.

The **Wildlife and Nature Protection Society** maintains some inexpensive bungalows in Yala National Park. They can be booked by phone 011 88 73 90; further information at www.wnpssl.org

Kumana Bird Kumana Bird Sanctuary is **part of Yala East National Park** and en-
Sanctuary tering it requires a special permit. It is home to a particularly diverse
bird world, including many species of water fowl, along with horn-
bills, herons, pelicans, eagles and more. This is also a good place to
encounter water buffalo, stags, wild pigs and various reptile species.

✶✶ Yapahuwa

✳ **B 6**

Province: North Western
Height of the rock fort: 92m/280ft

**Yapahuwa is neither a town nor a village, it is rather what re-
mains of an imposing 12th-century rock fort that rises up
abruptly from the wilderness to a height of 92m/280ft. The complex is a similarly bold and magnificent creation as the residence
of Sigiriya, designed with perspective and architectural symbolism in mind. In contrast to Sigiriya it is not at all overrun, so that
visitors can enjoy the wealth of attractions in peace and quiet.**

History Brahmi inscriptions in some of the plentiful caves prove that Buddhist hermits lived here, at least in the 2nd century AD. The kings of
Sri Lanka appear to have only noticed the strate-
gic location of this place in the 13th century; if
they did so earlier no records survive. When the
Kalinga prince Magha was the king of Sri Lanka
(1215–1236) resistance groups formed in several
parts of the country. One of them occupied the
rock that was named after their leader Subha –
Yapahuwa is the Sinhala word for Subhagiri or
Subhapatta. This group developed it into a defensive complex because they were able to observe
the rebels' movements in the south. King Bhuvanaike Bahu I put an army together from here
for his brother Vijaya Bahu II, who had been the kingdom's administrator since 1262. This army achieved a victory against the Malay
king Sri Dharamaraja from Ligor near Yapahuwa. In 1272, after his
brother had been murdered in Dambadeniya, Bhuvanaike Bahu fled
with his wife to Yapahuwa; it was only when he was proclaimed king
several months later that he chose the secure mountain fort to be his
residence and the capital of his kingdom. As a symbol of his power
he also possessed the **holy tooth**. His reign was marked by battles
against the southern Indian Pandya under Arya Chakravarti and
against enemies in his own country who were after the throne. Chi-

> **!** **MARCO ❂ POLO TIP**
>
> *Ask the monks* **Insider Tip**
>
> The caves are nor-
> mally closed but they
> are still used for
> prayer by the monks
> living here. Ask them
> for permission to vis-
> it.

nese coins found in Yapahuwa suggest that Bhuvanaike Bahu I maintained friendly relations to China and may have even asked the Chinese for help. Marco Polo for example reports that a party had come to Yapahuwa from the Mongol ruler Kublai Khan, who had conquered China.

When Bhuvanaike Bahu I died in 1284 it was also the end of the short golden age of Yapahuwa. The Pandyas even managed to conquer the fort and gain possession of the sacred tooth relic. King Parakrama Bahu II (1287–1293) however successfully negotiated to have it returned to Sri Lanka.

The Portuguese also knew of the existence of the old fort of Yapahuwa, while the Dutch probably did not. When an officer of the British army set up camp nearby he discovered the impressive complex. First excavations were undertaken in 1888.

Magnificent and tranquil: Yapahuwa Rock Fort

** ROCK FORT YAPAHUWA

Complex

Two parallel walls surround the southern section of the rock at a distance of 100m/110 yd. The outer wall, 14m/45 ft thick and 4.5m/14ft high consists of piled up earth covered in brick walls and stone blocks at the base. There is a 13m/40ft wide ditch on the outside of the 900m/990yd long wall, in which there are three gates. The main gate is opposite the palace access in the southwest. Remains of the buildings between the two walls are very scarce.

The lower town was located behind the inner wall. The temple at the eastern access was only built by a monk from Nettipologama in the 18th century; King Kirti Sri Raja Singha from Kandy is said to have acquiesced to its construction. Inside is a column that was found within the complex bearing an old inscription that testifies to this.

Cave temple

Somewhat further to the northeast is a cave temple with paintings from the 18th century, the Kandyan period. Amongst other things the paintings depict **Buddha's 24 visions**, the seven weeks after his enlightenment and his first sermon. The painting on the ceiling is

Yapahuwa

GETTING THERE

By car: from Kurunegala on the A 10 to Padeniya, continue on the A 28, turn right at Maho. Walk from Maho (scenic) or take a taxi. The bus only covers the first 3km/2mi to the Yapahuwa turning.
By train: Maho is a railway hub. The lines from Colombo to Trincomalee and Jaffna meet here.

WHERE TO STAY

There is a Rest House with basic rooms around 4km/2.5mi from Yapahuwa. A greater selection of accommodation, including higher-quality options can be found in "Kurunegala.

Yapahuwa Paradise £ £ – £ £ £
Yapahuwa
tel. 037 397 50 55
www.hotelyapahuwaparadise.com
Very well tended hotel right on a small lake not far from the impressive ruins of Yapahuwa. Comfortable rooms with all kinds of amenities. All rooms have sea views. There is a pool in the garden. The restaurant serves local and international fare. Excursions to the surrounding area and to many historic sites as well as nature trips are organized by the hotel.

equally remarkable. The two Buddha figures are depicted in the same pose unusual in Sri Lanka – arms crossed – as the Ananda statue in Polonnaruwa. The statues in the cave temple were probably made at the end of the 18th century, maybe even later. The bodhi tree that belongs to the temple was probably only planted in the 19th century. Somewhat further north is another cave with an interesting roof, around 15m/50 ft above ground. At the southern end of the interior a 7.5 x 3.6m (25 x 12ft) walled area was created, presumably for a Vihara. The temple also contains a large stone throne.

Mandapa Near the stairs to the palace are the remains of a building that housed 52 columns. The bases are still present. It is called the Mandapa or also Ambassador's Pavilion because it may have served as a guesthouse for foreign emissaries.

Stairs The most impressive feat to be admired in Yapahuwa today is the monumental staircase that is richly structured and adorned with lively sculptures in the upper section. It is the expression of a strong desire for display and of a strength that builds on legitimation as well as a sense of religious and political mission. This palace access consists of six stairway sections and the landings in between. The lower section of this staircase is unadorned. After a landing measuring 7.5m/25ft in width, the upper section begins, ornamented with magnificent sculptures. This section reaches its harmonious consummation in an impressive gate decorated with many figures, including sculptures of lions of outstanding quality. On either side of the entrance were windows artistically carved from granite; they are unique in all of Sri Lanka. One has survived and is now in the small archaeological museum in the lower town. It consists of 45 touching circular shapes; each circle contains a figure (lion, elephant, swan, dwarf, dancer) cut out in the silhouette manner. Also richly adorned is the makara arch above the window openings, below which is a scenic depiction: the goddess Lakshmi is sitting, legs crossed, holding a lotus in each hand, as she is being bathed by two elephants who are cupping containers with their trunks. The palace proper, a brick building with an area of 432sq m/516sq yd, was evidently very modest, which, by the way, also led to the conclusion that it may not have been a palace but a temple for the sacred tooth relic. On the other hand it was also assumed that after the construction of the magnificent stairs, events occurred that no longer permitted further buildings to be constructed.

PRACTICAL
INFORMATION

What to pack for a holiday to Sri Lanka? What vaccinations are advisable? On what side of the road do the cars drive? Why is it bad form to eat with the left hand? Find out here!

Arrival · Before the Journey

BY AIR

Flight time The distance between London and Sri Lanka is over 8000km/5000mi; the flying time is around nine hours. Non-stop flights are available with Sri Lankan Airlines. Routes run by Middle Eastern airlines or flights via India are worth considering.

Flight prices Ticket prices vary a great deal. Shopping around for the best deal is a good idea. It is important to book well in advance during the high season (Christmas–Easter). The weeks before and after this period are the cheapest.

Budget tickets Some tour operators (e.g. www.opodo.co.uk) have specialized in the sale of surplus or unused tickets. Taking advantage of these money-saving deals requires flexibility regarding the departure date and the type of accommodation in Sri Lanka.

Airport With the opening of the second international airport, Mattala Rajapaksa International Airport (MRIA) near Hambantota, app. 270 km/170mi southeast of Colombo, there are now two large airports in Sri Lanka. However, the new airport does not currently receive flights from Europe, meaning that most visitors will have to arrive via **Bandaranaike Airport** (international code CMB) app. 35km/22mi to the north of Colombo. The opening of a new fast road has significantly decreased travel times between the city centre and the airport as well as to seaside resorts to the south.

Transfer from or to the airport is generally organized by the booked hotel or the tour operator. Individual travellers will find buses and trains and licensed taxis waiting outside.

Security checks Travellers will still have to expect meticulous and therefore lengthy security checks at Bandaranaike Airport! Definitely plan for this by leaving enough time and arriving at the airport early.

SriLankan Airlines The award-winning SriLankan Airlines, the country's national airline, enjoys an excellent reputation as being one of the leading providers with regard to security and service. The company maintains an exclusively Airbus fleet flying A 340, A 330 and A 320s and currently serves 62 destinations in 34 countries. It is possible to book, get tickets and check in online on its website. There are bargains for frequent flyers on the website www.flysmiles.com.

Note
Premium service numbers that charge a fee are marked with a star: *0180 …

AIRLINES
SriLankan Airlines
In Canada
tel.4162279000
sales@srilankanca.com
www.srilankanca.com

In the United Kingdom
tel.02085382001
www.srilankan.com/en_en

In the USA
tel.8779152652 (nationwide toll-free)
E-mail: sales@srilankanusa.com
www.srilankanusa.com
www.srilankan.com

Cinnamon Air
tel. 0094 11 247 54 75
www.cinnamonair.com

VISA
Department of Immigration and Emigration
41, Ananda Rajakaruna Mw,
Colombo
tel. 011 532 93 00
www.immigration.gov.lk
Mon – Fri 9am – 3pm

ETA
www.eta.gov.lk

Domestic flights

The domestic airline Cinnamon Air offers daily connections between Colombo and the most important destinations on the island (such as Batticaloa, Kandy, Sigirya, Dickwella). This saves time and allows visitors to get to know the island from a new perspective.

ENTRY AND DEPARTURE REGULATIONS

Travel documents

Citizens of the UK, USA and most other English-speaking countries require a passport that has two months to run from the end of the visit and has one empty page. Since 2012 visas have had to be applied for via the **online ETA system** (www.eta.gov.lk). The visa fee is US$30 for a stay of up to 30 days with double entry. Children under the age of 12 do not have to pay visa fees.
Visas can also be obtained by post or in person at the **High Commission visa counter** (▶Information, p.397) for £35 (up to 30 days) or £45 (up to 90 days).

Visa extension

On entering the country visitors have to fill out a form that has to be handed in again upon departure. Visitors also need to produce a valid return flight ticket.
Travellers wishing to stay beyond the abovementioned times will have to renew their visa before the original visa expires. This can only be done at the Department of Immigration and Emigration in Colombo. To apply for a visa extension – the form can be downloaded from the department website prior to the appointment – visitors must bring two passport photos and proof of sufficient funds (e.g.

valid bank card or sufficient traveller's cheques) as well as enough patience. The process can take an hour or even more.

Lost passport The visa is stamped in the passport. As a result, loss of the passport means visitors will be denied exit from Sri Lanka. Therefore it is very sensible to make copies of travel documents and take two photographs and keep them separate from the originals. Visitors will also have to declare their loss to the police. Only then can they go to the embassy or consulate of their home country to get replacement documents.

CUSTOMS REGULATIONS

Entry to Sri Lanka Personal effects are exempt from duty. Visitors over the age of 18 can also bring in 200 cigarettes or 250g/9oz of tobacco or 50 cigars, 1 litre of wine or spirits, one camera and one video camera as well as goods worth up to US$250. Medication for personal use can also be brought in; in order to avoid misunderstandings it is best to carry medicine in the original packaging. Importing drugs and pornographic material is prohibited. The import of hunting weapons and munitions requires a permit. It is not permitted to bring harpoons for underwater hunting into the country.

Foreign currency Visitors carrying more than US$ 5000 or other foreign currency worth the equivalent amount will have to declare the amount to customs upon arrival. Indian and Pakistani rupees may not be imported. All unspent Sri Lankan rupees obtained by changing currency can be changed back upon departure. Visitors will have to produce the relevant receipts.

Pets Visitors wishing to bring their pets to Sri Lanka will have to apply for an import permit from the Animal Quarantine Officer. To get the permit, an international veterinary certificate of health has to confirm that the animal is healthy and free from parasites. In addition you will need a certificate proving the pet has a valid rabies vaccination. Dogs also have to be vaccinated against distemper, hepatitis, leptospirosis, parvovirosis and kennel cough. Cats against feline enteritis and against viral respiratory diseases. Animals that arrive in Sri Lanka without the relevant entry permit are immediately sent back to their country of origin at the owner's expense.

Re-entry into the EU When returning to the EU, EU citizens have to pay third-country duty and import tax (= VAT) on goods worth more than €430. Exempt from duty are all personal effects that were taken on the trip; it is a good idea to keep receipts for valuable items bought before the trip to avoid problems on re-entry. Travellers over the age of 18 are also permitted to import 200 cigarettes or 100 small cigars or

250g/9oz of tobacco as well as 250ml of eau de toilet or 50g of perfume. Also exempt from customs are 1 litre of spirits at more than 22% or 2 litres of sparkling or fortified wine, as well as 2 litres of table wine. The import of food has been prohibited since 2005.

In order to prevent the import of pests or the spread of diseases no food, fruit, vegetables, seeds, plants or animal products may be imported into Sri Lanka or into the EU. Luggage inspections are conducted. Violations are punishable with heavy fines.

Washington Convention

The Convention on International Trade in Endangered Species of Wild Flora and Fauna, also known as the Washington Convention or CITES, which came into effect in 1975, aims to secure the continued existence of threatened flora and fauna. It therefore prohibits the import of exotic animals, regardless of whether they are dead or alive. Not even parts of these protected species may be brought into the EU, and checks at airports could occur at any time. Anyone in violation of this convention faces heavy fines. When in doubt it is best to avoid buying protected animals or animal products, which include certain types of shell, corals, birds and reptiles (as well as crocodile-leather bags and shoes).

? Think about ...

MARCO POLO INSIGHT

A British tourist was questioned at the airport in 2012 because the officers had noticed his Buddha tattoo and because he spoke disrespectfully about the Buddhist faith. As a result he was refused entry with the justification that the tattoo could provoke the population.

Export

Visitors leaving the country are allowed to take 10kg of tea without incurring customs duties. Without a permit, the export of antiques, defined as objects that are more than 50 years old, such as rare books, palm leaf manuscripts and anthropological material, is prohibited. The purchase and export of all wild animals, birds and reptiles, regardless whether dead or alive, as well as the export of parts of animals, birds and reptiles such as hides, horns, scales and feathers is prohibited except with express permission, which is granted only for scientific purposes. It is not allowed to export specimens of the legally protected 450 plant species without a special permit. The export of corals, shells and other protected marine products is strictly prohibited. Expect meticulous checks at the airport!

TRAVEL INSURANCE

It is advisable to take out private travel insurance that also includes repatriation in the event of an Insurance for repatriation emergency. It is also a good idea to insure your luggage and take out accident and general liability insurance.

Insurance packages

Drugs

Strictly prohibited

Like everywhere in Asia, the possession and consumption of recreational drugs is strictly prohibited, as is dealing in drugs. The Sri Lankan police are very tough on these offences, even using decoys at times. Drug offences are punished with **long prison sentences**. Offenders should not expect much help from the diplomatic community.

Electricity

Electricity grid

The electricity grid in Sri Lanka operates on 230V alternating current (50 hertz). While power cuts do occur in rural regions, the supply is secure in all towns and tourist hotspots. It is a good idea to bring an **adapter** to deal with the different sockets and standards. If necessary, it is usually possible to get an international adapter from the hotel reception.

Emergency

There is no central emergency number outside of the capital. Turn to the closest police station.

Tourist police
Fort, Colombo 1
tel. 011 22 69 41 or 242 11 11

Police in Colombo
tel. 011 43 33 33

Fire brigade
tel. 011 42 22 22

Accident rescue
tel. 011 222 22

Traffic accident service
Ward Place, Colombo 7
tel. 011 69 31 84 und 69 31 85

Etiquette and Customs

Never mind how tolerant Asians are towards Western travellers; there are some forms of behaviour that strain even the proverbial Sri Lankan equanimity. Even though tourists might not be aware of this, it causes them to lose face and they will subsequently be considered contemptible.

Visitors who are invited to a Sri Lankan house should bring small gifts. The lady of the house will be pleased with a bunch of flowers, and if there are children sweets are a good idea. Shoes must be taken off before entering the house. When dealing with the authorities it is a good idea to wear a shirt and proper shoes. Overly casual clothes are frowned upon!

The left hand is considered impure because the locals use it to clean themselves on the toilet, many of which are built in the French style. For that reason nothing should be handed over or accepted with the left hand!

The left hand is unclean

Of course there are also taboos that should be observed in order to avoid hurting the feelings of the people of Sri Lanka. Monks do not always like having their picture taken; it should be common sense to allow people their privacy when practising their religion and not take photographs of them. The Sri Lankans really do not like it when religious objects are used as accessories for holiday snaps. Climbing up Buddhas or any other temple statues is strictly forbidden and is punished with sizable fines. Requests that no photographs be taken should be respected. Smooching in public is improper and nude bathing not allowed.

Taboos

> **?** MARCO ⊕ POLO INSIGHT
>
> *Reserved seats*
>
> If you see a sign saying »Reserved for Clergy« on a bus or train, do not use those seats. It is better to stand because these seats are for the exclusive use of monks.

During a conversation visitors should practise respectful restraint. Wild gesticulation and pointing at others is considered rude. Even amongst friends intimate subjects are unusual. It is best to answer questions about income or personal issues evasively. It is important never to forget the smile that is part of the conversation; the more non-committal the response, the friendlier the smile should be.

Conversation

When visiting sacred sites, wearing »decent« clothes is a must. Shoulders and knees should definitely be covered, sleeveless T-shirts, midriff-free tops, shorts and mini skirts are absolute »no nos«. This is also true for temple ruins even though their religious significant might not seem obvious to the unsuspecting visitor at first glance. For the devout population they still possess a highly symbolic value. There are some Hindu temples however that men can only enter stripped to the waist. Just follow the example of the locals. Always take off your shoes before entering shrines and temples.

Visiting religious sites

For some years now Sri Lanka has imposed a ban on smoking in air-conditioned buildings and restaurants.

Smoking

Tipping   Although the bill in most restaurants already contains a service charge of around 10% it is still customary to give an additional tip or to round up the bill when satisfied with the service. A small tip for room attendants at the beginning of a stay is recommended and guests who are still satisfied at the end can give a further tip then. Around 200 rupees per week is a good guideline. Taxi drivers will also be pleased if the fare is rounded up. But beware: giving less than twenty rupees could be considered an insult.

Health

Prior to departure   Going on holiday in the tropics requires preparations and certain precautions once there so that the trip has every chance of being a positive experience. The family doctor should be consulted in good time to eliminate health risks.

The body clock   »Jet lag« is the name given to the state of physical exhaustion that regularly occurs after long-haul flights to different time zones. It takes some time for the traveller's body clock to adjust. Give your body the rest it needs. Schedule at least one day of rest after arrival instead of plunging straight into major activities.

Tropical climate   The tropical climate also requires a certain adjustment, for which the body needs time. It is wise to avoid physical exertion during the first few days and not stay out in the strong sun for too long.

Fevers   A feverish cold that is particularly common during the first few days is a notorious problem for people travelling to Asia. Often the cause is not an infection but the carelessness of the traveller. Such colds are associated with a high temperature (over 39°C/102°F), but there are not generally any other symptoms. Taking a medication for the fever and staying in bed for two days will be helpful.

Vaccinations   There are no compulsory vaccinations for travellers coming straight from Europe. The following vaccinations are nevertheless recommended for anyone wishing to stay for any length of time or anyone visiting remote areas: typhoid, polio, tetanus, hepatitis A, hepatitis B and rabies. Children should also be vaccinated against diphtheria, whooping cough, measles, mumps and rubella. The low risk of contracting malaria only exists outside of the tourist centres.

Stomach problems   Since most gastrointestinal problems are the result of food that was not prepared hygienically, it is wise to only eat well-cooked food. It is a bad idea to any eat raw food, especially fish (shellfish in particular)

Ayurvedic medicine can help

and meat. Eating salads can also be risky, unless treated water was used to wash the ingredients. Be careful when it comes to ice cream, especially when buying it from street vendors. Sometimes there are power cuts, especially outside of the central areas, which shortens the lifespan of chilled foods.

There is medication to treat intestinal problems such as diarrhoea and amoebiasis as well as dengue fever. It can be purchased in pharmacies in Sri Lanka.

Water

Tap water is not, by and large, drinking water. The boiling and filtration efforts are often a bit lax so it is best to rely on bottled water. There are several brands in Sri Lanka. Most of the bottled water is spring water from the highlands. Make sure the bottles have an SLS certification and that the seal is only broken in your presence. To be on the safe side, use only this kind of water for brushing your teeth as well. The tap water in more expensive hotels is generally fine.

Sunburn

Sri Lanka is only around 600km/370mi from the equator. As a result the sun can be incredibly strong and cause painful sunburn. Therefore it is indispensable to pack a sunscreen of at least factor 30. However, even with sunscreen it is best to avoid spending any length of time in direct sunlight. The same advice applies for heatstrokes. They occur when the body temperature rises dramatically and it is no longer possible to cool the skin.

The symptoms include a high temperature, significant reddening of the skin, a severe headache and impaired co-ordination. To avoid heatstroke, take water to the beach. The milk of the thambili (king coconut), which can be bought in many places, is another tried and tested method.

Local healthcare

Sri Lanka's healthcare system is quite well organized. There is a sufficient number of trained doctors and well equipped private hospitals in Colombo and other large towns. There are doctors in rural areas as well, ensuring the sick get treated. In an emergency the hotel reception will have the address of the closest hospital.

Sri Lanka, like other Asian countries, has seen a rise in healthcare tourism, since medical treatments tend to be cheaper than in Europe. Some private hospitals as well as dentists have specialized in this market.

Information

INFORMATION AT HOME:
AUSTRALIA
Department of Foreign Affairs
www.dfat.gov.au for travel advice

CANADA
Department of Foreign Affairs
www.fco.gov.uk, for travel advice

IRELAND
Department of Foreign Affairs
www.dfa.ie for travel advice

UK
Sri Lanka Tourism Promotion Bureau in the UK
No.1, 3rd Floor, Devonshire Square
London EC2M 4WD
tel. 0845 880 6333 (ext. 201)
www.srilankatourism.org

UK Foreign Office
See www.fco.gov.uk for up-to-date travel advice about Sri Lanka.

USA
Sri Lanka Tourism Promotion Bureau in the USA
379 Thornall Street
6th Floor, Edison NJ 08837
tel. 732-608-2676
www.srilankatourism.org

U.S. Department of State
www.state.gov/travel for travel advice

IN SRI LANKA
Sri Lanka Tourism Promotion Bureau (SLTPB)
80, Galle Road, Colombo 03
Travel Information Hotline 1912

tel. 011 243 70 59-60
www.srilanka.travel (in English too)

DIPLOMATIC REPRESENTATIONS:
SRI LANKA
High Commission in Australia
35 Empire Circuit
Forrest, ACT 2603
tel. 02 6239 7041
www.slhcaust.org

High Commission in Canada
333 Laurier Avenue West Suite 1204
Ottawa, Ontario K1P 1C1
tel. 613-233-8449
www.srilankahcottawa.org

Consulate in Ireland
59 Ranelagh Road, Dublin
tel. 014968043
E-mail: aelred@ireland.com

High Commission in the United Kingdom
No.13, Hyde Park Gardens
London W2 2LU
tel. 020 72621841
www.slhc-london.co.uk

Embassy in the USA
2148, Wyoming Avenue NW
Washington DC 20008
tel. 202-483-4025
http://slembassyusa.org

AUSTRALIA
Australian High Commission
21, Srimath R. G., Senanayake Mawatha, Colombo 7
tel. 011 2463 200
www.srilanka.embassy.gov.au

CANADA
Canadian Embassy
Canada House, 254 Bauddhaolka,
Mawatha, Gregory's Road PO Box 1006
Colombo
tel. 011 695 841
www.canadianembassyinformation.com

IRELAND
Sri Lanka Honorary Consul
Pership House (ONE), No. 72C
Bauddhaloka Mawatha
Colombo 04
tel. 011 258 7895

UNITED KINGDOM
United Kingdom High Comission
Sri Lanka
389 Bauddhaloka Mawatha
Colombo
tel. 011 539 0694
www.gov.uk/government/world/sri-lanka

USA
U.S. Embassy
210 Galle Road, Colombo 03
tel. 011 249 8500
srilanka.usembassy.go

Language

Sri Lanka's official languages are Sinhala and Tamil. The latter is spo-   **Official**
ken in several dialects. As a result of regular contact with tourists   **languages**
many Sri Lankans have also picked up basic English-language skills.

Sinhala belongs to the Indo-Aryan branch of the Indo-European lan-   **Sinhala**
guage family but is actually an isolated dialect that developed from
the languages spoken in central India. The first evidence of Sinhala
dates back to the 3rd century BC. Over the following centuries words
borrowed from Pali, Sanskrit and Tamil were incorporated into the
language. The vocabulary and morphology maintained their resemblance to the Indo-Aryan languages spoken primarily on the Indian
subcontinent, despite being isolated, while the syntax and style con-
verged with the Dravidian dialects, the second-largest language family in India. In addition to Sinhala, which is also sometimes called
Elu, a literary language developed between the 2nd century BC and
the 2nd century AD. While what was probably the oldest literary
work from this period, a commentary on the Buddhist canon Tripitaka, is believed to be lost, old Sinhala poems in the form of rock
carvings made be-tween the 6th and 10th centuries AD have survived.

Tamil is one of the 16 official languages spoken in India, but also in   **Tamil**
Sri Lanka. With a more than 2000-year tradition, Tamil is one of the
oldest of the Dravidian languages. Like Sinhala, Tamil is also an official language of Sri Lanka (since 1965), a concession by the government to the most significant minority on the island. Tamil also has a

great literary past; in contrast to Sinhala, Tamil initially forwent Sanskrit models. It was only during the 11th century that Sanskrit words came into use. The extensive old Indian verse epics, the Mahabharata and the Ramayana, are seen as the most significant models. Tamil only took on the status of a widely used language in the 19th century when the poet Subramanya Bharati (1882–1921), one of the most important representatives of Tamil literature, helped it achieve a breakthrough.

The »upper crust« speak English It is noteworthy that members of the upper class use English to communicate with each other. This trend is countered by the fact that English is not a compulsory subject in schools (apart from high schools).

Sinhala Phrase Book

Address

Numbe	Address amongst equals
Thamuse	Used by someone of higher standing to address someone of lower standing
Oya	Customary, informal address amongst friends and relatives
Tho	Insulting address made to people of a very low social standing (watch out!)
Umba	Form of address for domestic staff but also for one's own children (if it is used in the latter sense it is meant affectionately)
Thamunnaanse	Only people of higher standing are addressed this way, such as monks

Important expressions

Address (only men)	Mahatmaya
Address (only women)	Nona mahatmaya
Greeting	Ayubovan
How are you?	Kohomada sahpa sahneepa?
Fine, thanks!	Sanee-pen innava
Please	Karunakarala
Thank you	Istuti
Yes	Ou
No	Nä

No, thank you	Ehpa, istutiy
Excuse me!	Samavena
I don't understand!	Mate terenne na
No, I don't want to!	Mata epa!
What's your name?	Nama mokak da?
The bill please!	Karunakara bila génda!
How much is it?	Máka gána kiyada!

Out and about

Bus	Bas eka
Where is the bus station?	Bas pola koheda?
Station	Dumriyapala
I would like a taxi	Mata täksi-yak ona
Car	Kareken
Bicycle	Baisikalaya
Road	Mawatha
What is the name of this road?	Mé Páre nama mokakda?
To the left	Ren-na
Right	Da-ku-na-ta
Straight ahead!	Ke-lin yan-na!

Accommodation

Hotel	Hótelaya
Guesthouse	Thánayama
Where is there a hotel?	Hótalayak koheda thiyenne?
Do you have a room available?	Hiskamara ti ye navada?
How much does a room cost?	Ekamara ya kiyada

Geographical words

Mountain	Kandé
Beach	Werala
Waterfall	Diya ella
Hot Springs	Unu diya Ulpotha
River (small)	Oya
River (big)	Ganga
Place, town	Pura
Road	Mawatha

Days of the week

Monday	Sanduda
Tuesday	Angeharuvada
Wednesday	Badada
Thursday	Brahaspatinda
Friday	Sikurada
Saturday/Sunday	Senesurada/Irida

Months

January	Janavari
February	Pebaravari
March	Martu
April	Apprel
May	May
June	Juni
July	Juli
August	Agostu
September	Settembara
October	Oktombara
November	Novembara
December	Desembara

Time Words

Today	ada
Yesterday	iye
Tomorrow	heta

Numbers

1	eka	2	deka
3	thuna	4	hathara
5	paha	6	haya
7	hatha	8	ata
9	namaya	10	dahaya

Literature

Fiction **Michael Ondaatje:** *Running in the Family.* Bloomsbury (2009)
Ondaatje made a name for himself with his bestseller »The English Patient«. In this book he tells the story of his family and their life in Sri Lanka during the colonial period. Charming and entertaining. A must read!

Shyan Selvadurai: *Cinnamon Gardens.* Anchor (1999)
Events from the lives of three generations, starting with the British colonial period in Sri Lanka. Gripping!

Nicolas Bouvier: *The Scorpion Fish.* Carcanet (2002)

Nicolas Bouvier moved to Ceylon temporarily in March 1955. Lonely, weakened and lethargic because of the hot and humid climate, his senses are heightened for the perception of small things. A spiritual turnaround for a man who tried to capture the magic phenomena of Ceylon's shadow and insect world from a Western perspective that left him torn between fascination and terror.

Gehan De Silva Wijeyeratne: *A Photographic Guide to Birds of Sri Lanka*. New Holland Publisher (2000).

For ornithologists

Peter Kuruvita: *Serendip: My Sri Lankan Kitchen*. Murdoch Books (2009)
More than just a cookbook. The author draws deep on family experience.

Cookbooks

Amadea Morningstar, Urmilla Desai: *The Ayurvedic Cookbook: A Personalized Guide to Good Nutrition and Health*. Motilal Banarsidass (2003)
This book is what it says: not just recipes, but it has them too of course.

Mahatma Gandhi: *A Guide to Health*. BiblioBazaar (2009)
The great Indian statesman reveals his experiences with ayurveda and its effects on his life.

Ayurveda

Vasant Lad: *Ayurveda, the Science of Self-healing: A Practical Guide*. Lotus (1987)
This book cannot replace an ayurveda cure in Sri Lanka but it gives many tips for a healthier life according to the rules of the ancient Indian medicine.

Rudolph Ludwig Carl Virchow: *The Veddas of Ceylon and their Relation to the Neighboring Tribes*. BiblioBazaar (2008)
A classic dating from 1888, but constantly (and recently) reprinted.

History/ politics

Robert Knox: *An Historical Relation of the Island Ceylon* (2 vols). Tisara Prakasakayo Ltd.
Definitive historical work in English about Sri Lanka, written in 1681. After being shipwrecked Knox was held captive by the kings of Kandy for 19 years. During this time he recorded the habits, customs and political events from his perspective.

Nira Wickramasinghe: *Sri Lanka in the Modern Age: A History of Contested Identity*. Hurst (2005)
The title says it all: the Sri Lankans and their relationships with colonists and each other.

Religion **Marvin Olasky:** *The Religions Next Door: What We Need to Know about Judaism, Hinduism, Buddhism, and Islam – And What Reporters Are Missing.* B & H (2004)
An interesting read for those travelling to parts of the world where Christianity is not taken for granted, by a Jewish convert to Christianity

Media

Newspapers and magazines
Of the Singhalese daily newspapers that are published in English, The Island and The Times are to be recommended. On Sundays far more extensive editions are published (such as the Sunday Times, the Sunday Observer and the Sunday Leader). All newspapers sold in Sri Lanka are subject to censorship.

Radio
The state-owned Sri Lanka Broadcasting Corporation acts as the umbrella organization for all other broadcasters in Sri Lanka. The FM programme is broadcast in various languages, including English. The English-language programmes of the BBC World Service get good reception in Sri Lanka with a suitable short-wave radio. Since the best SW frequencies depend on the time of day and the season, it is best to note all the alternatives. They can be found under http://www.bbc.co.uk, where you will also find a programme schedule. Satellite reception is much better, and many hotels provide it.

Television
The television stations ITN, Rupavahini and MTV are also under state control. The programme consists of news, reports about local events as well as broadcasts of preferably Indian films. Many hotels provide satellite reception of BBC World.

Internet radio and television
All BBC radio channels (but not BBC domestic TV) are available online. Go to www.bbc.co.uk, click on the tab »Radio« and select your channel or programme.

Money

Currency
The currency is the Sri Lankan rupee (abbreviated Rs, official LKR). The word comes from the Sanskrit word rupa, meaning silver. One rupee breaks down into 100 cents.
There are 2, 5, 10, 20, 50, 100, 500 and 1000-rupee notes, which can also be distinguished by their different sizes. There are 1, 2, 5 and 10-cent coins.

CONTACT DETAILS FOR CREDIT CARDS

In the event of lost bank or credit cards you can contact the following numbers in UK and USA (phone numbers when dialling from Sri Lanka)..
Have the bank sort code, account number and card number as well as the expiry date ready.

Eurocard/MasterCard
tel. 001 636 7227 111

Visa
tel. 001 410 581 336

American Express UK
tel. 0044 1273 696 933

American Express USA
tel. 001 800 528 4800

Diners Club UK
tel. 0044 1252 513 500

Diners Club USA
tel. 001 303 799 9000

The following numbers of UK banks (dialling from Sri Lanka) can be used to report and stop lost or stolen bank and credit cards issued by those banks:

HSBC
tel. 0044 1442 422 929

Barclaycard
tel. 0044 1604 230 230

NatWest
tel. 0044 142 370 0545

Lloyds TSB
tel. 0044 1702 278 270

EXCHANGE RATES

100 Rs = approx. £0.50 or US$0.75
£1.00 = approx. 200.00 Rs
US$1.00 = approx. 150 Rs
Current exchanges rates can be found on numerous websites including www.oanda.com

Foreign currency regulations

When entering or leaving Sri Lanka a maximum of 1000 Rs may be brought in or taken out. The import of foreign currency (with the exception of Indian and Pakistani money) is not restricted, but larger sums have to be declared on a special form when entering Sri Lanka. A receipt of exchange is needed to change the currency back.

Banks and bureaux de change

It is definitely more favourable to wait until arriving in Sri Lanka to change money because the exchange rate is significantly better. Money can be changed in the airport arrivals terminal. All banks will exchange foreign currency into Sri Lankan rupees. There are also private moneychangers, particularly in Colombo, who accept traveller's cheques. Hotels generally have less favourable exchange rates than banks.
Banks are open Mon–Fri 9am–4pm, official moneychanging counters are often open longer. The times during which money can be changed in towns and tourists resorts are also often extended. **Cash machines** (ATMs) are accessible around the clock.

Debit and credit cards The use of debit cards with the Maestro symbol is possible at many cash machines (ATMs). The following credit cards are accepted: American Express, Visa and Mastercard/Eurocard; Diners Club is only accepted in certain places. Visitors booking a package holiday will find that the brochure will list the credit cards that are accepted at the destination.

Traveller's cheques Traveller's cheques, preferably in pounds or dollars, work well. The insurance that comes with them provides fast help if they are lost or stolen, but only if they were well taken care of (it is a particularly good idea to keep receipts and traveller's cheques separate). In addition exchange rates for traveller's cheques are slightly more favourable than they are for cash.

National Parks

Categories Sri Lanka currently has twelve national parks as well as 70 nature reserves, which can be divided into three categories. Sanctuaries are protected areas where hunting is prohibited. Nature reserves may be visited without obtaining permission first; human interference here only assumes a regulatory role. Strict nature reserves are areas where the flora and fauna are to be kept free from any human interference, which is why they may only be accessed with special permits. They are generally only issued to scientists from the Wildlife and Nature Protection Society.

?

MARCO ⊕ POLO

First nature reserve in the world

The world's first nature reserve was set up on Sri Lanka. King Devanampiya Tissa declared a forested area near his capital Mihintale a refuge for all animals in the 3rd century BC.

Access Some national parks in the north and east were also affected by the civil war. The Sri Lanka Tourist Board in Colombo has information about whether it is possible to visit these parks safely now that the civil war is over (►Information).

Rules of conduct National parks may only be accessed in the company of a ranger as well as with a suitable vehicle. Rangers wait at the main entrances to the national parks. Their fee is already included in the entrance price. It is not allowed to leave the vehicle during the trip without the express permission of the ranger.

Trips and overnight stays The Wildlife and Nature Protection Society maintains chalets for visitors in some national parks or just on their outskirts. Camping is not permitted in any of the national parks. The Eco Team in Colombo runs trips to some national parks, in particular to Yala National Park (tel. 11 583 08 33, www.srilankaecotourism.com). Some hotels and guesthouses near the national parks also organize such trips.

NATIONAL PARKS

Wild Life and Nature Protection Society

tel. 11 288 73 90
www.wnpssl.org (English)
Unless otherwise stated the national parks can be visited without restrictions.

Bundala Bird Sanctuary

Relatively small protected area (app. 62sq km/24 sq mi) with lots of bird species

Chundilaka and Kokkilai Lagune Bird Sanctuary

The area is located on one of the main migratory routes of large flocks of migratory birds and is therefore a bird sanctuary.

Gal Oya National Park

The Senanayake reservoir within the 62,936ha/155,518 acre park is a place of refuge for many bird species; there are also wild elephants.

Horton Plains Nature Reserve

Plateau with interesting vegetation, protected by UNESCO. A great place for trips to the cliff called World's End.

Kumana Bird Sanctuary

Large bird sanctuary with a remarkable number of waterfowl

Lahugala National Park

Many wild elephants and bird species; explore it by car.

Maduru Oya National Park

Lots of bird species and wild elephants; ask about visiting this park in Colombo.

Minneriya Giritale Sanctuary

Small bird sanctuary. Elephants and bears.

Ritigala Strict Nature Reserve

A place of refuge for many mammals and birds; it cannot be visited because it is a strict nature reserve

Sinharaja Rain Forest Reserve

Remnants of tropical rainforest, UNESCO World Heritage Site; diverse flora, many animals

Uda Walawe National Park

The lake in the park is a preferred resting place for many bird species; fallow deer.

Udawattekelle National Park

Lots of bird species and monkeys

Wasgomuwa Strictly Nature Reserve

One of the main migratory routes of elephants runs through the park; this reserve cannot be visited because it is a strict nature reserve.

Wilpattu National Park

Largest national park on the island; more than 40 small and larger lakes. Home to birds, reptiles, leopards, bears, elephants and fallow deer.

Wirawila Tissa Bird Sanctuary

Very diverse bird world.

Yala (Ruhuna) National Park

Yala East is a Strictly Nature Reserve. Yala West can be visited. It is home to elephants, leopards, bears, reptiles, fallow deer and countless bird species.

National Parks and other Conservation Areas

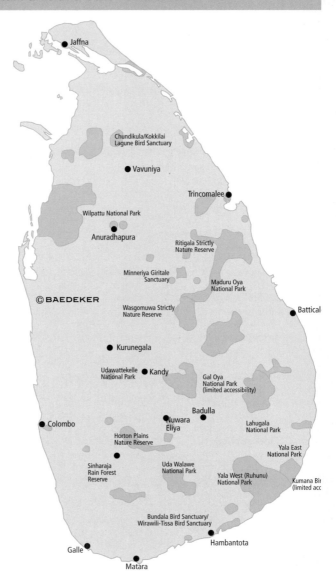

Jaffna

Chundikula/Kokkilai
Lagune Bird Sanctuary

Vavuniya

Trincomalee

Wilpattu National Park

Anuradhapura

Ritigala Strictly
Nature Reserve

Minneriya Giritale
Sanctuary

Maduru Oya
National Park

© BAEDEKER

Wasgomuwa Strictly
Nature Reserve

Battical

Kurunegala

Udawattekelle
National Park

Kandy

Gal Oya
National Park
(limited accessibility)

Badulla

Colombo

Nuwara
Eliya

Lahugala
National Park

Horton Plains
Nature Reserve

Yala East
National Park

Sinharaja
Rain Forest
Reserve

Uda Walawe
National Park

Yala West (Ruhunu)
National Park

Kumana Bir
(limited acc

Bundala Bird Sanctuary/
Wirawili-Tissa Bird Sanctuary

Hambantota

Galle

Matara

Post and Telecommunication

Post offices are normally open Mon – Fri from 8.30am – 5pm; on Saturdays only until 1pm.

Post offices

The Sri Lankan post office is generally reliable and speedy. Letters to Europe take six to ten day by air mail (par avion). If the letter is not marked »airmail« or it does not have enough stamps, it might be taken by land and sea, which can take up to three months.

Postal times

Postcards cost 20 Rs, letters weighing up to ten grams 45 Rs (every additional gram costs 10 Rs). Packages and parcels sent by airmail to the UK cost 1730 Rs (max. 500g, another 510Rs for every further 500g). Some mail can be sent as EMS (Express Mail Service) but this is significantly more expensive.
Sri Lanka also has branches of the international delivery services such as DHL, FedEx, TNT and UPS.

Postal charges

Since the state-run Sri Lanka Telekom was privatized, many other private operators have come on to the market. In addition it is possible to make IDD (International Direct Dialling) calls from almost every hotel, but because of the service fee they incur, they are more expensive than making calls from public phone boxes. Almost every town has a Communications Center, which offer inexpensive phone calls as well as internet and fax services.

Telephone

It is now possible to make calls with a mobile phone almost everywhere. However, making calls from Sri Lanka to Europe on a mobile is expensive. Although all the major mobile phone operators have signed roaming agreements, conversations still cost up to £4.50/US$6.50 per minute. It is better to buy a SIM card from a local provider (e.g. Dialog, www.dialog.lk or Mobitel, www.mobitel.com) after arrival. These providers both provide the best coverage on Sri Lanka and maintain desks where you can buy these SIM cards in the international airport in Colombo.

Mobile network

DIRECTORY
Domestic directory: 161
International directory: 134

DIALLING CODES TO AND FROM SRI LANKA
Sri Lanka: 00 94

UK: 00 44
US and Canada: 001

OPERATOR
Domestic calls: 101
International calls: 100

The cheapest option is to log into your hotel's wifi because then it is free to surf the web and send and receive emails. Almost all the better hotels offer this option, as do many guesthouses.

Internet cafés Every town in Sri Lanka has internet cafés and they often try to undercut each other in price. Go to one to use the internet and send/receive mails for a fee. It is important to clear the browsing history after logging off to prevent subsequent users from being able to see your internet activities. This is particularly true for anyone typing in usernames and passwords. It is not advisable to use internet cafés for sensitive communications, such as online banking.

Prices

Sri Lanka is an inexpensive destination, which is not least the result of its population's low per capita income. Food is cheap, alcoholic drinks on the other hand are relatively expensive (except for arrak, which is made locally) because they or the ingredients have to be imported.

> **MARCO POLO INSIGHT**
>
> **?**
>
> *How much does it cost?*
>
> Simple meals start at £ 1.20/US$1.80
> Three course meal: from £4/US$6
> Taxi: from £0.32/US$0.48
> 1 bottle of mineral water: £0.40–0.80/US$0.60–1.20
> Driver: from £20/US$30 per day (incl. car, fuel, accommodation and food)
> ▶Price categories for restaurants and hotels: p. 9

Tourists wishing to take **photographs in ancient ruins require permission** from the Department of Archaeology in Colombo (Sir Marcus Fernando Mawatha, Colombo - 07, tel. 011 269 2840/1. The fee of US$30 allows visitors to enter and take pictures of all of the country's historical sites for a month. This ticket is also available from the office of the Central Cultural Fund in Colombo (212/1, Bauddhaloka Mawatha, Colombo 07, tel. 011 267 9921, www.ccf.lk).

Prostitution

Sex tourism is increasing Sri Lanka has been a destination of international sex tourism for many years. After Thailand and the Philippines, Sri Lanka takes third place internationally. The sex tourists come from all around the world, particularly from Europe. Sex tourism exploits the economic poverty of many young island inhabitants, without taking their psychological development into account. Many victims come from rural areas and from the socially underprivileged classes. For them »selling« their body is often enough the last opportunity for survival. The often quoted opinion that prostitution is rooted in tradition in Asia is completely wrong, by the way. Child and adolescent prostitution has grown alarmingly in Sri Lanka. The country's government, which initially responded timidly to this phenomenon, has signed a United Nations treaty, not least because of vigorous demands by European countries. This treaty guarantees every child and adolescent under the age of 18 protection from sexual exploitation. The punishment for child abuse has also been severely increased. British citizens and residents can be prosecuted in the UK for sexual offences committed against children abroad under the Sexual Offences Act 2003, and similar legislation exists elsewhere. Well-known European tour operators have also declared themselves willing to face up to sex tourism and particularly child and adolescent prostitution. Sri Lanka's law enforcement authorities have recently started passing on the details of offenders to their home police authorities and banned the people in question from the island for life.

Safety

There is no more crime in Sri Lanka than elsewhere on earth. Often visitors' provocative behaviour makes them victims of theft. Often, for example, visitors carry more cash than Sri Lankans earn in an entire year of hard work. Sri Lanka is a developing country and when wealth is flaunted it can create envy.

Sri Lanka is a safe destination

Pickpockets are most common on markets. The best way to avoid becoming a victim is to carry cash and other valuables in a neck pouch or a special belt bag that cannot be seen from the outside.

Watch out for pickpockets

Visitors should be particularly careful when dealing with strangers. There have been cases in which locals robbed visitors by offering food or drink that at best made their victims lose consciousness temporarily. Refuse such offers in a friendly but firm manner if there is even the slightest doubt.

Protective measures

Every hotel has safes that are there to be used. It is a good idea to use them to keep cash etc. as well as travel documents as hotels accept no responsibility for valuables. It is also a good idea to hand in the room key at the reception before going out.

Valuables in the safe

Although or maybe because Sri Lankan society is generally considered conservative and sometimes even prudish, sexual assaults do

Sexual assault

The mugger crocodile looks lethargic but don't annoy it. That could be dangerous

occur and European women can be victims too. For this reason it is best to forgo revealing clothes and flirtatious words. Night-time walks on the beach or in shady areas should be avoided.

Wild animals There are several kinds of large animals that live in the wild in Sri Lanka (elephants, leopards, crocodiles etc.). In the interests of safety, do not approach them. They can be unpredictable in their behaviour, and if humans behave carelessly the animals could respond aggressively. It is also expressly forbidden for that reason to leave the vehicle within the boundary of a national park.

Transport

BY CAR

Sri Lankans **drive on the left**, and overtake on the right.

Road network The road network is fairly extensive. In recent years some national roads have been improved, especially the coastal road heading south from Colombo. The southeastern and northern parts of the island are still an exception. However, the efforts to raise the road standards in these regions is pushing ahead at full steam.

Only around a fifth of the total road network of approx. 152,000km/94,400mi is surfaced. Roads have soft verges, there are potholes. The surface is generally rough and there are sudden changes of surface materials. During the monsoon lower-lying roads and streets can flood.

Within towns the maximum speed limit is 50kmh/30mph. Outside towns vehicles may not go faster than70kmh/43mph. The police carry out regular speed checks. When planning a trip by car make calculations using an average speed of no more than 30kmh/20mph.

Speed limit

Officially Sri Lanka has a zero tolerance policy when it comes to drinking and driving. The blood alcohol limit is zero.

Blood alcohol limit

After a breakdown or accident drivers are dependent on the help of other drivers. There are no emergency telephones along the roads. In the event of a breakdown it is best to gain the attention of other drivers by waving. Since the locals are very helpful drivers will not generally have to wait very long. Vehicles that are unfit to drive may be towed to the closest garage. The situation is more difficult at night, particularly far away from towns. This is a further reason why driving at night should generally be avoided.

Breakdown and accident service

Filling-station coverage is not dense and it is not customary for drivers to serve themselves. Information on pumps is also given in English. Diesel is very cheap because it is subsidized by the state.

Filling stations

MODES OF TRANSPORT

The trains in Sri Lanka are a relic from the time of the British colonial rule and has not changed much since. The first line was opened between Colombo and Kandy in 1867. Over the decades a methodical expansion to a total of 1453km/903 mi has taken place so that now every larger town can be reached by rail. The trains are run by Sri Lanka Railways (SLR). Routes in the north and east that ceased to operate because of the civil war are to be reopened in the coming years. At the moment the line leaving Colombo northbound ends in Vavuniya.

Trains

There are three classes. It is necessary to book in advance for first class. Seats can always be reserved for a fee. Some long-distance trains have observation saloons. Seats have to be booked in advance for these carriages. Third class is not recommended since it is almost

THE MOST IMPORTANT TRAIN LINES

Colombo Fort – Negombo
133 km/83mi, app. 3 hrs.

Colombo Fort – Chilaw
82 km/51mi, app. 1.5 hrs.

Colombo Fort – Puttalam
135 km/84mi, app. 3 hrs.

Colombo Fort – Anuradhapura
206 km/128mi, app. 5 hrs.

Colombo Fort – Polonnaruwa
254 km/158mi, app. 7 hrs.

Colombo Fort – Vavuniya
310 km/193mi, app. 6 – 7 hrs.

Colombo Fort – Avissawella
61 km/38mi, app. 1.5 hrs.

Colombo Fort – Badulla
290 km/180mi, app. 11 hrs.

Colombo Fort – Kandy
120 km/75mi, app. 3 hrs.

Colombo Fort – Batticaloa
254 km/158mi, app. 9 hrs.

Colombo Fort – Trincomalee
248 km/154mi, app. 10 hrs.

Colombo Fort – Bentota
63 km/39mi, app. 1.5 – 2 hrs.

Colombo Fort – Hikkaduwa
92 km/57mi, app. 3 hrs.

Colombo Fort – Galle
112 km/70mi, app. 2 – 3 hrs.

Colombo Fort – Unawatuna
136 km/85mi, app. 3 Std

Colombo Fort – Matara
156 km/97mi, app. 3 – 3.5 hrs

always overcrowded. The second class carriages are more comfortable. They at least have padded seating instead of the somewhat uncomfortable wooden benches.

Although the trains run to fixed schedules, printed timetables for travellers are not always available. Current train times can be found online at **www.railway.gov.lk**. Trains are one of the cheapest modes of transport in Sri Lanka. A return trip between Colombo and Kandy (approx. 116km/72mi) only costs around GBP1.20/US$1.80 first class. Second class and third class are even cheaper but less advisable because they are overcrowded. Children up to the age of three travel free, between 3 and 12 they pay half price. Sri Lanka's government railway occasionally organizes round trips including accommodation and meals. More information is available at Colombo Fort station in the Railway Tourist Information Office (tel. 011 244 00 48 or 243 58 38, daily 9am – 5pm). There is the »**Viceroy Special**« round trip, for which the comfortable carriages are pulled by an historic steam engine from the year 1928, the »Sentinel Camel«. It runs from Colombo Fort to Kandy and Nuwara Eliya. This nostalgic experience can be booked via JF Tours & Travel (Cey) Ltd. (58 Havelock Road, Colombo 05, tel. 011 258 94 02, www.jftours.com).

Taxi Taxis with taximeters can only really be found in adequate numbers in Colombo and Kandy. They tend to be quite rare in other towns. Taximeters are not common outside Colombo, so the fare has to be negotiated in advance. A general rule of thumb is approx. 70–80 rupees per kilometre, while fixed prices can be agreed for longer trips (such as day trips).

These tuk tuks or trishaws, which are sometimes also called Bajaj af- **Three**
ter their manufacturers, are three-wheeled motorcycles and are a **Wheeler**
very popular and cheap mode of transport in all the larger towns and
seaside resorts. The three-wheeler is a typically Asian mode of transport. It has three wheels, a rattling two-stroke engine and possesses
an extraordinary cargo capacity. Negotiate a price in advance: expect
to pay app. 30 Rs for the first kilometer. Every additional kilometer
should not cost more than 10 Rs.

Buses are by far the most widespread and inexpensive mode of trans- **Buses**
port in Sri Lanka. They can also be used to reach remote parts of the
island. Every town on Sri Lanka has its own bus station, which is always located near the clock tower – a typical feature of a Sri Lankan
town centre. However, the buses are often in a sorry state of repair
and even more often they are completely overcrowded. The sometimes reckless driving style of some bus drivers is alarming. They occasionally seem to confuse narrow roads littered with potholes with
racetracks. A basic distinction is made between regular and express
services; the latter operate mainly between the large towns.
There is not necessarily a fixed bus timetable. Some drivers only leave
when enough passengers are on board. This is particularly true of
private buses, which can be recognized by their label »Intercity Express«. Unlike the buses run by the Sri Lanka Tourist Board, they
even have air-conditioning. Bus fares are very low. A trip from Colombo to Kandy for example only costs around 130 rupees.

Some places popular with tourists (such as the ruins of Polonnaruwa **Bicycles**
and Anuradhapura) have bicycle rental facilities. Some hotels also
offer this service. The prices are low. A bicycle costs around 60–80
rupees per day.

The seaside resorts along the west coast have some motorbike rental **Motorbikes**
places. This option should be avoided on principle. The unfamiliar
traffic conditions (bad roads etc.) can lead to serious accidents.

Time

Standard time is in place in Sri Lanka all year round. There is no
summer time. The time in Sri Lanka is 5.5 hours ahead of Green-
wich Mean Time (GMT) and 4.5 hours ahead of British Summer
Time.

Travelling with Disabilities

Trips are possible in principle
Travellers with particular needs should consider that the country makes very few provisions for people with disabilities, even though there is increased awareness and the situation is improving. Buildings, offices and banks have increasingly been fitted with wheelchair ramps. The locals are also very helpful.

Weights and Measures

Imperial system
Even after Sri Lanka gained its independence it maintained the imperial system of weights and measures. The metric system is also in use, however.

LENGTHS, AREAS AND VOLUMES
1 inch = 2.45 cm
1 foot = 0.305 m
1 acre = 0.405 ha
1 pound = 453 g
1 mile = 1.609 km
1 square mile = 2.59 km²

1 cubic foot = 0.028 m3
1 pound = 16 ounces

MEASURE OF CAPACITY
1 gallon (Imp.) = 4.54 l
1 quart = 1.135 l
1 gallon = 4 quarts
1 quart = 2 pints

When to Go

Tropical temperatures
Sri Lanka has a tropical climate with wet summers. The temperatures are almost consistently high. The seasonal changes in precipitation are marked. They are tied to the Indian monsoon circulation ("climate).

MARCO ◉ POLO TIP

! *Know when* **Insider Tip**

During the monsoon period and the period between monsoons it is best to start trips early in the morning. The best conditions exist between 10am and noon – before the showers start

For beach holidays on the southwest coast with trips to the Highlands, January to March offer the best weather conditions, while February to March is the best time for the island as a whole (lowest risk of rain and lowest temperatures). The best weather on the northeast coasts (dry but very hot) lasts from February to September. Absolutely avoid the wet months of October and November. It is a general rule of thumb that it gets wetter with increasing altitude and drier further north and east. Watch out: protection from the strong tropical sun is a must. In addition to a broad-brimmed hat, light cotton clothes are also a good idea.

Glossary of Religious and Cultural Terms

Abhaya mudra gesture of protection (made by Buddha statues)

Anuradha Indian deity (god of light)

Apsara female spirit

Avalokiteshvara bodhisattva in Mahayana Buddhism

Avatara incarnation of a deity

Ayurveda traditional, holistic natural medicine in Sri Lanka and India

Bikkhu Buddhist monk

Bikkhuni Buddhist nun

Bohdi tree a tree considered sacred since Siddharta Gautama reached enlighten-ment while sitting under such a tree (scientific name: Ficus religiosa)

Bodhigara temple where a ►bodhi tree is worshipped

Bodhi-maluwa terrace for a ►bodhi tree

Bodhisattva a person who is believed to be closest to ►nirvana, but who remains on earth to show other people the right path

Brahma creator of the world and the supreme deity of Hinduism; one of the three ►Trimurti

Brahman the world soul

Buddha Siddharta Gautama, creator of BuddhismCastes term for the different social classes

Chaitya originally an early Buddhist burial mound that over time developed into a temple with a wide central nave and two narrow side aisles

Chakra disc, emblem of the god ►Vishnu, also »wheel of law«, which was first set in motion by ►Buddha

Chattra a parasol, an honorary royal symbol, also used to crown a ►stupa or ►dagoba

Cella central room of a Buddhist temple

Chulavamsa continuation of the ►Mahavamsa

Dagoba sacred Buddhist building, developed from a burial or reliquary hill into a pagoda

Daladaga house of the sacred tooth relic (such as in Kandy and Polonnaruwa)

Devale Hindu temple

Devi female Hindu deity, original form of Parvati, Kali etc.

Dharamsala accommodation for pilgrims

Dharma Buddha's teachings, cosmic order

Diphavamsa chronicle of events on the island of Sri Lanka

Dravida style southern Indian architectural style

Enlightenment the insight obtained by ►Buddha about how human suffering can be overcome

Gana goblin in ►Shiva's retinue

Ganesha ►Shiva's vehicle, also seen as his son

Garuda sun bird, also ►Vishnu's vehicle

Guard stele panel with figurative depictions in front of the entrance to a temple

Gupta style northern Indian architectural style, named after the Gupta dynasty

Hanuman monkey god from the ►Ramayana

Hinayana also ►Theravada; Buddhist teaching of the »low vehicle«; in contrast to ►Mahayana Buddhism, humans can only reach the state of enlightenment through their own power

Incarnation »to be made flesh«; term for the rebirth of the souls in a human or animal body

Jataka the previous lives of ►Buddha (there are said to have been more than 500 existences in different guises)

Kailasa sacred Hindu mountain in Tibet

Kali terrifying manifestation of ►Devi

Kantaka Chaitya ►Siddharta Gautama's (►Buddha's) horse on which he is said to have left his parental palace

Karma »action«; the sum of all the mental and physical actions that are the basis for the current existenceKataragama another name for the god of war, ►Skanda

Ketumala flame of enlightenment (decoration on top of the heads of many   Buddha statues)

Kovil small Hindu temple that is not reserved for any specific deity (as opposed to ►Devale)

Krishna eighth manifestation of the god ►Vishnu (is often depicted as a   shepherd)

Kshattriya Indian warrior caste

Lakshmi female Hindu deity of affluence and beauty and ►Vishnu's wife

Lingam phallic symbol of the god ►Vishnu

Lohapasada »bronze palace«; a building decorated with or covered in metal

Mahabharata greatest epic of classical Indian literature

Mahapali alms house, this is where the poor were given their food by the monks

Mahavamsa old chronicle of the Singhalese kingdom from the 6th century

Mahayana Buddhist teaching of the »high vehicle«; it says that every human being can reach the desired state of enlightenment and thus ►nirvana, and ►Buddha and ►bodhisattvas can aid them in this (as opposed to ►Hinayana)

Maheshvara name of the god ►Shiva

Mahinda Indian monk who brought Buddhism to Sri Lanka

Mahout elephant driver

Makara architectural element in the form of a dragon (such as at the entrances to temples)

Mandapa prayer room for a relic

Meru according to Hinduism the mountain on which the gods of the Hindu   ►pantheon live

Moonstone semi-circular stone in front of temple entrances, symbol of the threshold between the material and the spiritual world (not to be confused with the semi-precious gem also called moonstone)

Moors descendants of Arab seafarers and merchants who still live on Sri Lanka today

Muchalinda a Hindu deity of the underworld (snake god, who covered Buddha as he meditated by fanning out his seven heads)

Mudra gesture or pose of Buddhist iconography

Naga Hindu deity of the underworld, depicted as a snake-like being with a human torso

Nirvana term from Buddhist teaching; »blowing out«; nirvana is the condition when a human being escapes the cycle of birth life – death – rebirth for good

Ola Buddhist texts written on palm leaves; the leaves of the talipot and Palmyra palms are used

Paria »untouchable«; term for a person who does not belong to any ►caste and is considered impure (»untouchable«) as a result

Parvati Hindu deity

Patimaghara picture house, part of the temple complex

Perahera Buddhist procession (also pilgrimage)

Pilimage statue house, part of the temple complex

Poya festival that takes place on the full moon of every month

Prakara stone fence around a temple

Prakriti term for the primordial matter from which the world is made

Prasada prayer hall in a temple complex

Puja Hindu ceremony in a temple

Purnagheta vase of abundance, a very popular image on Sri Lanka: symbol of the inexhaustible wealth of Buddhist teaching

Raja term for rulers

Ramayana classical Indian epic

Ravana king in the Indian epic ►Ramayana

Samahera Buddhist novice monk

Sangha Buddhist community of monks

Sanskrit the sacred language of ►Hinduism

Sarasvati female Hindu deity of science and wife of ►Brahma

Sari a gown for women, usually artistically woven, that is wrapped around the body several times

Sarong a simple gown for men worn around the lower part of the body

Shiva destroyer of the world, one of the three ►Trimurti

Shivalinga phallic symbol of the god ►Shiva

Siddharta civil name of the historical ►Buddha

Sikhara tower-like addition above the entrance to a Hindu temple

Singh(a) Indian: »lion«

Sita princess from the Indian epic ►Ramayana who is abducted by ►Ravana and brought to Sri Lanka

Skanda Hindu deity of war

Sri added to a name to mean »sacred«

Sri Pada symbolic and thus larger-than-lifesize footprint of ►Buddha (for example on Adam's Peak)

Stupa Thai and Burmese form of the dagoba

Sutra the literal tradition of ►Buddha's teachings

Tamil Eelam »land of the Tamils«; term for the independent republic desired by the Tamils living in the north of Sri Lanka

Tamil Tigers militant wing of the LTTE

Theravada also ►Hinayana; Buddhist teaching that in contrast to ►Mahayana Buddhism also claims to be the pure, unadulterated teaching

Thorani Hindu deity of the earth

Toddy palm sap; after toddy is distilled it becomes arrack

Trinity term for the three highest deities of ►Hinduism (►Brahma, ►Shiva and ►Vishnu)

Tripitaka the »threefold basket«, sacred manuscript cycle in which Buddha's teachings are summed up; the Tripitaka consist of three baskets (Vibayapitaka, Suttapitaka and Abhidhammapitala), which together with the commentaries written down by monks are used as the basis of recitations

Upasaka lay followers of the Buddhist teaching

Ushnisha snail-shaped plaited curl of hair as a symbol of a ►Buddha's enlightenment or omniscience

Vahalkada altar on which the sacrificial items were placed during ritual acts

Vahana the vehicle of a deity

Vatadage round, roofed temple building

Vedda »the hunters«, Sri Lanka's aboriginal population

Vedas »science«; the earliest Hindu texts

Vihara Buddhist monastery, term for the temple complex

Vishnu preserver of the world, a member of the ►trinityWatadage round, roofed temple building

Wewa artificial reservoir

Yaksha »demons«, terrifying creatures that stand at the entrances to temples to frighten evil spirits and keep them away

Yama Hindu god of death

Yoni indentation carved into the stone in which the ►lingam was placed

Index

A

accommodation **113**
Adam's Peak **22, 172**
administration **38**
Albuquerque, Alfonso de **60**
Alutnuvara **307**
Aluvihara **309**
Ambalangoda **175**
Ambalantota **253**
Ampara **177**
amulets **101**
animism **99**
Anuradhapura **57, 179**
Arankale **306**
arrival **388**
art periods **73**
Arugam Bay **348**
Ataragollawa **314**
Aukana **192**
Avissawella **194**
ayurveda **115, 117**
ayurveda hotels **115**

B

Baker's Falls **262**
Balangaloda culture **56**
ballooning **146**
Bandaranaike Airport **388**
Bandaranaike dynasty **66**
Bandaranaike, Sirimavo **103**
Bandaranaike, Solomon **103**
Bandarawela **195, 197**
banks **403**
Batticaloa **198**
Bawa, Geoffrey **105**
beaches **149**
Beliatta **366**
Beligela **299**
Bentota **202**

Beruwala **206**
Big World's End **262**
birds **24**
Blow Hole **366**
bodhi tree **85**
Brahman deities **83**
Brahman shrines **83**
British period **62**
Buddha poses **73**
Buddha's postures **87**
Buddha symbols **85**
buddhism **47**
buddhist temples **79**
Buduruvagala **238**
Bundala Bird Sanctuary **208, 405**
Bundala National Park **208**
Burgher **33**
buses **413**
Buttala **324**
butterflies **25**

C

car transport **410**
caste system **36**
Central Highlands **18**
Chenkaladi **199**
Chilaw **209**
children **123**
Chola kings period **74**
Christianity **53**
Chundilaka and Kokkilai Lagune Bird Sanctuary **405**
civil war **66**
climate **29**
Cloud Maidens of Sigiriya **365**
Colombo **211**
Colombo Plan **64**
colonial era **60**
consulates **396, 397**
cookshops **138**

credit cards **404**
curry **133**
customs **99**
customs regulations **390**

D

dagoba **79**
Dalada Maligawa **281**
Dambadeniya **306**
Dambegoda Vihara **323**
dance **96**
Dedigama **235**
Dehiwala **228**
Delft Island **270**
demons **100**
departure regulations **389**
Dhumarakkha Pabbata **348**
Dikoya **253, 254**
Dimbulagala **348**
Dipavamsa **96**
diving **148**
Diyaluma Falls **238**
Dodanduwa **256**
domestic flights **389**
Dondra Head **316**
Dowa Temple **196, 237**
drinks **138**
drugs **392**
Dutch period **60**
Dutch Canal **228**
Duwa **325**

E

economy **39**
education **36**
Elahera Canal **314**
electricity **392**
Elephant Orphanage **299**
elephants **27**
elevations **19**
Ella **236**

embassies **396, 397**
Embekke Devale **291**
emergency **392**
entry regulations **389**
ethnic groups **32**
etiquette **392**

F
fauna **22**
Fa Xian **58**
festival calendar **127**
flora **22**
flying foxes **25**
food **133**
full moon day **127**

G
Gadaladeniya Vihara **290**
Galagoda Temple **177**
Galebadda **323**
Galle **238**
Gal Oya National Park **247, 405**
Gampaha **327**
Gampola **292**
Giritale **249**
Giritale Minneriya Sanctuary **250**
golf **145**
government **38**
guesthouses **113**
Gunner's Coin **348**

H
Hakgala Sanctuary Botanical Gardens **334**
Hamangala Caves **178**
Hambantota **251**
handicrafts **98**
Hanguranketa **293**
Hantane Tea Factory **290**
Haputale **196**
Haputale Pass **196**
Hatton **253, 254**
health **394**

Henerathgoda Botanical Garden **327**
hiking **146**
Hikkaduwa **254**
hinduism **51**
history **55**
holidays **127**
homestays **114**
Horton Plains Nature Reserve **405**
Hunas Falls **293, 313**

I
Ibn Battuta **104**
independence **64**
information **396**
internet cafés **408**
irrigation **22**
Islam **52**
Istripura **196**

J
Jaffna **262**
Jaffna lowlands **19**
Jungle Beach **377**

K
Kalkudah **201**
Kallar **199**
Kalmunai **199**
Kalpitiya **353**
Kandy **272**
Kandy Highlands **292**
Kandy period **77**
Kanniyai hot springs **373**
Kantarodai **269**
Karaitivu **270**
Kayts **270**
Kelani Ganga **261**
Kirina **370**
Knuckles massif **293**
Kogalla **246**
Kotte period **77**
Kumana Bird Sanctuary **382, 405**
Kumarankanda Raja

Maha Vihara **236**
Kumbukkana **324**
Kunandaka Lena Cave **253**

L
Laguna Kitulana National Park **349**
Lahugala National Park **405**
Lake Ratgama **259**
Lake Tinapitiya **210**
landscapes **18**
language **397**
Lankatilaka Vihara **291**
Liberation Tigers of Tamil Eelam **67**
literature **94, 400**
Little World's End **262**

M
Maduru Oya National Park **405**
Magul Maha Vihara **349**
Mahabharata **95**
Mahaweli Ganga **261**
Mahiyangana **307**
Malayadi Temple Maligavila **323**
mantras **101**
Marawila **210**
Marco Polo **107**
Matale **309**
Matale mountains **293**
Matara **315**
Mattala Rajapaksa International Airport **388**
measures **414**
media **402**
Medirigiriya **317**
meditation **145**
centreigama Beach **378**
Mihintale **319**
Minneriya Giritale Sanctuary **405**
Mirissa **379**

Monaragala **323**
money **402**
monkeys **25**
monsoon **29, 30**
moonstone **80**
Moors **33**
mountain biking **145**
Mount Lavinia **228**
Mulkirigala Rock **366**
Munnesvaram Kovil **209**
music **96**

N
Nainativu **270**
Nalanda **313**
Nalanda Wewa **314**
Nallur Kandaswamy
  Kovil **269**
Namunkula **334**
national parks **404**
nature **17**
Nayipena Vihara **348**
newspapers **402**
Nillakgama **191**
Niyamgapaya Vihara
  293

O
Ondaatje, Michael **106**
Ondaatje, Philip Christo-
  pher **107**

P
painting **92**
Panama **351**
Passekudah **201**
Peradeniya Botanical
  Garden **288**
pets **390**
Pigeon Island **373**
Pinnawala **299**
Point Pedro **270**
Polgasduwa **259**
political parties **38**
Polonnaruwa **59**
Polonnaruwa period **75**

population **32**
post **407**
Pottuvil **348**
Pottuvil Point **349**
Premadasa, Ranasinghe
  108
prices **408**
prostitution **408**
Punkudutivu **270**
Puttalam **351**

R
rainforest **22**
Ramayana **95, 96**
Ramboda Pass **334**
Ranjangane **192**
Ravana Falls. **238**
religion **47**
reptiles **25**
restaurants **138**
rest houses **113**
Rhumassala Kanda **377**
rice **133**
Ritigala Strict Nature
  Reserve **405**
rivers **22**
Rock Fort of Sigiriya
  360
Rubber Research
  Institute **272**
Ruhuna National Park
  380

S
safety **409**
Sasseruwa **193**
Senanayake Dam **248**
Senanayake, Dudley
  Shelton **109**
Shiva **91**
shopping **141**
Siddharta Gautama **47,
  105**
Sigiriya **358**
Silver Temple **306**
Singhalese **32**

singing fishes **199**
Sinharaja Rain Forest
  Reserve **358, 405**
Sinigama Vihara **255**
snakes **26**
southeastern lowland
  19
sport **145**
Sri Pada **22, 172**
Sri Wijaya Sundarama
  Raja Maha Vihara
  306
stupa house **80**
Sunandaramaya
  Mahavihara **177**

T
Talawila **353**
Tamil **33, 57**
Tangalla **366**
taxis **412**
tea **138**
telephone **407**
Telwatta **255**
temperatures **30**
temple architecture **79**
Temple of the Tooth **281**
Thotupola Kanda **261**
time **413**
tipping **394**
Tissamaharama **368, 369**
tourism **43**
tourist police **392**
tours **153**
traditions **99**
trains **411**
transport **410**
travel documents **389**
travel insurance **391**
traveller's cheques **404**
travelling with disabili-
  ties **414**
Trincomalee **370**
tsunami **69**
tuk tuks **413**

U
Uda Walawe National
  Park **374, 405**
Udawattekelle National
  Par **405**
Una **375**
Unawatuna **375, 376**

V
Varana **327**
Vedda **32, 56, 248**
Vedda caves **248**
Vijithapura **193**

visual arts **85**

W
Wahakotte **314**
Walawe Ganga **261**
Wasgomuwa Strictly
  Nature Reserve **405**
Washington
  Convention **391**
water sports **148**
weights **414**
Weligama **378**
Wella Devale **377**

Wellawaya **238, 324**
Westminster Abbey **249**
Wilpattu National Park
  353, 405
Wiraketiya **366**
Wirawila Tissa Bird
  Sanctuary **405**

Y
Yala National Park (Ru-
  huna National Park)
  374, 376, 380, 405
Yapahuwa **382**

List of Maps and Illustrations

Sightseeing Highlights **2**
Tsunami – Large Wave in the Harbour
(Infographic) **20/21**
Facts and Figures
(Infographic) **34/35**
Three Typical Climates **31**
Foreign Rulers on Sri Lanka **61**
Sitting, Standing, Walking, Lying Down
... (Infographic) **88**
Tours on Sri Lanka **152**
Tour 1 **156**
Tour 2 **163**
Tour 3 **166**
Tour 4 **168**
Anuradhapura **183**
Colombo **213**
Colombo Fort **219**

Cave Temples of Dambulla (3D) **232**
Galle **245**
A Torn Country (Infographic) **266/267**
Kandy **277**
Dalada Maligawa (3D) **284**
Kandy Botanical Garden **289**
Dagobas (Infographic) **311/312**
Mihintale **321**
Nuwara Eliya **329**
A Delicious Drink (Infographic) **332/333**
Polonnaruwa **338**
Polonnaruwa Quadrangle **342**
Sigiriya **360**
Sigiriya Rock Fort (3D) **362**
National Parks Conservation Areas **406**
Overview map **back cover inside**

Photo Credits

AKG p. 75, 102, 107

Beck p. 3 (bottom left), 8, c7

Bey, Jens p. 67, 189, 232, 363 (centre)

Bildagentur Schuster p. 1

Dumont Bildarchiv p. 5 (bottom right), 85, 86, 95, 134 (above right), 139, 284, 285 (bottom left), 285 (bottom right), 357, 363 (left), 364, 380, c3

fotolia p. 91, 112, 144, 170, 260, 318, 330

fotolia/Eva Gruendemann p. 118

fotolia/vkph p. 120

Getty images p. 263

Gstaltmayr, Heiner p. 3 (centre left), 4 (bottom left), 5 (bottom left), 5 (above right), 6 (right), 7 (centre and bottom), 14, 15, 18, 28, 44, 45, 46, 50, 57, 65, 78, 81, 82, 121, 135 (right), 129, 132, 142, 146, 164, 172, 176, 190, 203, 247, 322, 341, 386, c8

Huber p.12, 292

interfoto p. 104

istock p. 6 (left), 110, 134 (left), 134 (bottom right), 135 (above left, bottomleft), 283, 293, 356, 376, c2, c4

istock/alwekelo p. 116

istock blueclue p. 395

Kefrig, Udo p. 148

Keusch p. 372

laif p. 2, 3 (above right), 3 (bottom right), 4 (above left und centre), 4 (above right), 7 (oben), 17, 26, 54, 67, 100, 134, 150, 155, 160, 180, 229, 239, 274, 285 (oben right), 290, 313, 335, 347, 365

look p. 4 (bottom right), 5 (above left), 43, 72, 97, 185, 225, 301, 359, 362, 363 (right), 383

mauritius images p. 41

mauritius images/Dieter Gerhard p. 233 (bottom left, above, bottom right)

mauritius images/Rene Mattes p. 3 (above left), 93

pa/stockfood p. 136 (right), 137 (left and right)

picture alliance/dpa p. 140, 297, 410

Schapowalow/Heaton p. 236

Silwen Randebrock p. 136 (left)

Sri Lanka Tourist Board p. 11, 125, 126, 130, 212, 256, c4

Cover photo: Huber-images/ Paolo Giosco

Publisher's Information

1st Edition 2015
Worldwide Distribution: Marco Polo
Travel Publishing Ltd
Pinewood, Chineham Business Park
Crockford Lane, Chineham
Basingstoke, Hampshire RG24 8AL,
United Kingdom.

Photos, illustrations, maps:
172 photos, 21 maps and and
illustrations, one large map
Text:
Heiner F. Gstaltmayr, Anita Rolf with
contributions by Gabriele Gaßmann,
Karen Schreitmüller, Reinhard Zakrze-
wski
Editing:
John Sykes Rainer Eisenschmid
Translation: Michael Scuffil
Cartography:
Klaus-Peter Lawall, Unterensingen;
MAIRDUMONT Ostfildern (city map)
3D illustrations:
jangled nerves, Stuttgart
Infographics:
Golden Section Graphics GmbH, Berlin
Design:
independent Medien-Design, Munich

Editor-in-chief:
Rainer Eisenschmid, Mairdumont
Ostfildern

Printed in China

Despite all of our authors' thorough
research, errors can creep in. The pub-
lishers do not accept any liability for thi
Whether you want to praise, alert us to
errors or give us a personal tip Please
contact us by email or post:

MARCO POLO Travel Publishing Ltd
Pinewood, Chineham Business Park
Crockford Lane, Chineham
Basingstoke, Hampshire RG24 8AL
United Kingdom
Email: sales@marcopolouk.com

FSC
www.fsc.org
MIX
Paper from
responsible sources
FSC® C011918

MARCO POLO

HANDBOOKS

MARCO POLO
TRAVEL HANDBOOK
ANDALUCÍA
INFOGRAPHICS · 3D ILLUSTRATIONS · PULL-OUT MAP
NEW

MARCO POLO
TRAVEL HANDBOOK
BARCELONA
Insider Tips
NEW

MARCO POLO
TRAVEL HANDBOOK
BERLIN
INFOGRAPHICS · 3D ILLUSTRATIONS · PULL-OUT MAP
Insider Tips
NEW

MARCO POLO
TRAVEL HANDBOOK
BUDAPEST
INFOGRAPHICS · 3D ILLUSTRATIONS · PULL-OUT MAP
Insider Tips
NEW

MARCO POLO
TRAVEL HANDBOOK
DRESDEN
INFOGRAPHICS · 3D ILLUSTRATIONS · PULL-OUT MAP
Insider Tips
NEW

MARCO POLO
TRAVEL HANDBOOK
FLORENCE
INFOGRAPHICS · 3D ILLUSTRATIONS · PULL-OUT MAP
Insider Tips
NEW

MARCO POLO
TRAVEL HANDBOOK
FLORIDA
Insider Tips
NEW

MARCO POLO
TRAVEL HANDBOOK
GRAN CANARIA
INFOGRAPHICS · 3D ILLUSTRATIONS · PULL-OUT MAP
Insider Tips
NEW

MARCO POLO
TRAVEL HANDBOOK
ICELAND
INFOGRAPHICS · 3D ILLUSTRATIONS · PULL-OUT MAP
Insider Tips
NEW

MARCO POLO
TRAVEL HANDBOOK
LONDON
INFOGRAPHICS · 3D ILLUSTRATIONS · PULL-OUT MAP
Insider Tips
NEW

MARCO POLO
TRAVEL HANDBOOK
MADEIRA
INFOGRAPHICS · 3D ILLUSTRATIONS · PULL-OUT MAP
Insider Tips
NEW

MARCO POLO
TRAVEL HANDBOOK
NEW YORK
INFOGRAPHICS · 3D ILLUSTRATIONS · PULL-OUT MAP
Insider Tips
NEW

MARCO POLO
TRAVEL HANDBOOK
NORWAY
INFOGRAPHICS · 3D ILLUSTRATIONS · PULL-OUT MAP
Insider Tips
NEW

MARCO POLO
TRAVEL HANDBOOK
PARIS
INFOGRAPHICS · 3D ILLUSTRATIONS · PULL-OUT MAP
Insider Tips
NEW

MARCO POLO
TRAVEL HANDBOOK
ROME
INFOGRAPHICS · 3D ILLUSTRATIONS · PULL-OUT MAP
Insider Tips
NEW

MARCO POLO
TRAVEL HANDBOOK
SRI LANKA
INFOGRAPHICS · 3D ILLUSTRATIONS · PULL-OUT MAP
NEW

MARCO POLO
TRAVEL HANDBOOK
VENICE
INFOGRAPHICS · 3D ILLUSTRATIONS · PULL-OUT MAP
Insider Tips
NEW

MARCO POLO
TRAVEL HANDBOOK
VIETNAM
INFOGRAPHICS · 3D ILLUSTRATIONS · PULL-OUT MAP
Insider Tips
NEW

www.marco-polo.com

Sri Lankan Curiosities

Different strokes for different folks. Of course on Sri Lanka some things are done differently than in other places. And some of them are quite special.

▶Only men dance
Even by family celebrations in Sri Lanka, especially in rural areas, men are often seen dancing alone while the women sit together and chat. A man would rather dance alone than with a woman.

▶Looking for a mate?
On Sri Lanka newspapers often run personal advertisements for marriage partners with certain requirements. Membership in certain castes, level of education or descent from a certain family are a must. If these are not fulfilled responding to the ad is useless.

▶Excuse me!
The head of the weather service on Sri Lanka apologized in public for the fact that the storm that caused extensive damage in May 2013 was named after King Maha Sena who ruled in the 3rd century and who is still honoured today. Political leaders and agricultural organisations were enraged because the reign of King Maha Sena is supposed to have ushered in an era of prosperity on Sri Lanka.

▶Yes or no? No or yes?
Sri Lankans have a unique characteristic when saying yes or no. Their response is in the form of a movement that looks like what Europeans call shaking your head. But when you look closely you can see that the head more or less rocks back and forth, which means yes.

▶Eating with your left hand is a no-go
It can be observed everywhere on Sri Lanka, even in the best restaurants that people eat only with their right hand. The reason is that the left hand is considered to be unclean since, especially in rural areas, it is used along with lots of water to clean up after a bowel movement. Of course there are toilets and toilet paper. But that doesn't change the fact that the right hand is reserved for eating.

▶... and another celebration
Newlyweds returning home from their honeymoon is another reason to have a party. It is called a Welcome Home Party and the family and friends gather to celebrate the safe return of the happy couple.